THE DOCTOR'S DILEMMA,
GETTING MARRIED, AND
THE SHEWING-UP OF
BLANCO POSNET

THE DOCTOR'S DILEMMA, GETTING MARRIED, AND THE SHEWING-UP OF BLANCO POSNET · BY BERNARD SHAW

WILDSIDE PRESS

Published by
Wildside Press, LLC
P.O. Box 301
Holicong, PA 18928-0301 USA
www.wildsidepress.com

Wildside Press Edition: MMIII

CONTENTS

The Doctor's Dilemma: a Tragedy . 1

  Preface on Doctors   v
  Doubtful Character borne by the
    Medical Profession . . .   vi
  Doctors' Consciences . . .   viii
  The Peculiar People   ix
  Recoil of the Dogma of Medical In-
    fallibility on the Doctor . . .   xi
  Why Doctors do not Differ . .   xiv
  The Craze for Operations . .   xv
  Credulity and Chloroform . .   xvii
  Medical Poverty   xviii
  The Successful Doctor . . .   xx
  The Psychology of Self-Respect in
    Surgeons   xxii
  Are Doctors Men of Science? . .   xxiv
  Bacteriology as a Superstition . .   xxvi
  Economic Difficulties of Immuniza-
    tion   xxix
  The Perils of Inoculation . . .   xxxi
  Trade Unionism and Science . .   xxxiv
  Doctors and Vivisection . . .   xxxvi
  The Primitive Savage Motive . .   xxxvii
  The Higher Motive. The Tree of
    Knowledge   xxxix
  The Flaw in the Argument . .   xl
  Limitations of the Right to Know-
    ledge   xli

Contents

A False Alternative	xlii
Cruelty for its own Sake . . .	xliv
Our Own Cruelties	xlv
The Scientific Investigation of Cruelty	xlvii
Suggested Laboratory Tests of the Vivisector's Emotions . . .	xlviii
Routine	xlix
The Old Line between Man and Beast	liii
Vivisecting the Human Subject .	liv
"The Lie is a European Power" .	lv
An Argument which would Defend any Crime	lvii
Thou Art the Man	lx
What the Public Wants and Will Not Get	lxi
The Vaccination Craze . . .	lxi
Statistical Illusions	lxii
The Surprises of Attention and Neglect	lxv
Stealing Credit from Civilization .	lxvii
Biometrika	lxix
Patient-made Therapeutics . .	lxx
The Reforms also come from the Laity	lxxi
Fashions and Epidemics . . .	lxxii
The Doctor's Virtues . . .	lxxii
The Doctor's Hardships . . .	lxxiii
The Public Doctor	lxxvi
Medical Organization . . .	lxxvii
The Social Solution of the Medical Problem	lxxix
The Future of Private Practice .	lxxx
The Technical Problem . . .	lxxxii
The Latest Theories	lxxxvi

Contents

Getting Married: a Comedy . . . 117

Preface—The Revolt against Marriage .	119
Marriage Nevertheless Inevitable .	120
What does the Word Marriage Mean?	121
Survivals of Sex Slavery . . .	123
The New Attack on Marriage . .	126
A Forgotten Conference of Married Men	127
Hearth and Home	131
Too Much of a Good Thing . .	134
Large and Small Families . . .	135
The Gospel of Laodicea . . .	136
For Better For Worse . . .	139
Wanted: an Immoral Statesman . .	141
The Limits of Democracy . . .	143
The Science and Art of Politics . .	144
Why Statesmen Shirk the Marriage Question	145
The Question of Population . .	146
The Right to Motherhood . . .	148
Monogamy, Polygyny, and Polyandry	149
The Male Revolt against Polygyny .	150
Difference between Oriental and Occidental Polygyny	151
The Old Maid's Right to Motherhood	153
Ibsen's Chain Stitch	154
Remoteness of the Facts from the Ideal	156
Difficulty of Obtaining Evidence .	157
Marriage as a Magic Spell . .	159
The Impersonality of Sex . . .	160
The Economic Slavery of Women .	163
Unpopularity of Impersonal Views .	164
Impersonality is not Promiscuity .	165
Domestic Change of Air . . .	166
Home Manners are Bad Manners .	168

Contents

Spurious "Natural" Affection	168
Carrying the War into the Enemy's Country	170
Shelley and Queen Victoria	171
A Probable Effect of Giving Women the Vote	172
The Personal Sentimental Basis of Monogamy	173
Divorce	177
Importance of Sentimental Grievances	179
Divorce Without Asking Why	180
Economic Slavery again the Root Difficulty	182
Labor Exchanges and the White Slavery	182
Divorce Favorable to Marriage	184
Male Economics and the Rights of Bachelors	186
The Pathology of Marriage	189
The Criminology of Marriage	191
Does it Matter?	192
Christian Marriage	193
Divorce a Sacramental Duty	195
Othello and Desdemona	196
What is to become of the Children?	198
The Cost of Divorce	203
Conclusions	204

The Shewing-Up of Blanco Posnet: a Melodrama 300

Preface—The Censorship	323
A Readable Bluebook	323
How Not to Do it	324
The Story of The Joint Select Committee	327

Contents

Why the Managers Love the Censorship	328
A Two Guinea Insurance Policy	330
Why the Government Interfered	331
The Peers on the Joint Select Committee	333
The Committee's Attitude toward the Theatre	334
A Bad Beginning	334
A Comic Interlude	336
An Anti-Shavian Panic	337
A Rare and Curious First Edition	338
The Times to the Rescue	339
The Council of Ten	340
The Sentence	341
The Execution	342
The Rejected Statement—The Witness's Qualifications	345
The Definition of Immorality	346
What Toleration means	349
The Case for Toleration	350
The Limits to Toleration	352
The Difference between Law and Censorship	354
Why the Lord Chamberlain?	358
The Diplomatic Objection to the Lord Chamberlain	359
The Objection of Court Etiquet	360
Why not an Enlightened Censorship?	361
The Weakness of the Lord Chamberlain's Department	364
An Enlightened Censorship still Worse than the Lord Chamberlain's	366
The Practical Impossibilities of Censorship	368
The Arbitration Proposal	371

Contents

The Licensing of Theatres—The Distinction between Licensing and Censorship	373
Prostitution and Drink in Theatres	374
Why the Managers dread Local Control	376
Desirable Limitations of Local Control	377
Summary of the Rejected Statement	381
Preface Resumed—Mr. George Alexander's Protest	385
Eliza and Her Bath	387
A King's Proctor	388
Counsel's Opinion	390
Wanted: A New Magna Charta	390
Proposed: A New Star Chamber	391
Possibilities of the Proposal	394
Star Chamber Sentimentality	396
Anything for a Quiet Life	398
Shall the Examiner of Plays Starve?	400
Lord Gorell's Awakening	401
Judges: Their Professional Limitations	403
Conclusion	403
Postscript	405

PREFACE ON DOCTORS

IT is not the fault of our doctors that the medical service of the community, as at present provided for, is a murderous absurdity. That any sane nation, having observed that you could provide for the supply of bread by giving bakers a pecuniary interest in baking for you, should go on to give a surgeon a pecuniary interest in cutting off your leg, is enough to make one despair of political humanity. But that is precisely what we have done. And the more appalling the mutilation, the more the mutilator is paid. He who corrects the ingrowing toe-nail receives a few shillings: he who cuts your inside out receives hundreds of guineas, except when he does it to a poor person for practice.

Scandalized voices murmur that these operations are necessary. They may be. It may also be necessary to hang a man or pull down a house. But we take good care not to make the hangman and the housebreaker the judges of that. If we did, no man's neck would be safe and no man's house stable. But we do make the doctor the judge, and fine him anything from sixpence to several hundred guineas if he decides in our favor. I cannot knock my shins severely without forcing on some surgeon the difficult question, "Could I not make a better use of a pocketful of guineas than this man is making of his leg? Could he not write as well—or even better—on one leg than on two? And the guineas would make all the difference in the world to me just now. My wife—my pretty ones—the leg may mortify—it is always safer to operate—he will be well in a fortnight —artificial legs are now so well made that they are really better than natural ones—evolution is towards motors and leglessness, &c., &c., &c."

Now there is no calculation that an engineer can make as to the behavior of a girder under a strain, or an astronomer as to the recurrence of a comet, more certain than the calculation that under such circumstances we shall be dismembered unnecessarily in all directions by surgeons who believe the operations to be necessary solely because they want to perform them. The process metaphorically called bleeding the rich man is performed not only metaphorically but literally every day by surgeons who are quite as honest as most of us. After all, what harm is there in it? The surgeon need not take off the rich man's (or woman's) leg or arm: he can remove the appendix or the uvula, and leave the patient none the worse after a fortnight or so in bed, whilst the nurse, the general practitioner, the apothecary, and the surgeon will be the better.

Doubtful Character borne by the Medical Profession

Again I hear the voices indignantly muttering old phrases about the high character of a noble profession and the honor and conscience of its members. I must reply that the medical profession has not a high character: it has an infamous character. I do not know a single thoughtful and well-informed person who does not feel that the tragedy of illness at present is that it delivers you helplessly into the hands of a profession which you deeply mistrust, because it not only advocates and practises the most revolting cruelties in the pursuit

Preface on Doctors

of knowledge, and justifies them on grounds which would equally justify practising the same cruelties on yourself or your children, or burning down London to test a patent fire extinguisher, but, when it has shocked the public, tries to reassure it with lies of breath-bereaving brazenness. That is the character the medical profession has got just now. It may be deserved or it may not: there it is at all events, and the doctors who have not realized this are living in a fool's paradise. As to the honor and conscience of doctors, they have as much as any other class of men, no more and no less. And what other men dare pretend to be impartial where they have a strong pecuniary interest on one side? Nobody supposes that doctors are less virtuous than judges; but a judge whose salary and reputation depended on whether the verdict was for plaintiff or defendant, prosecutor or prisoner, would be as little trusted as a general in the pay of the enemy. To offer me a doctor as my judge, and then weight his decision with a bribe of a large sum of money and a virtual guarantee that if he makes a mistake it can never be proved against him, is to go wildly beyond the ascertained strain which human nature will bear. It is simply unscientific to allege or believe that doctors do not under existing circumstances perform unnecessary operations and manufacture and prolong lucrative illnesses. The only ones who can claim to be above suspicion are those who are so much sought after that their cured patients are immediately replaced by fresh ones. And there is this curious psychological fact to be remembered: a serious illness or a death advertizes the doctor exactly as a hanging advertizes the barrister who defended the person hanged. Suppose, for example, a royal personage gets something wrong with his throat, or has a pain in his inside. If a doctor effects some trumpery cure with a wet compress or a peppermint lozenge nobody

takes the least notice of him. But if he operates on
the throat and kills the patient, or extirpates an internal organ and keeps the whole nation palpitating for
days whilst the patient hovers in pain and fever between
life and death, his fortune is made: every rich man who
omits to call him in when the same symptoms appear in
his household is held not to have done his utmost duty
to the patient. The wonder is that there is a king or
queen left alive in Europe.

Doctor's Consciences

There is another difficulty in trusting to the honor and
conscience of a doctor. Doctors are just like other
Englishmen: most of them have no honor and no conscience: what they commonly mistake for these is sentimentality and an intense dread of doing anything that
everybody else does not do, or omitting to do anything
that everybody else does. This of course does amount
to a sort of working or rule-of-thumb conscience; but
it means that you will do anything, good or bad, provided you get enough people to keep you in countenance
by doing it also. It is the sort of conscience that makes
it possible to keep order on a pirate ship, or in a troop
of brigands. It may be said that in the last analysis
there is no other sort of honor or conscience in existence
—that the assent of the majority is the only sanction
known to ethics. No doubt this holds good in political
practice. If mankind knew the facts, and agreed with
the doctors, then the doctors would be in the right; and
any person who thought otherwise would be a lunatic.
But mankind does not agree, and does not know the
facts. All that can be said for medical popularity is
that until there is a practicable alternative to blind trust
in the doctor, the truth about the doctor is so terrible
that we dare not face it. Molière saw through the doc-

Preface on Doctors

tors; but he had to call them in just the same. Napoleon had no illusions about them; but he had to die under their treatment just as much as the most credulous ignoramus that ever paid sixpence for a bottle of strong medicine. In this predicament most people, to save themselves from unbearable mistrust and misery, or from being driven by their conscience into actual conflict with the law, fall back on the old rule that if you cannot have what you believe in you must believe in what you have. When your child is ill or your wife dying, and you happen to be very fond of them, or even when, if you are not fond of them, you are human enough to forget every personal grudge before the spectacle of a fellow creature in pain or peril, what you want is comfort, reassurance, something to clutch at, were it but a straw. This the doctor brings you. You have a wildly urgent feeling that something must be done; and the doctor does something. Sometimes what he does kills the patient; but you do not know that; and the doctor assures you that all that human skill could do has been done. And nobody has the brutality to say to the newly bereft father, mother, husband, wife, brother, or sister, " You have killed your lost darling by your credulity."

The Peculiar People

Besides, the calling in of the doctor is now compulsory except in cases where the patient is an adult and not too ill to decide the steps to be taken. We are subject to prosecution for manslaughter or for criminal neglect if the patient dies without the consolations of the medical profession. This menace is kept before the public by the Peculiar People. The Peculiars, as they are called, have gained their name by believing that the Bible is infallible, and taking their belief quite seriously. The Bible is very clear as to the treatment of illness. The

Epistle of James, chapter v., contains the following explicit directions:

> 14. Is any sick among you? let him call for the elders of the Church; and let them pray over him, anointing him with oil in the name of the Lord:
> 15. And the prayer of faith shall save the sick, and the Lord shall raise him up; and if he have committed sins, they shall be forgiven him.

The Peculiars obey these instructions and dispense with doctors. They are therefore prosecuted for manslaughter when their children die.

When I was a young man, the Peculiars were usually acquitted. The prosecution broke down when the doctor in the witness box was asked whether, if the child had had medical attendance, it would have lived. It was, of course, impossible for any man of sense and honor to assume divine omniscience by answering this in the affirmative, or indeed pretending to be able to answer it at all. And on this the judge had to instruct the jury that they must acquit the prisoner. Thus a judge with a keen sense of law (a very rare phenomenon on the Bench, by the way) was spared the possibility of having to sentence one prisoner (under the Blasphemy Laws) for questioning the authority of Scripture, and another for ignorantly and superstitiously accepting it as a guide to conduct. To-day all this is changed. The doctor never hesitates to claim divine omniscience, nor to clamor for laws to punish any scepticism on the part of laymen. A modern doctor thinks nothing of signing the death certificate of one of his own diphtheria patients, and then going into the witness box and swearing a Peculiar into prison for six months by assuring the jury, on oath, that if the prisoner's child, dead of diphtheria, had been placed under his treatment instead of that of St. James, it would not have died. And he does so not only with impunity, but with public ap-

Preface on Doctors

plause, though the logical course would be to prosecute him either for the murder of his own patient or for perjury in the case of St. James. Yet no barrister, apparently, dreams of asking for the statistics of the relative case-mortality in diphtheria among the Peculiars and among the believers in doctors, on which alone any valid opinion could be founded. The barrister is as superstitious as the doctor is infatuated; and the Peculiar goes unpitied to his cell, though nothing whatever has been proved except that his child does without the interference of a doctor as effectually as any of the hundreds of children who die every day of the same diseases in the doctor's care.

Recoil of the Dogma of Medical Infallibility on the Doctor

On the other hand, when the doctor is in the dock, or is the defendant in an action for malpractice, he has to struggle against the inevitable result of his former pretences to infinite knowledge and unerring skill. He has taught the jury and the judge, and even his own counsel, to believe that every doctor can, with a glance at the tongue, a touch on the pulse, and a reading of the clinical thermometer, diagnose with absolute certainty a patient's complaint, also that on dissecting a dead body he can infalliby put his finger on the cause of death, and, in cases where poisoning is suspected, the nature of the poison used. Now all this supposed exactness and infallibility is imaginary; and to treat a doctor as if his mistakes were necessarily malicious or corrupt malpractices (an inevitable deduction from the postulate that the doctor, being omniscient, cannot make mistakes) is as unjust as to blame the nearest apothecary for not being prepared to supply you with sixpenny-worth of the elixir of life, or the nearest motor garage for not having perpetual motion on sale in gallon tins. But if apothecaries and motor car makers habitually advertized elixir of life and perpetual motion, and succeeded in creating a strong general belief that they could supply it, they would find themselves in an awkward position if they were indicted for allowing a customer to die, or for burning a chauffeur by putting petrol into his car. That is the predicament the doctor finds himself in when he has to defend himself against a charge of malpractice by a plea of ignorance and fallibility. His plea is received with flat credulity; and he gets little sympathy, even from laymen who know, because he has brought the incredulity on himself. If he escapes, he can only do so by opening the eyes of the jury to the facts that medical science is as yet very imperfectly differentiated from common curemongering witchcraft; that diagnosis, though it means in many instances (including even the identification of pathogenic bacilli under the microscope) only a choice among terms so loose that they would not be accepted as definitions in any really exact science, is, even at that, an uncertain and difficult matter on which doctors often differ; and that the very best medical opinion and treatment varies widely from doctor to doctor, one practitioner prescribing six or seven scheduled poisons for so familiar a disease as enteric fever where another will not tolerate drugs at all; one starving a patient whom another would stuff; one urging an operation which another would regard as unnecessary and dangerous; one giving alcohol and meat which another would sternly forbid, &c., &c., &c.: all these discrepancies arising not between the opinion of good doctors and bad ones (the medical contention is, of course, that a bad doctor is an impossibility), but between practitioners of equal eminence and authority. Usually it is impossible to persuade the jury that these facts are facts. Juries seldom notice facts; and they

Preface on Doctors

have been taught to regard any doubts of the omniscience and omnipotence of doctors as blasphemy. Even the fact that doctors themselves die of the very diseases they profess to cure passes unnoticed. We do not shoot out our lips and shake our heads, saying, "They save others: themselves they cannot save": their reputation stands, like an African king's palace, on a foundation of dead bodies; and the result is that the verdict goes against the defendant when the defendant is a doctor accused of malpractice.

Fortunately for the doctors, they very seldom find themselves in this position, because it is so difficult to prove anything against them. The only evidence that can decide a case of malpractice is expert evidence: that is, the evidence of other doctors; and every doctor will allow a colleague to decimate a whole countryside sooner than violate the bond of professional etiquet by giving him away. It is the nurse who gives the doctor away in private, because every nurse has some particular doctor whom she likes; and she usually assures her patients that all the others are disastrous noodles, and soothes the tedium of the sick-bed by gossip about their blunders. She will even give a doctor away for the sake of making the patient believe that she knows more than the doctor. But she dare not, for her livelihood, give the doctor away in public. And the doctors stand by one another at all costs. Now and then some doctor in an unassailable position, like the late Sir William Gull, will go into the witness box and say what he really thinks about the way a patient has been treated; but such behavior is considered little short of infamous by his colleagues.

Why Doctors do not Differ

The truth is, there would never be any public agreement among doctors if they did not agree to agree on the main point of the doctor being always in the right. Yet the two guinea man never thinks that the five shilling man is right: if he did, he would be understood as confessing to an overcharge of £1:17s.; and on the same ground the five shilling man cannot encourage the notion that the owner of the sixpenny surgery round the corner is quite up to his mark. Thus even the layman has to be taught that infallibility is not quite infallible, because there are two qualities of it to be had at two prices.

But there is no agreement even in the same rank at the same price. During the first great epidemic of influenza towards the end of the nineteenth century a London evening paper sent round a journalist-patient to all the great consultants of that day, and published their advice and prescriptions; a proceeding passionately denounced by the medical papers as a breach of confidence of these eminent physicians. The case was the same; but the prescriptions were different, and so was the advice. Now a doctor cannot think his own treatment right and at the same time think his colleague right in prescribing a different treatment when the patient is the same. Anyone who has ever known doctors well enough to hear medical shop talked without reserve knows that they are full of stories about each other's blunders and errors, and that the theory of their omniscience and omnipotence no more holds good among themselves than it did with Molière and Napoleon. But for this very reason no doctor dare accuse another of malpractice. He is not sure enough of his own opinion to ruin another man by it. He knows that if such conduct were tolerated in his profession no doctor's livelihood or reputation would

Preface on Doctors

be worth a year's purchase. I do not blame him: I should do the same myself. But the effect of this state of things is to make the medical profession a conspiracy to hide its own shortcomings. No doubt the same may be said of all professions. They are all conspiracies against the laity; and I do not suggest that the medical conspiracy is either better or worse than the military conspiracy, the legal conspiracy, the sacerdotal conspiracy, the pedagogic conspiracy, the royal and aristocratic conspiracy, the literary and artistic conspiracy, and the innumerable industrial, commercial, and financial conspiracies, from the trade unions to the great exchanges, which make up the huge conflict which we call society. But it is less suspected. The Radicals who used to advocate, as an indispensable preliminary to social reform, the strangling of the last king with the entrails of the last priest, substituted compulsory vaccination for compulsory baptism without a murmur.

The Craze for Operations

Thus everything is on the side of the doctor. When men die of disease they are said to die from natural causes. When they recover (and they mostly do) the doctor gets the credit of curing them. In surgery all operations are recorded as successful if the patient can be got out of the hospital or nursing home alive, though the subsequent history of the case may be such as would make an honest surgeon vow never to recommend or perform the operation again. The large range of operations which consist of amputating limbs and extirpating organs admits of no direct verification of their necessity. There is a fashion in operations as there is in sleeves and skirts: the triumph of some surgeon who has at last found out how to make a once desperate operation fairly safe is usually followed by a rage for that operation not only among the doctors, but actually among their patients. There are men and women whom the operating table seems to fascinate: half-alive people who through vanity, or hypochondria, or a craving to be the constant objects of anxious attention or what not, lose such feeble sense as they ever had of the value of their own organs and limbs. They seem to care as little for mutilation as lobsters or lizards, which at least have the excuse that they grow new claws and new tails if they lose the old ones. Whilst this book was being prepared for the press a case was tried in the Courts, of a man who sued a railway company for damages because a train had run over him and amputated both his legs. He lost his case because it was proved that he had deliberately contrived the occurrence himself for the sake of getting an idler's pension at the expense of the railway company, being too dull to realize how much more he had to lose than to gain by the bargain even if he had won his case and received damages above his utmost hopes.

This amazing case makes it possible to say, with some prospect of being believed, that there is in the classes who can afford to pay for fashionable operations a sprinkling of persons so incapable of appreciating the relative importance of preserving their bodily integrity (including the capacity for parentage) and the pleasure of talking about themselves and hearing themselves talked about as the heroes and heroines of sensational operations, that they tempt surgeons to operate on them not only with huge fees, but with personal solicitation. Now it cannot be too often repeated that when an operation is once performed, nobody can ever prove that it was unnecessary. If I refuse to allow my leg to be amputated, its mortification and my death may prove that I was wrong; but if I let the leg go, nobody can ever prove that it would not have mortified had I been obstinate. Operation is therefore the safe side for the

Preface on Doctors

surgeon as well as the lucrative side. The result is that we hear of "conservative surgeons" as a distinct class of practitioners who make it a rule not to operate if they can possibly help it, and who are sought after by the people who have vitality enough to regard an operation as a last resort. But no surgeon is bound to take the conservative view. If he believes that an organ is at best a useless survival, and that if he extirpates it the patient will be well and none the worse in a fortnight, whereas to await the natural cure would mean a month's illness, then he is clearly justified in recommending the operation even if the cure without operation is as certain as anything of the kind ever can be. Thus the conservative surgeon and the radical or extirpatory surgeon may both be right as far as the ultimate cure is concerned; so that their consciences do not help them out of their differences.

Credulity and Chloroform

There is no harder scientific fact in the world than the fact that belief can be produced in practically unlimited quantity and intensity, without observation or reasoning, and even in defiance of both, by the simple desire to believe founded on a strong interest in believing. Everybody recognizes this in the case of the amatory infatuations of the adolescents who see angels and heroes in obviously (to others) commonplace and even objectionable maidens and youths. But it holds good over the entire field of human activity. The hardest-headed materialist will become a consulter of table-rappers and slate-writers if he loses a child or a wife so beloved that the desire to revive and communicate with them becomes irresistible. The cobbler believes that there is nothing like leather. The Imperialist who regards the conquest of England by a foreign power as the worst of political misfortunes believes that the conquest of a foreign power by England would be a boon to the conquered. Doctors are no more proof against such illusions than other men. Can anyone then doubt that under existing conditions a great deal of unnecessary and mischievous operating is bound to go on, and that patients are encouraged to imagine that modern surgery and anesthesia have made operations much less serious matters than they really are? When doctors write or speak to the public about operations, they imply, and often say in so many words, that chloroform has made surgery painless. People who have been operated on know better. The patient does not feel the knife, and the operation is therefore enormously facilitated for the surgeon; but the patient pays for the anesthesia with hours of wretched sickness; and when that is over there is the pain of the wound made by the surgeon, which has to heal like any other wound. This is why operating surgeons, who are usually out of the house with their fee in their pockets before the patient has recovered consciousness, and who therefore see nothing of the suffering witnessed by the general practitioner and the nurse, occasionally talk of operations very much as the hangman in Barnaby Rudge talked of executions, as if being operated on were a luxury in sensation as well as in price.

Medical Poverty

To make matters worse, doctors are hideously poor. The Irish gentleman doctor of my boyhood, who took nothing less than a guinea, though he might pay you four visits for it, seems to have no equivalent nowadays in English society. Better be a railway porter than an ordinary English general practitioner. A railway porter has from eighteen to twenty-three shillings a week from the Company merely as a retainer; and his additional

Preface on Doctors

fees from the public, if we leave the third-class twopenny tip out of account (and I am by no means sure that even this reservation need be made), are equivalent to doctor's fees in the case of second-class passengers, and double doctor's fees in the case of first. Any class of educated men thus treated tends to become a brigand class, and doctors are no exception to the rule. They are offered disgraceful prices for advice and medicine. Their patients are for the most part so poor and so ignorant that good advice would be resented as impracticable and wounding. When you are so poor that you cannot afford to refuse eighteenpence from a man who is too poor to pay you any more, it is useless to tell him that what he or his sick child needs is not medicne, but more leisure, better clothes, better food, and a better drained and ventilated house. It is kinder to give him a bottle of something almost as cheap as water, and tell him to come again with another eighteenpence if it does not cure him. When you have done that over and over again every day for a week, how much scientific conscience have you left? If you are weak-minded enough to cling desperately to your eighteenpence as denoting a certain social superiority to the sixpenny doctor, you will be miserably poor all your life; whilst the sixpenny doctor, with his low prices and quick turnover of patients, visibly makes much more than you do and kills no more people.

A doctor's character can no more stand out against such conditions than the lungs of his patients can stand out against bad ventilation. The only way in which he can preserve his self-respect is by forgetting all he ever learnt of science, and clinging to such help as he can give without cost merely by being less ignorant and more accustomed to sick-beds than his patients. Finally, he acquires a certain skill at nursing cases under povertystricken domestic conditions, just as women who have been trained as domestic servants in some huge institution with lifts, vacuum cleaners, electric lighting, steam heating, and machinery that turns the kitchen into a laboratory and engine house combined, manage, when they are sent out into the world to drudge as general servants, to pick up their business in a new way, learning the slatternly habits and wretched makeshifts of homes where even bundles of kindling wood are luxuries to be anxiously economized.

The Successful Doctor

The doctor whose success blinds public opinion to medical poverty is almost as completely demoralized. His promotion means that his practice becomes more and more confined to the idle rich. The proper advice for most of their ailments is typified in Abernethy's "Live on sixpence a day and earn it." But here, as at the other end of the scale, the right advice is neither agreeable nor practicable. And every hypochondriacal rich lady or gentleman who can be persuaded that he or she is a lifelong invalid means anything from fifty to five hundred pounds a year for the doctor. Operations enable a surgeon to earn similar sums in a couple of hours; and if the surgeon also keeps a nursing home, he may make considerable profits at the same time by running what is the most expensive kind of hotel. These gains are so great that they undo much of the moral advantage which the absence of grinding pecuniary anxiety gives the rich doctor over the poor one. It is true that the temptation to prescribe a sham treatment because the real treatment is too dear for either patient or doctor does not exist for the rich doctor. He always has plenty of genuine cases which can afford genuine treatment; and these provide him with enough sincere scientific professional work to save him from the ignorance, obsolescence, and atrophy of scientific conscience into which his poorer colleagues sink. But on the other hand his expenses are enormous. Even as a bachelor, he must, at London west end rates, make over a thousand a year before he can afford even to insure his life. His house, his servants, and his equipage (or autopage) must be on the scale to which his patients are accustomed, though a couple of rooms with a camp bed in one of them might satisfy his own requirements. Above all, the income which provides for these outgoings stops the moment he himself stops working. Unlike the man of business, whose managers, clerks, warehousemen and laborers keep his business going whilst he is in bed or in his club, the doctor cannot earn a farthing by deputy. Though he is exceptionally exposed to infection, and has to face all weathers at all hours of the night and day, often not enjoying a complete night's rest for a week, the money stops coming in the moment he stops going out; and therefore illness has special terrors for him, and success no certain permanence. He dare not stop making hay while the sun shines; for it may set at any time. Men do not resist pressure of this intensity. When they come under it as doctors they pay unnecessary visits; they write prescriptions that are as absurd as the rub of chalk with which an Irish tailor once charmed away a wart from my father's finger; they conspire with surgeons to promote operations; they nurse the delusions of the *malade imaginaire* (who is always really ill because, as there is no such thing as perfect health, nobody is ever really well); they exploit human folly, vanity, and fear of death as ruthlessly as their own health, strength, and patience are exploited by selfish hypochondriacs. They must do all these things or else run pecuniary risks that no man can fairly be asked to run. And the healthier the world becomes, the more they are compelled to live by imposture and the less by that really helpful activity of which all doctors get enough to preserve them from utter corruption. For even the most hardened humbug who ever prescribed ether tonics to ladies whose need for tonics is of precisely the same character as the need of poorer women for a glass of gin, has to help a mother through child-bearing often enough to feel that he is not living wholly in vain.

The Psychology of Self-Respect in Surgeons

The surgeon, though often more unscrupulous than the general practitioner, retains his self-respect more easily. The human conscience can subsist on very questionable food. No man who is occupied in doing a very difficult thing, and doing it very well, ever loses his self-respect. The shirk, the duffer, the malingerer, the coward, the weakling, may be put out of countenance by his own failures and frauds; but the man who does evil skilfully, energetically, masterfully, grows prouder and bolder at every crime. The common man may have to found his self-respect on sobriety, honesty and industry; but a Napoleon needs no such props for his sense of dignity. If Nelson's conscience whispered to him at all in the silent watches of the night, you may depend on it it whispered about the Baltic and the Nile and Cape St. Vincent, and not about his unfaithfulness to his wife. A man who robs little children when no one is looking can hardly have much self-respect or even self-esteem; but an accomplished burglar must be proud of himself. In the play to which I am at present preluding I have represented an artist who is so entirely satisfied with his artistic conscience, even to the point of dying like a saint with its support, that he is utterly selfish and unscrupulous in every other relation without feeling at the smallest disadvantage. The same thing may be observed in women who have a genius for personal attractiveness: they expend more thought, labor, skill, inventiveness, taste and endurance on making themselves lovely than would suffice to keep a dozen ugly women honest; and this enables them to maintain a high opinion of themselves, and an angry contempt for unattractive and personally careless women, whilst they lie and cheat and slander and sell themselves without a blush. The truth is, hardly any of us have ethical energy enough for more than one really inflexible point of honor. Andrea del Sarto, like Louis Dubedat in my play, must have expended on the attainment of his great mastery of design and his originality in fresco painting more conscientiousness and industry than go to the making of the reputations of a dozen ordinary mayors and churchwardens; but (if Vasari is to be believed) when the King of France entrusted him with money to buy pictures for him, he stole it to spend on his wife. Such cases are not confined to eminent artists. Unsuccessful, unskilful men are often much more scrupulous than successful ones. In the ranks of ordinary skilled labor many men are to be found who earn good wages and are never out of a job because they are strong, indefatigable, and skilful, and who therefore are bold in a high opinion of themselves; but they are selfish and tyrannical, gluttonous and drunken, as their wives and children know to their cost.

Not only do these talented energetic people retain their self-respect through shameful misconduct: they do not even lose the respect of others, because their talents benefit and interest everybody, whilst their vices affect only a few. An actor, a painter, a composer, an author, may be as selfish as he likes without reproach from the public if only his art is superb; and he cannot fulfil this condition without sufficient effort and sacrifice to make him feel noble and martyred in spite of his selfishness. It may even happen that the selfishness of an artist may be a benefit to the public by enabling him to concentrate himself on their gratification with a recklessness of every other consideration that makes him highly dangerous to those about him. In sacrificing others to himself he is sacrificing them to the public he gratifies; and the public is quite content with that arrangement. The public actually has an interest in the artist's vices.

It has no such interest in the surgeon's vices. The surgeon's art is exercised at its expense, not for its gratification. We do not go to the operating table as we go to the theatre, to the picture gallery, to the concert room, to be entertained and delighted: we go to be tormented and maimed, lest a worse thing should befall us. It is of the most extreme importance to us that the experts on whose assurance we face this horror and suffer this mutilation should have no interests but our own to think of; should judge our cases scientifically; and should feel about them kindly. Let us see what guarantees we have: first for the science, and then for the kindness.

Are Doctors Men of Science?

I presume nobody will question the existence of a widely spread popular delusion that every doctor is a man of science. It is escaped only in the very small class which understands by science something more than conjuring with retorts and spirit lamps, magnets and microscopes, and discovering magical cures for disease. To a sufficiently ignorant man every captain of a trading schooner is a Galileo, every organ-grinder a Beethoven, every piano-tuner a Helmholtz, every Old Bailey barrister a Solon, every Seven Dials pigeon dealer a

Preface on Doctors

Darwin, every scrivener a Shakespear, every locomotive engine a miracle, and its driver no less wonderful than George Stephenson. As a matter of fact, the rank and file of doctors are no more scientific than their tailors; or, if you prefer to put it the reverse way, their tailors are no less scientific than they. Doctoring is an art, not a science: any layman who is interested in science sufficiently to take in one of the scientific journals and follow the literature of the scientific movement, knows more about it than those doctors (probably a large majority) who are not interested in it, and practise only to earn their bread. Doctoring is not even the art of keeping people in health (no doctor seems able to advise you what to eat any better than his grandmother or the nearest quack): it is the art of curing illnesses. It does happen exceptionally that a practising doctor makes a contribution to science (my play describes a very notable one); but it happens much oftener that he draws disastrous conclusions from his clinical experience because he has no conception of scientific method, and believes, like any rustic, that the handling of evidence and statistics needs no expertness. The distinction between a quack doctor and a qualified one is mainly that only the qualified one is authorized to sign death certificates, for which both sorts seem to have about equal occasion. Unqualified practitioners now make large incomes as hygienists, and are resorted to as frequently by cultivated amateur scientists who understand quite well what they are doing as by ignorant people who are simply dupes. Bone-setters make fortunes under the very noses of our greatest surgeons from educated and wealthy patients; and some of the most successful doctors on the register use quite heretical methods of treating disease, and have qualified themselves solely for convenience. Leaving out of account the village witches who prescribe spells and sell charms, the humblest professional healers in this country are the herbalists. These men wander through the fields on Sunday seeking for herbs with magic properties of curing disease, preventing childbirth, and the like. Each of them believes that he is on the verge of a great discovery, in which Virginia Snake Root will be an ingredient, heaven knows why! Virginia Snake Root fascinates the imagination of the herbalist as mercury used to fascinate the alchemists. On week days he keeps a shop in which he sells packets of pennyroyal, dandelion, &c., labelled with little lists of the diseases they are supposed to cure, and apparently do cure to the satisfaction of the people who keep on buying them. I have never been able to perceive any distinction between the science of the herbalist and that of the duly registered doctor. A relative of mine recently consulted a doctor about some of the ordinary symptoms which indicate the need for a holiday and a change. The doctor satisfied himself that the patient's heart was a little depressed. Digitalis being a drug labelled as a heart specific by the profession, he promptly administered a stiff dose. Fortunately the patient was a hardy old lady who was not easily killed. She recovered with no worse result than her conversion to Christian Science, which owes its vogue quite as much to public despair of doctors as to superstition. I am not, observe, here concerned with the question as to whether the dose of digitalis was judicious or not; the point is, that a farm laborer consulting a herbalist would have been treated in exactly the same way.

Bacteriology as a Superstition

The smattering of science that all—even doctors—pick up from the ordinary newspapers nowadays only makes the doctor more dangerous than he used to be. Wise men used to take care to consult doctors qualified

Preface on Doctors

before 1860, who were usually contemptuous of or indifferent to the germ theory and bacteriological therapeutics; but now that these veterans have mostly retired or died, we are left in the hands of the generations which, having heard of microbes much as St. Thomas Aquinas heard of angels, suddenly concluded that the whole art of healing could be summed up in the formula: Find the microbe and kill it. And even that they did not know how to do. The simplest way to kill most microbes is to throw them into an open street or river and let the sun shine on them, which explains the fact that when great cities have recklessly thrown all their sewage into the open river the water has sometimes been cleaner twenty miles below the city than thirty miles above it. But doctors instinctively avoid all facts that are reassuring, and eagerly swallow those that make it a marvel that anyone could possibly survive three days in an atmosphere consisting mainly of countless pathogenic germs. They conceive microbes as immortal until slain by a germicide administered by a duly qualified medical man. All through Europe people are adjured, by public notices and even under legal penalties, not to throw their microbes into the sunshine, but to collect them carefully in a handkerchief; shield the handkerchief from the sun in the darkness and warmth of the pocket; and send it to a laundry to be mixed up with everybody eles's handkerchiefs, with results only too familiar to local health authorities.

In the first frenzy of microbe killing, surgical instruments were dipped in carbolic oil, which was a great improvement on not dipping them in anything at all and simply using them dirty; but as microbes are so fond of carbolic oil that they swarm in it, it was not a success from the anti-microbe point of view. Formalin was squirted into the circulation of consumptives until it was discovered that formalin nourishes the tubercle bacillus handsomely and kills men. The popular theory of disease is the common medical theory: namely, that every disease had its microbe duly created in the garden of Eden, and has been steadily propagating itself and producing widening circles of malignant disease ever since. It was plain from the first that if this had been even approximately true, the whole human race would have been wiped out by the plague long ago, and that every epidemic, instead of fading out as mysteriously as it rushed in, would spread over the whole world. It was also evident that the characteristic microbe of a disease might be a symptom instead of a cause. An unpunctual man is always in a hurry; but it does not follow that hurry is the cause of unpunctuality: on the contrary, what is the matter with the patient is sloth. When Florence Nightingale said bluntly that if you overcrowded your soldiers in dirty quarters there would be an outbreak of smallpox among them, she was snubbed as an ignorant female who did not know that smallpox can be produced only by the importation of its specific microbe.

If this was the line taken about smallpox, the microbe of which has never yet been run down and exposed under the microscope by the bacteriologist, what must have been the ardor of conviction as to tuberculosis, tetanus, enteric fever, Maltese fever, diphtheria, and the rest of the diseases in which the characteristic bacillus had been identified! When there was no bacillus it was assumed that, since no disease could exist without a bacillus, it was simply eluding observation. When the bacillus was found, as it frequently was, in persons who were not suffering from the disease, the theory was saved by simply calling the bacillus an impostor, or pseudobacillus. The same boundless credulity which the public exhibit as to a doctor's power of diagnosis was shown by the doctors themselves as to the analytic microbe hunters. These witch finders would give you a certificate of the ultimate constitution of anything from a sample of the water from your well to a scrap of your lungs, for seven-and-sixpence. I do not suggest that the analysts were dishonest. No doubt they carried the analysis as far as they could afford to carry it for the money. No doubt also they could afford to carry it far enough to be of some use. But the fact remains that just as doctors perform for half-a-crown, without the least misgiving, operations which could not be thoroughly and safely performed with due scientific rigor and the requisite apparatus by an unaided private practitioner for less than some thousands of pounds, so did they proceed on the assumption that they could get the last word of science as to the constituents of their pathological samples for a two hours cab fare.

Economic Difficulties of Immunization

I have heard doctors affirm and deny almost every possible proposition as to disease and treatment. I can remember the time when doctors no more dreamt of consumption and pneumonia being infectious than they now dream of sea-sickness being infectious, or than so great a clinical observer as Sydenham dreamt of smallpox being infectious. I have heard doctors deny that there is such a thing as infection. I have heard them deny the existence of hydrophobia as a specific disease differing from tetanus. I have heard them defend prophylactic measures and prophylactic legislation as the sole and certain salvation of mankind from zymotic disease; and I have heard them denounce both as malignant spreaders of cancer and lunacy. But the one objection I have never heard from a doctor is the objection that prophylaxis by the inoculatory methods most in vogue is an economic impossibility under our private practice system. They buy some stuff from somebody for a shilling, and inject a pennyworth of it under their patient's skin for half-a-crown, concluding that, since this primitive rite pays the somebody and pays them, the problem of prophylaxis has been satisfactorily solved. The results are sometimes no worse than the ordinary results of dirt getting into cuts; but neither the doctor nor the patient is quite satisfied un'ess the inoculation "takes"; that is, unless it produces perceptible illness and disablement. Sometimes both doctor and patient get more value in this direction than they bargain for. The results of ordinary private-practice-inoculation at their worst are bad enough to be indistinguishable from those of the most discreditable and dreaded disease known; and doctors, to save the credit of the inoculation, have been driven to accuse their patient or their patient's parents of having contracted this disease independently of the inoculation, an excuse which naturally does not make the family any more resigned, and leads to public recriminations in which the doctors, forgetting everything but the immediate quarrel, naively excuse themselves by admitting, and even claiming as a point in their favor, that it is often impossible to distinguish the disease produced by their inoculation and the disease they have accused the patient of contracting. And both parties assume that what is at issue is the scientific soundness of the prophylaxis. It never occurs to them that the particular pathogenic germ which they intended to introduce into the patient's system may be quite innocent of the catastrophe, and that the casual dirt introduced with it may be at fault. When, as in the case of smallpox or cowpox, the germ has not yet been detected, what you inoculate is simply undefined matter that has been scraped off an anything but chemically clean calf suffering from the disease in question. You take your chance of the germ being in the scrapings, and, lest you should kill it, you take no precautions against other germs being in

Preface on Doctors

it as well. Anything may happen as the result of such an inoculation. Yet this is the only stuff of the kind which is prepared and supplied even in State establishments: that is, in the only establishments free from the commercial temptation to adulterate materials and scamp precautionary processes.

Even if the germ were identified, complete precautions would hardly pay. It is true that microbe farming is not expensive. The cost of breeding and housing two head of cattle would provide for the breeding and housing of enough microbes to inoculate the entire population of the globe since human life first appeared on it. But the precautions necessary to insure that the inoculation shall consist of nothing else but the required germ in the proper state of attenuation are a very different matter from the precautions necessary in the distribution and consumption of beefsteaks. Yet people expect to find vaccines and antitoxins and the like retailed at " popular prices " in private enterprise shops just as they expect to find ounces of tobacco and papers of pins.

The Perils of Inoculation

The trouble does not end with the matter to be inoculated. There is the question of the condition of the patient. The discoveries of Sir Almroth Wright have shewn that the appalling results which led to the hasty dropping in 1894 of Koch's tuberculin were not accidents, but perfectly orderly and inevitable phenomena following the injection of dangerously strong " vaccines " at the wrong moment, and reinforcing the disease instead of stimulating the resistance to it. To ascertain the right moment a laboratory and a staff of experts are needed. The general practitioner, having no such laboratory and no such experience, has always chanced it, and insisted, when he was unlucky, that the results were not due to the inoculation, but to some other cause: a favorite and not very tactful one being the drunkenness or licentiousness of the patient. But though a few doctors have now learnt the danger of inoculating without any reference to the patient's "opsonic index" at the moment of inoculation, and though those other doctors who are denouncing the danger as imaginary and opsonin as a craze or a fad, obviously do so because it involves an operation which they have neither the means nor the knowledge to perform, there is still no grasp of the economic change in the situation. They have never been warned that the practicability of any method of extirpating disease depends not only on its efficacy, but on its cost. For example, just at present the world has run raving mad on the subject of radium, which has excited our credulity precisely as the apparitions at Lourdes excited the credulity of Roman Catholics. Suppose it were ascertained that every child in the world could be rendered absolutely immune from all disease during its entire life by taking half an ounce of radium to every pint of its milk. The world would be none the healthier, because not even a Crown Prince—no, not even the son of a Chicago Meat King, could afford the treatment. Yet it is doubtful whether doctors would refrain from prescribing it on that ground. The recklessness with which they now recommend wintering in Egypt or at Davos to people who cannot afford to go to Cornwall, and the orders given for champagne jelly and old port in households where such luxuries must obviously be acquired at the cost of stinting necessaries, often make one wonder whether it is possible for a man to go through a medical training and retain a spark of common sense.

This sort of inconsiderateness gets cured only in the classes where poverty, pretentious as it is even at its worst, cannot pitch its pretences high enough to make it

Preface on Doctors

possible for the doctor (himself often no better off than the patient) to assume that the average income of an English family is about £2,000 a year, and that it is quite easy to break up a home, sell an old family seat at a sacrifice, and retire into a foreign sanatorium devoted to some "treatment" that did not exist two years ago and probably will not exist (except as a pretext for keeping an ordinary hotel) two years hence. In a poor practice the doctor must find cheap treatments for cheap people, or humiliate and lose his patients either by prescribing beyond their means or sending them to the public hospitals. When it comes to prophylactic inoculation, the alternative lies between the complete scientific process, which can only be brought down to a reasonable cost by being very highly organized as a public service in a public institution, and such cheap, nasty, dangerous and scientifically spurious imitations as ordinary vaccination, which seems not unlikely to be ended, like its equally vaunted forerunner, XVIII. century inoculation, by a purely reactionary law making all sorts of vaccination, scientific or not, criminal offences. Naturally, the poor doctor (that is, the average doctor) defends ordinary vaccination frantically, as it means to him the bread of his children. To secure the vehement and practically unanimous support of the rank and file of the medical profession for any sort of treatment or operation, all that is necessary is that it can be easily practised by a rather shabbily dressed man in a surgically dirty room in a surgically dirty house without any assistance, and that the materials for it shall cost, say, a penny, and the charge for it to a patient with £100 a year be half-a-crown. And, on the other hand, a hygienic measure has only to be one of such refinement, difficulty, precision and costliness as to be quite beyond the resources of private practice, to be ignored or angrily denounced as a fad.

Trade Unionism and Science

Here we have the explanation of the savage rancor that so amazes people who imagine that the controversy concerning vaccination is a scientific one. It has really nothing to do with science. The medical profession, consisting for the most part of very poor men struggling to keep up appearances beyond their means, find themselves threatened with the extinction of a considerable part of their incomes: a part, too, that is easily and regularly earned, since it is independent of disease, and brings every person born into the nation, healthy or not, to the doctors. To boot, there is the occasional windfall of an epidemic, with its panic and rush for revaccination. Under such circumstances, vaccination would be defended desperately were it twice as dirty, dangerous, and unscientific in method as it actually is. The note of fury in the defence, the feeling that the anti-vaccinator is doing a cruel, ruinous, inconsiderate thing in a mood of malignant folly: all this, so puzzling to the observer who knows nothing of the economic side of the question, and only sees that the anti-vaccinator, having nothing whatever to gain and a good deal to lose by placing himself in opposition to the law and to the outcry that adds private persecution to legal penalties, can have no interest in the matter except the interest of a reformer in abolishing a corrupt and mischievous superstition, becomes intelligible the moment the tragedy of medical poverty and the lucrativeness of cheap vaccination is taken into account.

In the face of such economic pressure as this, it is silly to expect that medical teaching, any more than medical practice, can possibly be scientific. The test to which all methods of treatment are finally brought is whether they are lucrative to doctors or not. It would be difficult to cite any proposition less obnoxious to science than that advanced by Hahnemann: to wit, that drugs which in large doses produce certain symptoms, counteract them in very small doses, just as in more modern practice it is found that a sufficiently small inoculation with typhoid rallies our powers to resist the disease instead of prostrating us with it. But Hahnemann and his followers were frantically persecuted for a century by generations of apothecary-doctors whose incomes depended on the quantity of drugs they could induce their patients to swallow. These two cases of ordinary vaccination and homeopathy are typical of all the rest. Just as the object of a trade union under existing conditions must finally be, not to improve the technical quality of the work done by its members, but to secure a living wage for them, so the object of the medical profession today is to secure an income for the private doctor; and to this consideration all concern for science and public health must give way when the two come into conflict. Fortunately they are not always in conflict. Up to a certain point doctors, like carpenters and masons, must earn their living by doing the work that the public wants from them; and as it is not in the nature of things possible that such public want should be based on unmixed disutility, it may be admitted that doctors have their uses, real as well as imaginary. But just as the best carpenter or mason will resist the introduction of a machine that is likely to throw him out of work, or the public technical education of unskilled laborers' sons to compete with him, so the doctor will resist with all his powers of persecution every advance of science that threatens his income. And as the advance of scientific hygiene tends to make the private doctor's visits rarer, and the public inspector's frequenter, whilst the advance of scientific therapeutics is in the direction of treatments that involve highly organized laboratories, hospitals, and public institutions generally, it unluckily happens that the organization of private practitioners which we call the medical profession is coming more and more to represent, not science, but desperate and embittered antiscience: a statement of things which is likely to get worse until the average doctor either depends upon or hopes for an appointment in the public health service for his livelihood.

So much for our guarantees as to medical science. Let us now deal with the more painful subject of medical kindness.

Doctors and Vivisection

The importance to our doctors of a reputation for the tenderest humanity is so obvious, and the quantity of benevolent work actually done by them for nothing (a great deal of it from sheer good nature) so large, that at first sight it seems unaccountable that they should not only throw all their credit away, but deliberately choose to band themselves publicly with outlaws and scoundrels by claiming that in the pursuit of their professional knowledge they should be free from the restraints of law, of honor, of pity, of remorse, of everything that distinguishes an orderly citizen from a South Sea buccaneer, or a philosopher from an inquisitor. For here we look in vain for either an economic or a sentimental motive. In every generation fools and blackguards have made this claim; and honest and reasonable men, led by the strongest contemporary minds, have repudiated it and exposed its crude rascality. From Shakespear and Dr. Johnson to Ruskin and Mark Twain, the natural abhorrence of sane mankind for the vivisector's cruelty, and the contempt of able thinkers for his imbecile casuistry, have been expressed by the most popular spokesmen of humanity. If the medical profession were to outdo the Anti-Vivisection Societies in a general professional protest against the practice and principles of the vivisectors, every doctor in the kingdom would gain substantially by the immense relief and reconciliation which would follow such a reassurance of the humanity of the doctor. Not one doctor in a thousand is a vivisector, or has any interest in vivisection, either pecuniary or intellectual, or would treat his dog cruelly or allow anyone else to do it. It is true that the doctor complies with the professional fashion of defending vivisection, and assuring you that people like Shakespear and Dr. Johnson and Ruskin and Mark Twain are ignorant sentimentalists, just as he complies with any other silly fashion: the mystery is, how it became the fashion in spite of its being so injurious to those who follow it. Making all possible allowance for the effect of the brazen lying of the few men who bring a rush of despairing patients to their doors by professing in letters to the newspapers to have learnt from vivisection how to cure certain diseases, and the assurances of the sayers of smooth things that the practice is quite painless under the law, it is still difficult to find any civilized motive for an attitude by which the medical profession has everything to lose and nothing to gain.

The Primitive Savage Motive

I say civilized motive advisedly; for primitive tribal motives are easy enough to find. Every savage chief who is not a Mahomet learns that if he wishes to strike the imagination of his tribe—and without doing that he cannot rule them—he must terrify or revolt them from time to time by acts of hideous cruelty or disgusting unnaturalness. We are far from being as superior to such tribes as we imagine. It is very doubtful indeed whether Peter the Great could have effected the changes he made in Russia if he had not fascinated and intimidated his people by his monstrous cruelties and grotesque escapades.

Had he been a nineteenth-century king of England, he would have had to wait for some huge accidental calamity: a cholera epidemic, a war, or an insurrection, before waking us up sufficiently to get anything done. Vivisection helps the doctor to rule us as Peter ruled the Russians. The notion that the man who does dreadful things is superhuman, and that therefore he can also do wonderful things either as ruler, avenger, healer, or what not, is by no means confined to barbarians. Just as the manifold wickednesses and stupidities of our criminal code are supported, not by any general comprehension of law or study of jurisprudence, not even by simple vindictiveness, but by the superstition that a calamity of any sort must be expiated by a human sacrifice; so the wickednesses and stupidities of our medicine men are rooted in superstitions that have no more to do with science than the traditional ceremony of christening an ironclad has to do with the effectiveness of its armament. We have only to turn to Macaulay's description of the treatment of Charles II. in his last illness to see how strongly his physicians felt that their only chance of cheating death was by outraging nature in tormenting and disgusting their unfortunate patient. True, this was more than two centuries ago; but I have heard my own nineteenth-century grandfather describe the cupping and firing and nauseous medicines of his time with perfect credulity as to their beneficial effects; and some more modern treatments appear to me quite as barbarous. It is in this way that vivisection pays the doctor. It appeals to the fear and credulity of the savage in us; and without fear and credulity half the private doctor's occupation and seven-eighths of his influence would be gone.

The Higher Motive. The Tree of Knowledge

But the greatest force of all on the side of vivisection is the mighty and indeed divine force of curiosity. Here we have no decaying tribal instinct which men strive to root out of themselves as they strive to root out the tiger's lust for blood. On the contrary, the curiosity of the ape, or of the child who pulls out the legs and wings of a fly to see what it will do without them, or who, on being told that a cat dropped out of the window will always fall on its legs, immediately tries the experiment on the nearest cat from the highest window in the house (I protest I did it myself from the first floor only), is as nothing compared to the thirst for knowledge of the philosopher, the poet, the biologist, and the naturalist. I have always despised Adam because he had to be tempted by the woman, as she was by the serpent, before he could be induced to pluck the apple from the tree of knowledge. I should have swallowed every apple on the tree the moment the owner's back was turned. When Gray said " Where ignorance is bliss, 'tis folly to be wise," he forgot that it is godlike to be wise; and since nobody wants bliss particularly, or could stand more than a very brief taste of it if it were attainable, and since everybody, by the deepest law of the Life Force, desires to be godlike, it is stupid, and indeed blasphemous and despairing, to hope that the thirst for knowledge will either diminish or consent to be subordinated to any other end whatsoever. We shall see later on that the claim that has arisen in this way for the unconditioned pursuit of knowledge is as idle as all dreams of unconditioned activity; but none the less the right to knowledge must be regarded as a fundamental human right. The fact that men of science have had to fight so hard to secure its recognition, and are still so vigorously persecuted when they discover anything that is not quite palatable to vulgar people, makes them sorely jealous for that right; and when they hear a popular outcry for the suppression of a method of research which has an air of being scientific, their first instinct is to rally to the defence of that method without further consideration, with the result that they sometimes, as in the case of vivisection, presently find themselves fighting on a false issue.

The Flaw in the Argument

I may as well pause here to explain their error. The right to know is like the right to live. It is fundamental and unconditional in its assumption that knowledge, like life, is a desirable thing, though any fool can prove that ignorance is bliss, and that "a little knowledge is a dangerous thing" (a little being the most that any of us can attain), as easily as that the pains of life are more numerous and constant than its pleasures, and that therefore we should all be better dead. The logic is unimpeachable; but its only effect is to make us say that if these are the conclusions logic leads to, so much the worse for logic, after which curt dismissal of Folly, we continue living and learning by instinct: that is, as of right. We legislate on the assumption that no man may be killed on the strength of a demonstration that he would be happier in his grave, not even if he is dying slowly of cancer and begs the doctor to despatch him quickly and mercifully. To get killed lawfully he must violate somebody else's right to live by committing murder. But he is by no means free to live unconditionally. In society he can exercise his right to live only under very stiff conditions. In countries where there is compulsory military service he may even have to throw away his individual life to save the life of the community.

It is just so in the case of the right to knowledge. It is a right that is as yet very imperfectly recognized in practice. But in theory it is admitted that an adult person in pursuit of knowledge must not be refused it on the ground that he would be better or happier without it. Parents and priests may forbid knowledge to those who accept their authority; and social taboo may be made effective by acts of legal persecution under cover of repressing blasphemy, obscenity, and sedition; but no government now openly forbids its subjects to pursue knowledge on the ground that knowledge is in itself a bad thing, or that it is possible for any of us to have too much of it.

Limitations of the Right to Knowledge

But neither does any government exempt the pursuit of knowledge, any more than the pursuit of life, liberty, and happiness (as the American Constitution puts it), from all social conditions. No man is allowed to put his mother into the stove because he desires to know how long an adult woman will survive at a temperature of 500° Fahrenheit, no matter how important or interesting that particular addition to the store of human knowledge may be. A man who did so would have short work made not only of his right to knowledge, but of his right to live and all his other rights at the same time. The right to knowledge is not the only right; and its exercise must be limited by respect for other rights, and for its own exercise by others. When a man says to Society, " May I torture my mother in pursuit of knowledge?" Society replies, " No." If he pleads, " What! Not even if I have a chance of finding out how to cure cancer by doing it?" Society still says, " Not even then." If the scientist, making the best of his disappointment, goes on to ask may he torture a dog, the stupid and callous people who do not realize that a dog is a fellow-creature and sometimes a good friend, may say Yes, though Shakespear, Dr. Johnson and their like may say No. But even those who say "You may torture *a* dog" never say "You may torture *my* dog." And nobody says, "Yes, because in the pursuit of knowledge you may do as you please." Just as even the stupidest people say, in effect, "If you cannot attain to knowledge without burning your mother you must do without knowledge," so the wisest people say, "If you cannot attain to knowledge without torturing a dog, you must do without knowledge."

A False Alternative

But in practice you cannot persuade any wise man that this alternative can ever be forced on anyone but a fool, or that a fool can be trusted to learn anything from any experiment, cruel or humane. The Chinaman who burnt down his house to roast his pig was no doubt honestly unable to conceive any less disastrous way of cooking his dinner; and the roast must have been spoiled after all (a perfect type of the average vivisectionist experiment); but this did not prove that the Chinaman was right: it only proved that the Chinaman was an incapable cook and, fundamentally, a fool.

Take another celebrated experiment: one in sanitary reform. In the days of Nero Rome was in the same predicament as London to-day. If some one would burn down London, and it were rebuilt, as it would now have to be, subject to the sanitary by-laws and Building Act provisions enforced by the London County Council, it would be enormously improved; and the average lifetime of Londoners would be considerably prolonged. Nero argued in the same way about Rome. He employed incendiaries to set it on fire; and he played the harp in

scientific raptures whilst it was burning. I am so far of
Nero's way of thinking that I have often said, when consulted by despairing sanitary reformers, that what London needs to make her healthy is an earthquake. Why,
then, it may be asked, do not I, as a public-spirited man,
employ incendiaries to set it on fire, with a heroic disregard of the consequences to myself and others? Any
vivisector would, if he had the courage of his opinions.
The reasonable answer is that London can be made
healthy without burning her down; and that as we have
not enough civic virtue to make her healthy in a humane
and economical way, we should not have enough to rebuild her in that way. In the old Hebrew legend, God
lost patience with the world as Nero did with Rome, and
drowned everybody except a single family. But the result was that the progeny of that family reproduced all
the vices of their predecessors so exactly that the misery
caused by the flood might just as well have been spared:
things went on just as they did before. In the same
way, the lists of diseases which vivisection claims to have
cured is long; but the returns of the Registrar-General
shew that people still persist in dying of them as if vivisection had never been heard of. Any fool can burn
down a ciy or cut an animal open; and an exceptionally
foolish fool is quite likely to promise enormous benefits
to the race as the result of such activities. But when the
constructive, benevolent part of the business comes to be
done, the same want of imagination, the same stupidity
and cruelty, the same laziness and want of perseverance
that prevented Nero or the vivisector from devising or
pushing through humane methods, prevents him from
bringing order out of the chaos and happiness out of the
misery he has made. At one time it seemed reasonable
enough to declare that it was impossible to find whether
or not there was a stone inside a man's body except by
exploring it with a knife, or to find out what the sun is

made of without visiting it in a balloon. Both these impossibilities have been achieved, but not by vivisectors. The Röntgen rays need not hurt the patient; and spectrum analysis involves no destruction. After such triumphs of humane experiment and reasoning, it is useless to assure us that there is no other key to knowledge except cruelty. When the vivisector offers us that assurance, we reply simply and contemptuously, "You mean that you are not clever or humane or energetic enough to find one."

Cruelty for its own Sake

It will now, I hope, be clear why the attack on vivisection is not an attack on the right to knowledge: why, indeed, those who have the deepest conviction of the sacredness of that right are the leaders of the attack. No knowledge is finally impossible of human attainment; for even though it may be beyond our present capacity, the needed capacity is not unattainable. Consequently no method of investigation is the only method; and no law forbidding any particular method can cut us off from the knowledge we hope to gain by it. The only knowledge we lose by forbidding cruelty is knowledge at first hand of cruelty itself, which is precisely the knowledge humane people wish to be spared.

But the question remains: Do we all really wish to be spared that knowledge? Are humane methods really to be preferred to cruel ones? Even if the experiments come to nothing, may not their cruelty be enjoyed for its own sake, as a sensational luxury? Let us face these questions boldly, not shrinking from the fact that cruelty is one of the primitive pleasures of mankind, and that the detection of its Protean disguises as law, education, medicine, discipline, sport and so forth, is one of the most difficult of the unending tasks of the legislator.

Our Own Cruelties

At first blush it may seem not only unnecessary, but even indecent, to discuss such a proposition as the elevation of cruelty to the rank of a human right. Unnecessary, because no vivisector confesses to a love of cruelty for its own sake or claims any general fundamental right to be cruel. Indecent, because there is an accepted convention to repudiate cruelty; and vivisection is only tolerated by the law on condition that, like judicial torture, it shall be done as mercifully as the nature of the practice allows. But the moment the controversy becomes embittered, the recriminations bandied between the opposed parties bring us face-to-face with some very ugly truths. On one occasion I was invited to speak at a large Anti-Vivisection meeting in the Queen's Hall in London. I found myself on the platform with fox hunters, tame stag hunters, men and women whose calendar was divided, not by pay days and quarter days, but by seasons for killing animals for sport: the fox, the hare, the otter, the partridge and the rest having each its appointed date for slaughter. The ladies among us wore hats and cloaks and head-dresses obtained by wholesale massacres, ruthless trappings, callous extermination of our fellow creatures. We insisted on our butchers supplying us with white veal, and were large and constant consumers of *pâte de foie gras;* both comestibles being obtained by revolting methods. We sent our sons to public schools where indecent flogging is a recognized method of taming the young human animal. Yet we were all in hysterics of indignation at the cruelties of the vivisectors. These, if any were present, must have smiled sardonically at such inhuman humanitarians, whose daily habits and fashionable amusements cause more suffering in England in a week than all the vivisectors of Europe do in a year. I made a very effective speech, not exclusively against vivisection, but against cruelty; and I have never been asked to speak since by that Society, nor do I expect to be, as I should probably give such offence to its most affluent subscribers that its attempts to suppress vivisection would be seriously hindered. But that does not prevent the vivisectors from freely using the " youre another " retort, and using it with justice.

We must therefore give ourselves no airs of superiority when denouncing the cruelties of vivisection. We all do just as horrible things, with even less excuse. But in making that admission we are also making short work of the virtuous airs with which we are sometimes referred to the humanity of the medical profession as a guarantee that vivisection is not abused—much as if our burglars should assure us that they are too honest to abuse the practice of burgling. We are, as a matter of fact, a cruel nation; and our habit of disguising our vices by giving polite names to the offences we are determined to commit does not, unfortunately for my own comfort, impose on me. Vivisectors can hardly pretend to be better than the classes from which they are drawn, or those above them; and if these classes are capable of sacrificing animals in various cruel ways under cover of sport, fashion, education, discipline, and even, when the cruel sacrifices are human sacrifices, of political economy, it is idle for the vivisector to pretend that he is incapable of practising cruelty for pleasure or profit or both under the cloak of science. We are all tarred with the same brush; and the vivisectors are not slow to remind us of it, and to protest vehemently against being branded as exceptionally cruel and as devisers of horrible instruments of torture by people whose main notion of enjoyment is cruel sport, and whose requirements in the way of villainously cruel traps occupy pages of the catalogue of the Army and Navy Stores.

The Scientific Investigation of Cruelty

There is in man a specific lust for cruelty which infects even his passion of pity and makes it savage. Simple disgust at cruelty is very rare. The people who turn sick and faint and those who gloat are often alike in the pains they take to witness executions, floggings, operations or any other exhibitions of suffering, especially those involving bloodshed, blows, and laceration. A craze for cruelty can be developed just as a craze for drink can; and nobody who attempts to ignore cruelty as a possible factor in the attraction of vivisection and even of antivivisection, or in the credulity with which we accept its excuses, can be regarded as a scientific investigator of it. Those who accuse vivisectors of indulging the well-known passion of cruelty under the cloak of research are therefore putting forward a strictly scientific psychological hypothesis, which is also simple, human, obvious, and probable. It may be as wounding to the personal vanity of the vivisector as Darwin's Origin of Species was to the people who could not bear to think that they were cousins to the monkeys (remember Goldsmith's anger when he was told that he could not move his upper jaw); but science has to consider only the truth of the hypothesis, and not whether conceited people will like it or not. In vain do the sentimental champions of vivisection declare themselves the most humane of men, inflicting suffering only to relieve it, scrupulous in the use of anesthetics, and void of all passion except the passion of pity for a disease-ridden world. The really scientific investigator answers that the question cannot be settled by hysterical protestations, and that if the vivisectionist rejects deductive reasoning, he had better clear his character by his own favorite method of experiment.

Suggested Laboratory Tests of the Vivisector's Emotions

Take the hackneyed case of the Italian who tortured mice, ostensibly to find out about the effects of pain rather less than the nearest dentist could have told him, and who boasted of the ecstatic sensations (he actually used the word love) with which he carried out his experiments. Or the gentleman who starved sixty dogs to death to establish the fact that a dog deprived of food gets progressively lighter and weaker, becoming remarkably emaciated, and finally dying: an undoubted truth, but ascertainable without laboratory experiments by a simple enquiry addressed to the nearest policeman, or, failing him, to any sane person in Europe. The Italian is diagnosed as a cruel voluptuary: the dog-starver is passed over as such a hopeless fool that it is impossible to take any interest in him. Why not test the diagnosis scientifically? Why not perform a careful series of experiments on persons under the influence of voluptuous ecstasy, so as to ascertain its physiological symptoms? Then perform a second series on persons engaged in mathematical work or machine designing, so as to ascertain the symptoms of cold scientific activity? Then note the symptoms of a vivisector performing a cruel experiment; and compare them with the voluptuary symptoms and the mathematical symptoms? Such experiments would be quite as interesting and important as any yet undertaken by the vivisectors. They might open a line of investigation which would finally make, for instance, the ascertainment of the guilt or innocence of an accused person a much exacter process than the very fallible methods of our criminal courts. But instead of proposing such an investigation, our vivisectors offer us all the pious protestations and all the huffy recriminations that any common unscientific mortal offers when he is accused of unworthy conduct.

Routine

Yet most vivisectors would probably come triumphant out of such a series of experiments, because vivisection is now a routine, like butchering or hanging or flogging; and many of the men who practise it do so only because it has been established as part of the profession they have adopted. Far from enjoying it, they have simply overcome their natural repugnance and become indifferent to it, as men inevitably become indifferent to anything they do often enough. It is this dangerous power of custom that makes it so difficult to convince the common sense of mankind that any established commercial or professional practice has its root in passion. Let a routine once spring from passion, and you will presently find thousands of routineers following it passionlessly for a livelihood. Thus it always seems strained to speak of the religious convictions of a clergyman, because nine out of ten clergymen have no religious convictions: they are ordinary officials carrying on a routine of baptizing, marrying, and churching; praying, reciting, and preaching; and, like solicitors or doctors, getting away from their duties with relief to hunt, to garden, to keep bees, to go into society, and the like. In the same way many people do cruel and vile things without being in the least cruel or vile, because the routine to which they have been brought up is superstitiously cruel and vile. To say that every man who beats his children and every schoolmaster who flogs a pupil is a conscious debauchee is absurd: thousands of dull, conscientious people beat their children conscientiously, because they were beaten themselves and think children ought to be beaten. The ill-tempered vulgarity that instinctively strikes at and hurts a thing

1 The Doctor's Dilemma

that annoys it (and all children are annoying), and the simple stupidity that requires from a child perfection beyond the reach of the wisest and best adults (perfect truthfulness coupled with perfect obedience is quite a common condition of leaving a child unwhipped), produce a good deal of flagellation among people who not only do not lust after it, but who hit the harder because they are angry at having to perform an uncomfortable duty. These people will beat merely to assert their authority, or to carry out what they conceive to be a divine order on the strength of the precept of Solomon recorded in the Bible, which carefully adds that Solomon completely spoilt his own son and turned away from the god of his fathers to the sensuous idolatry in which he ended his days.

In the same way we find men and women practising vivisection as senselessly as a humane butcher, who adores his fox terrier, will cut a calf's throat and hang it up by its heels to bleed slowly to death because it is the custom to eat veal and insist on its being white; or as a German purveyor nails a goose to a board and stuffs it with food because fashionable people eat *pâté de foie gras*; or as the crew of a whaler breaks in on a colony of seals and clubs them to death in wholesale massacre because ladies want sealskin jackets; or as fanciers blind singing birds with hot needles, and mutilate the ears and tails of dogs and horses. Let cruelty or kindness or anything else once become customary and it will be practised by people to whom it is not at all natural, but whose rule of life is simply to do only what everybody else does, and who would lose their employment and starve if they indulged in any peculiarity. A respectable man will lie daily, in speech and in print, about the qualities of the article he lives by selling, because it is customary to do so. He will flog his boy for telling a lie, because it is customary to do so. He will also flog him for not telling a lie if

Preface on Doctors

the boy tells inconvenient or disrespectful truths, because it is customary to do so. He will give the same boy a present on his birthday, and buy him a spade and bucket at the seaside, because it is customary to do so, being all the time neither particularly mendacious, nor particularly cruel, nor particularly generous, but simply incapable of ethical judgment or independent action.

Just so do we find a crowd of petty vivisectionists daily committing atrocities and stupidities, because it is the custom to do so. Vivisection is customary as part of the routine of preparing lectures in medical schools. For instance, there are two ways of making the action of the heart visible to students. One, a barbarous, ignorant, and thoughtless way, is to stick little flags into a rabbit's heart and let the students see the flags jump. The other, an elegant, ingenious, well-informed, and instructive way, is to put a sphygmograph on the student's wrist and let him see a record of his heart's action traced by a needle on a slip of smoked paper. But it has become the custom for lecturers to teach from the rabbit; and the lecturers are not original enough to get out of their groove. Then there are the demonstrations which are made by cutting up frogs with scissors. The most humane man, however repugnant the operation may be to him at first, cannot do it at lecture after lecture for months without finally—and that very soon—feeling no more for the frog than if he were cutting up pieces of paper. Such clumsy and lazy ways of teaching are based on the cheapness of frogs and rabbits. If machines were as cheap as frogs, engineers would not only be taught the anatomy of machines and the functions of their parts: they would also have machines misused and wrecked before them so that they might learn as much as possible by using their eyes, and as little as possible by using their brains and imaginations. Thus we have, as part of the routine of teaching, a routine of vivisection which soon produces complete indifference to it on the part even of those who are naturally humane. If they pass on from the routine of lecture preparation, not into general practice, but into research work, they carry this acquired indifference with them into the laboratory, where any atrocity is possible, because all atrocities satisfy curiosity. The routine man is in the majority in his profession always: consequently the moment his practice is tracked down to its source in human passion there is a great and quite sincere poohpoohing from himself, from the mass of the profession, and from the mass of the public, which sees that the average doctor is much too commonplace and decent a person to be capable of passionate wickedness of any kind.

Here then, we have in vivisection, as in all the other tolerated and instituted cruelties, this anti-climax: that only a negligible percentage of those who practise and consequently defend it get any satisfaction out of it. As in Mr. Galsworthy's play Justice the useless and detestable torture of solitary imprisonment is shewn at its worst without the introduction of a single cruel person into the drama, so it would be possible to represent all the torments of vivisection dramatically without introducing a single vivisector who had not felt sick at his first experience in the laboratory. Not that this can exonerate any vivisector from suspicion of enjoying his work (or *her* work: a good deal of the vivisection in medical schools is done by women). In every autobiography which records a real experience of school or prison life, we find that here and there among the routineers there is to be found the genuine amateur, the orgiastic flogging schoolmaster or the nagging warder, who has sought out a cruel profession for the sake of its cruelty. But it is the genuine routineer who is the bulwark of the practice, because, though you can excite public fury against a Sade, a Bluebeard, or a Nero, you cannot rouse any feeling against dull Mr.

Smith doing his duty: that is, doing the usual thing. He is so obviously no better and no worse than anyone else that it is difficult to conceive that the things he does are abominable. If you would see public dislike surging up in a moment against an individual, you must watch one who does something unusual, no matter how sensible it may be. The name of Jonas Hanway lives as that of a brave man because he was the first who dared to appear in the streets of this rainy island with an umbrella.

The Old Line between Man and Beast

But there is still a distinction to be clung to by those who dare not tell themselves the truth about the medical profession because they are so helplessly dependent on it when death threatens the household. That distinction is the line that separates the brute from the man in the old classification. Granted, they will plead, that we are all cruel; yet the tame-stag-hunter does not hunt men; and the sportsman who lets a leash of greyhounds loose on a hare would be horrified at the thought of letting them loose on a human child. The lady who gets her cloak by flaying a sable does not flay a negro; nor does it ever occur to her that her veal cutlet might be improved on by a slice of tender baby.

Now there was a time when some trust could be placed in this distinction. The Roman Catholic Church still maintains, with what it must permit me to call a stupid obstinacy, and in spite of St. Francis and St. Anthony, that animals have no souls and no rights; so that you cannot sin against an animal, or against God by anything you may choose to do to an animal. Resisting the temptation to enter on an argument as to whether you may not sin against your own soul if you are unjust or cruel to the least of those whom St. Francis called his little brothers, I have only to point out here that nothing could be more despicably superstitious in the opinion of a vivisector than the notion that science recognizes any such step in evolution as the step from a physical organism to an immortal soul. That conceit has been taken out of all our men of science, and out of all our doctors, by the evolutionists; and when it is considered how completely obsessed biological science has become in our days, not by the full scope of evolution, but by that particular method of it which has neither sense nor purpose nor life nor anything human, much less godlike, in it: by the method, that is, of so-called Natural Selection (meaning no selection at all, but mere dead accident and luck), the folly of trusting to vivisectors to hold the human animal any more sacred than the other animals becomes so clear that it would be waste of time to insist further on it. As a matter of fact the man who once concedes to the vivisector the right to put a dog outside the laws of honor and fellowship, concedes to him also the right to put himself outside them; for he is nothing to the vivisector but a more highly developed, and consequently more interesting-to-experiment-on vertebrate than the dog.

Vivisecting the Human Subject

I have in my hand a printed and published account by a doctor of how he tested his remedy for pulmonary tuberculosis, which was, to inject a powerful germicide directly into the circulation by stabbing a vein with a syringe. He was one of those doctors who are able to command public sympathy by saying, quite truly, that when they discovered that the proposed treatment was dangerous, they experimented thenceforth on themselves. In this case the doctor was devoted enough to carry his experiments to the point of running serious risks, and actually making himself very uncomfortable. But he did not begin with himself. His first experiment was on two hospital patients. On receiving a message from the hospital to the effect that these two martyrs to therapeutic science had all but expired in convulsions, he experimented on a rabbit, which instantly dropped dead. It was then, and not until then, that he began to experiment on himself, with the germicide modified in the direction indicated by the experiments made on the two patients and the rabbit. As a good many people countenance vivisection because they fear that if the experiments are not made on rabbits they will be made on themselves, it is worth noting that in this case, where both rabbits and men were equally available, the men, being, of course, enormously more instructive, and costing nothing, were experimented on first. Once grant the ethics of the vivisectionists and you not only sanction the experiment on the human subject, but make it the first duty of the vivisector. If a guinea pig may be sacrificed for the sake of the very little that can be learnt from it, shall not a man be sacrificed for the sake of the great deal that can be learnt from him? At all events, he *is* sacrificed, as this typical case shows. I may add (not that it touches the argument) that the doctor, the patients, and the rabbit all suffered in vain, as far as the hoped-for rescue of the race from pulmonary consumption is concerned.

"The Lie is a European Power"

Now at the very time when the lectures describing these experiments were being circulated in print and discussed eagerly by the medical profession, the customary denials that patients are experimented on were as loud, as indignant, as high-minded as ever, in spite of the few intelligent doctors who point out rightly that all treatments are experiments on the patient. And this brings us to an obvious but mostly overlooked weakness in the vivisector's position: that is, his inevitable forfeiture of all claim to have his word believed. It is hardly to be expected that a man who does not hesitate to vivisect for the sake of science will hesitate to lie about it afterwards to protect it from what he deems the ignorant sentimentality of the laity. When the public conscience stirs uneasily and threatens suppression, there is never wanting some doctor of eminent position and high character who will sacrifice himself devotedly to the cause of science by coming forward to assure the public on his honor that all experiments on animals are completely painless; although he must know that the very experiments which first provoked the anti-vivisection movement by their atrocity were experiments to ascertain the physiological effects of the sensation of extreme pain (the much more interesting physiology of pleasure remains uninvestigated) and that all experiments in which sensation is a factor are voided by its suppression. Besides, vivisection may be painless in cases where the experiments are very cruel. If a person scratches me with a poisoned dagger so gently that I do not feel the scratch, he has achieved a painless vivisection; but if I presently die in torment I am not likely to consider that his humanity is amply vindicated by his gentleness. A cobra's bite hurts so little that the creature is almost, legally speaking, a vivisector who inflicts no pain. By giving his victims chloroform before biting them he could comply with the law completely.

Here, then, is a pretty deadlock. Public support of vivisection is founded almost wholly on the assurances of the vivisectors that great public benefits may be expected from the practice. Not for a moment do I suggest that such a defence would be valid even if proved. But when the witnesses begin by alleging that in the cause of science all the customary ethical obligations (which include the obligation to tell the truth) are suspended, what weight can any reasonable person give to their testimony? I would rather swear fifty lies than take an animal which had licked my hand in good fellowship and torture it. If I did torture the dog, I should certainly not have the face to turn round and ask how any person dare suspect an honorable man like myself of telling lies. Most sensible and humane people would, I hope, reply flatly that honorable men do not behave dishonorably even to dogs. The murderer who, when asked by the chaplain whether he had any other crimes to confess, replied indignantly, "What do you take me for?" reminds us very strongly of the vivisectors who are so deeply hurt when their evidence is set aside as worthless.

An Argument which would Defend any Crime

The Achilles heel of vivisection, however, is not to be found in the pain it causes, but in the line of argument by which it is justified. The medical code regarding it is simply criminal anarchism at its very worst. Indeed no criminal has yet had the impudence to argue as every vivisector argues. No burglar contends that as it is admittedly important to have money to spend, and as the object of burglary is to provide the burglar with money to spend, and as in many instances it has achieved this object, therefore the burglar is a public benefactor and the police are ignorant sentimentalists. No highway robber has yet harrowed us with denunciations of the puling moralist who allows his child to suffer all the evils of poverty because certain faddists think it dishonest to garotte an alderman. Thieves and assassins understand quite well that there are paths of acquisition, even of the best things, that are barred to all men of honor. Again, has the silliest burglar ever pretended that to put a stop to burglary is to put a stop to industry? All the vivisections that have been performed since the world began have produced nothing so important as the innocent and honorable discovery of radiography; and one of the reasons why radiography was not discovered sooner was that the men whose business it was to discover new clinical methods were coarsening and stupefying themselves with the sensual villanies and cutthroat's casuistries of vivisection. The law of the conservation of energy holds good in physiology as in other things: every vivisector is a deserter from the army of honorable investigators. But the vivisector does not see this. He not only calls his methods scientific: he contends that there are no other scientific methods. When you express your natural loathing for his cruelty and your natural contempt for his stupidity, he imagines that you are attacking science. Yet he has no inkling of the method and temper of science. The point at issue being plainly whether he is a rascal or not, he not only insists that the real point is whether some hotheaded antivivisectionist is a liar (which he proves by ridiculously unscientific assumptions as to the degree of accuracy attainable in human statement), but never dreams of offering any scientific evidence by his own methods.

There are many paths to knowledge already discovered; and no enlightened man doubts that there are many more waiting to be discovered. Indeed, all paths lead to knowledge; because even the vilest and stupidest action teaches us something about vileness and stupidity, and may accidentally teach us a good deal more: for instance, a cutthroat learns (and perhaps teaches) the anatomy of the carotid artery and jugular vein; and there can be no question that the burning of St. Joan of Arc must have been a most instructive and interesting experiment to a good observer, and could have been made more so if it had been carried out by skilled physi-

Preface on Doctors

ologists under laboratory conditions. The earthquake in San Francisco proved invaluable as an experiment in the stability of giant steel buildings; and the ramming of the Victoria by the Camperdown settled doubtful points of the greatest importance in naval warfare. According to vivisectionist logic our builders would be justified in producing artificial earthquakes with dynamite, and our admirals in contriving catastrophes at naval manœuvres, in order to follow up the line of research thus accidentally discovered.

The truth is, if the acquisition of knowledge justifies every sort of conduct, it justifies any sort of conduct, from the illumination of Nero's feasts by burning human beings alive (another interesting experiment) to the simplest act of kindness. And in the light of that truth it is clear that the exemption of the pursuit of knowledge from the laws of honor is the most hideous conceivable enlargement of anarchy; worse, by far, than an exemption of the pursuit of money or political power, since these can hardly be attained without some regard for at least the appearances of human welfare, whereas a curious devil might destroy the whole race in torment, acquiring knowledge all the time from his highly interesting experiment. There is more danger in one respectable scientist countenancing such a monstrous claim than in fifty assassins or dynamitards. The man who makes it is ethically imbecile; and whoever imagines that it is a scientific claim has not the faintest conception of what science means. The paths to knowledge are countless. One of these paths is a path through darkness, secrecy, and cruelty. When a man deliberately turns from all other paths and goes down that one, it is scientific to infer that what attracts him is not knowledge, since there are other paths to that, but cruelty. With so strong and scientific a case against him, it is childish for him to stand on his honor and reputation and high

lx   The Doctor's Dilemma

character and the credit of a noble profession and so forth: he must clear himself either by reason or by experiment, unless he boldly contends that evolution has retained a passion of cruelty in man just because it is indispensable to the fulness of his knowledge.

Thou Art The Man

I shall not be at all surprised if what I have written above has induced in sympathetic readers a transport of virtuous indignation at the expense of the medical profession. I shall not damp so creditable and salutary a sentiment; but I must point out that the guilt is shared by all of us. It is not in his capacity of healer and man of science that the doctor vivisects or defends vivisection, but in his entirely vulgar lay capacity. He is made of the same clay as the ignorant, shallow, credulous, half-miseducated, pecuniarily anxious people who call him in when they have tried in vain every bottle and every pill the advertizing druggist can persuade them to buy. The real remedy for vivisection is the remedy for all the mischief that the medical profession and all the other professions are doing: namely, more knowledge. The juries which send the poor Peculiars to prison, and give vivisectionists heavy damages against humane persons who accuse them of cruelty; the editors and councillors and student-led mobs who are striving to make Vivisection one of the watchwords of our civilization, are not doctors: they are the British public, all so afraid to die that they will cling frantically to any idol which promises to cure all their diseases, and crucify anyone who tells them that they must not only die when their time comes, but die like gentlemen. In their paroxysms of cowardice and selfishness they force the doctors to humor their folly and ignorance. How complete and inconsiderate their ignorance is can only be realized by those

Preface on Doctors

lxi

who have some knowledge of vital statistics, and of the illusions which beset Public Health legislation.

What the Public Wants and Will Not Get

The demands of this poor public are not reasonable, but they are quite simple. It dreads disease and desires to be protected against it. But it is poor and wants to be protected cheaply. Scientific measures are too hard to understand, too costly, too clearly tending towards a rise in the rates and more public interference with the insanitary, because insufficiently financed, private house. What the public wants, therefore, is a cheap magic charm to prevent, and a cheap pill or potion to cure, all disease. It forces all such charms on the doctors.

The Vaccination Craze

Thus it was really the public and not the medical profession that took up vaccination with irresistible faith, sweeping the invention out of Jenner's hand and establishing it in a form which he himself repudiated. Jenner was not a man of science; but he was not a fool; and when he found that people who had suffered from cowpox either by contagion in the milking shed or by vaccination, were not, as he had supposed, immune from smallpox, he ascribed the cases of immunity which had formerly misled him to a disease of the horse, which, perhaps because we do not drink its milk and eat its flesh, is kept at a greater distance in our imagination than our foster mother the cow. At all events, the public, which had been boundlessly credulous about the cow, would not have the horse on any terms; and to this day the law which prescribes Jennerian vaccination is carried out with an anti-Jennerian inoculation because the public would have it so in spite of Jenner. All the grossest lies and superstitions which have disgraced the vaccination craze were taught to the doctors by the public. It was not the doctors who first began to declare that all our old men remember the time when almost every face they saw in the street was horribly pitted with smallpox, and that all this disfigurement has vanished since the introduction of vaccination. Jenner himself alluded to this imaginary phenomenon before the introduction of vaccination, and attributed it to the older practice of smallpox inoculation, by which Voltaire, Catherine II. and Lady Mary Wortley Montagu so confidently expected to see the disease made harmless. It was not Jenner who set people declaring that smallpox, if not abolished by vaccination, had at least been made much milder: on the contrary, he recorded a pre-vaccination epidemic in which none of the persons attacked went to bed or considered themselves as seriously ill. Neither Jenner, nor any other doctor ever, as far as I know, inculcated the popular notion that everybody got smallpox as a matter of course before vaccination was invented. That doctors get infected with these delusions, and are in their unprofessional capacity as members of the public subject to them like other men, is true; but if we had to decide whether vaccination was first forced on the public by the doctors or on the doctors by the public, we should have to decide against the public.

Statistical Illusions

Public ignorance of the laws of evidence and of statistics can hardly be exaggerated. There may be a doctor here and there who in dealing with the statistics of disease has taken at least the first step towards sanity by grasping the fact that as an attack of even the commonest disease is an exceptional event, apparently overwhelming statistical evidence in favor of any prophylactic can be produced by persuading the public that everybody caught the disease formerly. Thus if a disease is one which normally attacks fifteen per cent of the population, and if the effect of a prophylactic is actually to increase the proportion to twenty per cent, the publication of this figure of twenty per cent will convince the public that the prophylactic has reduced the percentage by eighty per cent instead of increasing it by five, because the public, left to itself and to the old gentlemen who are always ready to remember, on every possible subject, that things used to be much worse than they are now (such old gentlemen greatly outnumber the laudatores tempori acti), will assume that the former percentage was about 100. The vogue of the Pasteur treatment of hydrophobia, for instance, was due to the assumption by the public that every person bitten by a rabid dog necessarily got hydrophobia. I myself heard hydrophobia discussed in my youth by doctors in Dublin before a Pasteur Institute existed, the subject having been brought forward there by the scepticism of an eminent surgeon as to whether hydrophobia is really a specific disease or only ordinary tetanus induced (as tetanus was then supposed to be induced) by a lacerated wound. There were no statistics available as to the proportion of dog bites that ended in hydrophobia; but nobody ever guessed that the cases could be more than two or three per cent of the bites. On me, therefore, the results published by the Pasteur Institute produced no such effect as they did on the ordinary man who thinks that the bite of a mad dog means certain hydrophobia. It seemed to me that the proportion of deaths among the cases treated at the Institute was rather higher, if anything, than might have been expected had there been no Institute in existence. But to the public every Pasteur patient who did not die was miraculously saved from an agonizing death by the beneficent white magic of that most trusty of all wizards, the man of science.

Even trained statisticians often fail to appreciate the extent to which statistics are vitiated by the unrecorded assumptions of their interpreters. Their attention is too much occupied with the cruder tricks of those who make a corrupt use of statistics for advertizing purposes. There is, for example, the percentage dodge. In some hamlet, barely large enough to have a name, two people are attacked during a smallpox epidemic. One dies: the other recovers. One has vaccination marks: the other has none. Immediately either the vaccinists or the anti-vaccinists publish the triumphant news that at such and such a place not a single vaccinated person died of smallpox whilst 100 per cent of the unvaccinated perished miserably; or, as the case may be, that 100 per cent of the unvaccinated recovered whilst the vaccinated succumbed to the last man. Or, to take another common instance, comparisons which are really comparisons between two social classes with different standards of nutrition and education are palmed off as comparisons between the results of a certain medical treatment and its neglect. Thus it is easy to prove that the wearing of tall hats and the carrying of umbrellas enlarges the chest, prolongs life, and confers comparative immunity from disease; for the statistics shew that the classes which use these articles are bigger, healthier, and live longer than the class which never dreams of possessing such things. It does not take much perspicacity to see that what really makes this difference is not the tall hat and the umbrella, but the wealth and nourishment of which they are evidence, and that a gold watch or membership of a club in Pall Mall might be proved in the same way to have the like sovereign virtues. A university degree, a daily bath, the owning of thirty pairs of trousers, a knowledge of Wagner's music, a pew in

Preface on Doctors

church, anything, in short, that implies more means and better nurture than the mass of laborers enjoy, can be statistically palmed off as a magic-spell conferring all sorts of privileges.

In the case of a prophylactic enforced by law, this illusion is intensified grotesquely, because only vagrants can evade it. Now vagrants have little power of resisting any disease: their death rate and their case-mortality rate is always high relatively to that of respectable folk. Nothing is easier, therefore, than to prove that compliance with any public regulation produces the most gratifying results. It would be equally easy even if the regulation actually raised the death-rate, provided it did not raise it sufficiently to make the average householder, who cannot evade regulations, die as early as the average vagrant who can.

The Surprises of Attention and Neglect

There is another statistical illusion which is independent of class differences. A common complaint of houseowners is that the Public Health Authorities frequently compel them to instal costly sanitary appliances which are condemned a few years later as dangerous to health, and forbidden under penalties. Yet these discarded mistakes are always made in the first instance on the strength of a demonstration that their introduction has reduced the death-rate. The explanation is simple. Suppose a law were made that every child in the nation should be compelled to drink a pint of brandy per month, but that the brandy must be administered only when the child was in good health, with its digestion and so forth working normally, and its teeth either naturally or artificially sound. Probably the result would be an immediate and startling reduction in child mortality, leading to further legislation increasing the quantity of brandy to a gallon. Not until the brandy craze had been carried to a point at which the direct harm done by it would outweigh the incidental good, would an anti-brandy party be listened to. That incidental good would be the substitution of attention to the general health of children for the neglect which is now the rule so long as the child is not actually too sick to run about and play as usual. Even if this attention were confined to the children's teeth, there would be an improvement which it would take a good deal of brandy to cancel.

This imaginary case explains the actual case of the sanitary appliances which our local sanitary authorities prescribe today and condemn tomorrow. No sanitary contrivance which the mind of even the very worst plumber can devize could be as disastrous as that total neglect for long periods which gets avenged by pestilences that sweep through whole continents, like the black death and the cholera. If it were proposed at this time of day to discharge all the sewage of London crude and untreated into the Thames, instead of carrying it, after elaborate treatment, far out into the North Sea, there would be a shriek of horror from all our experts. Yet if Cromwell had done that instead of doing nothing, there would probably have been no Great Plague of London. When the Local Health Authority forces every householder to have his sanitary arrangements thought about and attended to by somebody whose special business it is to attend to such things, then it matters not how erroneous or even directly mischievous may be the specific measures taken: the net result at first is sure to be an improvement. Not until attention has been effectually substituted for neglect as the general rule, will the statistics begin to shew the merits of the particular methods of attention adopted. And as we are far from having arrived at this stage, being as to health legislation only at the beginning of things, we have practically no evidence yet as to the value of methods. Simple and obvious as this is, nobody seems as yet to discount the effect of substituting attention for neglect in drawing conclusions from health statistics. Everything is put to the credit of the particular method employed, although it may quite possibly be raising the death rate by five per thousand whilst the attention incidental to it is reducing the death rate fifteen per thousand. The net gain of ten per thousand is credited to the method, and made the excuse for enforcing more of it.

Stealing Credit from Civilization

There is yet another way in which specifics which have no merits at all, either direct or incidental, may be brought into high repute by statistics. For a century past civilization has been cleaning away the conditions which favor bacterial fevers. Typhus, once rife, has vanished: plague and cholera have been stopped at our frontiers by a sanitary blockade. We still have epidemics of smallpox and typhoid; and diphtheria and scarlet fever are endemic in the slums. Measles, which in my childhood was not regarded as a dangerous disease, has now become so mortal that notices are posted publicly urging parents to take it seriously. But even in these cases the contrast between the death and recovery rates in the rich districts and in the poor ones has led to the general conviction among experts that bacterial diseases are preventible; and they already are to a large extent prevented. The dangers of infection and the way to avoid it are better understood than they used to be. It is barely twenty years since people exposed themselves recklessly to the infection of consumption and pneumonia in the belief that these diseases were not "catching." Nowadays the troubles of consumptive patients are greatly increased by the growing disposition to treat them as lepers. No doubt there is a good deal of ignorant exaggeration and cowardly refusal to face a human and necessary share of the risk. That has always been the case. We now know that the medieval horror of leprosy was out of all proportion to the danger of infection, and was accompanied by apparent blindness to the infectiousness of smallpox, which has since been worked up by our disease terrorists into the position formerly held by leprosy. But the scare of infection, though it sets even doctors talking as if the only really scientific thing to do with a fever patient is to throw him into the nearest ditch and pump carbolic acid on him from a safe distance until he is ready to be cremated on the spot, has led to much greater care and cleanliness. And the net result has been a series of victories over disease.

Now let us suppose that in the early nineteenth century somebody had come forward with a theory that typhus fever always begins in the top joint of the little finger; and that if this joint be amputated immediately after birth, typhus fever will disappear. Had such a suggestion been adopted, the theory would have been triumphantly confirmed; for as a matter of fact, typhus fever *has* disappeared. On the other hand cancer and madness have increased (statistically) to an appalling extent. The opponents of the little finger theory would therefore be pretty sure to allege that the amputations were spreading cancer and lunacy. The vaccination controversy is full of such contentions. So is the controversy as to the docking of horses' tails and the cropping of dogs' ears. So is the less widely known controversy as to circumcision and the declaring certain kinds of flesh unclean by the Jews. To advertize any remedy or operation, you have only to pick out all the most reassuring advances made by civilization, and boldly present the two in the relation of cause and effect: the public will swallow the fallacy without a wry face. It has no idea of the

Preface on Doctors

need for what is called a control experiment. In Shakespear's time and for long after it, mummy was a favorite medicament. You took a pinch of the dust of a dead Egyptian in a pint of the hottest water you could bear to drink; and it did you a great deal of good. This, you thought, proved what a sovereign healer mummy was. But if you had tried the control experiment of taking the hot water without the mummy, you might have found the effect exactly the same, and that any hot drink would have done as well.

Biometrika

Another difficulty about statistics is the technical difficulty of calculation. Before you can even make a mistake in drawing your conclusion from the correlations established by your statistics you must ascertain the correlations. When I turn over the pages of Biometrika, a quarterly journal in which is recorded the work done in the field of biological statistics by Professor Karl Pearson and his colleagues, I am out of my depth at the first line, because mathematics are to me only a concept: I never used a logarithm in my life, and could not undertake to extract the square root of four without misgiving. I am therefore unable to deny that the statistical ascertainment of the correlations between one thing and another must be a very complicated and difficult technical business, not to be tackled successfully except by high mathematicians; and I cannot resist Professor Karl Pearson's immense contempt for, and indignant sense of grave social danger in, the unskilled guesses of the ordinary sociologist.

Now the man in the street knows nothing of Biometrika: all he knows is that "you can prove anything by figures," though he forgets this the moment figures are used to prove anything he wants to believe. If he did take in Biometrika he would probably become abjectly credulous as to all the conclusions drawn in it from the correlations so learnedly worked out; though the mathematician whose correlations would fill a Newton with admiration may, in collecting and accepting data and drawconclusions from them, fall into quite crude errors by just such popular oversights as I have been describing.

Patient-made Therapeutics

To all these blunders and ignorances doctors are no less subject than the rest of us. They are not trained in the use of evidence, nor in biometrics, nor in the psychology of human credulity, nor in the incidence of economic pressure. Further, they must believe, on the whole, what their patients believe, just as they must wear the sort of hat their patients wear. The doctor may lay down the law despotically enough to the patient at points where the patient's mind is simply blank; but when the patient has a prejudice the doctor must either keep it in countenance or lose his patient. If people are persuaded that night air is dangerous to health and that fresh air makes them catch cold, it will not be possible for a doctor to make his living in private practice if he prescribes ventilation. We have to go back no further than the days of The Pickwick Papers to find ourselves in a world where people slept in four-post beds with curtains drawn closely round to exclude as much air as possible. Had Mr. Pickwick's doctor told him that he would be much healthier if he slept on a camp bed by an open window, Mr. Pickwick would have regarded him as a crank and called in another doctor. Had he gone on to forbid Mr. Pickwick to drink brandy and water whenever he felt chilly, and assured him that if he were deprived of meat or salt for a whole year, he would not only not die, but would be none the worse, Mr. Pickwick would have fled from his presence as from that of a dangerous madman. And in these matters the doctor cannot cheat his patient. If he has no faith in drugs or vaccination, and the patient has, he can cheat him with colored water and pass his lancet through the flame of a spirit lamp before scratching his arm. But he cannot make him change his daily habits without knowing it.

The Reforms also come from the Laity

In the main, then, the doctor learns that if he gets ahead of the superstitions of his patients he is a ruined man; and the result is that he instinctively takes care not to get ahead of them. That is why all the changes come from the laity. It was not until an agitation had been conducted for many years by laymen, including quacks and faddists of all kinds, that the public was sufficiently impressed to make it possible for the doctors to open their minds and their mouths on the subject of fresh air, cold water, temperance, and the rest of the new fashions in hygiene. At present the tables have been turned on many old prejudices. Plenty of our most popular elderly doctors believe that cold tubs in the morning are unnatural, exhausting, and rheumatic; that fresh air is a fad and that everybody is the better for a glass or two of port wine every day; but they no longer dare say as much until they know exactly where they are; for many very desirable patients in country houses have lately been persuaded that their first duty is to get up at six in the morning and begin the day by taking a walk barefoot through the dewy grass. He who shews the least scepticism as to this practice is at once suspected of being "an old-fashioned doctor," and dismissed to make room for a younger man.

In short, private medical practice is governed not by

science but by supply and demand; and however scientific a treatment may be, it cannot hold its place in the market if there is no demand for it; nor can the grossest quackery be kept off the market if there is a demand for it.

Fashions and Epidemics

A demand, however, can be inculcated. This is thoroughly understood by fashionable tradesmen, who find no difficulty in persuading their customers to renew articles that are not worn out and to buy things they do not want. By making doctors tradesmen, we compel them to learn the tricks of trade; consequently we find that the fashions of the year include treatments, operations, and particular drugs, as well as hats, sleeves, ballads, and games. Tonsils, vermiform appendices, uvulas, even ovaries are sacrificed because it is the fashion to get them cut out, and because the operations are highly profitable. The psychology of fashion becomes a pathology; for the cases have every air of being genuine: fashions, after all, are only induced epidemics, proving that epidemics can be induced by tradesmen, and therefore by doctors.

The Doctor's Virtues

It will be admitted that this is a pretty bad state of things. And the melodramatic instinct of the public, always demanding that every wrong shall have, not its remedy, but its villain to be hissed, will blame, not its own apathy, superstition, and ignorance, but the depravity of the doctors. Nothing could be more unjust or mischievous. Doctors, if no better than other men, are certainly no worse. I was reproached during the performances of The Doctor's Dilemma at the Court Theatre in 1907 because I made the artist a rascal, the journalist an illiterate incapable, and all the doctors " angels." But I did

Preface on Doctors

not go beyond the warrant of my own experience. It has been my luck to have doctors among my friends for nearly forty years past (all perfectly aware of my freedom from the usual credulity as to the miraculous powers and knowledge attributed to them); and though I know that there are medical blackguards as well as military, legal, and clerical blackguards (one soon finds that out when one is privileged to hear doctors talking shop among themselves), the fact that I was no more at a loss for private medical advice and attendance when I had not a penny in my pocket than I was later on when I could afford fees on the highest scale, has made it impossible for me to share that hostility to the doctor as a man which exists and is growing as an inevitable result of the present condition of medical practice. Not that the interest in disease and aberrations which turns some men and women to medicine and surgery is not sometimes as morbid as the interest in misery and vice which turns some others to philanthropy and "rescue work." But the true doctor is inspired by a hatred of ill-health, and a divine impatience of any waste of vital forces. Unless a man is led to medicine or surgery through a very exceptional technical aptitude, or because doctoring is a family tradition, or because he regards it unintelligently as a lucrative and gentlemanly profession, his motives in choosing the career of a healer are clearly generous. However actual practice may disillusion and corrupt him, his selection in the first instance is not a selection of a base character.

The Doctor's Hardships

A review of the counts in the indictment I have brought against private medical practice will shew that they arise out of the doctor's position as a competitive private tradesman: that is, out of his poverty and dependence.

And it should be borne in mind that doctors are expected to treat other people specially well whilst themselves submitting to specially inconsiderate treatment. The butcher and baker are not expected to feed the hungry unless the hungry can pay; but a doctor who allows a fellow-creature to suffer or perish without aid is regarded as a monster. Even if we must dismiss hospital service as really venal, the fact remains that most doctors do a good deal of gratuitous work in private practice all through their careers. And in his paid work the doctor is on a different footing to the tradesman. Although the articles he sells, advice and treatment, are the same for all classes, his fees have to be graduated like the income tax. The successful fashionable doctor may weed his poorer patients out from time to time, and finally use the College of Physicians to place it out of his own power to accept low fees; but the ordinary general practitioner never makes out his bills without considering the taxable capacity of his patients.

Then there is the disregard of his own health and comfort which results from the fact that he is, by the nature of his work, an emergency man. We are polite and considerate to the doctor when there is nothing the matter, and we meet him as a friend or entertain him as a guest; but when the baby is suffering from croup, or its mother has a temperature of 104°, or its grandfather has broken his leg, nobody thinks of the doctor except as a healer and saviour. He may be hungry, weary, sleepy, run down by several successive nights disturbed by that instrument of torture, the night bell; but who ever thinks of this in the face of sudden sickness or accident? We think no more of the condition of a doctor attending a case than of the condition of a fireman at a fire. In other occupations night-work is specially recognized and provided for. The worker sleeps all day; has his breakfast in the evening; his lunch or dinner at midnight; his din-

Preface on Doctors

ner or supper before going to bed in the morning; and he changes to day-work if he cannot stand night-work. But a doctor is expected to work day and night. In practices which consist largely of workmen's clubs, and in which the patients are therefore taken on wholesale terms and very numerous, the unfortunate assistant, or the principal if he has no assistant, often does not undress, knowing that he will be called up before he has snatched an hour's sleep. To the strain of such inhuman conditions must be added the constant risk of infection. One wonders why the impatient doctors do not become savage and unmanageable, and the patient ones imbecile. Perhaps they do, to some extent. And the pay is wretched, and so uncertain that refusal to attend without payment in advance becomes often a necessary measure of self-defence, whilst the County Court has long ago put an end to the tradition that the doctor's fee is an honorarium. Even the most eminent physicians, as such biographies as those of Paget shew, are sometimes miserably, inhumanly poor until they are past their prime.

In short, the doctor needs our help for the moment much more than we often need his. The ridicule of Molière, the death of a well-informed and clever writer like the late Harold Frederic in the hands of Christian Scientists (a sort of sealing with his blood of the contemptuous disbelief in and dislike of doctors he had bitterly expressed in his books), the scathing and quite justifiable exposure of medical practice in the novel by Mr. Maarten Maartens entitled The New Religion: all these trouble the doctor very little, and are in any case well set off by the popularity of Sir Luke Fildes' famous picture, and by the verdicts in which juries from time to time express their conviction that the doctor can do no wrong. The real woes of the doctor are the shabby coat, the wolf at the door, the tyranny of ignorant patients, the work-day of 24 hours, and the uselessness of honestly prescribing what most of the patients really need: that is, not medicine, but money.

The Public Doctor

What then is to be done?

Fortunately we have not to begin absolutely from the beginning: we already have, in the Medical Officer of Health, a sort of doctor who is free from the worst hardships, and consequently from the worst vices, of the private practitioner. His position depends, not on the number of people who are ill, and whom he can keep ill, but on the number of people who are well. He is judged, as all doctors and treatments should be judged, by the vital statistics of his district. When the death rate goes up his credit goes down. As every increase in his salary depends on the issue of a public debate as to the health of the constituency under his charge, he has every inducement to strive towards the ideal of a clean bill of health. He has a safe, dignified, responsible, independent position based wholly on the public health; whereas the private practitioner has a precarious, shabby-genteel, irresponsible, servile position, based wholly on the prevalence of illness.

It is true, there are grave scandals in the public medical service. The public doctor may be also a private practitioner eking out his earnings by giving a little time to public work for a mean payment. There are cases in which the position is one which no successful practitioner will accept, and where, therefore, incapables or drunkards get automatically selected for the post, *faute de mieux*; but even in these cases the doctor is less disastrous in his public capacity than in his private one: besides, the conditions which produce these bad cases are doomed, as the evil is now recognized and understood. A popular but unstable remedy is to enable local authorities, when they are too small to require the undivided time of such men as the Medical Officers of our great municipalities, to combine for public health purposes so that each may share the services of a highly paid official of the best class; but the right remedy is a larger area as the sanitary unit.

Medical Organization

Another advantage of public medical work is that it admits of organization, and consequently of the distribution of the work in such a manner as to avoid wasting the time of highly qualified experts on trivial jobs. The individualism of private practice leads to an appalling waste of time on trifles. Men whose dexterity as operators or almost divinatory skill in diagnosis are constantly needed for difficult cases, are poulticing whitlows, vaccinating, changing unimportant dressings, prescribing ether drams for ladies with timid leanings towards dipsomania, and generally wasting their time in the pursuit of private fees. In no other profession is the practitioner expected to do all the work involved in it from the first day of his professional career to the last as the doctor is. The judge passes sentence of death; but he is not expected to hang the criminal with his own hands, as he would be if the legal profession were as unorganized as the medical. The bishop is not expected to blow the organ or wash the baby he baptizes. The general is not asked to plan a campaign or conduct a battle at half-past twelve and to play the drum at half-past two. Even if they were, things would still not be as bad as in the medical profession; for in it not only is the first-class man set to do third-class work, but, what is much more terrifying, the third-class man is expected to do first-class work. Every general practitioner is supposed to be capable of the whole range of medical and surgical work at a moment's notice; and the country doctor, who has not a specialist nor a crack consultant at the end of his telephone, often has to tackle without hesitation cases which no sane practitioner in a town would take in hand without assistance. No doubt this develops the resourcefulness of the country doctor, and makes him a more capable man than his suburban colleague; but it cannot develop the second-class man into a first-class one. If the practice of law not only led to a judge having to hang, but the hangman to judge, or if in the army matters were so arranged that it would be possible for the drummer boy to be in command at Waterloo whilst the Duke of Wellington was playing the drum in Brussels, we should not be consoled by the reflection that our hangmen were thereby made a little more judicial-minded, and our drummers more responsible, than in foreign countries where the legal and military professions recognized the advantages of division of labor.

Under such conditions no statistics as to the graduation of professional ability among doctors are available. Assuming that doctors are normal men and not magicians (and it is unfortunately very hard to persuade people to admit so much and thereby destroy the romance of doctoring) we may guess that the medical profession, like the other professions, consists of a small percentage of highly gifted persons at one end, and a small percentage of altogether disastrous duffers at the other. Between these extremes comes the main body of doctors (also, of course, with a weak and a strong end) who can be trusted to work under regulations with more or less aid from above according to the gravity of the case. Or, to put it in terms of the cases, there are cases that present no difficulties, and can be dealt with by a nurse or student at one end of the scale, and cases that require watching and handling by the very highest existing skill at the other; whilst between come the great mass of cases which need visits from the doctor of ordinary ability and from the chiefs of the profession in the proportion of, say, seven to none, seven to one, three to one, one to one, or, for a day or two, none to one. Such a service is organized at present only in hospitals; though in large towns the practice of calling in the consultant acts, to some extent, as a substitute for it. But in the latter case it is quite unregulated except by professional etiquet, which, as we have seen, has for its object, not the health of the patient or of the community at large, but the protection of the doctor's livelihood and the concealment of his errors. And as the consultant is an expensive luxury, he is a last resource rather, as he should be, than a matter of course, in all cases where the general practitioner is not equal to the occasion: a predicament in which a very capable man may find himself at any time through the cropping up of a case of which he has had no clinical experience.

The Social Solution of the Medical Problem

The social solution of the medical problem, then, depends on that large, slowly advancing, pettishly resisted integration of society called generally Socialism. Until the medical profession becomes a body of men trained and paid by the country to keep the country in health it will remain what it is at present: a conspiracy to exploit popular credulity and human suffering. Already our M.O.H.s (Medical Officers of Health) are in the new position: what is lacking is appreciation of the change, not only by the public but by the private doctors. For, as we have seen, when one of the first-rate posts becomes vacant in one of the great cities, and all the leading M.O.H.s compete for it, they must appeal to the good health of the cities of which they have been in charge, and not to the size of the incomes the local private doctors are making out of the ill-health of their patients. If a competitor can prove that he has utterly ruined every sort of medical private practice in a large city except obstetric practice and the surgery of accidents, his claims are irresistible; and this is the ideal at which every M.O.H should aim. But the profession at large should none the less welcome him and set its house in order for the social change which will finally be its own salvation. For the M.O.H. as we know him is only the beginning of that army of Public Hygiene which will presently take the place in general interest and honor now occupied by our military and naval forces. It is silly that an Englishman should be more afraid of a German soldier than of a British disease germ, and should clamor for more barracks in the same newspapers that protest against more school clinics, and cry out that if the State fights disease for us it makes us paupers, though they never say that if the State fights the Germans for us it makes us cowards. Fortunately, when a habit of thought is silly it only needs steady treatment by ridicule from sensible and witty people to be put out of countenance and perish. Every year sees an increase in the number of persons employed in the Public Health Service, who would formerly have been mere adventurers in the Private Illness Service. To put it another way, a host of men and women who have now a strong incentive to be mischievous and even murderous rogues will have a much stronger, because a much honester, incentive to be not only good citizens but active benefactors to the community. And they will have no anxiety whatever about their incomes.

The Future of Private Practice

It must not be hastily concluded that this involves the extinction of the private practitioner. What it will really

Preface on Doctors

mean for him is release from his present degrading and scientifically corrupting slavery to his patients. As I have already shewn, the doctor who has to live by pleasing his patients in competition with everybody who has walked the hospitals, scraped through the examinations, and bought a brass plate, soon finds himself prescribing water to teetotallers and brandy or champagne jelly to drunkards; beefsteaks and stout in one house, and "uric acid free" vegetarian diet over the way; shut windows, big fires, and heavy overcoats to old Colonels, and open air and as much nakedness as is compatible with decency to young faddists, never once daring to say either "I dont know," or "I dont agree." For the strength of the doctor's, as of every other man's position when the evolution of social organization at last reaches his profession, will be that he will always have open to him the alternative of public employment when the private employer becomes too tyrannous. And let no one suppose that the words doctor and patient can disguise from the parties the fact that they are employer and employee. No doubt doctors who are in great demand can be as high-handed and independent as employees are in all classes when a dearth in their labor market makes them indispensable; but the average doctor is not in this position: he is struggling for life in an overcrowded profession, and knows well that "a good bedside manner" will carry him to solvency through a morass of illness, whilst the least attempt at plain dealing with people who are eating too much, or drinking too much, or frowsting too much (to go no further in the list of intemperances that make up so much of family life) would soon land him in the Bankruptcy Court.

Private practice, thus protected, would itself protect individuals, as far as such protection is possible, against the errors and superstitions of State medicine, which are at worst no worse than the errors and superstitions of private practice, being, indeed, all derived from it. Such monstrosities as vaccination are, as we have seen, founded, not on science, but on half-crowns. If the Vaccination Acts, instead of being wholly repealed as they are already half repealed, were strengthened by compelling every parent to have his child vaccinated by a public officer whose salary was completely independent of the number of vaccinations performed by him, and for whom there was plenty of alternative public health work waiting, vaccination would be dead in two years, as the vaccinator would not only not gain by it, but would lose credit through the depressing effects on the vital statistics of his district of the illness and deaths it causes, whilst it would take from him all the credit of that freedom from smallpox which is the result of good sanitary administration and vigilant prevention of infection. Such absurd panic scandals as that of the last London epidemic, where a fee of half-a-crown per re-vaccination produced raids on houses during the absence of parents, and the forcible seizure and re-vaccination of children left to answer the door, can be prevented simply by abolishing the half-crown and all similar follies, paying, not for this or that ceremony of witchcraft, but for immunity from disease, and paying, too, in a rational way. The officer with a fixed salary saves himself trouble by doing his business with the least possible interference with the private citizen. The man paid by the job loses money by not forcing his job on the public as often as possible without reference to its results.

The Technical Problem

As to any technical medical problem specially involved, there is none. If there were, I should not be competent to deal with it, as I am not a technical expert in medicine: I deal with the subject as an economist, a politician, and

Preface on Doctors

a citizen exercising my common sense. Everything that I have said applies equally to all the medical techniques, and will hold good whether public hygiene be based on the poetic fancies of Christian Science, the tribal superstitions of the druggist and the vivisector, or the best we can make of our real knowledge. But I may remind those who confusedly imagine that the medical problem is also the scientific problem, that all problems are finally scientific problems. The notion that therapeutics or hygiene or surgery is any more or less scientific than making or cleaning boots is entertained only by people to whom a man of science is still a magician who can cure diseases, transmute metals, and enable us to live for ever. It may still be necessary for some time to come to practise on popular credulity, popular love and dread of the marvellous, and popular idolatry, to induce the poor to comply with the sanitary regulations they are too ignorant to understand. As I have elsewhere confessed, I have myself been responsible for ridiculous incantations with burning sulphur, experimentally proved to be quite useless, because poor people are convinced, by the mystical air of the burning and the horrible smell, that it exorcises the demons of smallpox and scarlet fever and makes it safe for them to return to their houses. To assure them that the real secret is sunshine and soap is only to convince them that you do not care whether they live or die, and wish to save money at their expense. So you perform the incantation; and back they go to their houses, satisfied. A religious ceremony—a poetic blessing of the threshold, for instance—would be much better; but unfortunately our religion is weak on the sanitary side. One of the worst misfortunes of Christendom was that reaction against the voluptuous bathing of the imperial Romans which made dirty habits a part of Christian piety, and in some unlucky places (the Sandwich Islands for example) made the introduction of Christianity also the introduction of disease, because the formulators of the superseded native religion, like Mahomet, had been enlightened enough to introduce as religious duties such sanitary measures as ablution and the most careful and reverent treatment of everything cast off by the human body, even to nail clippings and hairs; and our missionaries thoughtlessly discredited this godly doctrine without supplying its place, which was promptly taken by laziness and neglect. If the priests of Ireland could only be persuaded to teach their flocks that it is a deadly insult to the Blessed Virgin to place her image in a cottage that is not kept up to that high standard of Sunday cleanliness to which all her worshippers must believe she is accustomed, and to represent her as being especially particular about stables because her son was born in one, they might do more in one year than all the Sanitary Inspectors in Ireland could do in twenty; and they could hardly doubt that Our Lady would be delighted. Perhaps they do nowadays; for Ireland is certainly a transfigured country since my youth as far as clean faces and pinafores can transfigure it. In England, where so many of the inhabitants are too gross to believe in poetic faiths, too respectable to tolerate the notion that the stable at Bethany was a common peasant farmer's stable instead of a first-rate racing one, and too savage to believe that anything can really cast out the devil of disease unless it be some terrifying hoodoo of tortures and stinks, the M.O.H. will no doubt for a long time to come have to preach to fools according to their folly, promising miracles, and threatening hideous personal consequences of neglect of by-laws and the like; therefore it will be important that every M.O.H. shall have, with his (or her) other qualifications, a sense of humor, lest (he or she) should come at last to believe all the nonsense that must needs be talked. But he must, in his capacity of an expert advising the authorities, keep the government itself free of superstition. If Italian peasants are so ignorant that the Church can get no hold of them except by miracles, why, miracles there must be. The blood of St. Januarius must liquefy whether the Saint is in the humor or not. To trick a heathen into being a dutiful Christian is no worse than to trick a whitewasher into trusting himself in a room where a smallpox patient has lain, by pretending to exorcise the disease with burning sulphur. But woe to the Church if in deceiving the peasant it also deceives itself; for then the Church is lost, and the peasant too, unless he revolt against it. Unless the Church works the pretended miracle painfully against the grain, and is continually urged by its dislike of the imposture to strive to make the peasant susceptible to the true reasons for behaving well, the Church will become an instrument of his corruption and an exploiter of his ignorance, and will find itself launched upon that persecution of scientific truth of which all priesthoods are accused—and none with more justice than the scientific priesthood.

And here we come to the danger that terrifies so many of us: the danger of having a hygienic orthodoxy imposed on us. But we must face that: in such crowded and poverty ridden civilizations as ours any orthodoxy is better than laisser-faire. If our population ever comes to consist exclusively of well-to-do, highly cultivated, and thoroughly instructed free persons in a position to take care of themselves, no doubt they will make short work of a good deal of official regulation that is now of life-and-death necessity to us; but under existing circumstances, I repeat, almost any sort of attention that democracy will stand is better than neglect. Attention and activity lead to mistakes as well as to successes; but a life spent in making mistakes is not only more honorable but more useful than a life spent doing nothing. The one lesson that comes out of all our theorizing and experimenting is that there is only one really scientific progressive method;

and that is the method of trial and error. If you come to that, what is laisser-faire but an orthodoxy? the most tyrannous and disastrous of all the orthodoxies, since it forbids you even to learn.

The Latest Theories

Medical theories are so much a matter of fashion, and the most fertile of them are modified so rapidly by medical practice and biological research, which are international activities, that the play which furnishes the pretext for this preface is already slightly outmoded, though I believe it may be taken as a faithful record for the year (1906) in which it was begun. I must not expose any professional man to ruin by connecting his name with the entire freedom of criticism which I, as a layman, enjoy; but it will be evident to all experts that my play could not have been written but for the work done by Sir Almroth Wright in the theory and practice of securing immunization from bacterial diseases by the inoculation of " vaccines " made of their own bacteria: a practice incorrectly called vaccinetherapy (there is nothing vaccine about it) apparently because it is what vaccination ought to be and is not. Until Sir Almroth Wright, following up one of Metchnikoff's most suggestive biological romances, discovered that the white corpuscles or phagocytes which attack and devour disease germs for us do their work only when we butter the disease germs appetizingly for them with a natural sauce which Sir Almroth named opsonin, and that our production of this condiment continually rises and falls rhythmically from negligibility to the highest efficiency, nobody had been able even to conjecture why the various serums that were from time to time introduced as having effected marvellous cures, presently made such direful havoc of some unfortunate patient that they had to be dropped hastily. The

Preface on Doctors

quantity of sturdy lying that was necessary to save the credit of inoculation in those days was prodigious; and had it not been for the devotion shewn by the military authorities throughout Europe, who would order the entire disappearance of some disease from their armies, and bring it about by the simple plan of changing the name under which the cases were reported, or for our own Metropolitan Asylums Board, which carefully suppressed all the medical reports that revealed the sometimes quite appalling effects of epidemics of revaccination, there is no saying what popular reaction might not have taken place against the whole immunization movement in therapeutics.

The situation was saved when Sir Almroth Wright pointed out that if you inoculated a patient with pathogenic germs at a moment when his powers of cooking them for consumption by the phagocytes was receding to its lowest point, you would certainly make him a good deal worse and perhaps kill him, whereas if you made precisely the same inoculation when the cooking power was rising to one of its periodical climaxes, you would stimulate it to still further exertions and produce just the opposite result. And he invented a technique for ascertaining in which phase the patient happened to be at any given moment. The dramatic possibilities of this discovery and invention will be found in my play. But it is one thing to invent a technique: it is quite another to persuade the medical profession to acquire it. Our general practitioners, I gather, simply declined to acquire it, being mostly unable to afford either the acquisition or the practice of it when acquired. Something simple, cheap, and ready at all times for all comers, is, as I have shewn, the only thing that is economically possible in general practice, whatever may be the case in Sir Almroth's famous laboratory in St. Mary's Hospital. It would have become necessary to denounce opsonin in the trade papers as a fad and Sir Almroth as a dangerous man if his practice in the laboratory had not led him to the conclusion that the customary inoculations were very much too powerful, and that a comparatively infinitesimal dose would not precipitate a negative phase of cooking activity, and might induce a positive one. And thus it happens that the refusal of our general practitioners to acquire the new technique is no longer quite so dangerous in practice as it was when The Doctor's Dilemma was written: nay, that Sir Ralph Bloomfield Bonington's way of administering inoculations as if they were spoonfuls of squills may sometimes work fairly well. For all that, I find Sir Almroth Wright, on the 23rd May, 1910, warning the Royal Society of Medicine that "the clinician has not yet been prevailed upon to reconsider his positon," which means that the general practitioner (" the doctor," as he is called in our homes) is going on just as he did before, and could not afford to learn or practice a new technique even if he had ever heard of it. To the patient who does not know about it he will say nothing. To the patient who does, he will ridicule it, and disparage Sir Almroth. What else can he do, except confess his ignorance and starve?

But now please observe how "the whirligig of time brings its revenges." This latest discovery of the remedial virtue of a very, very tiny hair of the dog that bit you reminds us, not only of Arndt's law of protoplasmic reaction to stimuli, according to which weak and strong stimuli provoke opposite reactions, but of Hahnemann's homeopathy, which was founded on the fact alleged by Hahnemann that drugs which produce certain symptoms when taken in ordinary perceptible quantities, will, when taken in infinitesimally small quantities, provoke just the opposite symptoms; so that the drug that gives you a headache will also cure a headache if you take little enough of it. I have already explained that the savage opposition which homeopathy encountered from the medical profession was not a scientific opposition; for nobody seems to deny that some drugs act in the alleged manner. It was opposed simply because doctors and apothecaries lived by selling bottles and boxes of doctor's stuff to be taken in spoonfuls or in pellets as large as peas; and people would not pay as much for drops and globules no bigger than pins' heads. Nowadays, however, the more cultivated folk are beginning to be so suspicious of drugs, and the incorrigibly superstitious people so profusely supplied with patent medicines (the medical advice to take them being wrapped round the bottle and thrown in for nothing) that homeopathy has become a way of rehabilitating the trade of prescription compounding, and is consequently coming into professional credit. At which point the theory of opsonins comes very opportunely to shake hands with it.

Add to the newly triumphant homeopathist and the opsonist that other remarkable innovator, the Swedish masseur, who does not theorize about you, but probes you all over with his powerful thumbs until he finds out your sore spots and rubs them away, besides cheating you into a little wholesome exercise; and you have nearly everything in medical practice to-day that is not flat witchcraft or pure commercial exploitation of human credulity and fear of death. Add to them a good deal of vegetarian and teetotal controversy raging round a clamor for scientific eating and drinking, and resulting in little so far except calling digestion Metabolism and dividing the public between the eminent doctor who tells us that we do not eat enough fish, and his equally eminent colleague who warns us that a fish diet must end in leprosy, and you have all that opposes with any sort of countenance the rise of Christian Science with its cathedrals and congregations and zealots and miracles and cures: all very silly, no doubt, but sane and sensible, poetic and hopeful, compared to the pseudo science of the commercial general practitioner, who foolishly clamors for the prosecution and even the execution of the Christian Scientists when their patients die, forgetting the long death roll of his own patients.

By the time this preface is in print the kaleidoscope may have had another shake; and opsonin may have gone the way of phlogiston at the hands of its own restless discoverer. I will not say that Hahnemann may have gone the way of Diafoirus; for Diafoirus we have always with us. But we shall still pick up all our knowledge in pursuit of some Will o' the Wisp or other. What is called science has always pursued the Elixir of Life and the Philosopher's Stone, and is just as busy after them to-day as ever it was in the days of Paracelsus. We call them by different names: Immunization or Radiology or what not; but the dreams which lure us into the adventures from which we learn are always at bottom the same. Science becomes dangerous only when it imagines that it has reached its goal. What is wrong with priests and popes is that instead of being apostles and saints, they are nothing but empirics who say " I know " instead of " I am learning," and pray for credulity and inertia as wise men pray for scepticism and activity. Such abominations as the Inquisition and the Vaccination Acts are possible only in the famine years of the soul, when the great vital dogmas of honor, liberty, courage, the kinship of all life, faith that the unknown is greater than the known and is only the As Yet Unknown, and resolution to find a manly highway to it, have been forgotten in a paroxysm of littleness and terror in which nothing is active except concupiscence and the fear of death, playing on which any trader can filch a fortune, any blackguard gratify his cruelty, and any tyrant make us his slaves.

Lest this should seem too rhetorical a conclusion for our professional men of science, who are mostly trained

Preface on Doctors

not to believe anything unless it is worded in the jargon of those writers who, because they never really understand what they are trying to say, cannot find familiar words for it, and are therefore compelled to invent a new language of nonsense for every book they write, let me sum up my conclusions as dryly as is consistent with accurate thought and live conviction.

1. Nothing is more dangerous than a poor doctor: not even a poor employer or a poor landlord.

2. Of all the anti-social vested interests the worst is the vested interest in ill-health.

3. Remember that an illness is a misdemeanor; and treat the doctor as an accessory unless he notifies every case to the Public Health authority.

4. Treat every death as a possible and under our present system a probable murder, by making it the subject of a reasonably conducted inquest; and execute the doctor, if necessary, *as* a doctor, by striking him off the register.

5. Make up your mind how many doctors the community needs to keep it well. Do not register more or less than this number; and let registration constitute the doctor a civil servant with a dignified living wage paid out of public funds.

6. Municipalize Harley Street.

7. Treat the private operator exactly as you would treat a private executioner.

8. Treat persons who profess to be able to cure disease as you treat fortune tellers.

9. Keep the public carefully informed, by special statistics and announcements of individual cases, of all illnesses of doctors or in their families.

10. Make it compulsory for a doctor using a brass plate to have inscribed on it, in addition to the letters indicating his qualifications, the words " Remember that I too am mortal."

11. In legislation and social organization, proceed on the principle that invalids, meaning persons who cannot keep themselves alive by their own activities, cannot, beyond reason, expect to be kept alive by the activity of others. There is a point at which the most energetic policeman or doctor, when called upon to deal with an apparently drowned person, gives up artificial respiration, although it is never possible to declare with certainty, at any point short of decomposition, that another five minutes of the exercise would not effect resuscitation. The theory that every individual alive is of infinite value is legislatively impracticable. No doubt the higher the life we secure to the individual by wise social organization, the greater his value is to the community, and the more pains we shall take to pull him through any temporary danger or disablement. But the man who costs more than he is worth is doomed by sound hygiene as inexorably as by sound economics.

12. Do not try to live for ever. You will not succeed.

13. Use your health, even to the point of wearing it out. That is what it is for. Spend all you have before you die; and do not outlive yourself.

14. Take the utmost care to get well born and well brought up. This means that your mother must have a good doctor. Be careful to go to a school where there is what they call a school clinic, where your nutrition and teeth and eyesight and other matters of importance to you will be attended to. Be particularly careful to have all this done at the expense of the nation, as otherwise it will not be done at all, the chances being about forty to one against your being able to pay for it directly yourself, even if you know how to set about it. Otherwise you will be what most people are at present: an unsound citizen of an unsound nation, without sense enough to be ashamed or unhappy about it.

THE DOCTOR'S DILEMMA

XVI

1906

I am grateful to Hesba Stretton, the authoress of "Jessica's First Prayer," for permission to use the title of one of her stories for this play.

ACT I

On the 15th June 1903, in the early forenoon, a medical student, surname Redpenny, Christian name unknown and of no importance, sits at work in a doctor's consulting-room. He devils for the doctor by answering his letters, acting as his domestic laboratory assistant, and making himself indispensable generally, in return for unspecified advantages involved by intimate intercourse with a leader of his profession, and amounting to an informal apprenticeship and a temporary affiliation. Redpenny is not proud, and will do anything he is asked without reservation of his personal dignity if he is asked in a fellow-creaturely way. He is a wide-open-eyed, ready, credulous, friendly, hasty youth, with his hair and clothes in reluctant transition from the untidy boy to the tidy doctor.

Redpenny is interrupted by the entrance of an old serving-woman who has never known the cares, the preoccupations, the responsibilities, jealousies, and anxieties of personal beauty. She has the complexion of a never-washed gypsy, incurable by any detergent; and she has, not a regular beard and moustaches, which could at least be trimmed and waxed into a masculine presentableness, but a whole crop of small beards and moustaches, mostly springing from moles all over her face. She carries a

duster and toddles about meddlesomely, spying out dust
so diligently that whilst she is flicking off one speck she
is already looking elsewhere for another. In conversation she has the same trick, hardly ever looking at the
person she is addressing except when she is excited. She
has only one manner, and that is the manner of an old
family nurse to a child just after it has learnt to walk.
She has used her ugliness to secure indulgences unattainable by Cleopatra or Fair Rosamund, and has the further
great advantage over them that age increases her qualification instead of impairing it. Being an industrious,
agreeable, and popular old soul, she is a walking sermon
on the vanity of feminine prettiness. Just as Redpenny
has no discovered Christian name, she has no discovered
surname, and is known throughout the doctors' quarter
between Cavendish Square and the Marylebone Road
simply as Emmy.

The consulting-room has two windows looking on
Queen Anne Street. Between the two is a marble-topped
console, with haunched gilt legs ending in sphinx claws.
The huge pier-glass which surmounts it is mostly disabled from reflection by elaborate painting on its surface
of palms, ferns, lilies, tulips, and sunflowers. The ad-
joining wall contains the fireplace, with two arm-chairs
before it. As we happen to face the corner we see nothing of the other two walls. On the right of the fireplace,
or rather on the right of any person facing the fireplace,
is the door. On its left is the writing-table at which Redpenny sits. It is an untidy table with a microscope, several test tubes, and a spirit lamp standing up through its
litter of papers. There is a couch in the middle of the
room, at right angels to the console, and parallel to the
fireplace. A chair stands between the couch and the win-
dowed wall. The windows have green Venetian blinds
and rep curtains; and there is a gasalier; but it is a convert to electric lighting. The wall paper and carpets are

ACT I   The Doctor's Dilemma

mostly green, coeval with the gasalier and the Venetian blinds. The house, in fact, was so well furnished in the middle of the XIXth century that it stands unaltered to this day and is still quite presentable.

EMMY [*entering and immediately beginning to dust the couch*] Theres a lady bothering me to see the doctor.

REDPENNY [*distracted by the interruption*] Well, she cant see the doctor. Look here: whats the use of telling you that the doctor cant take any new patients, when the moment a knock comes to the door, in you bounce to ask whether he can see somebody?

EMMY. Who asked you whether he could see somebody?

REDPENNY. You did.

EMMY. I said theres a lady bothering me to see the doctor. That isnt asking. Its telling.

REDPENNY. Well, is the lady bothering you any reason for you to come bothering me when I'm busy?

EMMY. Have you seen the papers?

REDPENNY. No.

EMMY. Not seen the birthday honors?

REDPENNY [*beginning to swear*] What the—

EMMY. Now, now, ducky!

REDPENNY. What do you suppose I care about the birthday honors? Get out of this with your chattering. Dr Ridgeon will be down before I have these letters ready. Get out.

EMMY. Dr Ridgeon wont never be down any more, young man.

She detects dust on the console and is down on it immediately.

REDPENNY [*jumping up and following her*] What?

EMMY. He's been made a knight. Mind you dont go Dr Ridgeoning him in them letters. Sir Colenso Ridgeon is to be his name now.

REDPENNY. I'm jolly glad.

EMMY. I never was so taken aback. I always thought his great discoveries was fudge (let alone the mess of them) with his drops of blood and tubes full of Maltese fever and the like. Now he'll have a rare laugh at me.

REDPENNY. Serve you right! It was like your cheek to talk to him about science. [*He returns to his table and resumes his writing*].

EMMY. Oh, I dont think much of science; and neither will you when youve lived as long with it as I have. Whats on my mind is answering the door. Old Sir Patrick Cullen has been here already and left first congratulations—hadnt time to come up on his way to the hospital, but was determined to be first—coming back, he said. All the rest will be here too: the knocker will be going all day. What I'm afraid of is that the doctor'll want a footman like all the rest, now that he's Sir Colenso. Mind: dont you go putting him up to it, ducky; for he'll never have any comfort with anybody but me to answer the door. I know who to let in and who to keep out. And that reminds me of the poor lady. I think he ought to see her. She's just the kind that puts him in a good temper. [*She dusts Redpenny's papers*].

REDPENNY. I tell you he cant see anybody. Do go away, Emmy. How can I work with you dusting all over me like this?

EMMY. I'm not hindering you working—if you call writing letters working. There goes the bell. [*She looks out of the window*]. A doctor's carriage. Thats more congratulations. [*She is going out when Sir Colenso Ridgeon enters*]. Have you finished your two eggs, sonny?

RIDGEON. Yes.

EMMY. Have you put on your clean vest?

RIDGEON. Yes.

EMMY. Thats my ducky diamond! Now keep yourself tidy and dont go messing about and dirtying your hands: the people are coming to congratulate you. [*She goes out*].

Sir Colenso Ridgeon is a man of fifty who has never shaken off his youth. He has the off-handed manner and the little audacities of address which a shy and sensitive man acquires in breaking himself in to intercourse with all sorts and conditions of men. His face is a good deal lined; his movements are slower than, for instance, Redpenny's; and his flaxen hair has lost its lustre; but in figure and manner he is more the young man than the titled physician. Even the lines in his face are those of overwork and restless scepticism, perhaps partly of curiosity and appetite, rather than of age. Just at present the announcement of his knighthood in the morning papers makes him specially self-conscious, and consequently specially off-hand with Redpenny.

RIDGEON. Have you seen the papers? Youll have to alter the name in the letters if you havnt.

REDPENNY. Emmy has just told me. I'm awfully glad. I—

RIDGEON. Enough, young man, enough. You will soon get accustomed to it.

REDPENNY. They ought to have done it years ago.

RIDGEON. They would have; only they couldnt stand Emmy opening the door, I daresay.

EMMY [*at the door, announcing*] Dr Shoemaker. [*She withdraws*].

A middle-aged gentleman, well dressed, comes in with a friendly but propitiatory air, not quite sure of his reception. His combination of soft manners and responsive kindliness, with a certain unseizable reserve and a familiar yet foreign chiselling of feature, reveal the Jew: in this instance the handsome gentlemanly Jew, gone a little pigeon-breasted and stale after thirty, as handsome young Jews often do, but still decidedly good-looking.

THE GENTLEMAN. Do you remember me? Schutzmacher. University College school and Belsize Avenue. Loony Schutzmacher, you know.

RIDGEON. What! Loony! [*He shakes hands cordially*]. Why, man, I thought you were dead long ago. Sit down. [*Schutzmacher sits on the couch: Ridgeon on the chair between it and the window*]. Where have you been these thirty years?

SCHUTZMACHER. In general practice, until a few months ago. I've retired.

RIDGEON. Well done, Loony! I wish *I* could afford to retire. Was your practice in London?

SCHUTZMACHER. No.

RIDGEON. Fashionable coast practice, I suppose.

SCHUTZMACHER. How could I afford to buy a fashionable practice? I hadnt a rap. I set up in a manufacturing town in the midlands in a little surgery at ten shillings a week.

RIDGEON. And made your fortune?

SCHUTZMACHER. Well, I'm pretty comfortable. I have a place in Hertfordshire besides our flat in town. If you ever want a quiet Saturday to Monday, I'll take you down in my motor at an hour's notice.

RIDGEON. Just rolling in money! I wish you rich g.p.'s would teach me how to make some. Whats the secret of it?

SCHUTZMACHER. Oh, in my case the secret was simple enough, though I suppose I should have got into trouble if it had attracted any notice. And I'm afraid you'll think it rather infra dig.

RIDGEON. Oh, I have an open mind. What was the secret?

SCHUTZMACHER. Well, the secret was just two words.

RIDGEON. Not Consultation Free, was it?

SCHUTZMACHER [*shocked*] No, no. Really!

RIDGEON [*apologetic*] Of course not. I was only joking.

SCHUTZMACHER. My two words were simply Cure Guaranteed.

RIDGEON [*admiring*] Cure Guaranteed!

SCHUTZMACHER. Guaranteed. After all, thats what everybody wants from a doctor, isn't it?

RIDGEON. My dear Loony, it was an inspiration. Was it on the brass plate?

SCHUTZMACHER. There was no brass plate. It was a shop window: red, you know, with black lettering. Doctor Leo Schutzmacher, L.R.C.P.M.R.C.S. Advice and medicine sixpence. Cure Guaranteed.

RIDGEON. And the guarantee proved sound nine times out of ten, eh?

SCHUTZMACHER [*rather hurt at so moderate an estimate*] Oh, much oftener than that. You see, most people get well all right if they are careful and you give them a little sensible advice. And the medicine really did them good. Parrish's Chemical Food: phosphates, you know. One tablespoonful to a twelve-ounce bottle of water: nothing better, no matter what the case is.

RIDGEON. Redpenny: make a note of Parrish's Chemical Food.

SCHUTZMACHER. I take it myself, you know, when I feel run down. Good-bye. You dont mind my calling, do you? Just to congratulate you.

RIDGEON. Delighted, my dear Loony. Come to lunch on Saturday next week. Bring your motor and take me down to Hertford.

SCHUTZMACHER. I will. We shall be delighted. Thank you. Good-bye. [*He goes out with Ridgeon, who returns immediately*].

REDPENNY. Old Paddy Cullen was here before you were up, to be the first to congratulate you.

RIDGEON. Indeed. Who taught you to speak of Sir Patrick Cullen as old Paddy Cullen, you young ruffian?

REDPENNY. You never call him anything else.

RIDGEON. Not now that I am Sir Colenso. Next thing, you fellows will be calling me old Colly Ridgeon.

REDPENNY. We do, at St. Anne's.

RIDGEON. Yach! Thats what makes the medical student the most disgusting figure in modern civilization. No veneration, no manners—no—

EMMY [*at the door, announcing*] Sir Patrick Cullen. [*She retires*].

Sir Patrick Cullen is more than twenty years older than Ridgeon, not yet quite at the end of his tether, but near it and resigned to it. His name, his plain, downright, sometimes rather arid common sense, his large build and stature, the absence of those odd moments of ceremonial servility by which an old English doctor sometimes shews you what the status of the profession was in England in his youth, and an occasional turn of speech, are Irish; but he has lived all his life in England and is thoroughly acclimatized. His manner to Ridgeon, whom he likes, is whimsical and fatherly: to others he is a little gruff and uninviting, apt to substitute more or less expressive grunts for articulate speech, and generally indisposed, at his age, to make much social effort. He shakes Ridgeon's hand and beams at him cordially and jocularly.

SIR PATRICK. Well, young chap. Is your hat too small for you, eh?

RIDGEON. Much too small. I owe it all to you.

SIR PATRICK. Blarney, my boy. Thank you all the same. [*He sits in one of the arm-chairs near the fireplace. Ridgeon sits on the couch*]. Ive come to talk to you a bit. [*To Redpenny*] Young man: get out.

REDPENNY. Certainly, Sir Patrick [*He collects his papers and makes for the door*].

ACT I   The Doctor's Dilemma   11

SIR PATRICK. Thank you. Thats a good lad. [*Redpenny vanishes*]. They all put up with me, these young chaps, because I'm an old man, a real old man, not like you. Youre only beginning to give yourself the airs of age. Did you ever see a boy cultivating a moustache? Well, a middle-aged doctor cultivating a grey head is much the same sort of spectacle.

RIDGEON. Good Lord! yes: I suppose so. And I thought that the days of my vanity were past. Tell me: at what age does a man leave off being a fool?

SIR PATRICK. Remember the Frenchman who asked his grandmother at what age we get free from the temptations of love. The old woman said she didn't know. [*Ridgeon laughs*]. Well, I make you the same answer. But the world's growing very interesting to me now, Colly.

RIDGEON. You keep up your interest in science, do you?

SIR PATRICK. Lord! yes. Modern science is a wonderful thing. Look at your great discovery! Look at all the great discoveries! Where are they leading to? Why, right back to my poor dear old father's ideas and discoveries. He's been dead now over forty years. Oh, it's very interesting.

RIDGEON. Well, theres nothing like progress, is there?

SIR PATRICK. Dont misunderstand me, my boy. I'm not belittling your discovery. Most discoveries are made regularly every fifteen years; and it's fully a hundred and fifty since yours was made last. Thats something to be proud of. But your discovery's not new. It's only inoculation. My father practised inoculation until it was made criminal in eighteen-forty. That broke the poor old man's heart, Colly: he died of it. And now it turns out that my father was right after all. Youve brought us back to inoculation.

RIDGEON. I know nothing about smallpox. My line

is tuberculosis and typhoid and plague. But of course the principle of all vaccines is the same.

SIR PATRICK. Tuberculosis? M-m-m-m! Youve found out how to cure consumption, eh?

RIDGEON. I believe so.

SIR PATRICK. Ah yes. It's very interesting. What is it the old cardinal says in Browning's play? "I have known four and twenty leaders of revolt." Well, Ive known over thirty men that found out how to cure consumption. Why do people go on dying of it, Colly? Devilment, I suppose. There was my father's old friend George Boddington of Sutton Coldfield. He discovered the open-air cure in eighteen-forty. He was ruined and driven out of his practice for only opening the windows; and now we wont let a consumptive patient have as much as a roof over his head. Oh, it's very v e r y interesting to an old man.

RIDGEON. You old cynic, you dont believe a bit in my discovery.

SIR PATRICK. No, no: I dont go quite so far as that, Colly. But still, you remember Jane Marsh?

RIDGEON. Jane Marsh? No.

SIR PATRICK. You dont!

RIDGEON. No.

SIR PATRICK. You mean to tell me you dont remember the woman with the tuberculosus ulcer on her arm?

RIDGEON [*enlightened*] Oh, your washerwoman's daughter. Was her name Jane Marsh? I forgot.

SIR PATRICK. Perhaps youve forgotten also that you undertook to cure her with Koch's tuberculin.

RIDGEON. And instead of curing her, it rotted her arm right off. Yes: I remember. Poor Jane! However, she makes a good living out of that arm now by shewing it at medical lectures.

SIR PATRICK. Still, that wasnt quite what you intended, was it?

ACT I   The Doctor's Dilemma   13

RIDGEON. I took my chance of it.
SIR PATRICK. Jane did, you mean.
RIDGEON. Well, it's always the patient who has to take the chance when an experiment is necessary. And we can find out nothing without experiment.
SIR PATRICK. What did you find out from Jane's case?
RIDGEON. I found out that the inoculation that ought to cure sometimes kills.
SIR PATRICK. I could have told you that. Ive tried these modern inoculations a bit myself. Ive killed people with them; and Ive cured people with them; but I gave them up because I never could tell which I was going to do.
RIDGEON [*taking a pamphlet from a drawer in the writing-table and handing it to him*] Read that the next time you have an hour to spare; and youll find out why.
SIR PATRICK [*grumbling and fumbling for his spectacles*] Oh, bother your pamphlets. Whats the practice of it? [*Looking at the pamphlet*] Opsonin? What the devil is opsonin?
RIDGEON. Opsonin is what you butter the disease germs with to make your white blood corpuscles eat them. [*He sits down again on the couch*].
SIR PATRICK. Thats not new. Ive heard this notion that the white corpuscles—what is it that whats his name?—Metchnikoff—calls them?
RIDGEON. Phagocytes.
SIR PATRICK. Aye, phagocytes: yes, yes, yes. Well, I heard this theory that the phagocytes eat up the disease germs years ago: long before you came into fashion. Besides, they dont always eat them.
RIDGEON. They do when you butter them with opsonin.
SIR PATRICK. Gammon.

RIDGEON. No: it's not gammon. What it comes to in practice is this. The phagocytes wont eat the microbes unless the microbes are nicely buttered for them. Well, the patient manufactures the butter for himself all right; but my discovery is that the manufacture of that butter, which I call opsonin, goes on in the system by ups and downs—Nature being always rhythmical, you know— and that what the inoculation does is to stimulate the ups or downs, as the case may be. If we had inoculated Jane Marsh when her butter factory was on the up-grade, we should have cured her arm. But we got in on the down-grade and lost her arm for her. I call the up-grade the positive phase and the down-grade the negative phase. Everything depends on your inoculating at the right moment. Inoculate when the patient is in the negative phase and you kill: inoculate when the patient is in the positive phase and you cure.

SIR PATRICK. And pray how are you to know whether the patient is in the positive or the negative phase?

RIDGEON. Send a drop of the patient's blood to the laboratory at St. Anne's; and in fifteen minutes I'll give you his opsonin index in figures. If the figure is one, inoculate and cure: if it's under point eight, inoculate and kill. Thats my discovery: the most important that has been made since Harvey discovered the circulation of the blood. My tuberculosis patients dont die now.

SIR PATRICK. And mine do when my inoculation catches them in the negative phase, as you call it. Eh?

RIDGEON. Precisely. To inject a vaccine into a patient without first testing his opsonin is as near murder as a respectable practitioner can get. If I wanted to kill a man I should kill him that way.

EMMY [*looking in*] Will you see a lady that wants her husband's lungs cured?

RIDGEON [*impatiently*] No. Havnt I told you I will see nobody? [*To Sir Patrick*] I live in a state of siege

ACT I   The Doctor's Dilemma   15

ever since it got about that I'm a magician who can cure consumption with a drop of serum. [*To Emmy*] Dont come to me again about people who have no appointments. I tell you I can see nobody.

EMMY. Well, I'll tell her to wait a bit.

RIDGEON [*furious*] Youll tell her I cant see her, and send her away: do you hear?

EMMY [*unmoved*] Well, will you see Mr Cutler Walpole? He dont want a cure: he only wants to congratulate you.

RIDGEON. Of course. Shew him up. [*She turns to go*]. Stop. [*To Sir Patrick*] I want two minutes more with you between ourselves. [*To Emmy*] Emmy: ask Mr. Walpole to wait just two minutes, while I finish a consultation.

EMMY. Oh, he'll wait all right. He's talking to the poor lady. [*She goes out*].

SIR PATRICK. Well? what is it?

RIDGEON. Dont laugh at me. I want your advice.

SIR PATRICK. Professional advice?

RIDGEON. Yes. Theres something the matter with me. I dont know what it is.

SIR PATRICK. Neither do I. I suppose youve been sounded.

RIDGEON. Yes, of course. Theres nothing wrong with any of the organs: nothing special, anyhow. But I have a curious aching: I dont know where: I cant localize it. Sometimes I think it's my heart: sometimes I suspect my spine. It doesnt exactly hurt me; but it unsettles me completely. I feel that something is going to happen. And there are other symptoms. Scraps of tunes come into my head that seem to me very pretty, though theyre quite commonplace.

SIR PATRICK. Do you hear voices?

RIDGEON. No.

SIR PATRICK. I'm glad of that. When my patients

tell me that theyve made a greater discovery than Harvey, and that they hear voices, I lock them up.

RIDGEON. You think I'm mad! Thats just the suspicion that has come across me once or twice. Tell me the truth: I can bear it.

SIR PATRICK. Youre sure there are no voices?

RIDGEON. Quite sure

SIR PATRICK. Then it's only foolishness.

RIDGEON. Have you ever met anything like it before in your practice?

SIR PATRICK. Oh, yes: often. It's very common between the ages of seventeen and twenty-two. It sometimes comes on again at forty or thereabouts. Youre a bachelor, you see. It's not serious—if youre careful.

RIDGEON. About my food?

SIR PATRICK. No: about your behavior. Theres nothing wrong with your spine; and theres nothing wrong with your heart; but theres something wrong with your common sense. Youre not going to die; but you may be going to make a fool of yourself. So be careful.

RIDGEON. I see you dont believe in my discovery. Well, sometimes I dont believe in it myself. Thank you all the same. Shall we have Walpole up?

SIR PATRICK. Oh, have him up. [*Ridgeon rings*]. He's a clever operator, is Walpole, though he's only one of your chloroform surgeons. In my early days, you made your man drunk; and the porters and students held him down; and you had to set your teeth and finish the job fast. Nowadays you work at your ease; and the pain doesn't come until afterwards, when youve taken your cheque and rolled up your bag and left the house. I tell you, Colly, chloroform has done a lot of mischief. It's enabled every fool to be a surgeon.

RIDGEON [*to Emmy, who answers the bell*] Shew Mr Walpole up.

ACT I   The Doctor's Dilemma   17

EMMY. He's talking to the lady.
RIDGEON [*exasperated*] Did I not tell you—
Emmy goes out without heeding him. He gives it up, with a shrug, and plants himself with his back to the console, leaning resignedly against it.
SIR PATRICK. I know your Cutler Walpoles and their like. Theyve found out that a man's body's full of bits and scraps of old organs he has no mortal use for. Thanks to chloroform, you can cut half a dozen of them out without leaving him any the worse, except for the illness and the guineas it costs him. I knew the Walpoles well fifteen years ago. The father used to snip off the ends of people's uvulas for fifty guineas, and paint throats with caustic every day for a year at two guineas a time. His brother-in-law extirpated tonsils for two hundred guineas until he took up women's cases at double the fees. Cutler himself worked hard at anatomy to find something fresh to operate on; and at last he got hold of something he calls the nuciform sac, which he's made quite the fashion. People pay him five hundred guineas to cut it out. They might as well get their hair cut for all the difference it makes; but I suppose they feel important after it. You cant go out to dinner now without your neighbor bragging to you of some useless operation or other.
EMMY [*announcing*] Mr Cutler Walpole. [*She goes out*].
Cutler Walpole is an energetic, unhesitating man of forty, with a cleanly modelled face, very decisive and symmetrical about the shortish, salient, rather pretty nose, and the three trimly turned corners made by his chin and jaws. In comparison with Ridgeon's delicate broken lines, and Sir Patrick's softly rugged aged ones, his face looks machine-made and beeswaxed; but his scrutinizing, daring eyes give it life and force. He seems never at a loss, never in doubt: one feels that if he made

*a mistake he would make it thoroughly and firmly. He
has neat, well-nourished hands, short arms, and is built
for strength and compactness rather than for height. He
is smartly dressed with a fancy waistcoat, a richly colored scarf secured by a handsome ring, ornaments on his
watch chain, spats on his shoes, and a general air of the
well-to-do sportsman about him. He goes straight across
to Ridgeon and shakes hands with him.*

WALPOLE. My dear Ridgeon, best wishes! heartiest
congratulations! You deserve it.

RIDGEON. Thank you.

WALPOLE. As a man, mind you. You deserve it as a
man. The opsonin is simple rot, as any capable surgeon
can tell you; but we're all delighted to see your personal
qualities officially recognized. Sir Patrick: how are you?
I sent you a paper lately about a little thing I invented:
a new saw. For shoulder blades.

SIR PATRICK [*meditatively*] Yes: I got it. It's a
good saw: a useful, handy instrument.

WALPOLE [*confidently*] I knew youd see its points.

SIR PATRICK. Yes: I remember that saw sixty-five
years ago.

WALPOLE. What!

SIR PATRICK. It was called a cabinetmaker's jimmy
then.

WALPOLE. Get out! Nonsense! Cabinetmaker be—

RIDGEON. Never mind him, Walpole. He's jealous.

WALPOLE. By the way, I hope I'm not disturbing
you two in anything private.

RIDGEON. No no. Sit down. I was only consulting
him. I'm rather out of sorts. Overwork, I suppose.

WALPOLE [*swiftly*] I know whats the matter with you.
I can see it in your complexion. I can feel it in the grip
of your hand.

RIDGEON. What is it?

WALPOLE. Blood-poisoning.

Act I   The Doctor's Dilemma   19

RIDGEON. Blood-poisoning! Impossible.

WALPOLE. I tell you, blood-poisoning. Ninety-five per cent of the human race suffer from chronic blood-poisoning, and die of it. It's as simple as A.B.C. Your nuciform sac is full of decaying matter—undigested food and waste products—rank ptomaines. Now you take my advice, Ridgeon. Let me cut it out for you. You'll be another man afterwards.

SIR PATRICK. Dont you like him as he is?

WALPOLE. No I dont. I dont like any man who hasnt a healthy circulation. I tell you this: in an intelligently governed country people wouldnt be allowed to go about with nuciform sacs, making themselves centres of infection. The operation ought to be compulsory: it's ten times more important than vaccination.

SIR PATRICK. Have you had your own sac removed, may I ask?

WALPOLE [*triumphantly*] I havnt got one. Look at me! Ive no symptoms. I'm as sound as a bell. About five per cent of the population havnt got any; and I'm one of the five per cent. I'll give you an instance. You know Mrs Jack Foljambe: the smart Mrs Foljambe? I operated at Easter on her sister-in-law, Lady Gorran, and found she had the biggest sac I ever saw: it held about two ounces. Well, Mrs. Foljambe had the right spirit—the genuine hygienic instinct. She couldnt stand her sister-in-law being a clean, sound woman, and she simply a whited sepulchre. So she insisted on my operating on her, too. And by George, sir, she hadnt any sac at all. Not a trace! Not a rudiment!! I was so taken aback—so interested, that I forgot to take the sponges out, and was stitching them up inside her when the nurse missed them. Somehow, I'd made sure she'd have an exceptionally large one. [*He sits down on the couch, squaring his shoulders and shooting his hands out of his cuffs as he sets his knuckles akimbo*].

EMMY [*looking in*] Sir Ralph Bloomfield Bonington.
*A long and expectant pause follows this announcement.
All look to the door; but there is no Sir Ralph.*
  RIDGEON [*at last*] Where is he?
  EMMY [*looking back*] Drat him, I thought he was following me. He's stayed down to talk to that lady.
  RIDGEON [*exploding*] I told you to tell that lady— [*Emmy vanishes*].
  WALPOLE [*jumping up again*] Oh, by the way, Ridgeon, that reminds me. Ive been talking to that poor girl. It's her husband; and she thinks it's a case of consumption: the usual wrong diagnosis: these damned general practitioners ought never to be allowed to touch a patient except under the orders of a consultant. She's been describing his symptoms to me; and the case is as plain as a pikestaff: bad blood-poisoning. Now she's poor. She cant afford to have him operated on. Well, you send him to me: I'll do it for nothing. Theres room for him in my nursing home. I'll put him straight, and feed him up and make her happy. I like making people happy. [*He goes to the chair near the window*].
  EMMY [*looking in*] Here he is.
  Sir Ralph Bloomfield Bonington wafts himself into the room. He is a tall man, with a head like a tall and slender egg. He has been in his time a slender man; but now, in his sixth decade, his waistcoat has filled out somewhat. His fair eyebrows arch good-naturedly and uncritically. He has a most musical voice; his speech is a perpetual anthem; and he never tires of the sound of it. He radiates an enormous self-satisfaction, cheering, reassuring, healing by the mere incompatibility of disease or anxiety with his welcome presence. Even broken bones, it is said, have been known to unite at the sound of his voice: he is a born healer, as independent of mere treatment and skill as any Christian scientist. When he expands into oratory or scientific exposition, he is as ener-

getic as Walpole; but it is with a bland, voluminous, atmospheric energy, which envelops its subject and its audience, and makes interruption or inattention impossible, and imposes veneration and credulity on all but the strongest minds. He is known in the medical world as B. B.; and the envy roused by his success in practice is softened by the conviction that he is, scientifically considered, a colossal humbug: the fact being that, though he knows just as much (and just as little) as his contemporaries, the qualifications that pass muster in common men reveal their weakness when hung on his egregious personality.

B. B. Aha! Sir Colenso. Sir Colenso, eh? Welcome to the order of knighthood.

RIDGEON [shaking hands] Thank you, B. B.

B. B. What! Sir Patrick! And how are we to-day? a little chilly? a little stiff? but hale and still the cleverest of us all. [Sir Patrick grunts]. What! Walpole! the absent-minded beggar: eh?

WALPOLE. What does that mean?

B. B. Have you forgotten the lovely opera singer I sent you to have that growth taken off her vocal cords?

WALPOLE [springing to his feet] Great heavens, man, you dont mean to say you sent her for a throat operation!

B. B. [archly] Aha! Ha ha! Aha! [trilling like a lark as he shakes his finger at Walpole]. You removed her nuciform sac. Well, well! force of habit! force of habit! Never mind, ne-e-e-ver mind. She got back her voice after it, and thinks you the greatest surgeon alive; and so you are, so you are, so you are.

WALPOLE [in a tragic whisper, intensely serious] Blood-poisoning. I see. I see. [He sits down again].

SIR PATRICK. And how is a certain distinguished family getting on under your care, Sir Ralph?

B. B. Our friend Ridgeon will be gratified to hear

that I have tried his opsonin treatment on little Prince Henry with complete success.

RIDGEON [*startled and anxious*] But how——

B. B. [*continuing*] I suspected typhoid: the head gardener's boy had it; so I just called at St Anne's one day and got a tube of your very excellent serum. You were out, unfortunately.

RIDGEON. I hope they explained to you carefully——

B. B. [*waving away the absurd suggestion*] Lord bless you, my dear fellow, I didnt need any explanations. I'd left my wife in the carriage at the door; and I'd no time to be taught my business by your young chaps. I know all about it. Ive handled these anti-toxins ever since they first came out.

RIDGEON. But theyre not anti-toxins; and theyre dangerous unless you use them at the right time.

B. B. Of course they are. Everything is dangerous unless you take it at the right time. An apple at breakfast does you good: an apple at bedtime upsets you for a week. There are only two rules for anti-toxins. First, dont be afraid of them: second, inject them a quarter of an hour before meals, three times a day.

RIDGEON [*appalled*] Great heavens, B. B., no, no, no.

B. B. [*sweeping on irresistibly*] Yes, yes, yes, Colly. The proof of the pudding is in the eating, you know. It was an immense success. It acted like magic on the little prince. Up went his temperature; off to bed I packed him; and in a week he was all right again, and absolutely immune from typhoid for the rest of his life. The family were very nice about it: their gratitude was quite touching; but I said they owed it all to you, Ridgeon; and I am glad to think that your knighthood is the result.

RIDGEON. I am deeply obliged to you. [*Overcome, he sits down on the chair near the couch*].

B. B. Not at all, not at all. Your own merit. Come! come! come! dont give way.

RIDGEON. It's nothing. I was a little giddy just now. Overwork, I suppose.

WALPOLE. Blood-poisoning.

B. B. Overwork! Theres no such thing. I do the work of ten men. Am I giddy? No. NO. If youre not well, you have a disease. It may be a slight one; but it's a disease. And what is a disease? The lodgment in the system of a pathogenic germ, and the multiplication of that germ. What is the remedy? A very simple one. Find the germ and kill it.

SIR PATRICK. Suppose theres no germ?

B. B. Impossible, Sir Patrick: there must be a germ: else how could the patient be ill?

SIR PATRICK. Can you shew me the germ of overwork?

B. B. No; but why? Why? Because, my dear Sir Patrick, though the germ is there, it's invisible. Nature has given it no danger signal for us. These germs—these bacilli—are translucent bodies, like glass, like water. To make them visible you must stain them. Well, my dear Paddy, do what you will, some of them wont stain. They wont take cochineal: they wont take methylene blue; they wont take gentian violet: they wont take any coloring matter. Consequently, though we know, as scientific men, that they exist, we cannot see them. But can you disprove their existence? Can you conceive the disease existing without them? Can you, for instance, shew me a case of diphtheria without the bacillus?

SIR PATRICK. No; but I'll shew you the same bacillus, without the disease, in your own throat.

B. B. No, not the same, Sir Patrick. It is an entirely different bacillus; only the two are, unfortunately, so exactly alike that you cannot see the difference. You must understand, my dear Sir Patrick, that every one of these interesting little creatures has an imitator. Just as men imitate each other, germs imitate each other. There is the genuine diphtheria bacillus discovered by Lœffler; and there is the pseudo-bacillus, exactly like it, which you could find, as you say, in my own throat.

SIR PATRICK. And how do you tell one from the other?

B. B. Well, obviously, if the bacillus is the genuine Lœffler, you have diphtheria; and if it's the pseudo-bacillus, youre quite well. Nothing simpler. Science is always simple and always profound. It is only the half-truths that are dangerous. Ignorant faddists pick up some superficial information about germs; and they write to the papers and try to discredit science. They dupe and mislead many honest and worthy people. But science has a perfect answer to them on every point.

> A little learning is a dangerous thing;
> Drink deep ; or taste not the Pierian spring.

I mean no disrespect to your generation, Sir Patrick: some of you old stagers did marvels through sheer professional intuition and clinical experience; but when I think of the average men of your day, ignorantly bleeding and cupping and purging, and scattering germs over their patients from their clothes and instruments, and contrast all that with the scientific certainty and simplicity of my treatment of the little prince the other day, I cant help being proud of my own generation: the men who were trained on the germ theory, the veterans of the great struggle over Evolution in the seventies. We may have our faults; but at least we are men of science. That is why I am taking up your treatment, Ridgeon, and pushing it. It's scientific. [*He sits down on the chair near the couch*].

EMMY [*at the door, announcing*] Dr Blenkinsop.

Dr Blenkinsop is in very different case from the others. He is clearly not a prosperous man. He is flabby and shabby, cheaply fed and cheaply clothed. He has the lines made by a conscience between his eyes, and the lines made by continual money worries all over his face, cut all the deeper as he has seen better days, and hails his well-to-do colleagues as their contemporary and old hospital friend, though even in this he has to struggle with the diffidence of poverty and relegation to the poorer middle class.

RIDGEON. How are you, Blenkinsop?

BLENKINSOP. Ive come to offer my humble congratulations. Oh dear! all the great guns are before me.

B. B. [*patronizing, but charming*] How d'ye do, Blenkinsop? How d'ye do?

BLENKINSOP. And Sir Patrick, too! [*Sir Patrick grunts*].

RIDGEON. Youve met Walpole, of course?

WALPOLE. How d'ye do?

BLENKINSOP. It's the first time Ive had that honor. In my poor little practice there are no chances of meeting you great men. I know nobody but the St Anne's men of my own day. [*To Ridgeon*] And so youre Sir Colenso. How does it feel?

RIDGEON. Foolish at first. Dont take any notice of it.

BLENKINSOP. I'm ashamed to say I havnt a notion what your great discovery is; but I congratulate you all the same for the sake of old times.

B. B. [*shocked*] But, my dear Blenkinsop, you used to be rather keen on science.

BLENKINSOP. Ah, I used to be a lot of things. I used to have two or three decent suits of clothes, and flannels to go up the river on Sundays. Look at me now: this is my best; and it must last till Christmas. What can I do? Ive never opened a book since I was qualified thirty years ago. I used to read the medical papers at first; but you know how soon a man drops that; besides, I cant afford them; and what are they after all but trade papers, full of advertisements? Ive forgotten all my science: whats the use of my pretending I havnt? But I have great experience: clinical experience; and bedside experience is the main thing, isn't it?

B. B. No doubt; always provided, mind you, that you have a sound scientific theory to correlate your observations at the bedside. Mere experience by itself is nothing. If I take my dog to the bedside with me, he sees what I see. But he learns nothing from it. Why? Because he's not a scientific dog.

WALPOLE. It amuses me to hear you physicians and general practitioners talking about clinical experience. What do you see at the bedside but the outside of the patient? Well: it isnt his outside thats wrong, except perhaps in skin cases. What you want is a daily familiarity with people's insides; and that you can only get at the operating table. I know what I'm talking about: Ive been a surgeon and a consultant for twenty years; and Ive never known a general practitioner right in his diagnosis yet. Bring them a perfectly simple case; and they diagnose cancer, and arthritis, and appendicitis, and every other itis, when any really experienced surgeon can see that it's a plain case of blood-poisoning.

BLENKINSOP. Ah, it's easy for you gentlemen to talk; but what would you say if you had my practice? Except for the workmen's clubs, my patients are all clerks and shopmen. They darent be ill: they cant afford it. And when they break down, what can I do for them? You can send your people to St Moritz or to Egypt, or recommend horse exercise or motoring or champagne jelly or complete change and rest for six months. *I* might as well order my people a slice of the moon. And the worst of it is, I'm too poor to keep well myself on the cooking I have to put up with. Ive such a wretched digestion; and I look it. How am I to inspire confidence? [*He sits disconsolately on the couch*].

RIDGEON [*restlessly*] Dont, Blenkinsop: it's too painful. The most tragic thing in the world is a sick doctor.

WALPOLE. Yes, by George: its like a bald-headed man trying to sell a hair restorer. Thank God I'm a surgeon!

B. B. [*sunnily*] I am never sick. Never had a day's illness in my life. Thats what enables me to sympathize with my patients.

WALPOLE [*interested*] What! youre never ill?

B. B. Never.

WALPOLE. Thats interesting. I believe you have no nuciform sac. If you ever do feel at all queer, I should very much like to have a look.

B. B. Thank you, my dear fellow; but I'm too busy just now.

RIDGEON. I was just telling them when you came in, Blenkinsop, that I have worked myself out of sorts

BLENKINSOP. Well, it seems presumptuous of me to offer a prescription to a great man like you; but still I have great experience; and if I might recommend a pound of ripe greengages every day half an hour before lunch, I'm sure youd find a benefit. Theyre very cheap.

RIDGEON. What do you say to that B. B.?

B. B. [*encouragingly*] Very sensible, Blenkinsop: very sensible indeed. I'm delighted to see that you disapprove of drugs.

SIR PATRICK [*grunts*]!

B. B. [*archly*] Aha! Haha! Did I hear from the fireside armchair the bow-wow of the old school defending its drugs? Ah, believe me, Paddy, the world would be healthier if every chemist's shop in England were demolished. Look at the papers! full of scandalous advertisements of patent medicines! a huge commercial system of quackery and poison. Well, whose fault is it? Ours. I say, ours. We set the example. We spread the superstition. We taught the people to believe in bottles of doctor's stuff; and now they buy it at the stores instead of consulting a medical man.

WALPOLE. Quite true. Ive not prescribed a drug for the last fifteen years.

B. B. Drugs can only repress symptoms: they cannot eradicate disease. The true remedy for all diseases is Nature's remedy. Nature and Science are at one, Sir Patrick, believe me; though you were taught differently. Nature has provided, in the white corpuscles as you call them—in the phagocytes as we call them—a natural means of devouring and destroying all disease germs. There is at bottom only one genuinely scientific treatment for all diseases, and that is to stimulate the phagocytes. Stimulate the phagocytes. Drugs are a delusion. Find the germ of the disease; prepare from it a suitable anti-toxin; inject it three times a day quarter of an hour before meals; and what is the result? The phagocytes are stimulated; they devour the disease; and the patient recovers—unless, of course, he's too far gone. That, I take it, is the essence of Ridgeon's discovery.

SIR PATRICK [*dreamily*] As I sit here, I seem to hear my poor old father talking again.

B. B. [*rising in incredulous amazement*] Your father! But, Lord bless my soul, Paddy, your father must have been an older man than you.

SIR PATRICK. Word for word almost, he said what you say. No more drugs. Nothing but inoculation.

B. B. [*almost contemptuously*] Inoculation! Do you mean smallpox inoculation?

SIR PATRICK. Yes. In the privacy of our family circle, sir, my father used to declare his belief that smallpox inoculation was good, not only for smallpox, but for all fevers.

B. B. [*suddenly rising to the new idea with immense interest and excitement*] What! Ridgeon: did you hear that? Sir Patrick: I am more struck by what you have just told me than I can well express. Your father, sir, anticipated a discovery of my own. Listen, Walpole. Blenkinsop: attend one moment. You will all be intensely interested in this. I was put on the track by accident. I had a typhoid case and a tetanus case side by side in the hospital: a beadle and a city missionary. Think of what that meant for them, poor fellows! Can a beadle be dignified with typhoid? Can a missionary be eloquent with lockjaw? No. NO. Well, I got some typhoid anti-toxin from Ridgeon and a tube of Muldooley's anti-tetanus serum. But the missionary jerked all my things off the table in one of his paroxysms; and in replacing them I put Ridgeon's tube where Muldooley's ought to have been. The consequence was that I inoculated the typhoid case for tetanus and the tetanus case for typhoid. [*The doctors look greatly concerned. B. B., undamped, smiles triumphantly*]. Well, they recovered. THEY RECOVERED. Except for a touch of St Vitus's dance the missionary's as well to-day as ever; and the beadle's ten times the man he was.

BLENKINSOP. Ive known things like that happen. They cant be explained.

B. B. [*severely*] Blenkinsop: there is nothing that cannot be explained by science. What did I do? Did I fold my hands helplessly and say that the case could not be explained? By no means. I sat down and used my brains. I thought the case out on scientific principles. I asked myself why didnt the missionary die of typhoid on top of tetanus, and the beadle of tetanus on top of typhoid? Theres a problem for you, Ridgeon. Think, Sir Patrick. Reflect, Blenkinsop. Look at it without prejudice, Walpole. What is the real work of the antitoxin? Simply to stimulate the phagocytes. Very well. But so long as you stimulate the phagocytes, what does it matter which particular sort of serum you use for the purpose? Haha! Eh? Do you see? Do you grasp it? Ever since that Ive used all sorts of anti-toxins absolutely indiscriminately, with perfectly satisfactory results. I inoculated the little prince with your stuff, Ridgeon, because I wanted to give you a lift; but two years ago I tried the experiment of treating a scarlet fever case with a sample of hydrophobia serum from the Pasteur Institute, and it answered capitally. It stimulated the phagocytes; and the phagocytes did the rest. That is why Sir Patrick's father found that inoculation cured all fevers. It stimulated the phagocytes. [*He throws himself into his chair, exhausted with the triumph of his demonstration, and beams magnificently on them*].

EMMY [*looking in*] Mr Walpole: your motor's come for you; and it's frightening Sir Patrick's horses; so come along quick.

WALPOLE [*rising*] Good-bye, Ridgeon.

RIDGEON. Good-bye; and many thanks.

B. B. You see my point, Walpole?

EMMY. He cant wait, Sir Ralph. The carriage will be into the area if he dont come.

WALPOLE. I'm coming. [*To B. B.*] Theres nothing in your point: phagocytosis is pure rot: the cases are all blood-poisoning; and the knife is the real remedy. Bye-bye, Sir Paddy. Happy to have met you, Mr. Blenkinsop. Now, Emmy. [*He goes out, followed by Emmy*].

B. B. [*sadly*] Walpole has no intellect. A mere surgeon. Wonderful operator; but, after all, what is operating? Only manual labor. Brain—BRAIN remains master of the situation. The nuciform sac is utter nonsense: theres no such organ. It's a mere accidental kink in the membrane, occurring in perhaps two-and-a-half per cent of the population. Of course I'm glad for Walpole's sake that the operation is fashionable; for he's a

Act I   The Doctor's Dilemma   31

dear good fellow; and after all, as I always tell people, the operation will do them no harm: indeed, Ive known the nervous shake-up and the fortnight in bed do people a lot of good after a hard London season; but still it's a shocking fraud. [*Rising*] Well, I must be toddling. Good-bye, Paddy [*Sir Patrick grunts*] good-bye, good-bye. Good-bye, my dear Blenkinsop, good-bye! Good-bye, Ridgeon. Dont fret about your health: you know what to do: if your liver is sluggish, a little mercury never does any harm. If you feel restless, try bromide. If that doesnt answer, a stimulant, you know: a little phosphorus and strychnine. If you cant sleep, trional, trional, trion—

SIR PATRICK [*drily*] But no drugs, Colly, remember that.

B. B. [*firmly*] Certainly not. Quite right, Sir Patrick. As temporary expedients, of course; but as treatment, no, NO. Keep away from the chemist's shop, my dear Ridgeon, whatever you do.

RIDGEON [*going to the door with him*] I will. And thank you for the knighthood. Good-bye.

B. B. [*stopping at the door, with the beam in his eye twinkling a little*] By the way, who's your patient?

RIDGEON. Who?

B. B. Downstairs. Charming woman. Tuberculous husband.

RIDGEON. Is she there still?

EMMY [*looking in*] Come on, Sir Ralph: your wife's waiting in the carriage.

B. B. [*suddenly sobered*] Oh! Good-bye. [*He goes out almost precipitately*].

RIDGEON. Emmy: is that woman there still? If so, tell her once for all that I cant and wont see her. Do you hear?

EMMY. Oh, she aint in a hurry: she doesnt mind how long she waits. [*She goes out*].

BLENKINSOP. I must be off, too: every half-hour I spend away from my work costs me eighteenpence. Good-bye, Sir Patrick.

SIR PATRICK. Good-bye. Good-bye.

RIDGEON. Come to lunch with me some day this week.

BLENKINSOP. I cant afford it, dear boy; and it would put me off my own food for a week. Thank you all the same.

RIDGEON [*uneasy at Blenkinsop's poverty*] Can I do nothing for you?

BLENKINSOP. Well, if you have an old frock-coat to spare? you see what would be an old one for you would be a new one for me; so remember the next time you turn out your wardrobe. Good-bye. [*He hurries out*].

RIDGEON [*looking after him*] Poor chap! [*Turning to Sir Patrick*] So thats why they made me a knight! And thats the medical profession!

SIR PATRICK. And a very good profession, too, my lad. When you know as much as I know of the ignorance and superstition of the patients, youll wonder that we're half as good as we are.

RIDGEON. We're not a profession: we're a conspiracy.

SIR PATRICK. All professions are conspiracies against the laity. And we cant all be geniuses like you. Every fool can get ill; but every fool cant be a good doctor: there are not enough good ones to go round. And for all you know, Bloomfield Bonington kills less people than you do.

RIDGEON. Oh, very likely. But he really ought to know the difference between a vaccine and an anti-toxin. Stimulate the phagocytes! The vaccine doesnt affect the phagocytes at all. He's all wrong: hopelessly, dangerously wrong. To put a tube of serum into his hands is murder: simple murder.

EMMY [*returning*] Now, Sir Patrick. How long more are you going to keep them horses standing in the draught?

SIR PATRICK. Whats that to you, you old catamaran?

EMMY. Come, come, now! none of your temper to me. And it's time for Colly to get to his work.

RIDGEON. Behave yourself, Emmy. Get out.

EMMY. Oh, I learnt how to behave myself before I learnt you to do it. I know what doctors are: sitting talking together about themselves when they ought to be with their poor patients. And I know what horses are, Sir Patrick. I was brought up in the country. Now be good; and come along.

SIR PATRICK [*rising*] Very well, very well, very well. Good-bye, Colly. [*He pats Ridgeon on the shoulder and goes out, turning for a moment at the door to look meditatively at Emmy and say, with grave conviction*] You *are* an ugly old devil, and no mistake.

EMMY [*highly indignant, calling after him*] Youre no beauty yourself. [*To Ridgeon, much flustered*] Theyve no manners: they think they can say what they like to me; and you set them on, you do. I'll teach them their places. Here now: are you going to see that poor thing or are you not?

RIDGEON. I tell you for the fiftieth time I wont see anybody. Send her away.

EMMY. Oh, I'm tired of being told to send her away. What good will that do her?

RIDGEON. Must I get angry with you, Emmy?

EMMY [*coaxing*] Come now: just see her for a minute to please me: theres a good boy. She's given me half-a-crown. She thinks it's life and death to her husband for her to see you.

RIDGEON. Values her husband's life at half-a-crown!

EMMY. Well, it's all she can afford, poor lamb. Them

others think nothing of half-a-sovereign just to talk about themselves to you, the sluts! Besides, she'll put you in a good temper for the day, because it's a good deed to see her; and she's the sort that gets round you.

RIDGEON. Well, she hasnt done so badly. For half-a-crown she's had a consultation with Sir Ralph Bloomfield Bonington and Cutler Walpole. Thats six guineas' worth to start with. I dare say she's consulted Blenkinsop too: thats another eighteenpence.

EMMY. Then youll see her for me, wont you?

RIDGEON. Oh, send her up and be hanged. [*Emmy trots out, satisfied. Ridgeon calls*] Redpenny!

REDPENNY [*appearing at the door*] What is it?

RIDGEON. Theres a patient coming up. If she hasnt gone in five minutes, come in with an urgent call from the hospital for me. You understand: she's to have a strong hint to go.

REDPENNY. Right O! [*He vanishes*].

Ridgeon goes to the glass, and arranges his tie a little.

EMMY [*announcing*] Mrs Doobidad [*Ridgeon leaves the glass and goes to the writing-table*].

The lady comes in. Emmy goes out and shuts the door. Ridgeon, who has put on an impenetrable and rather distant professional manner, turns to the lady, and invites her, by a gesture, to sit down on the couch.

Mrs Dubedat is beyond all demur an arrestingly good-looking young woman. She has something of the grace and romance of a wild creature, with a good deal of the elegance and dignity of a fine lady. Ridgeon, who is extremely susceptible to the beauty of women, instinctively assumes the defensive at once, and hardens his manner still more. He has an impression that she is very well dressed; but she has a figure on which any dress would look well, and carries herself with the unaffected distinction of a woman who has never in her life suffered from those doubts and fears as to her social posi-

tion which spoil the manners of most middling people. She is tall, slender, and strong; has dark hair, dressed so as to look like hair and not like a bird's nest or a pantaloon's wig (fashion wavering just then between these two models); has unexpectedly narrow, subtle, dark-fringed eyes that alter her expression disturbingly when she is excited and flashes them wide open; is softly impetuous in her speech and swift in her movements; and is just now in mortal anxiety. She carries a portfolio.

MRS DUBEDAT [in low urgent tones] Doctor—

RIDGEON [curtly] Wait. Before you begin, let me tell you at once that I can do nothing for you. My hands are full. I sent you that message by my old servant. You would not take that answer.

MRS DUBEDAT. How could I?

RIDGEON. You bribed her.

MRS DUBEDAT. I—

RIDGEON. That doesnt matter. She coaxed me to see you. Well, you must take it from me now that with all the good will in the world, I cannot undertake another case.

MRS DUBEDAT. Doctor: you must save my husband. You must. When I explain to you, you will see that you must. It is not an ordinary case, not like any other case. He is not like anybody else in the world: oh, believe me, he is not. I can prove it to you: [fingering her portfolio] I have brought some things to shew you. And you can save him: the papers say you can.

RIDGEON. Whats the matter? Tuberculosis?

MRS DUBEDAT. Yes. His left lung—

RIDGEON. Yes: you neednt tell me about that.

MRS DUBEDAT. You can cure him, if only you will. It is true that you can, isnt it? [In great distress] Oh, tell me, please.

RIDGEON [warningly] You are going to be quiet and self-possessed, arnt you?

MRS DUBEDAT. Yes. I beg your pardon. I know I shouldnt—[*Giving way again*] Oh, please, say that you can; and then I shall be all right.

RIDGEON [*huffily*] I am not a curemonger: if you want cures, you must go to the people who sell them. [*Recovering himself, ashamed of the tone of his own voice*] But I have at the hospital ten tuberculous patients whose lives I believe I can save.

MRS DUBEDAT. Thank God!

RIDGEON. Wait a moment. Try to think of those ten patients as ten shipwrecked men on a raft—a raft that is barely large enough to save them—that will not support one more. Another head bobs up through the waves at the side. Another man begs to be taken aboard. He implores the captain of the raft to save him. But the captain can only do that by pushing one of his ten off the raft and drowning him to make room for the new comer. That is what you are asking me to do.

MRS DUBEDAT. But how can that be? I dont understand. Surely—

RIDGEON. You must take my word for it that it is so. My laboratory, my staff, and myself are working at full pressure. We are doing our utmost. The treatment is a new one. It takes time, means, and skill; and there is not enough for another case. Our ten cases are already chosen cases. Do you understand what I mean by chosen?

MRS DUBEDAT. Chosen. No: I cant understand.

RIDGEON [*sternly*] You must understand. Youve got to understand and to face it. In every single one of those ten cases I have had to consider, not only whether the man could be saved, but whether he was worth saving. There were fifty cases to choose from; and forty had to be condemned to death. Some of the forty had young wives and helpless children. If the hardness of their cases could have saved them they would have been saved ten times over. Ive no doubt your case is a hard one: I can see the tears in your eyes [*she hastily wipes her eyes*]: I know that you have a torrent of entreaties ready for me the moment I stop speaking; but it's no use. You must go to another doctor.

MRS DUBEDAT. But can you give me the name of another doctor who understands your secret?

RIDGEON. I have no secret: I am not a quack.

MRS DUBEDAT. I beg your pardon: I didnt mean to say anything wrong. I dont understand how to speak to you. Oh, pray dont be offended.

RIDGEON [*again a little ashamed*] There! there! never mind. [*He relaxes and sits down*]. After all, I'm talking nonsense: I daresay I am a quack, a quack with a qualification. But my discovery is not patented.

MRS DUBEDAT. Then can any doctor cure my husband? Oh, why dont they do it? I have tried so many: I have spent so much. If only you would give me the name of another doctor.

RIDGEON. Every man in this street is a doctor. But outside myself and the handful of men I am training at St Anne's, there is nobody as yet who has mastered the opsonin treatment. And we are full up? I'm sorry; but that is all I can say. [*Rising*] Good morning.

MRS DUBEDAT [*suddenly and desperately taking some drawings from her portfolio*] Doctor: look at these. You understand drawings: you have good ones in your waiting-room. Look at them. They are his work.

RIDGEON. It's no use my looking. [*He looks, all the same*] Hallo! [*He takes one to the window and studies it*]. Yes: this is the real thing. Yes, yes. [*He looks at another and returns to her*]. These are very clever. Theyre unfinished, arnt they?

MRS DUBEDAT. He gets tired so soon. But you see, dont you, what a genius he is? You see that he is worth saving. Oh, doctor, I married him just to help him to begin: I had money enough to tide him over the hard years at the beginning—to enable him to follow his inspiration until his genius was recognized. And I was useful to him as a model: his drawings of me sold quite quickly.

RIDGEON. Have you got one?

MRS DUBEDAT [*producing another*] Only this one. It was the first.

RIDGEON [*devouring it with his eyes*] Thats a wonderful drawing. Why is it called Jennifer?

MRS DUBEDAT. My name is Jennifer.

RIDGEON. A strange name.

MRS DUBEDAT. Not in Cornwall. I am Cornish. It's only what you call Guinevere.

RIDGEON [*repeating the names with a certain pleasure in them*] Guinevere. Jennifer. [*Looking again at the drawing*] Yes: it's really a wonderful drawing. Excuse me; but may I ask is it for sale? I'll buy it.

MRS DUBEDAT. Oh, take it. It's my own: he gave it to me. Take it. Take them all. Take everything; ask anything; but save him. You can: you will: you must.

REDPENNY [*entering with every sign of alarm*] Theyve just telephoned from the hospital that youre to come instantly—a patient on the point of death. The carriage is waiting.

RIDGEON [*intolerantly*] Oh, nonsense: get out. [*Greatly annoyed*] What do you mean by interrupting me like this?

REDPENNY. But—

RIDGEON. Chut! cant you see I'm engaged? Be off. *Redpenny, bewildered, vanishes.*

MRS DUBEDAT [*rising*] Doctor: one instant only before you go—

RIDGEON. Sit down. It's nothing.

ACT I   The Doctor's Dilemma   39

MRS DUBEDAT. But the patient. He said he was dying.

RIDGEON. Oh, he's dead by this time. Never mind. Sit down.

MRS DUBEDAT [*sitting down and breaking down*] Oh, you none of you care. You see people die every day.

RIDGEON [*petting her*] Nonsense! it's nothing: I told him to come in and say that. I thought I should want to get rid of you.

MRS DUBEDAT [*shocked at the falsehood*] Oh!

RIDGEON [*continuing*] Dont look so bewildered: theres nobody dying.

MRS DUBEDAT. My husband is.

RIDGEON [*pulling himself together*] Ah, yes: I had forgotten your husband. Mrs Dubedat: you are asking me to do a very serious thing?

MRS DUBEDAT. I am asking you to save the life of a great man.

RIDGEON. You are asking me to kill another man for his sake; for as surely as I undertake another case, I shall have to hand back one of the old ones to the ordinary treatment. Well, I dont shrink from that. I have had to do it before; and I will do it again if you can convince me that his life is more important than the worst life I am now saving. But you must convince me first.

MRS DUBEDAT. He made those drawings; and they are not the best—nothing like the best; only I did not bring the really best: so few people like them. He is twenty-three: his whole life is before him. Wont you let me bring him to you? wont you speak to him? wont you see for yourself?

RIDGEON. Is he well enough to come to a dinner at the Star and Garter at Richmond?

MRS DUBEDAT. Oh yes. Why?

RIDGEON. I'll tell you. I am inviting all my old friends to a dinner to celebrate my knighthood—youve seen about it in the papers, havnt you?

MRS DUBEDAT. Yes, oh yes. That was how I found out about you.

RIDGEON. It will be a doctors' dinner; and it was to have been a bachelors' dinner. I'm a bachelor. Now if you will entertain for me, and bring your husband, he will meet me; and he will meet some of the most eminent men in my profession: Sir Patrick Cullen, Sir Ralph Bloomfield Bonington, Cutler Walpole, and others. I can put the case to them; and your husband will have to stand or fall by what we think of him. Will you come?

MRS DUBEDAT. Yes, of course I will come. Oh, thank you, thank you. And may I bring some of his drawings—the really good ones?

RIDGEON. Yes. I will let you know the date in the course of to-morrow. Leave me your address.

MRS DUBEDAT. Thank you again and again. You have made me so happy: I know you will admire him and like him. This is my address. [*She gives him her card*].

RIDGEON. Thank you. [*He rings*].

MRS DUBEDAT [*embarrassed*] May I—is there—should I—I mean—[*she blushes and stops in confusion*].

RIDGEON. Whats the matter?

MRS DUBEDAT. Your fee for this consultation?

RIDGEON. Oh, I forgot that. Shall we say a beautiful drawing of his favorite model for the whole treatment, including the cure?

MRS DUBEDAT. You are very generous. Thank you. I know you will cure him. Good-bye.

RIDGEON. I will. Good-bye. [*They shake hands*]. By the way, you know, dont you, that tuberculosis is catching. You take every precaution, I hope.

MRS DUBEDAT. I am not likely to forget it. They treat us like lepers at the hotels.

EMMY [*at the door*] Well, deary: have you got round him?

RIDGEON. Yes. Attend to the door and hold your tongue.

EMMY. Thats a good boy. [*She goes out with Mrs Dubedat*].

RIDGEON [*alone*] Consultation free. Cure guaranteed. [*He heaves a great sigh*].

ACT II

After dinner on the terrace at the Star and Garter, Richmond. Cloudless summer night; nothing disturbs the stillness except from time to time the long trajectory of a distant train and the measured clucking of oars coming up from the Thames in the valley below. The dinner is over; and three of the eight chairs are empty. Sir Patrick, with his back to the view, is at the head of the square table with Ridgeon. The two chairs opposite them are empty. On their right come, first, a vacant chair, and then one very fully occupied by B. B., who basks blissfully in the moonbeams. On their left, Schutzmacher and Walpole. The entrance to the hotel is on their right, behind B. B. The five men are silently enjoying their coffee and cigarets, full of food, and not altogether void of wine.

Mrs Dubedat, wrapped up for departure, comes in. They rise, except Sir Patrick; but she takes one of the vacant places at the foot of the table, next B. B.; and they sit down again.

MRS DUBEDAT [*as she enters*] Louis will be here presently. He is shewing Dr Blenkinsop how to work the telephone. [*She sits.*] Oh, I am so sorry we have to go. It seems such a shame, this beautiful night. And we have enjoyed ourselves so much.

RIDGEON. I dont believe another half-hour would do Mr Dubedat a bit of harm.

SIR PATRICK. Come now, Colly, come! come! none of that. You take your man home, Mrs Dubedat; and get him to bed before eleven.

B. B. Yes, yes. Bed before eleven. Quite right, quite right. Sorry to lose you, my dear lady; but Sir Patrick's orders are the laws of—er—of Tyre and Sidon.

WALPOLE. Let me take you home in my motor.

SIR PATRICK. No. You ought to be ashamed of yourself, Walpole. Your motor will take Mr and Mrs Dubedat to the station, and quite far enough too for an open carriage at night.

MRS DUBEDAT. Oh, I am sure the train is best.

RIDGEON. Well, Mrs Dubedat, we have had a most enjoyable evening.

WALPOLE. ⎱ Most enjoyable.
B. B. ⎰ Delightful. Charming. Unforgettable.

MRS DUBEDAT [*with a touch of shy anxiety*] What did you think of Louis? Or am I wrong to ask?

RIDGEON. Wrong! Why, we are all charmed with him.

WALPOLE. Delighted.

B. B. Most happy to have met him. A privilege, a real privilege.

SIR PATRICK [*grunts*]!

MRS DUBEDAT [*quickly*] Sir Patrick: are you uneasy about him?

SIR PATRICK [*discreetly*] I admire his drawings greatly, maam.

MRS DUBEDAT. Yes; but I meant—

RIDGEON. You shall go away quite happy. He's worth saving. He must and shall be saved.

Mrs Dubedat rises and gasps with delight, relief, and gratitude. They all rise except Sir Patrick and Schutzmacher, and come reassuringly to her.

B. B. Certainly, cer-tainly.

WALPOLE. Theres no real difficulty, if only you know what to do.

MRS DUBEDAT. Oh, how can I ever thank you! From this night I can begin to be happy at last. You dont know what I feel.

She sits down in tears. They crowd about her to console her.

B. B. My dear lady: come come! come come! [*very persuasively*] come come!

WALPOLE. Dont mind us. Have a good cry.

RIDGEON. No: dont cry. Your husband had better not know that weve been talking about him.

MRS DUBEDAT [*quickly pulling herself together*] No, of course not. Please dont mind me. What a glorious thing it must be to be a doctor! [*They laugh*]. Dont laugh. You dont know what youve done for me. I never knew until now how deadly afraid I was—how I had come to dread the worst. I never dared let myself know. But now the relief has come: now I know.

Louis Dubedat comes from the hotel, in his overcoat, his throat wrapped in a shawl. He is a slim young man of 23, physically still a stripling, and pretty, though not effeminate. He has turquoise blue eyes, and a trick of looking you straight in the face with them, which, combined with a frank smile, is very engaging. Although he is all nerves, and very observant and quick of apprehension, he is not in the least shy. He is younger than Jennifer; but he patronizes her as a matter of course. The doctors do not put him out in the least: neither Sir Patrick's years nor Bloomfield Bonington's majesty have the smallest apparent effect on him: he is as natural as a cat: he moves among men as most men move among things, though he is intentionally making himself agreeable to them on this occasion. Like all people who can be depended on to take care of themselves, he is welcome

ACT II   The Doctor's Dilemma   45

company; and his artist's power of appealing to the imagination gains him credit for all sorts of qualities and powers, whether he possesses them or not.

LOUIS [*pulling on his gloves behind Ridgeon's chair*] Now, Jinny-Gwinny: the motor has come round.

RIDGEON. Why do you let him spoil your beautiful name like that, Mrs Dubedat?

MRS DUBEDAT. Oh, on grand occasions I am Jennifer.

B. B. You are a bachelor: you do not understand these things, Ridgeon. Look at me [*They look*]. I also have two names. In moments of domestic worry, I am simple Ralph. When the sun shines in the home, I am Beedle-Deedle-Dumkins. Such is married life! Mr Dubedat: may I ask you to do me a favor before you go. Will you sign your name to this menu card, under the sketch you have made of me?

WALPOLE. Yes; and mine too, if you will be so good.

LOUIS. Certainly. [*He sits down and signs the cards*].

MRS DUBEDAT. Wont you sign Dr Schutzmacher's for him, Louis?

LOUIS. I dont think Dr Schutzmacher is pleased with his portrait. I'll tear it up. [*He reaches across the table for Schutzmacher's menu card, and is about to tear it. Schutzmacher makes no sign*].

RIDGEON. No, no: if Loony doesnt want it, I do.

LOUIS. I'll sign it for you with pleasure. [*He signs and hands it to Ridgeon*]. Ive just been making a little note of the river to-night: it will work up into something good [*he shews a pocket sketch-book*]. I think I'll call it the Silver Danube.

B. B. Ah, charming, charming.

WALPOLE. Very sweet. Youre a nailer at pastel.

Louis coughs, first out of modesty, then from tuberculosis.

SIR PATRICK. Now then, Mr Dubedat: youve had enough of the night air. Take him home, maam.

MRS DUBEDAT. Yes. Come, Louis.

RIDGEON. Never fear. Never mind. I'll make that cough all right.

B. B. We will stimulate the phagocytes. [*With tender effusion, shaking her hand*] Good-night, Mrs Dubedot. Good-night. Good-night.

WALPOLE. If the phagocytes fail, come to me. I'll put you right.

LOUIS. Good-night, Sir Patrick. Happy to have met you.

SIR PATRICK. 'Night [*half a grunt*].

MRS DUBEDAT. Good-night, Sir Patrick.

SIR PATRICK. Cover yourself well up. Dont think your lungs are made of iron because theyre better than his. Good-night.

MRS DUBEDAT. Thank you. Thank you. Nothing hurts me. Good-night.

Louis goes out through the hotel without noticing Schutzmacher. Mrs Dubedat hesitates, then bows to him. Schutzmacher rises and bows formally, German fashion. She goes out, attended by Ridgeon. The rest resume their seats, ruminating or smoking quietly.

B. B. [*harmoniously*] Dee-lightful couple! Charming woman! Gifted lad! Remarkable talent! Graceful outlines! Perfect evening! Great success! Interesting case! Glorious night! Exquisite scenery! Capital dinner! Stimulating conversation! Restful outing! Good wine! Happy ending! Touching gratitude! Lucky Ridgeon—

RIDGEON [*returning*] Whats that? Calling me, B. B.? [*He goes back to his seat next Sir Patrick*].

B. B. No, no. Only congratulating you on a most successful evening! Enchanting woman! Thorough breeding! Gentle nature! Refined—

Act II The Doctor's Dilemma

Blenkinsop comes from the hotel and takes the empty chair next Ridgeon.

BLENKINSOP. I'm so sorry to have left you like this, Ridgeon; but it was a telephone message from the police. Theyve found half a milkman at our level crossing with a prescription of mine in its pocket. Wheres Mr Dubedat?

RIDGEON. Gone.

BLENKINSOP [*rising, very pale*] Gone!

RIDGEON. Just this moment—

BLENKINSOP. Perhaps I could overtake him—[*he rushes into the hotel*].

WALPOLE [*calling after him*] He's in the motor, man, miles off. You can—[*giving it up*]. No use.

RIDGEON. Theyre really very nice people. I confess I was afraid the husband would turn out an appalling bounder. But he's almost as charming in his way as she is in hers. And theres no mistake about his being a genius. It's something to have got a case really worth saving. Somebody else will have to go; but at all events it will be easy to find a worse man.

SIR PATRICK. How do you know?

RIDGEON. Come now, Sir Paddy, no growling. Have something more to drink.

SIR PATRICK. No, thank you.

WALPOLE. Do you see anything wrong with Dubedat, B. B.?

B. B. Oh, a charming young fellow. Besides, after all, what could be wrong with him? Look at him. What could be wrong with him?

SIR PATRICK. There are two things that can be wrong with any man. One of them is a cheque. The other is a woman. Until you know that a man's sound on these two points, you know nothing about him.

B. B. Ah, cynic, cynic!

WALPOLE. He's all right as to the cheque, for a while

at all events. He talked to me quite frankly before dinner as to the pressure of money difficulties on an artist. He says he has no vices and is very economical, but that theres one extravagance he cant afford and yet cant resist; and that is dressing his wife prettily. So I said, bang plump out, " Let me lend you twenty pounds, and pay me when your ship comes home." He was really very nice about it. He took it like a man; and it was a pleasure to see how happy it made him, poor chap.

B. B. [*who has listened to Walpole with growing perturbation*] But—but—but—when was this, may I ask?

WALPOLE. When I joined you that time down by the river.

B. B. But, my dear Walpole, he had just borrowed ten pounds from me.

WALPOLE. What!

SIR PATRICK [*grunts*]!

B. B. [*indulgently*] Well, well, it was really hardly borrowing; for he said heaven only knew when he could pay me. I couldnt refuse. It appears that Mrs Dubedat has taken a sort of fancy to me—

WALPOLE [*quickly*] No: it was to me.

B. B. Certainly not. Your name was never mentioned between us. He is so wrapped up in his work that he has to leave her a good deal alone; and the poor innocent young fellow—he has of course no idea of my position or how busy I am—actually wanted me to call occasionally and talk to her.

WALPOLE. Exactly what he said to me!

B. B. Pooh! Pooh pooh! Really, I must say.
[*Much disturbed, he rises and goes up to the balustrade, contemplating the landscape vexedly*].

WALPOLE. Look here, Ridgeon! this is beginning to look serious.

Blenkinsop, very anxious and wretched, but trying to look unconcerned, comes back.

Act II   The Doctor's Dilemma

RIDGEON. Well, did you catch him?

BLENKINSOP. No. Excuse my running away like that. [*He sits down at the foot of the table, next Bloomfield Bonington's chair*].

WALPOLE. Anything the matter?

BLENKINSOP. Oh no. A trifle—something ridiculous. It cant be helped. Never mind.

RIDGEON. Was it anything about Dubedat?

BLENKINSOP [*almost breaking down*] I ought to keep it to myself, I know. I cant tell you, Ridgeon, how ashamed I am of dragging my miserable poverty to your dinner after all your kindness. It's not that you wont ask me again; but it's so humiliating. And I did so look forward to one evening in my dress clothes (theyre still presentable, you see) with all my troubles left behind, just like old times.

RIDGEON. But what has happened?

BLENKINSOP. Oh, nothing. It's too ridiculous. I had just scraped up four shillings for this little outing; and it cost me one-and-fourpence to get here. Well, Dubedat asked me to lend him half-a-crown to tip the chambermaid of the room his wife left her wraps in, and for the cloakroom. He said he only wanted it for five minutes, as she had his purse. So of course I lent it to him. And he's forgotten to pay me. I've just tuppence to get back with.

RIDGEON. Oh, never mind that—

BLENKINSOP [*stopping him resolutely*] No: I know what youre going to say; but I wont take it. Ive never borrowed a penny; and I never will. Ive nothing left but my friends; and I wont sell them. If none of you were to be able to meet me without being afraid that my civility was leading up to the loan of five shillings, there would be an end of everything for me. I'll take your old clothes, Colly, sooner than disgrace you by talking to you in the street in my own; but I wont borrow money.

I'll train it as far as the twopence will take me; and I'll tramp the rest.

WALPOLE. Youll do the whole distance in my motor. [*They are all greatly relieved; and Walpole hastens to get away from the painful subject by adding*] Did he get anything out of you, Mr Schutzmacher?

SCHUTZMACHER [*shakes his head in a most expressive negative*].

WALPOLE. You didnt appreciate his drawing, I think.

SCHUTZMACHER. Oh yes I did. I should have liked very much to have kept the sketch and got it autographed.

B. B. But why didnt you?

SCHUTZMACHER. Well, the fact is, when I joined Dubedat after his conversation with Mr Walpole, he said the Jews were the only people who knew anything about art, and that though he had to put up with your Philistine twaddle, as he called it, it was what I said about the drawings that really pleased him. He also said that his wife was greatly struck with my knowledge, and that she always admired Jews. Then he asked me to advance him £50 on the security of the drawings.

B. B.		No, no. Positively! Seriously!
WALPOLE	[*All exclaiming together*]	What! Another fifty!
BLENKINSOP		Think of that!
SIR PATRICK		[*grunts*]!

SCHUTZMACHER. Of course I couldnt lend money to a stranger like that.

B. B. I envy you the power to say No, Mr Schutzmacher. Of course, I knew I oughtnt to lend money to a young fellow in that way; but I simply hadnt the nerve to refuse. I couldnt very well, you know, could I?

SCHUTZMACHER. I dont understand that. *I* felt that I couldnt very well lend it.

WALPOLE. What did he say?

SCHUTZMACHER. Well, he made a very uncalled-for

Act II The Doctor's Dilemma 51

remark about a Jew not understanding the feelings of a gentleman. I must say you Gentiles are very hard to please. You say we are no gentlemen when we lend money; and when we refuse to lend it you say just the same. I didnt mean to behave badly. As I told him, I might have lent it to him if he had been a Jew himself.

SIR PATRICK [*with a grunt*] And what did he say to that?

SCHUTZMACHER. Oh, he began trying to persuade me that he was one of the chosen people—that his artistic faculty shewed it, and that his name was as foreign as my own. He said he didnt really want £50; that he was only joking; that all he wanted was a couple of sovereigns.

B. B. No, no, Mr Schutzmacher. You invented that last touch. Seriously, now?

SCHUTZMACHER. No. You cant improve on Nature in telling stories about gentlemen like Mr Dubedat.

BLENKINSOP. You certainly do stand by one another, you chosen people, Mr Schutzmacher.

SCHUTZMACHER. Not at all. Personally, I like Englishmen better than Jews, and always associate with them. Thats only natural, because, as I am a Jew, theres nothing interesting in a Jew to me, whereas there is always something interesting and foreign in an Englishman. But in money matters it's quite different. You see, when an Englishman borrows, all he knows or cares is that he wants money; and he'll sign anything to get it, without in the least understanding it, or intending to carry out the agreement if it turns out badly for him. In fact, he thinks you a cad if you ask him to carry it out under such circumstances. Just like the Merchant of Venice, you know. But if a Jew makes an agreement, he means to keep it and expects you to keep it. If he wants money for a time, he borrows it and knows he must pay it at the end of the time. If he knows he cant pay, he begs it as a gift.

RIDGEON. Come, Loony! do you mean to say that Jews are never rogues and thieves?

SCHUTZMACHER. Oh, not at all. But I was not talking of criminals. I was comparing honest Englishmen with honest Jews.

One of the hotel maids, a pretty, fair-haired woman of about 25, comes from the hotel, rather furtively. She accosts Ridgeon.

THE MAID. I beg your pardon, sir—

RIDGEON. Eh?

THE MAID. I beg pardon, sir. It's not about the hotel. I'm not allowed to be on the terrace; and I should be discharged if I were seen speaking to you, unless you were kind enough to say you called me to ask whether the motor has come back from the station yet.

WALPOLE. Has it?

THE MAID. Yes, sir.

RIDGEON. Well, what do you want?

THE MAID. Would you mind, sir, giving me the address of the gentleman that was with you at dinner?

RIDGEON [*sharply*] Yes, of course I should mind very much. You have no right to ask.

THE MAID. Yes, sir, I know it looks like that. But what am I to do?

SIR PATRICK. Whats the matter with you?

THE MAID. Nothing, sir. I want the address: thats all.

B. B. You mean the young gentleman?

THE MAID. Yes, sir: that went to catch the train with the woman he brought with him.

RIDGEON. The woman! Do you mean the lady who dined here? the gentleman's wife?

THE MAID. Dont believe them, sir. She cant be his wife. I'm his wife.

ACT II   The Doctor's Dilemma   53

B. B. ⎫⎧ [*in amazed remonstrance*] My good girl!
RIDGEON ⎬⎨ You his wife!
WALPOLE ⎭⎩ What! whats that? Oh, this is getting
         perfectly fascinating, Ridgeon.

THE MAID. I could run upstairs and get you my marriage lines in a minute, sir, if you doubt my word. He's Mr Louis Dubedat, isnt he?

RIDGEON. Yes.

THE MAID. Well, sir, you may believe me or not; but I'm the lawful Mrs Dubedat.

SIR PATRICK. And why arnt you living with your husband?

THE MAID. We couldnt afford it, sir. I had thirty pounds saved; and we spent it all on our honeymoon in three weeks, and a lot more that he borrowed. Then I had to go back into service, and he went to London to get work at his drawing; and he never wrote me a line or sent me an address. I never saw nor heard of him again until I caught sight of him from the window going off in the motor with that woman.

SIR PATRICK. Well, thats two wives to start with.

B. B. Now upon my soul I dont want to be uncharitable; but really I'm beginning to suspect that our young friend is rather careless.

SIR PATRICK. Beginning to think! How long will it take you, man, to find out that he's a damned young blackguard?

BLENKINSOP. Oh, thats severe, Sir Patrick, very severe. Of course it's bigamy; but still he's very young; and she's very pretty. Mr Walpole: may I spunge on you for another of those nice cigarets of yours? [*He changes his seat for the one next Walpole*].

WALPOLE. Certainly. [*He feels in his pockets*]. Oh bother! Where—? [*Suddenly remembering*] I say: I recollect now: I passed my cigaret case to Dubedat and he didnt return it. It was a gold one.

THE MAID. He didnt mean any harm: he never thinks about things like that, sir. I'll get it back for you, sir, if youll tell me where to find him.

RIDGEON. What am I to do? Shall I give her the address or not?

SIR PATRICK. Give her your own address; and then we'll see. [*To the maid*] Youll have to be content with that for the present, my girl. [*Ridgeon gives her his card*]. Whats your name?

THE MAID. Minnie Tinwell, sir.

SIR PATRICK. Well, you write him a letter to care of this gentleman; and it will be sent on. Now be off with you.

THE MAID. Thank you, sir. I'm sure you wouldnt see me wronged. Thank you all, gentlemen; and excuse the liberty.

She goes into the hotel. They watch her in silence.

RIDGEON [*when she is gone*] Do you realize, you chaps, that we have promised Mrs Dubedat to save this fellow's life?

BLENKINSOP. Whats the matter with him?

RIDGEON. Tuberculosis.

BLENKINSOP [*interested*] And can you cure that?

RIDGEON. I believe so.

BLENKINSOP. Then I wish youd cure me. My right lung is touched, I'm sorry to say.

RIDGEON		What! your lung is going!
B. B.	[*all together*]	My dear Blenkinsop, what do you tell me? [*full of concern for Blenkinsop, he comes back from the balustrade*].
SIR PATRICK		Eh? Eh? whats that?
WALPOLE		Hullo! you mustnt neglect this, you know.

Act II   The Doctor's Dilemma   55

BLENKINSOP [*putting his fingers in his ears*] No, no: it's no use. I know what youre going to say: Ive said it often to others. I cant afford to take care of myself; and theres an end of it. If a fortnight's holiday would save my life, I'd have to die. I shall get on as others have to get on. We cant all go to St Moritz or to Egypt, you know, Sir Ralph. Dont talk about it.
Embarrassed silence.
SIR PATRICK [*grunts and looks hard at Ridgeon*]!
SCHUTZMACHER [*looking at his watch and rising*] I must go. It's been a very pleasant evening, Colly. You might let me have my portrait if you dont mind. I'll send Mr Dubedat that couple of sovereigns for it.
RIDGEON [*giving him the menu card*] Oh dont do that, Loony. I don't think he'd like that.
SCHUTZMACHER. Well, of course I shant if you feel that way about it. But I dont think you understand Dubedat. However, perhaps thats because I'm a Jew. Good-night, Dr Blenkinsop [*shaking hands*].
BLENKINSOP. Good-night, sir—I mean—Good-night.
SCHUTZMACHER [*waving his hand to the rest*] Good-night, everybody.
WALPOLE
B. B.
SIR PATRICK
RIDGEON
} Good-night.

B. B. repeats the salutation several times, in varied musical tones. Schutzmacher goes out.

SIR PATRICK. It's time for us all to move. [*He rises and comes between Blenkinsop and Walpole. Ridgeon also rises*]. Mr Walpole: take Blenkinsop home: he's had enough of the open air cure for to-night. Have you a thick overcoat to wear in the motor, Dr Blenkinsop?
BLENKINSOP. Oh, theyll give me some brown paper

in the hotel; and a few thicknesses of brown paper across
the chest are better than any fur coat.

WALPOLE. Well, come along. Good-night, Colly.
Youre coming with us, arnt you, B. B.?

B. B. Yes: I'm coming. [*Walpole and Blenkinsop
go into the hotel*]. Good-night, my dear Ridgeon [*shaking hands affectionately*]. Dont let us lose sight of your
interesting patient and his very charming wife. We must
not judge him too hastily, you know. [*With unction*]
Goooooood-night, Paddy. Bless you, dear old chap.
[*Sir Patrick utters a formidable grunt. B. B. laughs and
pats him indulgently on the shoulder*] Good-night.
Good-night. Good-night. Good-night. [*He good-nights
himself into the hotel*].

*The others have meanwhile gone without ceremony.
Ridgeon and Sir Patrick are left alone together. Ridgeon, deep in thought, comes down to Sir Patrick.*

SIR PATRICK. Well, Mr Savior of Lives: which is it
to be? that honest decent man Blenkinsop, or that rotten
blackguard of an artist, eh?

RIDGEON. It's not an easy case to judge, is it?
Blenkinsop's an honest decent man; but is he any use?
Dubedat's a rotten blackguard; but he's a genuine source
of pretty and pleasant and good things.

SIR PATRICK. What will he be a source of for
that poor innocent wife of his, when she finds him
out?

RIDGEON. Thats true. Her life will be a hell.

SIR PATRICK. And tell me this. Suppose you had
this choice put before you: either to go through life and
find all the pictures bad but all the men and women
good, or to go through life and find all the pictures good
and all the men and women rotten. Which would you
choose?

RIDGEON. Thats a devilishly difficult question, Paddy.
The pictures are so agreeable, and the good people so

Act II   The Doctor's Dilemma   57

infernally disagreeable and mischievous, that I really cant undertake to say offhand which I should prefer to do without.

SIR PATRICK. Come come! none of your cleverness with me: I'm too old for it. Blenkinsop isnt that sort of good man; and you know it.

RIDGEON. It would be simpler if Blenkinsop could paint Dubedat's pictures.

SIR PATRICK. It would be simpler still if Dubedat had some of Blenkinsop's honesty. The world isnt going to be made simple for you, my lad: you must take it as it is. Youve to hold the scales between Blenkinsop and Dubedat. Hold them fairly.

RIDGEON. Well, I'll be as fair as I can. I'll put into one scale all the pounds Dubedat has borrowed, and into the other all the half-crowns that Blenkinsop hasnt borrowed.

SIR PATRICK. And youll take out of Dubedat's scale all the faith he has destroyed and the honor he has lost, and youll put into Blenkinsop's scale all the faith he has justified and the honor he has created.

RIDGEON. Come come, Paddy! none of your claptrap with me: I'm too sceptical for it. I'm not at all convinced that the world wouldnt be a better world if everybody behaved as Dubedat does than it is now that everybody behaves as Blenkinsop does.

SIR PATRICK. Then why dont you behave as Dubedat does?

RIDGEON. Ah, that beats me. Thats the experimental test. Still, it's a dilemma. It's a dilemma. You see theres a complication we havnt mentioned.

SIR PATRICK. Whats that?

RIDGEON. Well, if I let Blenkinsop die, at least nobody can say I did it because I wanted to marry his widow.

SIR PATRICK. Eh? Whats that?

RIDGEON. Now if I let Dubedat die, I'll marry his widow.

SIR PATRICK. Perhaps she wont have you, you know.

RIDGEON [*with a self-assured shake of the head*] I've a pretty good flair for that sort of thing. I know when a woman is interested in me. She is.

SIR PATRICK. Well, sometimes a man knows best; and sometimes he knows worst. Youd much better cure them both.

RIDGEON. I cant. I'm at my limit. I can squeeze in one more case, but not two. I must choose.

SIR PATRICK. Well, you must choose as if she didnt exist: thats clear.

RIDGEON. Is that clear to you? Mind: it's not clear to me. She troubles my judgment.

SIR PATRICK. To me, it's a plain choice between a man and a lot of pictures.

RIDGEON. It's easier to replace a dead man than a good picture.

SIR PATRICK. Colly: when you live in an age that runs to pictures and statues and plays and brass bands because its men and women are not good enough to comfort its poor aching soul, you should thank Providence that you belong to a profession which is a high and great profession because its business is to heal and mend men and women.

RIDGEON. In short, as a member of a high and great profession, I'm to kill my patient.

SIR PATRICK. Dont talk wicked nonsense. You cant kill him. But you can leave him in other hands.

RIDGEON. In B. B.'s, for instance: eh? [*looking at him significantly*].

SIR PATRICK [*demurely facing his look*] Sir Ralph Bloomfield Bonington is a very eminent physician.

RIDGEON. He is.

SIR PATRICK. I'm going for my hat.

Ridgeon strikes the bell as Sir Patrick makes for the hotel. A waiter comes.
RIDGEON [*to the waiter*] My bill, please.
WAITER. Yes, sir.
He goes for it.

ACT III

In Dubedat's studio. Viewed from the large window the outer door is in the wall on the left at the near end. The door leading to the inner rooms is in the opposite wall, at the far end. The facing wall has neither window nor door. The plaster on all the walls is uncovered and undecorated, except by scrawlings of charcoal sketches and memoranda. There is a studio throne (a chair on a dais) a little to the left, opposite the inner door, and an easel to the right, opposite the outer door, with a dilapidated chair at it. Near the easel and against the wall is a bare wooden table with bottles and jars of oil and medium, paint-smudged rags, tubes of color, brushes, charcoal, a small lay figure, a kettle and spirit-lamp, and other odds and ends. By the table is a sofa, littered with drawing blocks, sketch-books, loose sheets of paper, newspapers, books, and more smudged rags. Next the outer door is an umbrella and hat stand, occupied partly by Louis' hats and cloak and muffler, and partly by odds and ends of costumes. There is an old piano stool on the near side of this door. In the corner near the inner door is a little tea-table. A lay figure, in a cardinal's robe and hat, with an hour-glass in one hand and a scythe slung on its back, smiles with inane malice at Louis, who, in a milkman's smock much smudged with colors, is painting a piece of brocade which he has draped about his wife. She is sitting on the throne, not interested in the paint-

ACT III   The Doctor's Dilemma   61

ing, and appealing to him very anxiously about another matter.

MRS DUBEDAT. Promise.

LOUIS [*putting on a touch of paint with notable skill and care and answering quite perfunctorily*]   I promise, my darling.

MRS DUBEDAT. When you want money, you will always come to me.

LOUIS. But it's so sordid, dearest. I hate money. I cant keep always bothering you for money, money, money. Thats what drives me sometimes to ask other people, though I hate doing it.

MRS DUBEDAT. It is far better to ask me, dear. It gives people a wrong idea of you.

LOUIS. But I want to spare your little fortune, and raise money on my own work. Dont be unhappy, love: I can easily earn enough to pay it all back. I shall have a one-man-show next season; and then there will be no more money troubles. [*Putting down his palette*] There! I mustnt do any more on that until it's bone-dry; so you may come down.

MRS DUBEDAT [*throwing off the drapery as she steps down, and revealing a plain frock of tussore silk*] But you have promised, remember, seriously and faithfully, never to borrow again until you have first asked me.

LOUIS. Seriously and faithfully. [*Embracing her*] Ah, my love, how right you are! how much it means to me to have you by me to guard me against living too much in the skies. On my solemn oath, from this moment forth I will never borrow another penny.

MRS DUBEDAT [*delighted*] Ah, thats right. Does his wicked worrying wife torment him and drag him down from the clouds. [*She kisses him*]. And now, dear, wont you finish those drawings for Maclean?

LOUIS. Oh, they dont matter. Ive got nearly all the money from him in advance.

MRS DUBEDAT. But, dearest, that is just the reason why you should finish them. He asked me the other day whether you really intended to finish them.

LOUIS. Confound his impudence! What the devil does he take me for? Now that just destroys all my interest in the beastly job. Ive a good mind to throw up the commission, and pay him back his money.

MRS DUBEDAT. We cant afford that, dear. You had better finish the drawings and have done with them. I think it is a mistake to accept money in advance.

LOUIS. But how are we to live?

MRS DUBEDAT. Well, Louis, it is getting hard enough as it is, now that they are all refusing to pay except on delivery.

LOUIS. Damn those fellows! they think of nothing and care for nothing but their wretched money.

MRS DUBEDAT. Still, if they pay us, they ought to have what they pay for.

LOUIS [*coaxing*] There now: thats enough lecturing for to-day. Ive promised to be good, havnt I?

MRS DUBEDAT [*putting her arms round his neck*] You know that I hate lecturing, and that I dont for a moment misunderstand you, dear, dont you?

LOUIS [*fondly*] I know. I know. I'm a wretch; and youre an angel. Oh, if only I were strong enough to work steadily, I'd make my darling's house a temple, and her shrine a chapel more beautiful than was ever imagined. I cant pass the shops without wrestling with the temptation to go in and order all the really good things they have for you.

MRS DUBEDAT. I want nothing but you, dear. [*She gives him a caress, to which he responds so passionately that she disengages herself*]. There! be good now: remember that the doctors are coming this morning. Isnt

Act III   The Doctor's Dilemma   63

it extraordinarily kind of them, Louis, to insist on coming? all of them, to consult about you?

LOUIS [*coolly*] Oh, I daresay they think it will be a feather in their cap to cure a rising artist. They wouldnt come if it didnt amuse them, anyhow. [*Someone knocks at the door*]. I say: it's not time yet, is it?

MRS DUBEDAT. No, not quite yet.

LOUIS [*opening the door and finding Ridgeon there*] Hello, Ridgeon. Delighted to see you. Come in.

MRS DUBEDAT [*shaking hands*] It's so good of you to come, doctor.

LOUIS. Excuse this place, wont you? It's only a studio, you know: theres no real convenience for living here. But we pig along somehow, thanks to Jennifer.

MRS DUBEDAT. Now I'll run away. Perhaps later on, when youre finished with Louis, I may come in and hear the verdict. [*Ridgeon bows rather constrainedly*]. Would you rather I didnt?

RIDGEON. Not at all. Not at all.

Mrs Dubedat looks at him, a little puzzled by his formal manner; then goes into the inner room.

LOUIS [*flippantly*] I say: dont look so grave. Theres nothing awful going to happen, is there?

RIDGEON. No.

LOUIS. Thats all right. Poor Jennifer has been looking forward to your visit more than you can imagine. Shes taken quite a fancy to you, Ridgeon. The poor girl has nobody to talk to: I'm always painting. [*Taking up a sketch*] Theres a little sketch I made of her yesterday.

RIDGEON. She shewed it to me a fortnight ago when she first called on me.

LOUIS [*quite unabashed*] Oh! did she? Good Lord! how time does fly! I could have sworn I'd only just finished it. It's hard for her here, seeing me piling up drawings and nothing coming in for them. Of course I shall sell them next year fast enough, after my one-man-show; but while the grass grows the steed starves. I hate to have her coming to me for money, and having none to give her. But what can I do?

RIDGEON. I understood that Mrs Dubedat had some property of her own.

LOUIS. Oh yes, a little; but how could a man with any decency of feeling touch that? Suppose I did, what would she have to live on if I died? I'm not insured: cant afford the premiums. [*Picking out another drawing*] How do you like that?

RIDGEON [*putting it aside*] I have not come here today to look at your drawings. I have more serious and pressing business with you.

LOUIS. You want to sound my wretched lung. [*With impulsive candor*] My dear Ridgeon: I'll be frank with you. Whats the matter in this house isnt lungs but bills. It doesnt matter about me; but Jennifer has actually to economize in the matter of food. Youve made us feel that we can treat you as a friend. Will you lend us a hundred and fifty pounds?

RIDGEON. No.

LOUIS [*surprised*] Why not?

RIDGEON. I am not a rich man; and I want every penny I can spare and more for my researches.

LOUIS. You mean youd want the money back again.

RIDGEON. I presume people sometimes have that in view when they lend money.

LOUIS [*after a moment's reflection*] Well, I can manage that for you. I'll give you a cheque—or see here: theres no reason why you shouldnt have your bit too: I'll give you a cheque for two hundred.

RIDGEON. Why not cash the cheque at once without troubling me?

LOUIS. Bless you! they wouldnt cash it: I'm overdrawn as it is. No: the way to work it is this. I'll postdate the cheque next October. In October Jennifer's dividends come in. Well, you present the cheque. It will be returned marked "refer to drawer" or some rubbish of that sort. Then you can take it to Jennifer, and hint that if the cheque isnt taken up at once I shall be put in prison. She'll pay you like a shot. Youll clear £50; and youll do me a real service; for I do want the money very badly, old chap, I assure you.

RIDGEON [*staring at him*] You see no objection to the transaction; and you anticipate none from me!

LOUIS. Well, what objection can there be? It's quite safe. I can convince you about the dividends.

RIDGEON. I mean on the score of its being—shall I say dishonorable?

LOUIS. Well, of course I shouldnt suggest it if I didnt want the money.

RIDGEON. Indeed! Well, you will have to find some other means of getting it.

LOUIS. Do you mean that you refuse?

RIDGEON. Do I mean—! [*letting his indignation loose*] Of course I refuse, man. What do you take me for? How dare you make such a proposal to me?

LOUIS. Why not?

RIDGEON. Faugh! You would not understand me if I tried to explain. Now, once for all, I will not lend you a farthing. I should be glad to help your wife; but lending you money is no service to her.

LOUIS. Oh well, if youre in earnest about helping her, I'll tell you what you might do. You might get your patients to buy some of my things, or to give me a few portrait commissions.

RIDGEON. My patients call me in as a physician, not as a commercial traveller.

A knock at the door. Louis goes unconcernedly to open it, pursuing the subject as he goes.

LOUIS. But you must have great influence with them. You must know such lots of things about them—private things that they wouldnt like to have known. They wouldnt dare to refuse you.

RIDGEON [*exploding*] Well, upon my—

Louis opens the door, and admits Sir Patrick, Sir Ralph, and Walpole.

RIDGEON [*proceeding furiously*] Walpole: Ive been here hardly ten minutes; and already he's tried to borrow £150 from me. Then he proposed that I should get the money for him by blackmailing his wife; and youve just interrupted him in the act of suggesting that I should blackmail my patients into sitting to him for their portraits.

LOUIS. Well, Ridgeon, if this is what you call being an honorable man! I spoke to you in confidence.

SIR PATRICK. We're all going to speak to you in confidence, young man.

WALPOLE [*hanging his hat on the only peg left vacant on the hat-stand*] We shall make ourselves at home for half an hour, Dubedat. Dont be alarmed: youre a most fascinating chap; and we love you.

LOUIS. Oh, all right, all right. Sit down—anywhere you can. Take this chair, Sir Patrick [*indicating the one on the throne*]. Up-z-z-z! [*helping him up: Sir Patrick grunts and enthrones himself*]. Here you are, B. B. [*Sir Ralph glares at the familiarity; but Louis, quite undisturbed, puts a big book and a sofa cushion on the dais, on Sir Patrick's right; and B. B. sits down, under protest*]. Let me take your hat. [*He takes B. B.'s hat unceremoniously, and substitutes it for the cardinal's hat on the head of the lay figure, thereby ingeniously destroying the dignity of the conclave. He then draws the piano stool from the wall and offers it to Walpole*]. You dont mind this, Walpole, do you? [*Walpole accepts the stool, and puts his hand into his pocket for his cigaret case. Missing it, he is reminded of his loss*].

Act III   The Doctor's Dilemma

WALPOLE. By the way, I'll trouble you for my cigaret case, if you dont mind?

LOUIS. What cigaret case?

WALPOLE. The gold one I lent you at the Star and Garter.

LOUIS [*surprised*]   Was that yours?

WALPOLE. Yes.

LOUIS. I'm awfully sorry, old chap. I wondered whose it was. I'm sorry to say this is all thats left of it. [*He hitches up his smock; produces a card from his waistcoat pocket; and hands it to Walpole*].

WALPOLE. A pawn ticket!

LOUIS [*reassuringly*]   It's quite safe: he cant sell it for a year, you know. I say, my dear Walpole, I am sorry. [*He places his hand ingenuously on Walpole's shoulder and looks frankly at him*].

WALPOLE [*sinking on the stool with a gasp*]   Dont mention it. It adds to your fascination.

RIDGEON [*who has been standing near the easel*]   Before we go any further, you have a debt to pay, Mr Dubedat.

LOUIS. I have a precious lot of debts to pay, Ridgeon. I'll fetch you a chair. [*He makes for the inner door*].

RIDGEON [*stopping him*]   You shall not leave the room until you pay it. It's a small one; and pay it you must and shall. I dont so much mind your borrowing £10 from one of my guests and £20 from the other—

WALPOLE. I walked into it, you know. I offered it.

RIDGEON. —they could afford it. But to clean poor Blenkinsop out of his last half-crown was damnable. I intend to give him that half-crown and to be in a position to pledge him my word that you paid it. I'll have that out of you, at all events.

B. B. Quite right, Ridgeon. Quite right. Come, young man! down with the dust. Pay up.

LOUIS. Oh, you neednt make such a fuss about it.

Of course I'll pay it. I had no idea the poor fellow was hard up. I'm as shocked as any of you about it. [*Putting his hand into his pocket*] Here you are. [*Finding his pocket empty*] Oh, I say, I havnt any money on me just at present. Walpole: would you mind lending me half-a-crown just to settle this.

WALPOLE. Lend you half— [*his voice faints away*].

LOUIS. Well, if you dont, Blenkinsop wont get it; for I havnt a rap: you may search my pockets if you like.

WALPOLE. Thats conclusive. [*He produces half-a-crown*].

LOUIS [*passing it to Ridgeon*] There! I'm really glad thats settled: it was the only thing that was on my conscience. Now I hope youre all satisfied.

SIR PATRICK. Not quite, Mr Dubedat. Do you happen to know a young woman named Minnie Tinwell?

LOUIS. Minnie! I should think I do; and Minnie knows me too. She's a really nice good girl, considering her station. Whats become of her?

WALPOLE. It's no use bluffing, Dubedat. Weve seen Minnie's marriage lines.

LOUIS [*coolly*] Indeed? Have you seen Jennifer's?

RIDGEON [*rising in irrepressible rage*] Do you dare insinuate that Mrs Dubedat is living with you without being married to you?

LOUIS. Why not?

B. B.   ⎫ [*echoing him in*   ⎧ Why not!
SIR PATRICK ⎬ *various tones of*   ⎨ Why not!
RIDGEON   ⎪ *scandalized*   ⎪ Why not!
WALPOLE   ⎭ *amazement*]   ⎩ Why not!

LOUIS. Yes, why not? Lots of people do it: just as good people as you. Why dont you learn to think, instead of bleating and baahing like a lot of sheep when you come up against anything youre not accustomed to? [*Contemplating their amazed faces with a chuckle*] I say: I should like to draw the lot of you now: you do

Act III   The Doctor's Dilemma   69

look jolly foolish. Especially you, Ridgeon. I had you that time, you know.

RIDGEON. How, pray?

LOUIS. Well, you set up to appreciate Jennifer, you know. And you despise me, dont you?

RIDGEON [*curtly*] I loathe you. [*He sits down again on the sofa*].

LOUIS. Just so. And yet you believe that Jennifer is a bad lot because you think I told you so.

RIDGEON. Were you lying?

LOUIS. No; but you were smelling out a scandal instead of keeping your mind clean and wholesome. I can just play with people like you. I only asked you had you seen Jennifer's marriage lines; and you concluded straight away that she hadnt got any. You dont know a lady when you see one.

B. B. [*majestically*] What do you mean by that, may I ask?

LOUIS. Now, I'm only an immoral artist; but if youd told me that Jennifer wasnt married, I'd have had the gentlemanly feeling and artistic instinct to say that she carried her marriage certificate in her face and in her character. But you are all moral men; and Jennifer is only an artist's wife—probably a model; and morality consists in suspecting other people of not being legally married. Arnt you ashamed of yourselves? Can one of you look me in the face after it?

WALPOLE. It's very hard to look you in the face, Dubedat; you have such a dazzling cheek. What about Minnie Tinwell, eh?

LOUIS. Minnie Tinwell is a young woman who has had three weeks of glorious happiness in her poor little life, which is more than most girls in her position get, I can tell you. Ask her whether she'd take it back if she could. She's got her name into history, that girl. My little sketches of her will be fought by collectors at Christie's. She'll have a page in my biography. Pretty good, that, for a still-room maid at a seaside hotel, I think. What have you fellows done for her to compare with that?

RIDGEON. We havnt trapped her into a mock marriage and deserted her.

LOUIS. No: you wouldnt have the pluck. But dont fuss yourselves. *I* didnt desert little Minnie. We spent all our money—

WALPOLE. All her money. Thirty pounds.

LOUIS. I said all our money: hers and mine too. Her thirty pounds didnt last three days. I had to borrow four times as much to spend on her. But I didnt grudge it; and she didnt grudge her few pounds either, the brave little lassie. When we were cleaned out, we'd had enough of it: you can hardly suppose that we were fit company for longer than that: I an artist, and she quite out of art and literature and refined living and everything else. There was no desertion, no misunderstanding, no police court or divorce court sensation for you moral chaps to lick your lips over at breakfast. We just said, Well, the money's gone: weve had a good time that can never be taken from us; so kiss; part good friends; and she back to service, and I back to my studio and my Jennifer, both the better and happier for our holiday.

WALPOLE. Quite a little poem, by George!

B. B. If you had been scientifically trained, Mr Dubedat, you would know how very seldom an actual case bears out a principle. In medical practice a man may die when, scientifically speaking, he ought to have lived. I have actually known a man die of a disease from which he was scientifically speaking, immune. But that does not affect the fundamental truth of science. In just the same way, in moral cases, a man's behavior may be quite harmless and even beneficial, when he is morally

ACT III   The Doctor's Dilemma   71

behaving like a scoundrel. And he may do great harm when he is morally acting on the highest principles. But that does not affect the fundamental truth of morality.

SIR PATRICK. And it doesnt affect the criminal law on the subject of bigamy.

LOUIS. Oh bigamy! bigamy! bigamy! What a fascination anything connected with the police has for you all, you moralists! Ive proved to you that you were utterly wrong on the moral point: now I'm going to shew you that youre utterly wrong on the legal point; and I hope it will be a lesson to you not to be so jolly cocksure next time.

WALPOLE. Rot! You were married already when you married her; and that settles it.

LOUIS. Does it! Why cant you think? How do you know she wasnt married already too?

B. B.	[*all*	Walpole! Ridgeon!
RIDGEON	*crying*	This is beyond everything!
WALPOLE	*out*	Well, damn me!
SIR PATRICK	*together*]	You young rascal.

LOUIS [*ignoring their outcry*] She was married to the steward of a liner. He cleared out and left her; and she thought, poor girl, that it was the law that if you hadnt heard of your husband for three years you might marry again. So as she was a thoroughly respectable girl and refused to have anything to say to me unless we were married I went through the ceremony to please her and to preserve her self-respect.

RIDGEON. Did you tell her you were already married?

LOUIS. Of course not. Dont you see that if she had known, she wouldnt have considered herself my wife? You dont seem to understand, somehow.

SIR PATRICK. You let her risk imprisonment in her ignorance of the law?

LOUIS. Well, *I* risked imprisonment for her sake. I

could have been had up for it just as much as she. But when a man makes a sacrifice of that sort for a woman, he doesnt go and brag about it to her; at least, not if he's a gentleman.

WALPOLE. What are we to do with this daisy?

LOUIS [*impatiently*] Oh, go and do whatever the devil you please. Put Minnie in prison. Put me in prison. Kill Jennifer with the disgrace of it all. And then, when youve done all the mischief you can, go to church and feel good about it. [*He sits down pettishly on the old chair at the easel, and takes up a sketching block, on which he begins to draw*]

WALPOLE. He's got us.

SIR PATRICK [*grimly*] He has.

B. B. But is he to be allowed to defy the criminal law of the land?

SIR PATRICK. The criminal law is no use to decent people. It only helps blackguards to blackmail their families. What are we family doctors doing half our time but conspiring with the family solicitor to keep some rascal out of jail and some family out of disgrace?

B. B. But at least it will punish him.

SIR PATRICK. Oh, yes: itll punish him. Itll punish not only him but everybody connected with him, innocent and guilty alike. Itll throw his board and lodging on our rates and taxes for a couple of years, and then turn him loose on us a more dangerous blackguard than ever. Itll put the girl in prison and ruin her: itll lay his wife's life waste. You may put the criminal law out of your head once for all: it's only fit for fools and savages.

LOUIS. Would you mind turning your face a little more this way, Sir Patrick. [*Sir Patrick turns indignantly and glares at him*]. Oh, thats too much.

SIR PATRICK. Put down your foolish pencil, man; and think of your position. You can defy the laws made

ACT III The Doctor's Dilemma 73

by men; but there are other laws to reckon with. Do you know that youre going to die?

LOUIS. We're all going to die, arnt we?

WALPOLE. We're not all going to die in six months.

LOUIS. How do you know?

This for B. B. is the last straw. He completely loses his temper and begins to walk excitedly about.

B. B. Upon my soul, I will not stand this. It is in questionable taste under any circumstances or in any company to harp on the subject of death; but it is a dastardly advantage to take of a medical man. [*Thundering at Dubedat*] I will not allow it, do you hear?

LOUIS. Well, I didn't begin it: you chaps did. It's always the way with the inartistic professions: when theyre beaten in argument they fall back on intimidation. I never knew a lawyer who didnt threaten to put me in prison sooner or later. I never knew a parson who didnt threaten me with damnation. And now you threaten me with death. With all your talk youve only one real trump in your hand, and thats Intimidation. Well, I'm not a coward; so it's no use with me.

B. B. [*advancing upon him*] I'll tell you what you are, sir. Youre a scoundrel.

LOUIS. Oh, I don't mind you calling me a scoundrel a bit. It's only a word: a word that you dont know the meaning of. What is a scoundrel?

B. B. You are a scoundrel, sir.

LOUIS. Just so. What is a scoundrel? I am. What am I? A scoundrel. It's just arguing in a circle. And you imagine youre a man of science!

B. B. I—I—I—I have a good mind to take you by the scruff of your neck, you infamous rascal, and give you a sound thrashing.

LOUIS. I wish you would. Youd pay me something handsome to keep it out of court afterwards. [*B. B.*, *baffled, flings away from him with a snort*]. Have you any more civilities to address to me in my own house? I should like to get them over before my wife comes back. [*He resumes his sketching*].

RIDGEON. My mind's made up. When the law breaks down, honest men must find a remedy for themselves. I will not lift a finger to save this reptile.

B. B. That is the word I was trying to remember. Reptile.

WALPOLE. I cant help rather liking you, Dubedat. But you certainly are a thoroughgoing specimen.

SIR PATRICK. You know our opinion of you now, at all events.

LOUIS [*patiently putting down his pencil*] Look here. All this is no good. You dont understand. You imagine that I'm simply an ordinary criminal.

WALPOLE. Not an ordinary one, Dubedat. Do yourself justice.

LOUIS. Well youre on the wrong tack altogether. I'm not a criminal. All your moralizings have no value for me. I don't believe in morality. I'm a disciple of Bernard Shaw.

SIR PATRICK. [*puzzled*] Eh?
B. B. [*waving his hand as if the subject were now disposed of*] Thats enough: I wish to hear no more.

LOUIS. Of course I havnt the ridiculous vanity to set up to be exactly a Superman; but still, it's an ideal that I strive towards just as any other man strives towards his ideal.

B. B. [*intolerant*] Dont trouble to explain. I now understand you perfectly. Say no more, please. When a man pretends to discuss science, morals, and religion, and then avows himself a follower of a notorious and avowed anti-vaccinationist, there is nothing more to be said. [*Suddenly putting in an effusive saving clause in*

Act III   The Doctor's Dilemma

parenthesis to Ridgeon] Not, my dear Ridgeon, that I believe in vaccination in the popular sense any more than you do: I neednt tell you that. But there are things that place a man socially; and anti-vaccination is one of them. [*He resumes his seat on the dais*].

SIR PATRICK. Bernard Shaw? I never heard of him. He's a Methodist preacher, I suppose.

LOUIS [*scandalized*] No, no. He's the most advanced man now living: he isn't anything.

SIR PATRICK. I assure you, young man, my father learnt the doctrine of deliverance from sin from John Wesley's own lips before you or Mr. Shaw were born. It used to be very popular as an excuse for putting sand in sugar and water in milk. Youre a sound Methodist, my lad; only you don't know it.

LOUIS [*seriously annoyed for the first time*] It's an intellectual insult. I don't believe theres such a thing as sin.

SIR PATRICK. Well, sir, there are people who dont believe theres such a thing as disease either. They call themselves Christian Scientists, I believe. Theyll just suit your complaint. We can do nothing for you. [*He rises*]. Good afternoon to you.

LOUIS [*running to him piteously*] Oh dont get up, Sir Patrick. Don't go. Please dont. I didnt mean to shock you, on my word. Do sit down again. Give me another chance. Two minutes more: thats all I ask.

SIR PATRICK [*surprised by this sign of grace, and a little touched*] Well— [*He sits down*]—

LOUIS [*gratefully*] Thanks awfully.

SIR PATRICK [*continuing*] —I don't mind giving you two minutes more. But dont address yourself to me; for Ive retired from practice; and I dont pretend to be able to cure your complaint. Your life is in the hands of these gentlemen.

RIDGEON. Not in mine. My hands are full. I have no time and no means available for this case.

SIR PATRICK. What do you say, Mr. Walpole?

WALPOLE. Oh, I'll take him in hand: I dont mind. I feel perfectly convinced that this is not a moral case at all: it's a physical one. Theres something abnormal about his brain. That means, probably, some morbid condition affecting the spinal cord. And that means the circulation. In short, it's clear to me that he's suffering from an obscure form of blood-poisoning, which is almost certainly due to an accumulation of ptomaines in the nuciform sac. I'll remove the sac—

LOUIS [changing color] Do you mean, operate on me? Ugh! No, thank you.

WALPOLE. Never fear: you wont feel anything. Youll be under an anæsthetic, of course. And it will be extraordinarily interesting.

LOUIS. Oh, well, if it would interest you, and if it wont hurt, thats another matter. How much will you give me to let you do it?

WALPOLE [rising indignantly] How much! What do you mean?

LOUIS. Well, you don't expect me to let you cut me up for nothing, do you?

WALPOLE. Will you paint my portrait for nothing?

LOUIS. No; but I'll give you the portrait when it's painted; and you can sell it afterwards for perhaps double the money. But I cant sell my nuciform sac when youve cut it out.

WALPOLE. Ridgeon: did you ever hear anything like this! [To Louis] Well, you can keep your nuciform sac, and your tubercular lung, and your diseased brain: Ive done with you. One would think I was not conferring a favor on the fellow! [He returns to his stool in high dudgeon].

SIR PATRICK. That leaves only one medical man who

Act III   The Doctor's Dilemma   77

has not withdrawn from your case, Mr. Dubedat. You have nobody left to appeal to now but Sir Ralph Bloomfield Bonington.

WALPOLE. If I were you, B. B., I shouldnt touch him with a pair of tongs. Let him take his lungs to the Brompton Hospital. They wont cure him; but theyll teach him manners.

B. B. My weakness is that I have never been able to say No, even to the most thoroughly undeserving people. Besides, I am bound to say that I dont think it is possible in medical practice to go into the question of the value of the lives we save. Just consider, Ridgeon. Let me put it to you, Paddy. Clear your mind of cant, Walpole.

WALPOLE [*indignantly*] My mind is clear of cant.

B. B. Quite so. Well now, look at my practice. It is what I suppose you would call a fashionable practice, a smart practice, a practice among the best people. You ask me to go into the question of whether my patients are of any use either to themselves or anyone else. Well, if you apply any scientific test known to me, you will achieve a reductio ad absurdum. You will be driven to the conclusion that the majority of them would be, as my friend Mr J. M. Barrie has tersely phrased it, better dead. Better dead. There are exceptions, no doubt. For instance, there is the court, an essentially social-democratic institution, supported out of public funds by the public because the public wants it and likes it. My court patients are hard-working people who give satisfaction, undoubtedly. Then I have a duke or two whose estates are probably better managed than they would be in public hands. But as to most of the rest, if I once began to argue about them, unquestionably the verdict would be, Better dead. When they actually do die, I sometimes have to offer that consolation, thinly disguised, to the family. [*Lulled by the cadences of his own voice, he becomes drowsier and drowsier*]. The fact that they spend money so extravagantly on medical attendance really would not justify me in wasting my talents—such as they are—in keeping them alive. After all, if my fees are high, I have to spend heavily. My own tastes are simple: a camp bed, a couple of rooms, a crust, a bottle of wine; and I am happy and contented. My wife's tastes are perhaps more luxurious; but even she deplores an expenditure the sole object of which is to maintain the state my patients require from their medical attendant. The—er—er—er— [*suddenly waking up*] I have lost the thread of these remarks. What was I talking about, Ridgeon?

RIDGEON. About Dubedat.

B. B. Ah yes. Precisely. Thank you. Dubedat, of course. Well, what is our friend Dubedat? A vicious and ignorant young man with a talent for drawing.

LOUIS. Thank you. Dont mind me.

B. B. But then, what are many of my patients? Vicious and ignorant young men without a talent for anything. If I were to stop to argue about their merits I should have to give up three-quarters of my practice. Therefore I have made it a rule not so to argue. Now, as an honorable man, having made that rule as to paying patients, can I make an exception as to a patient who, far from being a paying patient, may more fitly be described as a borrowing patient? No. I say No. Mr Dubedat: your moral character is nothing to me. I look at you from a purely scientific point of view. To me you are simply a field of battle in which an invading army of tubercle bacilli struggles with a patriotic force of phagocytes. Having made a promise to your wife, which my principles will not allow me to break, to stimulate those phagocytes, I will stimulate them. And I take no further responsibility. [*He flings himself back in his seat exhausted*].

SIR PATRICK. Well, Mr Dubedat, as Sir Ralph has very kindly offered to take charge of your case, and as the two minutes I promised you are up, I must ask you to excuse me. [*He rises*].

LOUIS. Oh, certainly. Ive quite done with you. [*Rising and holding up the sketch block*] There! While youve been talking, Ive been doing. What is there left of your moralizing? Only a little carbonic acid gas which makes the room unhealthy. What is there left of my work? That. Look at it [*Ridgeon rises to look at it*].

SIR PATRICK [*who has come down to him from the throne*] You young rascal, was it drawing me you were?

LOUIS. Of course. What else?

SIR PATRICK [*takes the drawing from him and grunts approvingly*] Thats rather good. Dont you think so, Colly?

RIDGEON. Yes. So good that I should like to have it.

SIR PATRICK. Thank you; but I should like to have it myself. What d'ye think, Walpole?

WALPOLE [*rising and coming over to look*] No, by Jove: *I* must have this.

LOUIS. I wish I could afford to give it to you, Sir Patrick. But I'd pay five guineas sooner than part with it.

RIDGEON. Oh, for that matter, I will give you six for it.

WALPOLE. Ten.

LOUIS. I think Sir Patrick is morally entitled to it, as he sat for it. May I send it to your house, Sir Patrick, for twelve guineas?

SIR PATRICK. Twelve guineas! Not if you were President of the Royal Academy, young man. [*He gives him back the drawing decisively and turns away, taking up his hat*].

LOUIS [*to B. B.*] Would you like to take it at twelve, Sir Ralph?

B. B. [*coming between Louis and Walpole*] Twelve guineas? Thank you: I'll take it at that. [*He takes it and presents it to Sir Patrick*]. Accept it from me, Paddy; and may you long be spared to contemplate it.

SIR PATRICK. Thank you. [*He puts the drawing into his hat*].

B. B. I neednt settle with you now, Mr Dubedat: my fees will come to more than that. [*He also retrieves his hat*].

LOUIS [*indignantly*] Well, of all the mean—[*words fail him*]! I'd let myself be shot sooner than do a thing like that. I consider youve stolen that drawing.

SIR PATRICK [*drily*] So weve converted you to a belief in morality after all, eh?

LOUIS. Yah! [*To Walpole*] I'll do another one for you, Walpole, if youll let me have the ten you promised.

WALPOLE. Very good. I'll pay on delivery.

LOUIS. Oh! What do you take me for? Have you no confidence in my honor?

WALPOLE. None whatever.

LOUIS. Oh well, of course if you feel that way, you cant help it. Before you go, Sir Patrick, let me fetch Jennifer. I know she'd like to see you, if you dont mind. [*He goes to the inner door*]. And now, before she comes in, one word. Youve all been talking here pretty freely about me—in my own house too. *I* dont mind that: I'm a man and can take care of myself. But when Jennifer comes in, please remember that she's a lady, and that you are supposed to be gentlemen. [*He goes out*].

WALPOLE. Well!!! [*He gives the situation up as indescribable, and goes for his hat*].

RIDGEON. Damn his impudence!

B. B. I shouldnt be at all surprised to learn that he's well connected. Whenever I meet dignity and self-

ACT III   The Doctor's Dilemma   81

possession without any discoverable basis, I diagnose good family.

RIDGEON. Diagnose artistic genius, B. B. Thats what saves his self-respect.

SIR PATRICK. The world is made like that. The decent fellows are always being lectured and put out of countenance by the snobs.

B. B. [*altogether refusing to accept this*] I am not out of countenance. I should like, by Jupiter, to see the man who could put me out of countenance. [*Jennifer comes in*]. Ah, Mrs. Dubedat! And how are we to-day?

MRS DUBEDAT [*shaking hands with him*] Thank you all so much for coming. [*She shakes Walpole's hand*]. Thank you, Sir Patrick [*she shakes Sir Patrick's*]. Oh, life has been worth living since I have known you. Since Richmond I have not known a moment's fear. And it used to be nothing but fear. Wont you sit down and tell me the result of the consultation?

WALPOLE. I'll go, if you dont mind, Mrs. Dubedat. I have an appointment. Before I go, let me say that I am quite agreed with my colleagues here as to the character of the case. As to the cause and the remedy, thats not my business: I'm only a surgeon; and these gentlemen are physicians and will advise you. I may have my own views: in fact I have them; and they are perfectly well known to my colleagues. If I am needed —and needed I shall be finally—they know where to find me; and I am always at your service. So for to-day, good-bye. [*He goes out, leaving Jennifer much puzzled by his unexpected withdrawal and formal manner*].

SIR PATRICK. I also will ask you to excuse me, Mrs Dubedat.

RIDGEON [*anxiously*] Are you going?

SIR PATRICK. Yes: I can be of no use here; and I must be getting back. As you know, maam, I'm not in practice now; and I shall not be in charge of the case. It rests between Sir Colenso Ridgeon and Sir Ralph Bloomfield Bonington. They know my opinion. Good afternoon to you, maam. [*He bows and makes for the door*].

MRS DUBEDAT [*detaining him*] Theres nothing wrong, is there? You dont think Louis is worse, do you?

SIR PATRICK. No: he's not worse. Just the same as at Richmond.

MRS DUBEDAT. Oh, thank you: you frightened me. Excuse me.

SIR PATRICK. Dont mention it, maam. [*He goes out*].

B. B. Now, Mrs Dubedat, if I am to take the patient in hand—

MRS DUBEDAT [*aprehensively, with a glance at Ridgeon*] You! But I thought that Sir Colenso—

B. B. [*beaming with the conviction that he is giving her a most gratifying surprise*] My dear lady, your husband shall have Me.

MRS DUBEDAT. But—

B. B. Not a word: it is a pleasure to me, for your sake. Sir Colenso Ridgeon will be in his proper place, in the bacteriological laboratory. *I* shall be in my proper place, at the bedside. Your husband shall be treated exactly as if he were a member of the royal family. [*Mrs Dubedat uneasy, again is about to protest*]. No gratitude: it would embarrass me, I assure you. Now, may I ask whether you are particularly tied to these apartments. Of course, the motor has annihilated distance; but I confess that if you were rather nearer to me, it would be a little more convenient.

MRS DUBEDAT. You see, this studio and flat are self-contained. I have suffered so much in lodgings. The servants are so frightfully dishonest.

ACT III   The Doctor's Dilemma   83

B. B. Ah! Are they? Are they? Dear me!

MRS DUBEDAT. I was never accustomed to lock things up. And I missed so many small sums. At last a dreadful thing happened. I missed a five-pound note. It was traced to the housemaid; and she actually said Louis had given it to her. And he wouldnt let me do anything: he is so sensitive that these things drive him mad.

B. B. Ah—hm—ha—yes—say no more, Mrs. Dubedat: you shall not move. If the mountain will not come to Mahomet, Mahomet must come to the mountain. Now I must be off. I will write and make an appointment. We shall begin stimulating the phagocytes on—on—probably on Tuesday next; but I will let you know. Depend on me; dont fret; eat regularly; sleep well; keep your spirits up; keep the patient cheerful; hope for the best; no tonic like a charming woman; no medicine like cheerfulness; no resource like science; good-bye, good-bye, good-bye. [*Having shaken hands—she being too overwhelmed to speak—he goes out, stopping to say to Ridgeon*] On Tuesday morning send me down a tube of some really stiff anti-toxin. Any kind will do. Dont forget. Good-bye, Colly. [*He goes out*].

RIDGEON. You look quite discouraged again. [*She is almost in tears*]. What's the matter? Are you disappointed?

MRS DUBEDAT. I know I ought to be very grateful. Believe me, I am very grateful. But—but—

RIDGEON. Well?

MRS DUBEDAT. I had set my heart on your curing Louis.

RIDGEON. Well, Sir Ralph Bloomfield Bonington—

MRS DUBEDAT. Yes, I know, I know. It is a great privilege to have him. But oh, I wish it had been you. I know it's unreasonable; I cant explain; but I had such a strong instinct that you would cure him. I dont—I cant feel the same about Sir Ralph. You promised me. Why did you give Louis up?

RIDGEON. I explained to you. I cannot take another case.

MRS DUBEDAT. But at Richmond?

RIDGEON. At Richmond I thought I could make room for one more case. But my old friend Dr Blenkinsop claimed that place. His lung is attacked.

MRS DUBEDAT [*attaching no importance whatever to Blenkinsop*] Do you mean that elderly man—that rather silly—

RIDGEON [*sternly*] I mean the gentleman that dined with us: an excellent and honest man, whose life is as valuable as anyone else's. I have arranged that I shall take his case, and that Sir Ralph Bloomfield Bonington shall take Mr Dubedat's.

MRS DUBEDAT [*turning indignantly on him*] I see what it is. Oh! it is envious, mean, cruel. And I thought that you would be above such a thing.

RIDGEON. What do you mean?

MRS DUBEDAT. Oh, do you think I dont know? do you think it has never happened before? Why does everybody turn against him? Can you not forgive him for being superior to you? for being cleverer? for being braver? for being a great artist?

RIDGEON. Yes: I can forgive him for all that.

MRS DUBEDAT. Well, have you anything to say against him? I have challenged everyone who has turned against him—challenged them face to face to tell me any wrong thing he has done, any ignoble thought he has uttered. They have always confessed that they could not tell me one. I challenge you now. What do you accuse him of?

RIDGEON. I am like all the rest. Face to face, I cannot tell you one thing against him.

MRS DUDEBAT [*not satisfied*] But your manner is

Act III   The Doctor's Dilemma   85

changed. And you have broken your promise to me to make room for him as your patient.

RIDGEON. I think you are a little unreasonable. You have had the very best medical advice in London for him; and his case has been taken in hand by a leader of the profession. Surely—

MRS DUBEDAT. Oh, it is so cruel to keep telling me that. It seems all right; and it puts me in the wrong. But I am not in the wrong. I have faith in you; and I have no faith in the others. We have seen so many doctors: I have come to know at last when they are only talking and can do nothing. It is different with you. I feel that you know. You must listen to me, doctor. [*With sudden misgiving*] Am I offending you by calling you doctor instead of remembering your title?

RIDGEON. Nonsense. I am a doctor. But mind you, dont call Walpole one.

MRS DUBEDAT. I dont care about Mr Walpole: it is you who must befriend me. Oh, will you please sit down and listen to me just for a few minutes. [*He assents with a grave inclination, and sits on the sofa. She sits on the easel chair*] Thank you. I wont keep you long; but I must tell you the whole truth. Listen. I know Louis as nobody else in the world knows him or ever can know him. I am his wife. I know he has little faults: impatiences, sensitivenesses, even little selfishnesses that are too trivial for him to notice. I know that he sometimes shocks people about money because he is so utterly above it, and cant understand the value ordinary people set on it. Tell me: did he—did he borrow any money from you?

RIDGEON. He asked me for some—once.

MRS DUBEDAT [*tears again in her eyes*] Oh, I am so sorry—so sorry. But he will never do it again: I pledge you my word for that. He has given me his promise: here in this room just before you came; and he is incapable of breaking his word. That was his only real weakness; and now it is conquered and done with for ever.

RIDGEON. Was that really his only weakness?

MRS DUDEBAT. He is perhaps sometimes weak about women, because they adore him so, and are always laying traps for him. And of course when he says he doesnt believe in morality, ordinary pious people think he must be wicked. You can understand, cant you, how all this starts a great deal of gossip about him, and gets repeated until even good friends get set against him?

RIDGEON. Yes: I understand.

MRS DUDEBAT. Oh, if you only knew the other side of him as I do! Do you know, doctor, that if Louis dishonored himself by a really bad action, I should kill myself.

RIDGEON. Come! dont exaggerate.

MRS DUBEDAT. I should. You don't understand that, you east country people.

RIDGEON. You did not see much of the world in Cornwall, did you?

MRS DUDEBAT [*naïvely*] Oh yes. I saw a great deal every day of the beauty of the world—more than you ever see here in London. But I saw very few people, if that is what you mean. I was an only child.

RIDGEON. That explains a good deal.

MRS DUBEDAT. I had a great many dreams; but at last they all came to one dream.

RIDGEON [*with half a sigh*] Yes, the usual dream.

MRS DUBEDAT [*surprised*] Is it usual?

RIDGEON. As I guess. You havnt yet told me what it was.

MRS DUBEDAT. I didn't want to waste myself. I could do nothing myself; but I had a little property and I could help with it. I had even a little beauty: dont think me vain for knowing it. I knew that men of genius always had a terrible struggle with poverty and neglect at first. My dream was to save one of them from that, and bring some charm and happiness into his life. I prayed Heaven to send me one. I firmly believe that Louis was guided to me in answer to my prayer. He was no more like the other men I had met than the Thames Embankment is like our Cornish coasts. He saw everything that I saw, and drew it for me. He understood everything. He came to me like a child. Only fancy, doctor: he never even wanted to marry me: he never thought of the things other men think of! I had to propose it myself. Then he said he had no money. When I told him I had some, he said "Oh, all right," just like a boy. He is still like that, quite unspoiled, a man in his thoughts, a great poet and artist in his dreams, and a child in his ways. I gave him myself and all I had that he might grow to his full height with plenty of sunshine. If I lost faith in him, it would mean the wreck and failure of my life. I should go back to Cornwall and die. I could show you the very cliff I should jump off. You must cure him: you must make him quite well again for me. I know that you can do it and that nobody else can. I implore you not to refuse what I am going to ask you to do. Take Louis yourself; and let Sir Ralph cure Dr Blenkinsop.

RIDGEON [*slowly*] Mrs Dubedat: do you really believe in my knowledge and skill as you say you do?

MRS DUBEDAT. Absolutely. I do not give my trust by halves.

RIDGEON. I know that. Well, I am going to test you —hard. Will you believe me when I tell you that I understand what you have just told me; that I have no desire but to serve you in the most faithful friendship; and that your hero must be preserved to you.

MRS DUBEDAT. Oh forgive me. Forgive what I said. You will preserve him to me.

RIDGEON. At all hazards. [*She kisses his hand. He rises hastily*]. No: you have not heard the rest. [*She rises too*]. You must believe me when I tell you that the one chance of preserving the hero lies in Louis being in the care of Sir Ralph.

MRS DUBEDAT [*firmly*] You say so: I have no more doubt: I believe you. Thank you.

RIDGEON. Good-bye. [*She takes his hand*]. I hope this will be a lasting friendship.

MRS DUBEDAT. It will. My friendships end only with death.

RIDGEON. Death ends everything, doesnt it? Good-bye.

With a sigh and a look of pity at her which she does not understand, he goes.

ACT IV

The studio. The easel is pushed back to the wall. Cardinal Death, holding his scythe and hour-glass like a sceptre and globe, sits on the throne. On the hat-stand hang the hats of Sir Patrick and Bloomfield Bonington. Walpole, just come in, is hanging up his beside them. There is a knock. He opens the door and finds Ridgeon there.

WALPOLE. Hallo, Ridgeon!
They come into the middle of the room together, taking off their gloves.
RIDGEON. Whats the matter! Have you been sent for, too?
WALPOLE. Weve all been sent for. Ive only just come: I havnt seen him yet. The charwoman says that old Paddy Cullen has been here with B. B. for the last half-hour. [*Sir Patrick, with bad news in his face, enters from the inner room*]. Well: whats up?
SIR PATRICK. Go in and see. B. B. is in there with him.
Walpole goes. Ridgeon is about to follow him; but Sir Patrick stops him with a look.
RIDGEON. What has happened?
SIR PATRICK. Do you remember Jane Marsh's arm?
RIDGEON. Is that whats happened?
SIR PATRICK. Thats whats happened. His lung has

gone like Jane's arm. I never saw such a case. He has got through three months galloping consumption in three days.

RIDGEON. B. B. got in on the negative phase.

SIR PATRICK. Negative or positive, the lad's done for. He wont last out the afternoon. He'll go suddenly: Ive often seen it.

RIDGEON. So long as he goes before his wife finds him out, *I* dont care. I fully expected this.

SIR PATRICK [*drily*] It's a little hard on a lad to be killed because his wife has too high an opinion of him. Fortunately few of us are in any danger of that.

Sir Ralph comes from the inner room and hastens between them, humanely concerned, but professionally elate and communicative.

B. B. Ah, here you are, Ridgeon. Paddy's told you, of course.

RIDGEON. Yes.

B. B. It's an enormously interesting case. You know, Colly, by Jupiter, if I didnt know as a matter of scientific fact that I'd been stimulating the phagocytes, I should say I'd been stimulating the other things. What is the explanation of it, Sir Patrick? How do you account for it, Ridgeon? Have we over-stimulated the phagocytes? Have they not only eaten up the bacilli, but attacked and destroyed the red corpuscles as well? a possibility suggested by the patient's pallor. Nay, have they finally begun to prey on the lungs themselves? Or on one another? I shall write a paper about this case.

Walpole comes back, very serious, even shocked. He comes between B. B. and Ridgeon.

WALPOLE. Whew! B. B.: youve done it this time.

B. B. What do you mean?

WALPOLE. Killed him. The worst case of neglected blood-poisoning I ever saw. It's too late now to do anything. He'd die under the anæsthetic.

B. B. [*offended*] Killed! Really, Walpole, if your monomania were not well known, I should take such an expression very seriously.

SIR PATRICK. Come come! When youve both killed as many people as I have in my time youll feel humble enough about it. Come and look at him, Colly.

Ridgeon and Sir Patrick go into the inner room.

WALPOLE. I apologize, B. B. But it's blood-poisoning.

B. B. [*recovering his irresistible good nature*] My dear Walpole, everything is blood-poisoning. But upon my soul, I shall not use any of that stuff of Ridgeon's again. What made me so sensitive about what you said just now is that, strictly between ourselves, Ridgeon has cooked our young friend's goose.

Jennifer, worried and distressed, but always gentle, comes between them from the inner room. She wears a nurse's apron.

MRS DUBEDAT. Sir Ralph: what am I to do? That man who insisted on seeing me, and sent in word that his business was important to Louis, is a newspaper man. A paragraph appeared in the paper this morning saying that Louis is seriously ill; and this man wants to interview him about it. How can people be so brutally callous?

WALPOLE [*moving vengefully towards the door*] You just leave me to deal with him!

MRS DUBEDAT [*stopping him*] But Louis insists on seeing him: he almost began to cry about it. And he says he cant bear his room any longer. He says he wants to [*she struggles with a sob*]—to die in his studio. Sir Patrick says let him have his way: it can do no harm. What shall we do?

B. B. [*encouragingly*] Why, follow Sir Patrick's excellent advice, of course. As he says, it can do him no harm; and it will no doubt do him good—a great deal of good. He will be much the better for it.

Mrs Dubedat [*a little cheered*] Will you bring the man up here, Mr Walpole, and tell him that he may see Louis, but that he mustnt exhaust him by talking? [*Walpole nods and goes out by the outer door*]. Sir Ralph, dont be angry with me; but Louis will die if he stays here. I must take him to Cornwall. He will recover there.

B. B. [*brightening wonderfully, as if Dubedat were already saved*] Cornwall! The very place for him! Wonderful for the lungs. Stupid of me not to think of it before. You are his best physician after all, dear lady. An inspiration! Cornwall: of course, yes, yes, yes.

Mrs Dubedat [*comforted and touched*] You are so kind, Sir Ralph. But dont give me much or I shall cry; and Louis cant bear that.

B. B. [*gently putting his protecting arm round her shoulders*] Then let us come back to him and help to carry him in. Cornwall! of course, of course. The very thing! [*They go together into the bedroom*].

Walpole returns with The Newspaper Man, a cheerful, affable young man who is disabled for ordinary business pursuits by a congenital erroneousness which renders him incapable of describing accurately anything he sees, or understanding or reporting accurately anything he hears. As the only employment in which these defects do not matter is journalism (for a newspaper, not having to act on its description and reports, but only to sell them to idly curious people, has nothing but honor to lose by inaccuracy and unveracity), he has perforce become a journalist, and has to keep up an air of high spirits through a daily struggle with his own illiteracy and the precariousness of his employment. He has a note-book, and ocasionally attempts to make a note; but as he cannot write shorthand, and does not write with ease in any hand, he generally gives it up as a bad job before he succeeds in finishing a sentence.

Act IV   The Doctor's Dilemma   93

THE NEWSPAPER MAN [*looking round and making indecisive attempts at notes*] This is the studio, I suppose.
WALPOLE. Yes.
THE NEWSPAPER MAN [*wittily*] Where he has his models, eh?
WALPOLE [*grimly irresponsive*] No doubt.
THE NEWSPAPER MAN. Cubicle, you said it was?
WALPOLE. Yes, tubercle.
THE NEWSPAPER MAN. Which way do you spell it: is it c-u-b-i-c-a-l or c-l-e?
WALPOLE. Tubercle, man, not cubical. [*Spelling it for him*] T-u-b-e-r-c-l-e.
THE NEWSPAPER MAN. Oh! tubercle. Some disease, I suppose. I thought he had consumption. Are you one of the family or the doctor?
WALPOLE. I'm neither one nor the other. I am Mister Cutler Walpole. Put that down. Then put down Sir Colenso Ridgeon.
THE NEWSPAPER MAN. Pigeon?
WALPOLE. Ridgeon. [*Contemptuously snatching his book*] Here: youd better let me write the names down for you: youre sure to get them wrong. That comes of belonging to an illiterate profession, with no qualifications and no public register. [*He writes the particulars*].
THE NEWSPAPER MAN. Oh, I say: you have got your knife into us, havnt you?
WALPOLE [*vindictively*] I wish I had: I'd make a better man of you. Now attend. [*Shewing him the book*] These are the names of the three doctors. This is the patient. This is the address. This is the name of the disease. [*He shuts the book with a snap which makes the journalist blink, and returns it to him*]. Mr Dubedat will be brought in here presently. He wants to see you because he doesnt know how bad he is. We'll

allow you to wait a few minutes to humor him; but if you talk to him, out you go. He may die at any moment.

THE NEWSPAPER MAN [*interested*] Is he as bad as that? I say: I am in luck to-day. Would you mind letting me photograph you? [*He produces a camera*]. Could you have a lancet or something in your hand?

WALPOLE. Put it up. If you want my photograph you can get it in Baker Street in any of the series of celebrities.

THE NEWSPAPER MAN. But theyll want to be paid. If you wouldnt mind [*fingering the camera*]—?

WALPOLE. I would. Put it up, I tell you. Sit down there and be quiet.

The Newspaper Man quickly sits down on the piano stool as Dubedat, in an invalid's chair, is wheeled in by Mrs Dubedat and Sir Ralph. They place the chair between the dais and the sofa, where the easel stood before. Louis is not changed as a robust man would be; and he is not scared. His eyes look larger; and he is so weak physically that he can hardly move, lying on his cushions with complete languor; but his mind is active; it is making the most of his condition, finding voluptuousness in languor and drama in death. They are all impressed, in spite of themselves, except Ridgeon, who is implacable. B. B. is entirely sympathetic and forgiving. Ridgeon follows the chair with a tray of milk and stimulants. Sir Patrick, who accompanies him, takes the tea-table from the corner and places it behind the chair for the tray. B. B. takes the easel chair and places it for Jennifer at Dubedat's side, next the dais, from which the lay figure ogles the dying artist. B. B. then returns to Dubedat's left. Jennifer sits. Walpole sits down on the edge of the dais. Ridgeon stands near him.

LOUIS [*blissfully*] Thats happiness. To be in a studio! Hapiness!

Act IV   The Doctor's Dilemma   95

MRS DUBEDAT. Yes, dear. Sir Patrick says you may stay here as long as you like.

LOUIS. Jennifer.

MRS DUBEDAT. Yes, my darling.

LOUIS. Is the newspaper man here?

THE NEWSPAPER MAN [*glibly*] Yes, Mr Dubedat: I'm here, at your service. I represent the press. I thought you might like to let us have a few words about —about—er—well, a few words on your illness, and your plans for the season.

LOUIS. My plans for the season are very simple. I'm going to die.

MRS DUBEDAT [*tortured*] Louis—dearest—

LOUIS. My darling: I'm very weak and tired. Dont put on me the horrible strain of pretending that I dont know. Ive been lying there listening to the doctors—laughing to myself. They know. Dearest: dont cry. It makes you ugly; and I cant bear that. [*She dries her eyes and recovers herself with a proud effort*]. I want you to promise me something.

MRS DUBEDAT. Yes, yes: you know I will. [*Imploringly*] Only, my love, my love, dont talk: it will waste your strength.

LOUIS. No: it will only use it up. Ridgeon: give me something to keep me going for a few minutes—not one of your confounded anti-toxins, if you dont mind. I have some things to say before I go.

RIDGEON [looking at Sir Patrick] I suppose it can do no harm? [*He pours out some spirit, and is about to add soda water when Sir Patrick corrects him*].

SIR PATRICK. In milk. Dont set him coughing.

LOUIS [*after drinking*] Jennifer.

MRS DUBEDAT. Yes, dear.

LOUIS. If theres one thing I hate more than another, it's a widow. Promise me that youll never be a widow.

MRS DUBEDAT. My dear, what do you mean?

Louis. I want you to look beautiful. I want people to see in your eyes that you were married to me. The people in Italy used to point at Dante and say " There goes the man who has been in hell." I want them to point at you and say " There goes a woman who has been in heaven." It has been heaven, darling, hasnt it—sometimes?

Mrs Dubedat. Oh yes, yes. Always, always.

Louis. If you wear black and cry, people will say " Look at that miserable woman: her husband made her miserable."

Mrs Dubedat. No, never. You are the light and the blessing of my life. I never lived until I knew you.

Louis [*his eyes glistening*] Then you must always wear beautiful dresses and splendid magic jewels. Think of all the wonderful pictures I shall never paint. [*She wins a terrible victory over a sob*] Well, you must be transfigured with all the beauty of those pictures. Men must get such dreams from seeing you as they never could get from any daubing with paints and brushes. Painters must paint you as they never painted any mortal woman before. There must be a great tradition of beauty, a great atmosphere of wonder and romance. That is what men must always think of when they think of me. That is the sort of immortality I want. You can make that for me, Jennifer. There are lots of things you dont understand that every woman in the street understands; but you can understand that and do it as nobody else can. Promise me that immortality. Promise me you will not make a little hell of crape and crying and undertaker's horrors and withering flowers and all that vulgar rubbish.

Mrs Dubedat. I promise. But all that is far off, dear. You are to come to Cornwall with me and get well. Sir Ralph says so.

Louis. Poor old B. B.

B. B. [*affected to tears, turns away and whispers to Sir Patrick*] Poor fellow! Brain going.

LOUIS. Sir Patrick's there, isn't he?

SIR PATRICK. Yes, yes. I'm here.

LOUIS. Sit down, wont you? It's a shame to keep you standing about.

SIR PATRICK. Yes, yes. Thank you. All right.

LOUIS. Jennifer.

MRS DUBEDAT. Yes, dear.

LOUIS [*with a strange look of delight*] Do you remember the burning bush?

MRS DUBEDAT. Yes, yes. Oh, my dear, how it strains my heart to remember it now!

LOUIS. Does it? It fills me with joy. Tell them about it.

MRS DUBEDAT. It was nothing—only that once in my old Cornish home we lit the first fire of the winter; and when we looked through the window we saw the flames dancing in a bush in the garden.

LOUIS. Such a color! Garnet color. Waving like silk. Liquid lovely flame flowing up through the bay leaves, and not burning them. Well, I shall be a flame like that. I'm sorry to disappoint the poor little worms; but the last of me shall be the flame in the burning bush. Whenever you see the flame, Jennifer, that will be me. Promise me that I shall be burnt.

MRS DUBEDAT. Oh, if I might be with you, Louis!

LOUIS. No: you must always be in the garden when the bush flames. You are my hold on the world: you are my immortality. Promise.

MRS DUBEDAT. I'm listening. I shall not forget. You know that I promise.

LOUIS. Well, thats about all; except that you are to hang my pictures at the one-man show. I can trust your eye. You wont let anyone else touch them.

MRS DUBEDAT. You can trust me.

LOUIS. Then theres nothing more to worry about, is there? Give me some more of that milk. I'm fearfully tired; but if I stop talking I shant begin again. [*Sir Ralph gives him a drink. He takes it and looks up quaintly*]. I say, B. B., do you think anything would stop you talking?

B. B. [*almost unmanned*] He confuses me with you, Paddy. Poor fellow! Poor fellow!

LOUIS [*musing*] I used to be awfully afraid of death; but now it's come I have no fear; and I'm perfectly happy. Jennifer.

MRS DUBEDAT. Yes, dear?

LOUIS. I'll tell you a secret. I used to think that our marriage was all an affectation, and that I'd break loose and run away some day. But now that I'm going to be broken loose whether I like it or not, I'm perfectly fond of you, and perfectly satisfied because I'm going to live as part of you and not as my troublesome self.

MRS DUBEDAT [*heartbroken*] Stay with me, Louis. Oh, dont leave me, dearest.

LOUIS. Not that I'm selfish. With all my faults I dont think Ive ever been really selfish. No artist can: Art is too large for that. You will marry again, Jennifer.

MRS DUBEDAT. Oh, how can you, Louis?

LOUIS [*insisting childishly*] Yes, because people who have found marriage happy always marry again. Ah, *I* shant be jealous. [*Slyly.*] But dont talk to the other fellow too much about me: he wont like it. [*Almost chuckling*] I shall be your lover all the time; but it will be a secret from him, poor devil!

SIR PATRICK. Come! youve talked enough. Try to rest awhile.

LOUIS [*wearily*] Yes: I'm fearfully tired; but I shall have a long rest presently. I have something to say to you fellows. Youre all there, arnt you? I'm too weak to see anything but Jennifer's bosom. That promises rest.

RIDGEON. We are all here.

LOUIS [*startled*] That voice sounded devilish. Take care, Ridgeon: my ears hear things that other people's ears cant. Ive been thinking—thinking. I'm cleverer than you imagine.

SIR PATRICK [*whispering to Ridgeon*] Youve got on his nerves, Colly. Slip out quietly.

RIDGEON [*apart to Sir Patrick*] Would you deprive the dying actor of his audience?

LOUIS [*his face lighting up faintly with mischievous glee*] I heard that, Ridgeon. That was good. Jennifer, dear: be kind to Ridgeon always; because he was the last man who amused me.

RIDGEON [*relentless*] Was I?

LOUIS. But it's not true. It's you who are still on the stage. I'm half way home already.

MRS DUBEDAT [*to Ridgeon*] What did you say?

LOUIS [*answering for him*] Nothing, dear. Only one of those little secrets that men keep among themselves. Well, all you chaps have thought pretty hard things of me, and said them.

B. B. [*quite overcome*] No, no, Dubedat. Not at all.

LOUIS. Yes, you have. I know what you all think of me. Dont imagine I'm sore about it. I forgive you.

WALPOLE [*involuntarily*] Well, damn me! [*Ashamed*] I beg your pardon.

LOUIS. That was old Walpole, I know. Don't grieve, Walpole. I'm perfectly happy. I'm not in pain. I dont want to live. Ive escaped from myself. I'm in heaven, immortal in the heart of my beautiful Jennifer. I'm not afraid, and not ashamed. [*Reflectively, puzzling it out for himself weakly*] I know that in an accidental sort of way, struggling through the unreal part of life, I havnt always been able to live up to my ideal. But in my own real world I have never done anything wrong, never denied my faith, never been untrue to myself. Ive been threatened and blackmailed and insulted and starved. But Ive played the game. Ive fought the good fight. And now it's all over, theres an indescribable peace. [*He feebly folds his hands and utters his creed*] I believe in Michael Angelo, Velasquez, and Rembrandt; in the might of design, the mystery of color, the redemption of all things by Beauty everlasting, and the message of Art that has made these hands blessed. Amen. Amen. [*He closes his eyes and lies still*].

MRS DUBEDAT [*breathless*] Louis: are you—
Walpole rises and comes quickly to see whether he is dead.

LOUIS. Not yet, dear. Very nearly, but not yet. I should like to rest my head on your bosom; only it would tire you.

MRS DUBEDAT. No, no, no, darling: how could you tire me? [*She lifts him so that he lies on her bosom*].

LOUIS. Thats good. Thats real.

MRS DUBEDAT. Dont spare me, dear. Indeed, indeed you will not tire me. Lean on me with all your weight.

LOUIS [*with a sudden half return of his normal strength and comfort*] Jinny Gwinny: I think I shall recover after all. [*Sir Patrick looks significantly at Ridgeon, mutely warning him that this is the end*].

MRS DUBEDAT [*hopefully*] Yes, yes: you shall.

LOUIS. Because I suddenly want to sleep. Just an ordinary sleep.

MRS DUBEDAT [*rocking him*] Yes, dear. Sleep. [*He seems to go to sleep. Walpole makes another movement. She protests*]. Sh-sh: please dont disturb him.

ACT IV   The Doctor's Dilemma   101

[*His lips move*]. What did you say, dear? [*In great distress*] I cant listen without moving him. [*His lips move again: Walpole bends down and listens*].

WALPOLE. He wants to know is the newspaper man here.

THE NEWSPAPER MAN [*excited; for he has been enjoying himself enormously*] Yes, Mr Dubedat. Here I am.

Walpole raises his hand warningly to silence him. Sir Ralph sits down quietly on the sofa and frankly buries his face in his handkerchief.

MRS DUBEDAT [*with great relief*] Oh thats right, dear: dont spare me: lean with all your weight on me. Now you are really resting.

Sir Patrick quickly comes forward and feels Louis's pulse; then takes him by the shoulders.

SIR PATRICK. Let me put him back on the pillow, maam. He will be better so.

MRS DUBEDAT [*piteously*] Oh no, please, please, doctor. He is not tiring me; and he will be so hurt when he wakes if he finds I have put him away.

SIR PATRICK. He will never wake again. [*He takes the body from her and replaces it in the chair. Ridgeon, unmoved, lets down the back and makes a bier of it*].

MRS DUBEDAT [*who has unexpectedly sprung to her feet, and stands dry-eyed and stately*] Was that death?

WALPOLE. Yes.

MRS DUBEDAT [*with complete dignity*] Will you wait for me a moment? I will come back. [*She goes out*].

WALPOLE. Ought we to follow her? Is she in her right senses?

SIR PATRICK [*with quiet conviction*]. Yes. Shes all right. Leave her alone. She'll come back.

RIDGEON [*callously*] Let us get this thing out of the way before she comes.

B. B. [*rising, shocked*] My dear Colly! The poor lad! He died splendidly.

SIR PATRICK. Aye! that is how the wicked die.

> For there are no bands in their death;
> But their strength is firm:
> They are not in trouble as other men.

No matter: it's not for us to judge. He's in another world now.

WALPOLE. Borrowing his first five-pound note there, probably.

RIDGEON. I said the other day that the most tragic thing in the world is a sick doctor. I was wrong. The most tragic thing in the world is a man of genius who is not also a man of honor.

Ridgeon and Walpole wheel the chair into the recess.

THE NEWSPAPER MAN [*to Sir Ralph*] I thought it shewed a very nice feeling, his being so particular about his wife going into proper mourning for him and making her promise never to marry again.

B. B. [*impressively*] Mrs Dubedat is not in a position to carry the interview any further. Neither are we.

SIR PATRICK. Good afternoon to you.

THE NEWSPAPER MAN. Mrs. Dubedat said she was coming back.

B. B. After you have gone.

THE NEWSPAPER MAN. Do you think she would give me a few words on How It Feels to be a Widow? Rather a good title for an article, isnt it?

B. B. Young man: if you wait until Mrs Dubedat comes back, you will be able to write an article on How It Feels to be Turned Out of the House.

THE NEWSPAPER MAN [*unconvinced*] You think she'd rather not—

B. B. [*cutting him short*] Good day to you. [*Giving*

him a visiting-card] Mind you get my name correctly. Good day.

THE NEWSPAPER MAN. Good day. Thank you. [*Vaguely trying to read the card*] Mr—

B. B. No, not Mister. This is your hat, I think [*giving it to him*]. Gloves? No, of course: no gloves. Good day to you. [*He edges him out at last; shuts the door on him; and returns to Sir Patrick as Ridgeon and Walpole come back from the recess, Walpole crossing the room to the hat-stand, and Ridgeon coming between Sir Ralph and Sir Patrick*]. Poor fellow! Poor young fellow! How well he died! I feel a better man, really.

SIR PATRICK. When youre as old as I am, youll know that it matters very little how a man dies. What matters is, how he lives. Every fool that runs his nose against a bullet is a hero nowadays, because he dies for his country. Why dont he live for it to some purpose?

B. B. No, please, Paddy: dont be hard on the poor lad. Not now, not now. After all, was he so bad? He had only two failings: money and women. Well, let us be honest. Tell the truth, Paddy. Dont be hypocritical, Ridgeon. Throw off the mask, Walpole. Are these two matters so well arranged at present that a disregard of the usual arrangements indicates real depravity?

WALPOLE. I dont mind his disregarding the usual arrangements. Confound the usual arrangements! To a man of science theyre beneath contempt both as to money and women. What I mind is his disregarding everything except his own pocket and his own fancy. He didnt disregard the usual arrangements when they paid him. Did he give us his pictures for nothing? Do you suppose he'd have hesitated to blackmail me if I'd compromised myself with his wife? Not he.

SIR PATRICK. Dont waste your time wrangling over him. A blackguard's a blackguard; an honest man's an honest man; and neither of them will ever be at a loss

for a religion or a morality to prove that their ways are
the right ways. It's the same with nations, the same
with professions, the same all the world over and always
will be.

B. B. Ah, well, perhaps, perhaps, perhaps. Still,
de mortuis nil nisi bonum. He died extremely well,
remarkably well. He has set us an example: let us en-
deavor to follow it rather than harp on the weaknesses
that have perished with him. I think it is Shakespear
who says that the good that most men do lives after
them: the evil lies interréd with their bones. Yes: interréd with their bones. Believe me, Paddy, we are all
mortal. It is the common lot, Ridgeon. Say what you
will, Walpole, Nature's debt must be paid. If tis not
to-day, twill be to-morrow.

> To-morrow and to-morrow and to-morrow
> After life's fitful fever they sleep well
> And like this insubstantial bourne from which
> No traveller returns
> Leave not a wrack behind.

*Walpole is about to speak, but B. B., suddenly and
vehemently proceeding, extinguishes him.*

> Out, out, brief candle:
> For nothing canst thou to damnation add
> The readiness is all.

WALPOLE [*gently; for B. B.'s feeling, absurdly expressed as it is, is too sincere and humane to be ridiculed*] Yes, B. B. Death makes people go on like that.
I dont know why it should; but it does. By the way,
what are we going to do? Ought we to clear out; or
had we better wait and see whether Mrs Dubedat will
come back?

SIR PATRICK. I think we'd better go. We can tell
the charwoman what to do.

Act IV The Doctor's Dilemma

They take their hats and go to the door.

Mrs Dubedat [*coming from the inner door wonderfully and beautifully dressed, and radiant, carrying a great piece of purple silk, handsomely embroidered, over her arm*] I'm so sorry to have kept you waiting.

Sir Patrick
B. B.
Ridgeon
Walpole
  [*amazed, all together in a confused murmur*]
Dont mention it, madam.
Not at all, not at all.
By no means.
It doesnt matter in the least.

Mrs Dubedat [*coming to them*] I felt that I must shake hands with his friends once before we part to-day. We have shared together a great privilege and a great happiness. I dont think we can ever think of ourselves as ordinary people again. We have had a wonderful experience; and that gives us a common faith, a common ideal, that nobody else can quite have. Life will always be beautiful to us: death will always be beautiful to us. May we shake hands on that?

Sir Patrick [*shaking hands*] Remember: all letters had better be left to your solicitor. Let him open everything and settle everything. Thats the law, you know.

Mrs Dubedat. Oh, thank you: I didnt know. [*Sir Patrick goes*].

Walpole. Good-bye. I blame myself: I should have insisted on operating. [*He goes*].

B. B. I will send the proper people: they will know what to do: you shall have no trouble. Good-bye, my dear lady. [*He goes*].

Ridgeon. Good-bye. [*He offers his hand*].

Mrs Dubedat [*drawing back with gentle majesty*] I said his friends, Sir Colenso. [*He bows and goes*].

She unfolds the great piece of silk, and goes into the recess to cover her dead.

ACT V

One of the smaller Bond Street Picture Galleries. The entrance is from a picture shop. Nearly in the middle of the gallery there is a writing-table, at which the Secretary, fashionably dressed, sits with his back to the entrance, correcting catalogue proofs. Some copies of a new book are on the desk, also the Secretary's shining hat and a couple of magnifying glasses. At the side, on his left, a little behind him, is a small door marked PRIVATE. *Near the same side is a cushioned bench parallel to the walls, which are covered with Dubedat's works. Two screens, also covered with drawings, stand near the corners right and left of the entrance.*

Jennifer, beautifully dressed and apparently very happy and prosperous, comes into the gallery through the private door.

JENNIFER. Have the catalogues come yet, Mr Danby?

THE SECRETARY. Not yet.

JENNIFER. What a shame! It's a quarter past: the private view will begin in less than half an hour.

THE SECRETARY. I think I'd better run over to the printers to hurry them up.

JENNIFER. Oh, if you would be so good, Mr Danby. I'll take your place while youre away.

THE SECRETARY. If anyone should come before the time dont take any notice. The commissionaire wont let anyone through unless he knows him. We have a few people who like to come before the crowd—people who really buy; and of course we're glad to see them. Have

ACT V   The Doctor's Dilemma   107

you seen the notices in Brush and Crayon and in The Easel?

JENNIFER [*indignantly*] Yes: most disgraceful. They write quite patronizingly, as if they were Mr Dubedat's superiors. After all the cigars and sandwiches they had from us on the press day, and all they drank, I really think it is infamous that they should write like that. I hope you have not sent them tickets for to-day.

THE SECRETARY. Oh, they wont come again: theres no lunch to-day. The advance copies of your book have come. [*He indicates the new books*].

JENNIFER [*pouncing on a copy, wildly excited*] Give it to me. Oh! excuse me a moment [*she runs away with it through the private door*].

The Secretary takes a mirror from his drawer and smartens himself before going out. Ridgeon comes in.

RIDGEON. Good morning. May I look round, as usual, before the doors open?

THE SECRETARY. Certainly, Sir Colenso. I'm sorry the catalogues have not come: I'm just going to see about them. Heres my own list, if you dont mind.

RIDGEON. Thanks. Whats this? [*He takes up one of the new books*].

THE SECRETARY. Thats just come in. An advance copy of Mrs Dubedat's Life of her late husband.

RIDGEON [*reading the title*] The Story of a King of Men. By His Wife. [*He looks at the portrait frontispiece*]. Ay: there he is. You knew him here, I suppose.

THE SECRETARY. Oh, we knew him. Better than she did, Sir Colenso, in some ways, perhaps.

RIDGEON. So did I. [*They look significantly at one another*]. I'll take a look round.

The Secretary puts on the shining hat and goes out. Ridgeon begins looking at the pictures. Presently he comes back to the table for a magnifying glass, and scrutinizes a drawing very closely. He sighs; shakes his head, *as if constrained to admit the extraordinary fascination and merit of the work; then marks the Secretary's list. Proceeding with his survey, he disappears behind the screen. Jennifer comes back with her book. A look round satisfies her that she is alone. She seats herself at the table and admires the memoir—her first printed book—to her heart's content. Ridgeon re-appears, face to the wall, scrutinizing the drawings. After using his glass again, he steps back to get a more distant view of one of the larger pictures. She hastily closes the book at the sound; looks round; recognizes him; and stares, petrified. He takes a further step back which brings him nearer to her.*

RIDGEON [*shaking his head as before, ejaculates*] Clever brute! [*She flushes as though he had struck her. He turns to put the glass down on the desk, and finds himself face to face with her intent gaze*]. I beg your pardon. I thought I was alone.

JENNIFER [*controlling herself, and speaking steadily and meaningly*] I am glad we have met, Sir Colenso Ridgeon. I met Dr Blenkinsop yesterday. I congratulate you on a wonderful cure.

RIDGEON [*can find no words: makes an embarrassed gesture of assent after a moment's silence, and puts down the glass and the Secretary's list on the table*].

JENNIFER. He looked the picture of health and strength and prosperity. [*She looks for a moment at the walls, contrasting Blenkinsop's fortune with the artist's fate*].

RIDGEON [*in low tones, still embarrassed*] He has been fortunate.

JENNIFER. Very fortunate. His life has been spared.

RIDGEON. I mean that he has been made a Medical Officer of Health. He cured the Chairman of the Borough Council very successfully.

JENNIFER. With your medicines?

ACT V   The Doctor's Dilemma

RIDGEON. No. I believe it was with a pound of ripe greengages.

JENNIFER [*with deep gravity*] Funny!

RIDGEON. Yes. Life does not cease to be funny when people die any more than it ceases to be serious when people laugh.

JENNIFER. Dr Blenkinsop said one very strange thing to me.

RIDGEON. What was that?

JENNIFER. He said that private practice in medicine ought to be put down by law. When I asked him why, he said that private doctors were ignorant licensed murderers.

RIDGEON. That is what the public doctor always thinks of the private doctor. Well, Blenkinsop ought to know. He was a private doctor long enough himself. Come! you have talked at me long enough. Talk to me. You have something to reproach me with. There is reproach in your face, in your voice: you are full of it. Out with it.

JENNIFER. It is too late for reproaches now. When I turned and saw you just now, I wondered how you could come here coolly to look at his pictures. You answered the question. To you, he was only a clever brute.

RIDGEON [*quivering*] Oh, dont. You know I did not know you were here.

JENNIFER [*raising her head a little with a quite gentle impulse of pride*] You think it only mattered because I heard it. As if it could touch me, or touch him! Dont you see that what is really dreadful is that to you living things have no souls.

RIDGEON [*with a sceptical shrug*] The soul is an organ I have not come across in the course of my anatomical work.

JENNIFER. You know you would not dare to say such a silly thing as that to anybody but a woman whose mind you despise. If you dissected me you could not find my conscience. Do you think I have got none?

RIDGEON. I have met people who had none.

JENNIFER. Clever brutes? Do you know, doctor, that some of the dearest and most faithful friends I ever had were only brutes! You would have vivisected them. The dearest and greatest of all my friends had a sort of beauty and affectionateness that only animals have. I hope you may never feel what I felt when I had to put him into the hands of men who defend the torture of animals because they are only brutes.

RIDGEON. Well, did you find us so very cruel, after all? They tell me that though you have dropped me, you stay for weeks with the Bloomfield Boningtons and the Walpoles. I think it must be true, because they never mention you to me now.

JENNIFER. The animals in Sir Ralph's house are like spoiled children. When Mr. Walpole had to take a splinter out of the mastiff's paw, I had to hold the poor dog myself; and Mr Walpole had to turn Sir Ralph out of the room. And Mrs. Walpole has to tell the gardener not to kill wasps when Mr. Walpole is looking. But there are doctors who are naturally cruel; and there are others who get used to cruelty and are callous about it. They blind themselves to the souls of animals; and that blinds them to the souls of men and women. You made a dreadful mistake about Louis; but you would not have made it if you had not trained yourself to make the same mistake about dogs. You saw nothing in them but dumb brutes; and so you could see nothing in him but a clever brute.

RIDGEON [*with sudden resolution*] I made no mistake whatever about him.

JENNIFER. Oh, doctor!

RIDGEON [*obstinately*] I made no mistake whatever about him.

ACT V   The Doctor's Dilemma   111

JENNIFER. Have you forgotten that he died?

RIDGEON [*with a sweep of his hand towards the pictures*] He is not dead. He is there. [*Taking up the book*] And there.

JENNIFER [*springing up with blazing eyes*] Put that down. How dare you touch it?

Ridgeon, amazed at the fierceness of the outburst, puts it down with a deprecatory shrug. She takes it up and looks at it as of he had profaned a relic.

RIDGEON. I am very sorry. I see I had better go.

JENNIFER [*putting the book down*] I beg your pardon. I—I forgot myself. But it is not yet—it is a private copy.

RIDGEON. But for me it would have been a very different book.

JENNIFER. But for you it would have been a longer one.

RIDGEON. You know then that I killed him?

JENNIFER [*suddenly moved and softened*] Oh, doctor, if you acknowledge that—if you have confessed it to yourself—if you realize what you have done, then there is forgiveness. I trusted in your strength instinctively at first; then I thought I had mistaken callousness for strength. Can you blame me? But if it was really strength—if it was only such a mistake as we all make sometimes—it will make me so happy to be friends with you again.

RIDGEON. I tell you I made no mistake. I cured Blenkinsop: was there any mistake there?

JENNIFER. He recovered. Oh, dont be foolishly proud, doctor. Confess to a failure, and save our friendship. Remember, Sir Ralph gave Louis your medicine; and it made him worse.

RIDGEON. I cant be your friend on false pretences. Something has got me by the throat: the truth must come out. I used that medicine myself on Blenkinsop. It did no make him worse. It is a dangerous medicine: it cured Blenkinsop: it killed Louis Dubedat. When I handle it, it cures. When another man handles it, it kills—sometimes.

JENNIFER [*naïvely: not yet taking it all in*] Then why did you let Sir Ralph give it to Louis?

RIDGEON. I'm going to tell you. I did it because I was in love with you.

JENNIFER [*innocently surprised*] In lo— You! an elderly man!

RIDGEON [*thunderstruck, raising his fists to heaven*] Dubedat: thou art avenged! [*He drops his hands and collapses on the bench*]. I never thought of that. I suppose I appear to you a ridiculous old fogey.

JENNIFER. But surely—I did not mean to offend you, indeed—but you must be at least twenty years older than I am.

RIDGEON. Oh, quite. More, perhaps. In twenty years you will understand how little difference that makes.

JENNIFER. But even so, how could you think that I —his wife—could ever think of you—

RIDGEON [*stopping her with a nervous waving of his fingers*] Yes, yes, yes, yes: I quite understand: you neednt rub it in.

JENNIFER. But—oh, it is only dawning on me now— I was so surprised at first—do you dare to tell me that it was to gratify a miserable jealousy that you deliberately—oh! oh! you murdered him.

RIDGEON. I think I did. It really comes to that.

> Thou shalt not kill, but needst not strive
> Officiously to keep alive.

I suppose—yes: I killed him.

ACT V   The Doctor's Dilemma   113

JENNIFER. And you tell me that! to my face! callously! You are not afraid!

RIDGEON. I am a doctor: I have nothing to fear. It is not an indictable offence to call in B. B. Perhaps it ought to be; but it isnt.

JENNIFER. I did not mean that. I meant afraid of my taking the law into my own hands, and killing you.

RIDGEON. I am so hopelessly idiotic about you that I should not mind it a bit. You would always remember me if you did that.

JENNIFER. I shall remember you always as a little man who tried to kill a great one.

RIDGEON. Pardon me. I succeeded.

JENNIFER [*with quiet conviction*] No. Doctors think they hold the keys of life and death; but it is not their will that is fulfilled. I dont believe you made any difference at all.

RIDGEON. Perhaps not. But I intended to.

JENNIFER [*looking at him amazedly: not without pity*] And you tried to destroy that wonderful and beautiful life merely because you grudged him a woman whom you could never have expected to care for you!

RIDGEON. Who kissed my hands. Who believed in me. Who told me her friendship lasted until death.

JENNIFER. And whom you were betraying.

RIDGEON. No. Whom I was saving.

JENNIFER [*gently*] Pray, doctor, from what?

RIDGEON. From making a terrible discovery. From having your life laid waste.

JENNIFER. How?

RIDGEON. No matter. I have saved you. I have been the best friend you ever had. You are happy. You are well. His works are an imperishable joy and pride for you.

JENNIFER. And you think that is your doing. Oh doctor, doctor! Sir Patrick is right: you do think you are a little god. How can you be so silly? You did not paint those pictures which are my imperishable joy and pride: you did not speak the words that will always be heavenly music in my ears. I listen to them now whenever I am tired or sad. That is why I am always happy.

RIDGEON. Yes, now that he is dead. Were you always happy when he was alive?

JENNIFER [*wounded*] Oh, you are cruel, cruel. When he was alive I did not know the greatness of my blessing. I worried meanly about little things. I was unkind to him. I was unworthy of him.

RIDGEON [*laughing bitterly*] Ha!

JENNIFER. Dont insult me: dont blaspheme. [*She snatches up the book and presses it to her heart in a paroxysm of remorse, exclaiming*] Oh, my King of Men!

RIDGEON. King of Men! Oh, this is too monstrous, too grotesque. We cruel doctors have kept the secret from you faithfully; but it is like all secrets: it will not not keep itself. The buried truth germinates and breaks through to the light.

JENNIFER. What truth?

RIDGEON. What truth! Why, that Louis Dubedat, King of Men, was the most entire and perfect scoundrel, the most miraculously mean rascal, the most callously selfish blackguard that ever made a wife miserable.

JENNIFER [*unshaken: calm and lovely*] He made his wife the happiest woman in the world, doctor.

RIDGEON. No: by all thats true on earth, he made his widow the happiest woman in the world; but it was I who made her a widow. And her happiness is my justification and my reward. Now you know what I did and what I thought of him. Be as angry with me as you like: at least you know me as I really am. If you ever come to care for an elderly man, you will know what you are caring for.

JENNIFER [*kind and quiet*] I am not angry with you

Act V   The Doctor's Dilemma   115

any more, Sir Colenso. I knew quite well that you did not like Louis; but it is not your fault: you dont understand: that is all. You never could have believed in him. It is just like your not believing in my religion: it is a sort of sixth sense that you have not got. And [*with a gentle reassuring movement towards him*] dont think that you have shocked me so dreadfully. I know quite well what you mean by his selfishness. He sacrificed everything for his art. In a certain sense he had even to sacrifice everybody—

RIDGEON. Everybody except himself. By keeping that back he lost the right to sacrifice you, and gave me the right to sacrifice him. Which I did.

JENNIFER [*shaking her head, pitying his error*] He was one of the men who know what women know: that self-sacrifice is vain and cowardly.

RIDGEON. Yes, when the sacrifice is rejected and thrown away. Not when it becomes the food of godhead.

JENNIFER. I dont understand that. And I cant argue with you: you are clever enough to puzzle me, but not to shake me. You are so utterly, so wildly wrong; so incapable of appreciating Louis—

RIDGEON. Oh! [*taking up the Secretary's list*] I have marked five pictures as sold to me.

JENNIFER. They will not be sold to you. Louis' creditors insisted on selling them; but this is my birthday; and they were all bought in for me this morning by my husband.

RIDGEON. By whom? ! ! !

JENNIFER. By my husband.

RIDGEON [*gabbling and stuttering*] What husband? Whose husband? Which husband? Whom? how? what? Do you mean to say that you have married again?

JENNIFER. Do you forget that Louis disliked widows, and that people who have married happily once always marry again?

RIDGEON. Then I have committed a purely disinterested murder!

The Secretary returns with a pile of catalogues.

THE SECRETARY. Just got the first batch of catalogues in time. The doors are open.

JENNIFER [*to Ridgeon, politely*] So glad you like the pictures, Sir Colenso. Good morning.

RIDGEON. Good morning. [*He goes towards the door; hesitates; turns to say something more; gives it up as a bad job; and goes*].

GETTING MARRIED

XVII

1908

N.B.—There is a point of some technical interest to be noted in this play. The customary division into acts and scenes has been disused, and a return made to unity of time and place, as observed in the ancient Greek drama. In the foregoing tragedy, The Doctor's Dilemma, there are five acts; the place is altered five times; and the time is spread over an undetermined period of more than a year. No doubt the strain on the attention of the audience and on the ingenuity of the playwright is much less; but I find in practice that the Greek form is inevitable when drama reaches a certain point in poetic and intellectual evolution. Its adoption was not, on my part, a deliberate display of virtuosity in form, but simply the spontaneous falling of a play of ideas into the form most suitable to it, which turned out to be the classical form. Getting Married, in several acts and scenes, with the time spread over a long period, would be impossible.

PREFACE TO GETTING MARRIED

The Revolt against Marriage

THERE is no subject on which more dangerous nonsense is talked and thought than marriage. If the mischief stopped at talking and thinking it would be bad enough; but it goes further, into disastrous anarchical action. Because our marriage law is inhuman and unreasonable to the point of downright abomination, the bolder and more rebellious spirits form illicit unions, defiantly sending cards round to their friends announcing what they have done. Young women come to me and ask me whether I think they ought to consent to marry the man they have decided to live with; and they are perplexed and astonished when I, who am supposed (heaven knows why!) to have the most advanced views attainable on the subject, urge them on no account to compromize themselves without the security of an authentic wedding ring. They cite the example of George Eliot, who formed an illicit union with Lewes. They quote a saying attributed to Nietzsche, that a married philosopher is ridiculous, though the men of their choice are not philosophers. When they finally give up the idea of reforming our marriage institutions by private enterprise and personal righteousness, and consent to be led to the Registry or even to the altar, they insist on first arriving at an explicit understanding that both parties are to be perfectly free to sip every flower and change every hour, as their fancy may dictate, in spite of the legal bond. I do not observe that their unions prove less monogamic than other people's: rather the contrary, in fact; consequently, I do not know whether they make less fuss than ordinary people when either party claims the benefit of the treaty; but the existence of the treaty shews the same anarchical notion that the law can be set aside by any two private persons by the simple process of promising one another to ignore it.

Marriage Nevertheless Inevitable

Now most laws are, and all laws ought to be, stronger than the strongest individual. Certainly the marriage law is. The only people who successfully evade it are those who actually avail themselves of its shelter by pretending to be married when they are not, and by Bohemians who have no position to lose and no career to be closed. In every other case open violation of the marriage laws means either downright ruin or such inconvenience and disablement as a prudent man or woman would get married ten times over rather than face. And these disablements and inconveniences are not even the price of freedom; for, as Brieux has shewn so convincingly in Les Hannetons, an avowedly illicit union is often found in practice to be as tyrannical and as hard to escape from as the worst legal one.

We may take it then that when a joint domestic establishment, involving questions of children or property, is contemplated, marriage is in effect compulsory upon all normal people; and until the law is altered there is nothing for us but to make the best of it as it stands. Even when no such establishment is desired, clandestine irregularities are negligible as an alternative to marriage. How common they are nobody knows; for in spite of the powerful protection afforded to the parties by the law of libel, and the readiness of society on various other grounds to be hoodwinked by the keeping up of the very thinnest appearances, most of them are probably never suspected. But they are neither dignified nor safe and comfortable, which at once rules them out for normal decent people. Marriage remains practically inevitable; and the sooner we acknowledge this, the sooner we shall set to work to make it decent and reasonable.

What does the Word Marriage Mean

However much we may all suffer through marriage, most of us think so little about it that we regard it as a fixed part of the order of nature, like gravitation. Except for this error, which may be regarded as constant, we use the word with reckless looseness, meaning a dozen different things by it, and yet always assuming that to a respectable man it can have only one meaning. The pious citizen, suspecting the Socialist (for example) of unmentionable things, and asking him heatedly whether he wishes to abolish marriage, is infuriated by a sense of unanswerable quibbling when the Socialist asks him what particular variety of marriage he means: English civil marriage, sacramental marriage, indissoluble Roman Catholic marriage, marriage of divorced persons, Scotch marriage, Irish marriage, French, German, Turkish, or South Dakotan marriage. In Sweden, one of the most highly civilized countries in the world, a marriage is dissolved if both parties wish it, without any question of conduct. That is what marriage means in Sweden. In Clapham that is what they call by the senseless name of Free Love. In the British Empire we have unlimited Kulin polygamy, Muslim polygamy limited to four wives, child marriages, and, nearer home, marriages of first cousins: all of them abominations in the eyes of many worthy persons. Not only may the respectable British champion of marriage mean any of these widely different institutions; sometimes he does not mean marriage at all. He means monogamy, chastity, temperance, respectability, morality, Christianity, anti-socialism, and a dozen other things that have no necessary connection with marriage. He often means something that he dare not avow: ownership of the person of another human being, for instance. And he never tells the truth about his own marriage either to himself or any one else.

With those individualists who in the mid-XIXth century dreamt of doing away with marriage altogether on the ground that it is a private concern between the two parties with which society has nothing to do, there is now no need to deal. The vogue of "the self-regarding action" has passed; and it may be assumed without argument that unions for the purpose of establishing a family will continue to be registered and regulated by the State. Such registration is marriage, and will continue to be called marriage long after the conditions of the registration have changed so much that no citizen now living would recognize them as marriage conditions at all if he revisited the earth. There is therefore no question of abolishing marriage; but there is a very pressing question of improving its conditions. I have never met anybody really in favor of maintaining marriage as it exists in England to-day. A Roman Catholic may obey his Church by assenting verbally to the doctrine of indissoluble marriage. But nobody worth counting believes directly, frankly, and instinctively that when a person commits a murder and is put into prison for twenty years for it, the free and innocent husband or wife of that murderer should remain bound by the marriage. To put it briefly, a contract for better for worse is a contract that should not be tolerated. As a matter of fact it is not tolerated fully even by the Roman Catholic Church; for Roman Catholic marriages can be dissolved, if not by the temporal Courts, by the Pope. Indissoluble marriage is

an academic figment, advocated only by celibates and by
comfortably married people who imagine that if other
couples are uncomfortable it must be their own fault, just
as rich people are apt to imagine that if other people are
poor it serves them right. There is always some means
of dissolution. The conditions of dissolution may vary
widely, from those on which Henry VIII. procured his
divorce from Katharine of Arragon to the pleas on which
American wives obtain divorces (for instance, "mental
anguish" caused by the husband's neglect to cut his toe-
nails); but there is always some point at which the theory of the inviolable better-for-worse marriage breaks
down in practice. South Carolina has indeed passed
what is called a freak law declaring that a marriage shall
not be dissolved under any circumstances; but such an
absurdity will probably be repealed or amended by sheer
force of circumstances before these words are in print.
The only question to be considered is, What shall the
conditions of the dissolution be?

Survivals of Sex Slavery

If we adopt the common romantic assumption that the
object of marriage is bliss, then the very strongest reason for dissolving a marriage is that it shall be disagreeable to one or other or both of the parties. If we accept
the view that the object of marriage is to provide for the
production and rearing of children, then childlessness
should be a conclusive reason for dissolution. As neither
of these causes entitles married persons to divorce it is
at once clear that our marriage law is not founded on
either assumption. What it is really founded on is the
morality of the tenth commandment, which Englishwomen will one day succeed in obliterating from the
walls of our churches by refusing to enter any building
where they are publicly classed with a man's house, his

ox, and his ass, as his purchased chattels. In this morality female adultery is malversation by the woman and theft by the man, whilst male adultery with an unmarried woman is not an offence at all. But though this is not only the theory of our marriage laws, but the practical morality of many of us, it is no longer an avowed morality, nor does its persistence depend on marriage; for the abolition of marriage would, other things remaining unchanged, leave women more effectually enslaved than they now are. We shall come to the question of the economic dependence of women on men later on; but at present we had better confine ourselves to the theories of marriage which we are not ashamed to acknowledge and defend, and upon which, therefore, marriage reformers will be obliged to proceed.

We may, I think, dismiss from the field of practical politics the extreme sacerdotal view of marriage as a sacred and indissoluble covenant, because though reinforced by unhappy marriages as all fanaticisms are reinforced by human sacrifices, it has been reduced to a private and socially inoperative eccentricity by the introduction of civil marriage and divorce. Theoretically, our civilly married couples are to a Catholic as unmarried couples are: that is, they are living in open sin. Practically, civilly married couples are received in society, by Catholics and everyone else, precisely as sacramentally married couples are; and so are people who have divorced their wives or husbands and married again. And yet marriage is enforced by public opinion with such ferocity that the least suggestion of laxity in its support is fatal to even the highest and strongest reputations, although laxity of conduct is winked at with grinning indulgence; so that we find the austere Shelley denounced as a fiend in human form, whilst Nelson, who openly left his wife and formed a *menage à trois* with Sir William and Lady Hamilton, was idolized. Shelley might have had an ille-

Preface

gi\lmate child in every county in England if he had done so frankly as a sinner. His unpardonable offence was that he attacked marriage as an institution. We feel a strange anguish of terror and hatred against him, as against one who threatens us with a mortal injury. What is the element in his proposals that produces this effect?

The answer of the specialists is the one already alluded to: that the attack on marriage is an attack on property; so that Shelley was something more hateful to a husband than a horse thief: to wit, a wife thief, and something more hateful to a wife than a burglar: namely, one who would steal her husband's house from over her head, and leave her destitute and nameless on the streets. Now, no doubt this accounts for a good deal of anti-Shelleyan prejudice: a prejudice so deeply rooted in our habits that, as I have shewn in my play, men who are bolder freethinkers than Shelley himself can no more bring themselves to commit adultery than to commit any common theft, whilst women who loathe sex slavery more fiercely than Mary Wollstonecraft are unable to face the insecurity and discredit of the vagabondage which is the masterless woman's only alternative to celibacy. But in spite of all this there is a revolt against marriage which has spread so rapidly within my recollection that though we all still assume the existence of a huge and dangerous majority which regards the least hint of scepticism as to the beauty and holiness of marriage as infamous and abhorrent, I sometimes wonder why it is so difficult to find an authentic living member of this dreaded army of convention outside the ranks of the people who never think about public questions at all, and who, for all their numerical weight and apparently invincible prejudices, accept social changes to-day as tamely as their forefathers accepted the Reformation under Henry and Edward, the Restoration under Mary, and, after Mary's death, the shandygaff which Elizabeth compounded from both doctrines and called the Articles of the Church of England. If matters were left to these simple folk, there would never be any changes at all; and society would perish like a snake that could not cast its skins. Nevertheless the snake does change its skin in spite of them; and there are signs that our marriage-law skin is causing discomfort to thoughtful people and will presently be cast whether the others are satisfied with it or not. The question therefore arises: What is there in marriage that makes the thoughtful people so uncomfortable?

The New Attack on Marriage

The answer to this question is an answer which everybody knows and nobody likes to give. What is driving our ministers of religion and statesmen to blurt it out at last is the plain fact that marriage is now beginning to depopulate the country with such alarming rapidity that we are forced to throw aside our modesty like people who, awakened by an alarm of fire, rush into the streets in their nightdresses or in no dresses at all. The fictitious Free Lover, who was supposed to attack marriage because it thwarted his inordinate affections and prevented him from making life a carnival, has vanished and given place to the very real, very strong, very austere avenger of outraged decency who declares that the licentiousness of marriage, now that it no longer recruits the race, is destroying it.

As usual, this change of front has not yet been noticed by our newspaper controversialists and by the suburban season-ticket holders whose minds the newspapers make. They still defend the citadel on the side on which nobody is attacking it, and leave its weakest front undefended.

The religious revolt against marriage is a very old one. Christianity began with a fierce attack on marriage; and to this day the celibacy of the Roman Catholic priesthood is a standing protest against its compatibility with the higher life. St. Paul's reluctant sanction of marriage; his personal protest that he countenanced it of necessity and against his own conviction; his contemptuous " better to marry than to burn " is only out of date in respect of his belief that the end of the world was at hand and that there was therefore no longer any population question. His instinctive recoil from its worst aspect as a slavery to pleasure which induces two people to accept slavery to one another has remained an active force in the world to this day, and is now stirring more uneasily than ever. We have more and more Pauline celibates whose objection to marriage is the intolerable indignity of being supposed to desire or live the married life as ordinarily conceived. Every thoughtful and observant minister of religion is troubled by the determination of his flock to regard marriage as a sanctuary for pleasure, seeing as he does that the known libertines of his parish are visibly suffering much less from intemperance than many of the married people who stigmatize them as monsters of vice.

A Forgotten Conference of Married Men

The late Hugh Price Hughes, an eminent Methodist divine, once organized in London a conference of respectable men to consider the subject. Nothing came of it (nor indeed could have come of it in the absence of women); but it had its value as giving the young sociologists present, of whom I was one, an authentic notion of what a picked audience of respectable men understood by married life. It was certainly a staggering revelation. Peter the Great would have been shocked; Byron would have been horrified; Don Juan would have fled from the conference into a monastery. The respectable men all regarded the marriage ceremony as a rite which absolved them from the laws of health and temperance; inaugurated a life-long honeymoon; and placed their pleasures on exactly the same footing as their prayers. It seemed entirely proper and natural to them that out of every twenty-four hours of their lives they should pass eight shut up in one room with their wives alone, and this, not birdlike, for the mating season, but all the year round and every year. How they settled even such minor questions as to which party should decide whether and how much the window should be open and how many blankets should be on the bed, and at what hour they should go to bed and get up so as to avoid disturbing one another's sleep, seemed insoluble questions to me. But the members of the conference did not seem to mind. They were content to have the whole national housing problem treated on a basis of one room for two people. That was the essence of marriage for them.

Please remember, too, that there was nothing in their circumstances to check intemperance. They were men of business: that is, men for the most part engaged in routine work which exercized neither their minds nor their bodies to the full pitch of their capacities. Compared with statesmen, first-rate professional men, artists, and even with laborers and artisans as far as muscular exertion goes, they were underworked, and could spare the fine edge of their faculties and the last few inches of their chests without being any the less fit for their daily routine. If I had adopted their habits, a startling deterioration would have appeared in my writing before the end of a fortnight, and frightened me back to what they would have considered an impossible asceticism. But they paid no penalty of which they were conscious. They had as much health as they wanted: that is, they did not feel the need of a doctor. They enjoyed their smokes, their meals, their respectable clothes, their affectionate games with their children, their prospects of larger profits or higher salaries, their Saturday half holidays and Sunday walks, and the rest of it. They did less than two hours work a day and took from seven to nine office hours to do it in. And they were no good for any mortal purpose except to go on doing it. They were respectable only by the standard they themselves had set. Considered seriously as electors governing an empire through their votes, and choosing and maintaining its religious and moral institutions by their powers of social persecution, they were a black-coated army of calamity. They were incapable of comprehending the industries they were engaged in, the laws under which they lived, or the relation of their country to other countries. They lived the lives of old men contentedly. They were timidly conservative at the age at which every healthy human being ought to be obstreperously revolutionary. And their wives went through the routine of the kitchen, nursery, and drawing-room just as they went through the routine of the office. They had all, as they called it, settled down, like balloons that had lost their lifting margin of gas; and it was evident that the process of settling down would go on until they settled into their graves. They read old-fashioned newspapers with effort, and were just taking with avidity to a new sort of paper, costing a halfpenny, which they believed to be extraordinarily bright and attractive, and which never really succeeded until it became extremely dull, discarding all serious news and replacing it by vapid tittle-tattle, and substituting for political articles informed by at least some pretence of knowledge of economics, history, and constitutional law, such paltry follies and sentimentalities, snobberies and partisaneries, as ignorance can understand and irresponsibility relish.

What they called patriotism was a conviction that because they were born in Tooting or Camberwell, they were the natural superiors of Beethoven, of Rodin, of Ibsen, of Tolstoy and all other benighted foreigners. Those of them who did not think it wrong to go to the theatre liked above everything a play in which the hero was called Dick; was continually fingering a briar pipe; and, after being overwhelmed with admiration and affection through three acts, was finally rewarded with the legal possession of a pretty heroine's person on the strength of a staggering lack of virtue. Indeed their only conception of the meaning of the word virtue was abstention from stealing other men's wives or from refusing to marry their daughters.

As to law, religion, ethics, and constitutional government, any counterfeit could impose on them. Any atheist could pass himself off on them as a bishop, any anarchist as a judge, any despot as a Whig, any sentimental socialist as a Tory, any philtre-monger or witch-finder as a man of science, any phrase-maker as a statesman. Those who did not believe the story of Jonah and the great fish were all the readier to believe that metals can be transmuted and all diseases cured by radium, and that men can live for two hundred years by drinking sour milk. Even these credulities involved too severe an intellectual effort for many of them: it was easier to grin and believe nothing. They maintained their respect for themselves by " playing the game " (that is, doing what everybody else did), and by being good judges of hats, ties, dogs, pipes, cricket, gardens, flowers, and the like. They were capable of discussing each other's solvency and respectability with some shrewdness, and could carry out quite complicated systems of paying visits and " knowing " one another. They felt a little vulgar when they spent a day at Margate, and quite distinguished and travelled when they spent it at Boulogne. They were, except as to their clothes, " not particular ": that is, they could put up with ugly sights and sounds, unhealthy smells, and inconvenient houses, with inhuman apathy and callousness. They had, as to adults, a theory that human nature is so poor that it is useless to try to make the world any better, whilst as to children they believed that if they were only sufficiently lectured and whipped, they could be brought to a state of moral perfection such as no fanatic has ever ascribed to his deity. Though they were not intentionally malicious, they practised the most appalling cruelties from mere thoughtlessness, thinking nothing of imprisoning men and women for periods up to twenty years for breaking into their houses; of treating their children as wild beasts to be tamed by a system of blows and imprisonment which they called education; and of keeping pianos in their houses, not for musical purposes, but to torment their daughters with a senseless stupidity that would have revolted an inquisitor.

In short, dear reader, they were very like you and me. I could fill a hundred pages with the tale of our imbecilities and still leave much untold; but what I have set down here haphazard is enough to condemn the system that produced us. The corner stone of that system was the family and the institution of marriage as we have it to-day in England.

Hearth and Home

There is no shirking it: if marriage cannot be made to produce something better than we are, marriage will have to go, or else the nation will have to go. It is no use talking of honor, virtue, purity, and wholesome, sweet, clean, English home lives when what is meant is simply the habits I have described. The flat fact is that English home life to-day is neither honorable, virtuous, wholesome, sweet, clean, nor in any creditable way distinctively English. It is in many respects conspicuously the reverse; and the result of withdrawing children from it completely at an early age, and sending them to a public school and then to a university, does, in spite of the fact that these institutions are class warped and in some respects quite abominably corrupt, produce sociabler men. Women, too, are improved by the escape from home provided by women's colleges; but as very few of them are fortunate enough to enjoy this advantage, most women are so thoroughly home-bred as to be unfit for human society. So little is expected of them that in Sheridan's School for Scandal we hardly notice that the heroine is a female cad, as detestable and dishonorable in her repentance as she is vulgar and silly in her naughtiness. It was left to an abnormal critic like George Gissing to point out the glaring fact that in the remarkable set of life studies of XIXth century women to be found in the novels of Dickens, the most convincingly real ones are either vilely unamiable or comically contemptible; whilst his attempts to manufacture admirable heroines by idealizations of home-bred womanhood are not only absurd but not even pleasantly absurd: one has no patience with them.

As all this is corrigible by reducing home life and domestic sentiment to something like reasonable proportions in the life of the individual, the danger of it does not lie in human nature. Home life as we understand it is no more natural to us than a cage is natural to a cockatoo. Its grave danger to the nation lies in its narrow views, its unnaturally sustained and spitefully jealous concupiscences, its petty tyrannies, its false social pretences, its endless grudges and squabbles, its sacrifice of the boy's future by setting him to earn money to help the family when he should be in training for his adult life (remember the boy Dickens and the blacking factory), and of the girl's chances by making her a slave to sick or selfish parents, its unnatural packing into little

Preface

brick boxes of little parcels of humanity of ill-assorted ages, with the old scolding or beating the young for behaving like young people, and the young hating and thwarting the old for behaving like old people, and all the other ills, mentionable and unmentionable, that arise from excessive segregation. It sets these evils up as benefits and blessings representing the highest attainable degree of honor and virtue, whilst any criticism of or revolt against them is savagely persecuted as the extremity of vice. The revolt, driven under ground and exacerbated, produces debauchery veiled by hypocrisy, an overwhelming demand for licentious theatrical entertainments which no censorship can stem, and, worst of all, a confusion of virtue with the mere morality that steals its name until the real thing is loathed because the imposture is loathsome. Literary traditions spring up in which the libertine and profligate—Tom Jones and Charles Surface are the heroes, and decorous, law-abiding persons—Blifil and Joseph Surface—are the villains and butts. People like to believe that Nell Gwynne has every amiable quality and the Bishop's wife every odious one. Poor Mr. Pecksniff, who is generally no worse than a humbug with a turn for pompous talking, is represented as a criminal instead of as a very typical English paterfamilias keeping a roof over the head of himself and his daughters by inducing people to pay him more for his services than they are worth. In the extreme instances of reaction against convention, female murderers get sheaves of offers of marriage; and when Nature throws up that rare phenomenon, an unscrupulous libertine, his success among " well brought-up " girls is so easy, and the devotion he inspires so extravagant, that it is impossible not to see that the revolt against conventional respectability has transfigured a commonplace rascal into a sort of Anarchist Saviour. As to the respectable voluptuary, who joins Omar Khayyam clubs and vibrates to Swinburne's invocation of Dolores to "come down and redeem us from virtue," he is to be found in every suburb.

Too Much of a Good Thing

We must be reasonable in our domestic ideals. I do not think that life at a public school is altogether good for a boy any more than barrack life is altogether good for a soldier. But neither is home life altogether good. Such good as it does, I should say, is due to its freedom from the very atmosphere it professes to supply. That atmosphere is usually described as an atmosphere of love; and this definition should be sufficient to put any sane person on guard against it. The people who talk and write as if the highest attainable state is that of a family stewing in love continuously from the cradle to the grave, can hardly have given five minutes serious consideration to so outrageous a proposition. They cannot have even made up their minds as to what they mean by love; for when they expatiate on their thesis they are sometimes talking about kindness, and sometimes about mere appetite. In either sense they are equally far from the realities of life. No healthy man or animal is occupied with love in any sense for more than a very small fraction indeed of the time he devotes to business and to recreations wholly unconnected with love. A wife entirely preoccupied with her affection for her husband, a mother entirely preoccupied with her affection for her children, may be all very well in a book (for people who like that kind of book); but in actual life she is a nuisance. Husbands may escape from her when their business compels them to be away from home all day; but young children may be, and quite often are, killed by her cuddling and coddling and doctoring and preaching: above all, by her continuous attempts to excite precocious sentimentality, a practice as objectionable, and possibly as mischievous, as the worst tricks of the worst nursemaids.

Large and Small Families

In most healthy families there is a revolt against this tendency. The exchanging of presents on birthdays and the like is barred by general consent, and the relations of the parties are placed by express treaty on an unsentimental footing.

Unfortunately this mitigation of family sentimentality is much more characteristic of large families than small ones. It used to be said that members of large families get on in the world; and it is certainly true that for purposes of social training a household of twenty surpasses a household of five as an Oxford College surpasses an eight-roomed house in a cheap street. Ten children, with the necessary adults, make a community in which an excess of sentimentality is impossible. Two children make a doll's house, in which both parents and children become morbid if they keep to themselves. What is more, when large families were the fashion, they were organized as tyrannies much more than as "atmospheres of love." Francis Place tells us that he kept out of his father's way because his father never passed a child within his reach without striking it; and though the case was an extreme one, it was an extreme that illustrated a tendency. Sir Walter Scott's father, when his son incautiously expressed some relish for his porridge, dashed a handful of salt into it with an instinctive sense that it was his duty as a father to prevent his son enjoying himself. Ruskin's mother gratified the sensual side of her maternal passion, not by cuddling her son, but by whipping him when he fell downstairs or was slack in learning the Bible off by heart; and this grotesque safety-valve for voluptuousness, mischievous as it was in many

ways, had at least the advantage that the child did not
enjoy it and was not debauched by it, as he would have
been by transports of sentimentality.

But nowadays we cannot depend on these safeguards,
such as they were. We no longer have large families: all
the families are too small to give the children the necessary social training. The Roman father is out of fashion; and the whip and the cane are becoming discredited,
not so much by the old arguments against corporal punishment (sound as these were) as by the gradual wearing
away of the veil from the fact that flogging is a form of
debauchery. The advocate of flogging as a punishment
is now exposed to very disagreeable suspicions; and ever
since Rousseau rose to the effort of making a certain very
ridiculous confession on the subject, there has been a
growing perception that child whipping, even for the
children themselves, is not always the innocent and high-
minded practice it professes to be. At all events there
is no getting away from the facts that families are
smaller than they used to be, and that passions which
formerly took effect in tyranny have been largely di-
verted into sentimentality. And though a little sentimentality may be a very good thing, chronic sentimentality
is a horror, more dangerous, because more possible, than
the erotomania which we all condemn when we are not
thoughtlessly glorifying it as the ideal married state.

The Gospel of Laodicea

Let us try to get at the root error of these false domes-
tice doctrines. Why was it that the late Samuel Butler,
with a conviction that increased with his experience of
life, preached the gospel of Laodicea, urging people to be
temperate in what they called goodness as in everything
else? Why is it that I, when I hear some well-meaning
person exhort young people to make it a rule to do at

least one kind action every day, feel very much as I
should if I heard them persuade children to get drunk at
least once every day? Apart from the initial absurdity
of accepting as permanent a state of things in which
there would be in this country misery enough to supply
occasion for several thousand million kind actions per
annum, the effect on the character of the doers of the
actions would be so appalling, that one month of any
serious attempt to carry out such counsels would probably bring about more stringent legislation against actions
going beyond the strict letter of the law in the way of
kindness than we have now against excess in the opposite
direction.

There is no more dangerous mistake than the mistake
of supposing that we cannot have too much of a good
thing. The truth is, an immoderately good man is very
much more dangerous than an immoderately bad man:
that is why Savonarola was burnt and John of Leyden
torn to pieces with red-hot pincers whilst multitudes of
unredeemed rascals were being let off with clipped ears,
burnt palms, a flogging, or a few years in the galleys.
That is why Christianity never got any grip of the world
until it virtually reduced its claims on the ordinary citizen's attention to a couple of hours every seventh day,
and let him alone on week-days. If the fanatics who
are preoccupied day in and day out with their salvation
were healthy, virtuous, and wise, the Laodiceanism of the
ordinary man might be regarded as a deplorable shortcoming; but, as a matter of fact, no more frightful misfortune could threaten us than a general spread of fanaticism. What people call goodness has to be kept in
check just as carefully as what they call badness; for
the human constitution will not stand very much of either
without serious psychological mischief, ending in insanity
or crime. The fact that the insanity may be privileged,
as Savonarola's was up to the point of wrecking the social

life of Florence, does not alter the case. We always
hesitate to treat a dangerously good man as a lunatic because he may turn out to be a prophet in the true sense:
that is, a man of exceptional sanity who is in the right
when we are in the wrong. However necessary it may
have been to get rid of Savonarola, it was foolish to poison Socrates and burn St. Joan of Arc. But it is none
the less necessary to take a firm stand against the monstrous proposition that because certain attitudes and sentiments may be heroic and admirable at some momentous
crisis, they should or can be maintained at the same pitch
continuously through life. A life spent in prayer and
almsgiving is really as insane as a life spent in cursing
and picking pockets: the effect of everybody doing it
would be equally disastrous. The superstitious tolerance
so long accorded to monks and nuns is inevitably giving
way to a very general and very natural practice of confiscating their retreats and expelling them from their
country, with the result that they come to England and
Ireland, where they are partly unnoticed and partly encouraged because they conduct technical schools and
teach our girls softer speech and gentler manners than
our comparatively ruffianly elementary teachers. But
they are still full of the notion that because it is possible
for men to attain the summit of Mont Blanc and stay
there for an hour, it is possible for them to live there.
Children are punished and scolded for not living there;
and adults take serious offence if it is not assumed that
they live there.

As a matter of fact, ethical strain is just as bad for
us as physical strain. It is desirable that the normal
pitch of conduct at which men are not conscious of being
particularly virtuous, although they feel mean when they
fall below it, should be raised as high as possible; but it
is not desirable that they should attempt to live above this
pitch any more than that they should habitually walk at

the rate of five miles an hour or carry a hundredweight continually on their backs. Their normal condition should be in nowise difficult or remarkable; and it is a perfectly sound instinct that leads us to mistrust the good man as much as the bad man, and to object to the clergyman who is pious extra-professionally as much as to the professional pugilist who is quarrelsome and violent in private life. We do not want good men and bad men any more than we want giants and dwarfs. What we do want is a high quality for our normal: that is, people who can be much better than what we now call respectable without self-sacrifice. Conscious goodness, like conscious muscular effort, may be of use in emergencies; but for everyday national use it is negligible; and its effect on the character of the individual may easily be disastrous.

For Better For Worse

It would be hard to find any document in practical daily use in which these obvious truths seem so stupidly overlooked as they are in the marriage service. As we have seen, the stupidity is only apparent: the service was really only an honest attempt to make the best of a commercial contract of property and slavery by subjecting it to some religious restraint and elevating it by some touch of poetry. But the actual result is that when two people are under the influence of the most violent, most insane, most delusive, and most transient of passions, they are required to swear that they will remain in that excited, abnormal, and exhausting condition continuously until death do them part. And though of course nobody expects them to do anything so impossible and so unwholesome, yet the law that regulates their relations, and the public opinion that regulates that law, is actually founded on the assumption that the marriage

vow is not only feasible but beautiful and holy, and that
if they are false to it, they deserve no sympathy and no
relief. If all married people really lived together, no
doubt the mere force of facts would make an end to this
inhuman nonsense in a month, if not sooner; but it is
very seldom brought to that test. The typical British
husband sees much less of his wife than he does of his
business partner, his fellow clerk, or whoever works beside him day by day. Man and wife do not as a rule,
live together: they only breakfast together, dine together,
and sleep in the same room. In most cases the woman
knows nothing of the man's working life and he knows
nothing of her working life (he calls it her home life).
It is remarkable that the very people who romance most
absurdly about the closeness and sacredness of the marriage tie are also those who are most convinced that the
man's sphere and the woman's sphere are so entirely
separate that only in their leisure moments can they ever
be together. A man as intimate with his own wife as a
magistrate is with his clerk, or a Prime Minister with the
leader of the Opposition, is a man in ten thousand. The
majority of married couples never get to know one another at all: they only get accustomed to having the same
house, the same children, and the same income, which is
quite a different matter. The comparatively few men
who work at home—writers, artists, and to some extent
clergymen—have to effect some sort of segregation within the house or else run a heavy risk of overstraining
their domestic relations. When the pair is so poor that
it can afford only a single room, the strain is intolerable:
violent quarrelling is the result. Very few couples can
live in a single-roomed tenement without exchanging
blows quite frequently. In the leisured classes there is
often no real family life at all. The boys are at a public
school; the girls are in the schoolroom in charge of a
governess; the husband is at his club or in a set which is

Preface

not his wife's; and the institution of marriage enjoys the credit of a domestic peace which is hardly more intimate than the relations of prisoners in the same gaol or guests at the same garden party. Taking these two cases of the single room and the unearned income as the extremes, we might perhaps locate at a guess whereabout on the scale between them any particular family stands. But it is clear enough that the one-roomed end, though its conditions enable the marriage vow to be carried out with the utmost attainable exactitude, is far less endurable in practice, and far more mischievous in its effect on the parties concerned, and through them on the community, than the other end. Thus we see that the revolt against marriage is by no means only a revolt against its sordidness as a survival of sex slavery. It may even plausibly be maintained that this is precisely the part of it that works most smoothly in practice. The revolt is also against its sentimentality, its romance, its Amorism, even against its enervating happiness.

Wanted: an Immoral Statesman

We now see that the statesman who undertakes to deal with marriage will have to face an amazingly complicated public opinion. In fact, he will have to leave opinion as far as possible out of the question, and deal with human nature instead. For even if there could be any real public opinion in a society like ours, which is a mere mob of classes, each with its own habits and prejudices, it would be at best a jumble of superstitions and interests, taboos and hypocrisies, which could not be reconciled in any coherent enactment. It would probably proclaim passionately that it does not matter in the least what sort of children we have, or how few or how many, provided the children are legitimate. Also that it does not matter in the least what sort of adults we have, provided they are married. No statesman worth the name can possibly act on these views. He is bound to prefer one healthy illegitimate child to ten rickety legitimate ones, and one energetic and capable unmarried couple to a dozen inferior apathetic husbands and wives. If it could be proved that illicit unions produce three children each and marriages only one and a half, he would be bound to encourage illicit unions and discourage and even penalize marriage. The common notion that the existing forms of marriage are not political contrivances, but sacred ethical obligations to which everything, even the very existence of the human race, must be sacrificed if necessary (and this is what the vulgar morality we mostly profess on the subject comes to) is one on which no sane Government could act for a moment; and yet it influences, or is believed to influence, so many votes, that no Government will touch the marriage question if it can possibly help it, even when there is a demand for the extension of marriage, as in the case of the recent long-delayed Act legalizing marriage with a deceased wife's sister. When a reform in the other direction is needed (for example, an extension of divorce), not even the existence of the most unbearable hardships will induce our statesmen to move so long as the victims submit sheepishly, though when they take the remedy into their own hands an inquiry is soon begun. But what is now making some action in the matter imperative is neither the sufferings of those who are tied for life to criminals, drunkards, physically unsound and dangerous mates, and worthless and unamiable people generally, nor the immorality of the couples condemned to celibacy by separation orders which do not annul their marriages, but the fall in the birth rate. Public opinion will not help us out of this difficulty: on the contrary, it will, if it be allowed, punish anybody who mentions it. When Zola tried to repopulate France by writing a novel in praise of parentage, the only comment made here was that the book could not possibly be translated into English, as its subject was too improper.

The Limits of Democracy

Now if England had been governed in the past by statesmen willing to be ruled by such public opinion as that, she would have been wiped off the political map long ago. The modern notion that democracy means governing a country according to the ignorance of its majorities is never more disastrous than when there is some question of sexual morals to be dealt with. The business of a democratic statesman is not, as some of us seem to think, to convince the voters that he knows no better than they as to the methods of attaining their common ends, but on the contrary to convince them that he knows much better than they do, and therefore differs from them on every possible question of method. The voter's duty is to take care that the Government consists of men whom he can trust to devize or support institutions making for the common welfare. This is highly skilled work; and to be governed by people who set about it as the man in the street would set about it is to make straight for "red ruin and the breaking up of laws." Voltaire said that Mr Everybody is wiser than anybody; and whether he is or not, it is his will that must prevail; but the will and the way are two very different things. For example, it is the will of the people on a hot day that the means of relief from the effects of the heat should be within the reach of everybody. Nothing could be more innocent, more hygienic, more important to the social welfare. But the way of the people on such occasions is mostly to drink large quantities of beer, or, among the more luxurious classes, iced claret cup, lemon squashes, and the like. To take a moral illustration, the will to suppress misconduct and secure efficiency in work is general and salutary; but the notion that the best and only effective way is by complaining, scolding, punishing, and revenging is equally general. When Mrs Squeers opened an abscess on her pupil's head with an inky penknife, her object was entirely laudable: her heart was in the right place: a statesman interfering with her on the ground that he did not want the boy cured would have deserved impeachment for gross tyranny. But a statesman tolerating amateur surgical practice with inky penknives in school would be a very bad Minister of Education. It is on the question of method that your expert comes in; and though I am democrat enough to insist that he must first convince a representative body of amateurs that his way is the right way and Mrs Squeers's way the wrong way, yet I very strongly object to any tendency to flatter Mrs Squeers into the belief that her way is in the least likely to be the right way, or that any other test is to be applied to it except the test of its effect on human welfare.

The Science and Art of Politics

Political Science means nothing else than the devizing of the best ways of fulfilling the will of the world; and, I repeat, it is skilled work. Once the way is discovered, the methods laid down, and the machinery provided, the work of the statesman is done, and that of the official begins. To illustrate, there is no need for the police officer who governs the street traffic to be or to know any better than the people who obey the wave of his hand. All concerted action involves subordination and the appointment of directors at whose signal the others will act. There is no more need for them to be superior to the rest than for the keystone of an arch to be of harder stone than the coping. But when it comes to devizing the directions which are to be obeyed: that is, to making new institutions and scraping old ones, then you need aristocracy in the sense of government by the best. A military state organized so as to carry out exactly the impulses of the average soldier would not last a year. The result of trying to make the Church of England reflect the notions of the average churchgoer has reduced it to a cipher except for the purposes of a petulantly irreligious social and political club. Democracy as to the thing to be done may be inevitable (hence the vital need for a democracy of supermen); but democracy as to the way to do it is like letting the passengers drive the train: it can only end in collision and wreck. As a matter of act, we obtain reforms (such as they are), not by allowing the electorate to draft statutes, but by persuading it that a certain minister and his cabinet are gifted with sufficient political sagacity to find out how to produce the desired result. And the usual penalty of taking advantage of this power to reform our institutions is defeat by a vehement " swing of the pendulum " at the next election. Therein lies the peril and the glory of democratic statesmanship. A statesman who confines himself to popular legislation—or, for the matter of that, a playwright who confines himself to popular plays—is like a blind man's dog who goes wherever the blind man pulls him, on the ground that both of them want to go to the same place.

Why Statesmen Shirk the Marriage Question

The reform of marriage, then, will be a very splendid and very hazardous adventure for the Prime Minister who takes it in hand. He will be posted on every hoarding and denounced in every Opposition paper, especially in the sporting papers, as the destroyer of the home, the family, of decency, of morality, of chastity and what not. All the commonplaces of the modern antiSocialist Noodle's Oration will be hurled at him. And he will have to proceed without the slightest concession to it, giving the noodles nothing but their due in the assurance "I know how to attain our ends better than you," and staking his political life on the conviction carried by that assurance, which conviction will depend a good deal on the certainty with which it is made, which again can be attained only by studying the facts of marriage and understanding the needs of the nation. And, after all, he will find that the pious commonplaces on which he and the electorate are agreed conceal an utter difference in the real ends in view: his being public, far-sighted, and impersonal, and those of multitudes of the electorate narrow, personal, jealous, and corrupt. Under such circumstances, it is not to be wondered at that the mere mention of the marriage question makes a British Cabinet shiver with apprehension and hastily pass on to safer business. Nevertheless the reform of marriage cannot be put off for ever. When its hour comes, what are the points the Cabinet will have to take up?

The Question of Population

First, it will have to make up its mind as to how many people we want in the country. If we want less than at present, we must ascertain how many less; and if we allow the reduction to be made by the continued operation of the present sterilization of marriage, we must settle how the process is to be stopped when it has gone far enough. But if we desire to maintain the population at its present figure, or to increase it, we must take immediate steps to induce people of moderate means to marry earlier and to have more children. There is less urgency in the case of the very poor and the very rich. They breed recklessly: the rich because they can afford it, and the poor because they cannot afford the precautions by which the artisans and the middle classes avoid big families. Nevertheless the population declines, because the high birth rate of the very poor is counterbalanced by a huge infantile-mortality in the slums, whilst the very rich are also the very few, and are becoming sterilized by the spreading revolt of their women against excessive childbearing—sometimes against any childbearing.

This last cause is important. It cannot be removed by any economic readjustment. If every family were provided with £10,000 a year tomorrow, women would still refuse more and more to continue bearing children until they are exhausted whilst numbers of others are bearing no children at all. Even if every woman bearing and rearing a valuable child received a handsome series of payments, thereby making motherhood a real profession as it ought to be, the number of women able or willing to give more of their lives to gestation and nursing than three or four children would cost them might not be very large if the advance in social organization and conscience indicated by such payments involved also the opening up of other means of livelihood to women. And it must be remembered that urban civilization itself, insofar as it is a method of evolution (and when it is not this, it is simply a nuisance), is a sterilizing process as far as numbers go. It is harder to keep up the supply of elephants than of sparrows and rabbits; and for the same reason it will be harder to keep up the supply of highly cultivated men and women than it now is of agricultural laborers. Bees get out of this difficulty by a special system of feeding which enables a queen bee to produce 4,000 eggs a day whilst the other females lose their sex altogether and become workers supporting the males in luxury and idleness until the queen has found her mate, when the queen kills him and the quondam females kill all the rest (such at least are the accounts given by romantic naturalists of the matter).

The Right to Motherhood

This system certainly shews a much higher development of social intelligence than our marriage system; but if it were physically possible to introduce it into human society it would be wrecked by an opposite and not less important revolt of women: that is, the revolt against compulsory barrenness. In this two classes of women are concerned: those who, though they have no desire for the presence or care of children, nevertheless feel that motherhood is an experience necessary to their complete psychical development and understanding of themselves and others, and those who, though unable to find or unwilling to entertain a husband, would like to occupy themselves with the rearing of children. My own experience of discussing this question leads me to believe that the one point on which all women are in furious secret rebellion against the existing law is the saddling of the right to a child with the obligation to become the servant of a man. Adoption, or the begging or buying or stealing of another woman's child, is no remedy: it does not provide the supreme experience of bearing the child. No political constitution will ever succeed or deserve to succeed unless it includes the recognition of an absolute right to sexual experience, and is untainted by the Pauline or romantic view of such experience as sinful in itself. And since this experience in its fullest sense must be carried in the case of women to the point of childbearing, it can only be reconciled with the acceptance of marriage with the child's father by legalizing polygyny, because there are more adult women in the country than men. Now though polygyny prevails throughout the greater part of the British Empire, and is as practicable here as in India, there is a good deal to be said against it, and still more to be felt. However, let us put our feelings aside for a moment, and consider the question politically.

Monogamy, Polygyny, and Polyandry

The number of wives permitted to a single husband or of husbands to a single wife under a marriage system, is not an ethical problem: it depends solely on the proportion of the sexes in the population. If in consequence of a great war three-quarters of the men in this country were killed, it would be absolutely necessary to adopt the Mohammedan allowance of four wives to each man in order to recruit the population. The fundamental reason for not allowing women to risk their lives in battle and for giving them the first chance of escape in all dangerous emergencies: in short, for treating their lives as more valuable than male lives, is not in the least a chivalrous reason, though men may consent to it under the illusion of chivalry. It is a simple matter of necessity; for if a large proportion of women were killed or disabled, no possible readjustment of our marriage law could avert the depopulation and consequent political ruin of the country, because a woman with several husbands bears fewer children than a woman with one, whereas a man can produce as many families as he has wives. The natural foundation of the institution of monogamy is not any inherent viciousness in polygyny or polyandry, but the hard fact that men and women are born in about equal numbers. Unfortunately, we kill so many of our male children in infancy that we are left with a surplus of adult women which is sufficiently large to claim attention, and yet not large enough to enable every man to have two wives. Even if it were, we should be met by an economic difficulty. A Kaffir is rich in proportion to the number of his wives, because the women are the breadwinners. But in our civilization women are not paid for their social work in the bearing and rearing of children and the ordering of households; they are quartered on the wages of their husbands. At least four out of five of our men could not afford two wives unless their wages were nearly doubled. Would it not then be well to try unlimited polygyny; so that the remaining fifth could have as many wives apiece as they could afford? Let us see how this would work.

The Male Revolt Against Polygyny

Experience shews that women do not object to polygyny when it is customary: on the contrary, they are its most ardent supporters. The reason is obvious. The question, as it presents itself in practice to a woman, is whether it is better to have, say, a whole share in a tenth-rate man or a tenth share in a first-rate man. Substitute the word Income for the word Man, and you will have the question as it presents itself economically to the dependent woman. The woman whose instincts are maternal, who desires superior children more than anything else, never hesitates. She would take a thousandth share, if necessary, in a husband who was a man in a thousand, rather than have some comparatively weedy weakling all to herself. It is the comparatively weedy weakling, left mateless by polygyny, who objects. Thus, it was not the women of Salt Lake City nor even of America who attacked Mormon polygyny. It was the men. And very naturally. On the other hand, women object to polyandry, because polyandry enables the best women to monopolize all the men, just as polygyny enables the best men to monopolize all the women. That is why all our ordinary men and women are unanimous in defence of monogamy, the men because it excludes

Preface

polygyny, and the women because it excludes polyandry. The women, left to themselves, would tolerate polygyny. The men, left to themselves, would tolerate polyandry. But polygyny would condemn a great many men, and polyandry a great many women, to the celibacy of neglect. Hence the resistance any attempt to establish unlimited polygyny always provokes, not from the best people, but from the mediocrities and the inferiors. If we could get rid of our inferiors and screw up our average quality until mediocrity ceased to be a reproach, thus making every man reasonably eligible as a father and every woman reasonably desirable as a mother, polygyny and polyandry would immediately fall into sincere disrepute, because monogamy is so much more convenient and economical that nobody would want to share a husband or a wife if he (or she) could have a sufficiently good one all to himself (or herself). Thus it appears that it is the scarcity of husbands or wives of high quality that leads woman to polygyny and men to polyandry, and that if this scarcity were cured, monogamy, in the sense of having only one husband or wife at a time (facilities for changing are another matter), would be found satisfactory.

Difference between Oriental and Occidental Polygyny

It may now be asked why the polygynist nations have not gravitated to monogamy, like the latter-day saints of Salt Lake City. The answer is not far to seek: their polygyny is limited. By the Mohammedan law a man cannot marry more than four wives; and by the unwritten law of necessity no man can keep more wives than he can afford; so that a man with four wives must be quite as exceptional in Asia as a man with a carriage-and-pair or a motor car is in Europe, where, nevertheless, we may all have as many carriages and motors as we can afford to pay for. Kulin polygyny, though unlimited, is not really a popular institution: if you are a person of high caste you pay another person of very august caste indeed to make your daughter momentarily one of his sixty or seventy momentary wives for the sake of ennobling your grandchildren; but this fashion of a small and intensely snobbish class is negligible as a general precedent. In any case, men and women in the East do not marry anyone they fancy, as in England and America. Women are secluded and marriages are arranged. In Salt Lake City the free unsecluded woman could see and meet the ablest man of the community, and tempt him to make her his tenth wife by all the arts peculiar to women in English-speaking countries. No eastern woman can do anything of the sort. The man alone has any initiative; but he has no access to the woman; besides, as we have seen, the difficulty created by male license is not polygyny but polyandry, which is not allowed.

Consequently, if we are to make polygyny a success, we must limit it. If we have two women to every one man, we must allow each man only two wives. That is simple; but unfortunately our own actual proportion is, roughly, something like $1\frac{1}{11}$ woman to 1 man. Now you cannot enact that each man shall be allowed $1\frac{1}{11}$ wives, or that each woman who cannot get a husband all to herself shall divide herself between eleven already married husbands. Thus there is no way out for us through polygyny. There is no way at all out of the present system of condemning the superfluous women to barrenness, except by legitimizing the children of women who are not married to the fathers.

Preface

The Old Maid's Right to Motherhood

Now the right to bear children without taking a husband could not be confined to women who are superfluous in the monogamic reckoning. There is the practical difficulty that although in our population there are about a million monogamically superfluous women, yet it is quite impossible to say of any given unmarried woman that she is one of the superfluous. And there is the difficulty of principle. The right to bear a child, perhaps the most sacred of all women's rights, is not one that should have any conditions attached to it except in the interests of race welfare. There are many women of admirable character, strong, capable, independent, who dislike the domestic habits of men; have no natural turn for mothering and coddling them; and find the concession of conjugal rights to any person under any conditions intolerable by their self-respect. Yet the general sense of the community recognizes in these very women the fittest people to have charge of children, and trusts them, as schoolmistresses and matrons of institutions, more than women of any other type when it is possible to procure them for such work. Why should the taking of a husband be imposed on these women as the price of their right to maternity? I am quite unable to answer that question. I see a good deal of first-rate maternal ability and sagacity spending itself on bees and poultry and village schools and cottage hospitals; and I find myself repeatedly asking myself why this valuable strain in the national breed should be sterilized. Unfortunately, the very women whom we should tempt to become mothers for the good of the race are the very last people to press their services on their country in that way. Plato long ago pointed out the importance of being governed by men with sufficient sense of responsibility and comprehension of public duties to be very reluctant to undertake the work of governing; and yet we have taken his instruction so little to heart that we are at present suffering acutely from government by gentlemen who will stoop to all the mean shifts of electioneering and incur all its heavy expenses for the sake of a seat in Parliament. But what our sentimentalists have not yet been told is that exactly the same thing applies to maternity as to government. The best mothers are not those who are so enslaved by their primitive instincts that they will bear children no matter how hard the conditions are, but precisely those who place a very high price on their services, and are quite prepared to become old maids if the price is refused, and even to feel relieved at their escape. Our democratic and matrimonial institutions may have their merits: at all events they are mostly reforms of something worse; but they put a premium on want of self-respect in certain very important matters; and the consequence is that we are very badly governed and are, on the whole, an ugly, mean, ill-bred race.

Ibsen's Chain Stitch

Let us not forget, however, in our sympathy for the superfluous women, that their children must have fathers as well as mothers. Who are the fathers to be? All monogamists and married women will reply hastily: either bachelors or widowers; and this solution will serve as well as another; for it would be hypocritical to pretend that the difficulty is a practical one. None the less, the monogamists, after due reflection, will point out that if there are widowers enough the superfluous women are not really superfluous, and therefore there is no reason why the parties should not marry respectably like other people. And they might in that case be right if the reasons were purely numerical: that is, if every woman were willing to take a husband if one could be found for her,

Preface

and every man willing to take a wife on the same terms; also, please remember, if widows would remain celibate to give the unmarried women a chance. These ifs will not work. We must recognize two classes of old maids: one, the really superfluous women, and the other, the women who refuse to accept maternity on the (to them) unbearable condition of taking a husband. From both classes may, perhaps, be subtracted for the present the large proportion of women who could not afford the extra expense of one or more children. I say "perhaps," because it is by no means sure that within reasonable limits mothers do not make a better fight for subsistence, and have not, on the whole, a better time than single women. In any case, we have two distinct cases to deal with: the superfluous and the voluntary; and it is the voluntary whose grit we are most concerned to fertilize. But here, again, we cannot put our finger on any particular case and pick out Miss Robinson's as superfluous, and Miss Wilkinson's as voluntary. Whether we legitimize the child of the unmarried woman as a duty to the superfluous or as a bribe to the voluntary, the practical result must be the same: to wit, that the condition of marriage now attached to legitimate parentage will be withdrawn from all women, and fertile unions outside marriage recognized by society. Now clearly the consequences would not stop there. The strong-minded ladies who are resolved to be mistresses in their own houses would not be the only ones to take advantage of the new law. Even women to whom a home without a man in it would be no home at all, and who fully intended, if the man turned out to be the right one, to live with him exactly as married couples live, would, if they were possessed of independent means, have every inducement to adopt the new conditions instead of the old ones. Only the women whose sole means of livelihood was wifehood would insist on marriage: hence a tendency would set in to make marriage more and more one of the customs imposed by necessity on the poor, whilst the freer form of union, regulated, no doubt, by settlements and private contracts of various kinds, would become the practice of the rich: that is, would become the fashion. At which point nothing but the achievement of economic independence by women, which is already seen clearly ahead of us, would be needed to make marriage disappear altogether, not by formal abolition, but by simple disuse. The private contract stage of this process was reached in ancient Rome. The only practicable alternative to it seems to be such an extension of divorce as will reduce the risks and obligations of marriage to a degree at which they will be no worse than those of the alternatives to marriage. As we shall see, this is the solution to which all the arguments tend. Meanwhile, note how much reason a statesman has to pause before meddling with an institution which, unendurable as its drawbacks are, threatens to come to pieces in all directions if a single thread of it be cut. Ibsen's similitude of the machine-made chain stitch, which unravels the whole seam at the first pull when a single stitch is ripped, is very applicable to the knot of marriage.

Remoteness of the Facts from the Ideal

But before we allow this to deter us from touching the sacred fabric, we must find out whether it is not already coming to pieces in all directions by the continuous strain of circumstances. No doubt, if it were all that it pretends to be, and human nature were working smoothly within its limits, there would be nothing more to be said: it would be let alone as it always is let alone during the cruder stages of civilization. But the moment we refer to the facts, we discover that the ideal matrimony and domesticity which our bigots implore us to preserve as

Preface

the corner stone of our society is a figment: what we have really got is something very different, questionable at its best, and abominable at its worst. The word pure, so commonly applied to it by thoughtless people, is absurd; because if they do not mean celibate by it, they mean nothing; and if they do mean celibate, then marriage is legalized impurity, a conclusion which is offensive and inhuman. Marriage as a fact is not in the least like marriage as an ideal. If it were, the sudden changes which have been made on the continent from indissoluble Roman Catholic marriage to marriage that can be dissolved by a box on the ear as in France, by an epithet as in Germany, or simply at the wish of both parties as in Sweden, not to mention the experiments made by some of the American States, would have shaken society to its foundations. Yet they have produced so little effect that Englishmen open their eyes in surprise when told of their existence.

Difficulty of Obtaining Evidence

As to what actual marriage is, one would like evidence instead of guesses; but as all departures from the ideal are regarded as disgraceful, evidence cannot be obtained; for when the whole community is indicted, nobody will go into the witness-box for the prosecution. Some guesses we can make with some confidence. For example, if it be objected to any change that our bachelors and widowers would no longer be Galahads, we may without extravagance or cynicism reply that many of them are not Galahads now, and that the only change would be that hypocrisy would no longer be compulsory. Indeed, this can hardly be called guessing: the evidence is in the streets. But when we attempt to find out the truth about our marriages, we cannot even guess with any confidence. Speaking for myself, I can say that I know the inside history of perhaps half a dozen marriages. Any family solicitor knows more than this; but even a family solicitor, however large his practice, knows nothing of the million households which have no solicitors, and which nevertheless make marriage what it really is. And all he can say comes to no more than I can say: to wit, that no marriage of which I have any knowledge is in the least like the ideal marriage. I do not mean that it is worse: I mean simply that it is different. Also, far from society being organized in a defence of its ideal so jealous and implacable that the least step from the straight path means exposure and ruin, it is almost impossible by any extravagance of misconduct to provoke society to relax its steady pretence of blindness, unless you do one or both of two fatal things. One is to get into the newspapers; and the other is to confess. If you confess misconduct to respectable men or women, they must either disown you or become virtually your accomplices: that is why they are so angry with you for confessing. If you get into the papers, the pretence of not knowing becomes impossible. But it is hardly too much to say that if you avoid these two perils, you can do anything you like, as far as your neighbors are concerned. And since we can hardly flatter ourselves that this is the effect of charity, it is difficult not to suspect that our extraordinary forbearance in the matter of stone throwing is that suggested in the well-known parable of the women taken in adultery which some early freethinker slipped into the Gospel of St John: namely, that we all live in glass houses. We may take it, then, that the ideal husband and the ideal wife are no more real human beings than the cherubim. Possibly the great majority keeps its marriage vows in the technical divorce court sense. No husband or wife yet born keeps them or ever can keep them in the ideal sense.

Preface

Marriage as a Magic Spell

The truth which people seem to overlook in this matter is that the marriage ceremony is quite useless as a magic spell for changing in an instant the nature of the relations of two human beings to one another. If a man marries a woman after three weeks acquaintance, and the day after meets a woman he has known for twenty years, he finds, sometimes to his own irrational surprise and his wife's equally irrational indignation, that his wife is a stranger to him, and the other woman an old friend. Also, there is no hocus pocus that can possibly be devized with rings and veils and vows and benedictions that can fix either a man's or woman's affection for twenty minutes, much less twenty years. Even the most affectionate couples must have moments during which they are far more conscious of one another's faults than of one another's attractions. There are couples who dislike one another furiously for several hours at a time; there are couples who dislike one another permanently; and there are couples who never dislike one another; but these last are people who are incapable of disliking anybody. If they do not quarrel, it is not because they are married, but because they are not quarrelsome. The people who are quarrelsome quarrel with their husbands and wives just as easily as with their servants and relatives and acquaintances: marriage makes no difference. Those who talk and write and legislate as if all this could be prevented by making solemn vows that it shall not happen, are either insincere, insane, or hopelessly stupid. There is some sense in a contract to perform or abstain from actions that are reasonably within voluntary control; but such contracts are only needed to provide against the possibility of either party being no longer desirous of the specified performance or abstention. A person proposing or accepting a contract not only to do something but to like doing it would be certified as mad. Yet popular superstition credits the wedding rite with the power of fixing our fancies or affections for life even under the most unnatural conditions.

The Impersonality of Sex

It is necessary to lay some stress on these points, because few realize the extent to which we proceed on the assumption that marriage is a short cut to perfect and permanent intimacy and affection. But there is a still more unworkable assumption which must be discarded before discussions of marriage can get into any sort of touch with the facts of life. That assumption is that the specific relation which marriage authorizes between the parties is the most intimate and personal of human relations, and embraces all the other high human relations. Now this is violently untrue. Every adult knows that the relation in question can and does exist between entire strangers, different in language, color, tastes, class, civilization, morals, religion, character: in everything, in short, except their bodily homology and the reproductive appetite common to all living organisms. Even hatred, cruelty, and contempt are not incompatible with it; and jealousy and murder are as near to it as affectionate friendship. It is true that it is a relation beset with wildly extravagant illusions for inexperienced people, and that even the most experienced people have not always sufficient analytic faculty to disentangle it from the sentiments, sympathetic or abhorrent, which may spring up through the other relations which are compulsorily attached to it by our laws, or sentimentally associated with it in romance. But the fact remains that the most disastrous marriages are those founded exclusively on it, and the most successful those in which it has been least considered, and in which the decisive considerations have had nothing to do with sex, such as liking, money, congeniality of tastes, similarity of habits, suitability of class, &c., &c.

It is no doubt necessary under existing circumstances for a woman without property to be sexually attractive, because she must get married to secure a livelihood; and the illusions of sexual attraction will cause the imagination of young men to endow her with every accomplishment and virtue that can make a wife a treasure. The attraction being thus constantly and ruthlessly used as a bait, both by individuals and by society, any discussion tending to strip it of its illusions and get at its real natural history is nervously discouraged. But nothing can well be more unwholesome for everybody than the exaggeration and glorification of an instinctive function which clouds the reason and upsets the judgment more than all the other instincts put together. The process may be pleasant and romantic; but the consequences are not. It would be far better for everyone, as well as far honester, if young people were taught that what they call love is an appetite which, like all other appetites, is destroyed for the moment by its gratification; that no profession, promise, or proposal made under its influence should bind anybody; and that its great natural purpose so completely transcends the personal interests of any individual or even of any ten generations of individuals that it should be held to be an act of prostitution and even a sort of blasphemy to attempt to turn it to account by exacting a personal return for its gratification, whether by process of law or not. By all means let it be the subject of contracts with society as to its consequences; but to make marriage an open trade in it as at present, with money, board and lodging, personal slavery, vows of eternal exclusive personal sentimentalities and the rest of it as the price, is neither virtuous, dignified, nor decent. No husband ever secured his domestic happiness and honor, nor has any wife ever secured hers, by relying on it. No private claims of any sort should be founded on it: the real point of honor is to take no corrupt advantage of it. When we hear of young women being led astray and the like, we find that what has led them astray is a sedulously inculcated false notion that the relation they are tempted to contract is so intensely personal, and the vows made under the influence of its transient infatuation so sacred and enduring, that only an atrociously wicked man could make light of or forget them. What is more, as the same fantastic errors are inculcated in men, and the conscientious ones therefore feel bound in honor to stand by what they have promised, one of the surest methods to obtain a husband is to practise on his susceptibilities until he is either carried away into a promise of marriage to which he can be legally held, or else into an indiscretion which he must repair by marriage on pain of having to regard himself as a scoundrel and a seducer, besides facing the utmost damage the lady's relatives can do him.

Such a transaction is not an entrance into a "holy state of matrimony": it is as often as not the inauguration of a lifelong squabble, a corroding grudge, that causes more misery and degradation of character than a dozen entirely natural "desertions" and "betrayals." Yet the number of marriages effected more or less in this way must be enormous. When people say that love should be free, their words, taken literally, may be foolish; but they are only expressing inaccurately a very real need for the disentanglement of sexual relations from a mass of exorbitant and irrelevant conditions imposed on them on false pretences to enable needy parents to get their daughters "off their hands" and to keep those who are already married effectually enslaved by one another.

Preface

The Economic Slavery of Women

One of the consequences of basing marriage on the considerations stated with cold abhorrence by Saint Paul in the seventh chapter of his epistle to the Corinthians, as being made necessary by the unlikeness of most men to himself, is that the sex slavery involved has become complicated by economic slavery; so that whilst the man defends marriage because he is really defending his pleasures, the woman is even more vehement on the same side because she is defending her only means of livelihood. To a woman without property or marketable talent a husband is more necessary than a master to a dog. There is nothing more wounding to our sense of human dignity than the husband hunting that begins in every family when the daughters become marriageable; but it is inevitable under existing circumstances; and the parents who refuse to engage in it are bad parents, though they may be superior individuals. The cubs of a humane tigress would starve; and the daughters of women who cannot bring themselves to devote several years of their lives to the pursuit of sons-in-law often have to expatiate their mother's squeamishness by lifelong celibacy and indigence. To ask a young man his intentions when you know he has no intentions, but is unable to deny that he has paid attentions; to threaten an action for breach of promise of marriage; to pretend that your daughter is a musician when she has with the greatest difficulty been coached into playing three pianoforte pieces which she loathes; to use your own mature charms to attract men to the house when your daughters have no aptitude for that department of sport; to coach them, when they have, in the arts by which men can be led to compromize themselves; and to keep all the skeletons carefully locked up in the family cupboard until the prey is duly hunted down and bagged: all this is a mother's duty today; and a very revolting duty it is: one that disposes of the conventional assumption that it is in the faithful discharge of her home duties that a woman finds her self-respect. The truth is that family life will never be decent, much less ennobling, until this central horror of the dependence of women on men is done away with. At present it reduces the difference between marriage and prostitution to the difference between Trade Unionism and unorganized casual labor: a huge difference, no doubt, as to order and comfort, but not a difference in kind.

However, it is not by any reform of the marriage laws that this can be dealt with. It is in the general movement for the prevention of destitution that the means for making women independent of the compulsory sale of their persons, in marriage or otherwise, will be found; but meanwhile those who deal specifically with the marriage laws should never allow themselves for a moment to forget this abomination that "plucks the rose from the fair forehead of an innocent love, and sets a blister there," and then calmly calls itself purity, home, motherhood, respectability, honor, decency, and any other fine name that happens to be convenient, not to mention the foul epithets it hurls freely at those who are ashamed of it.

Unpopularity of Impersonal Views

Unfortunately it is very hard to make an average citizen take impersonal views of any sort in matters affecting personal comfort or conduct. We may be enthusiastic Liberals or Conservatives without any hope of seats in Parliament, knighthoods, or posts in the Government, because party politics do not make the slightest difference in our daily lives and therefore cost us nothing. But to take a vital process in which we are keenly interested personal instruments, and ask us to regard it, and feel about it, and legislate on it, wholly as if it were an impersonal one, is to make a higher demand than most people seem capable of responding to. We all have personal interests in marriage which we are not prepared to sink. It is not only the women who want to get married: the men do too, sometimes on sentimental grounds, sometimes on the more sordid calculation that bachelor life is less comfortable and more expensive, since a wife pays for her status with domestic service as well as with the other services expected of her. Now that children are avoidable, this calculation is becoming more common and conscious than it was: a result which is regarded as " a steady improvement in general morality."

Impersonality is not Promiscuity

There is, too, a really appalling prevalence of the superstition that the sexual instinct in men is utterly promiscuous, and that the least relaxation of law and custom must produce a wild outbreak of licentiousness. As far as our moralists can grasp the proposition that we should deal with the sexual relation as impersonal, it seems to them to mean that we should encourage it to be promiscuous: hence their recoil from it. But promiscuity and impersonality are not the same thing. No man ever fell in love with the entire female sex, nor any woman with the entire male sex. We often do not fall in love at all; and when we do we fall in love with one person and remain indifferent to thousands of others who pass before our eyes every day. Selection, carried even to such fastidiousness as to induce people to say quite commonly that there is only one man or woman in the world for them, is the rule in nature. If anyone doubts this, let him open a shop for the sale of picture postcards, and, when an enamoured lady customer demands a portrait of her favorite actor or a gentleman of his favorite actress, try to substitute some other portrait on the ground that since the sexual instinct is promiscuous, one portrait is as pleasing as another. I suppose no shopkeeper has ever been foolish enough to do such a thing; and yet all our shopkeepers, the moment a discussion arises on marriage, will passionately argue against all reform on the ground that nothing but the most severe coercion can save their wives and daughters from quite indiscriminate rapine.

Domestic Change of Air

Our relief at the morality of the reassurance that man is not promiscuous in his fancies must not blind us to the fact that he is (to use the word coined by certain American writers to describe themselves) something of a Varietist. Even those who say there is only one man or woman in the world for them, find that it is not always the same man or woman. It happens that our law permits us to study this phenomenon among entirely law-abiding people. I know one lady who has been married five times. She is, as might be expected, a wise, attractive, and interesting woman. The question is, is she wise, attractive, and interesting because she has been married five times, or has she been married five times because she is wise, attractive, and interesting? Probably some of the truth lies both ways. I also know of a household consisting of three families, A having married first B, and then C, who afterwards married D. All three unions were fruitful; so that the children had a change both of fathers and mothers. Now I cannot honestly say that these and similar cases have convinced me that people are the worse for a change. The lady who has married and managed five husbands must be much more expert at it than most monogamic ladies; and as a companion and counsellor she probably leaves them nowhere. Mr Kipling's question

What can they know of England that only England know?

disposes not only of the patriots who are so patriotic that they never leave their own country to look at another, but of the citizens who are so domestic that they have never married again and never loved anyone except their own husbands and wives. The domestic doctrinaires are also the dull people. The impersonal relation of sex may be judicially reserved for one person; but any such reservation of friendship, affection, admiration, sympathy and so forth is only possible to a wretchedly narrow and jealous nature; and niether history nor contemporary society shews us a single amiable and respectable character capable of it. This has always been recognized in cultivated society: that is why poor people accuse cultivated society of profligacy, poor people being often so ignorant and uncultivated that they have nothing to offer each other but the sex relationship, and cannot conceive why men and women should associate for any other purpose.

As to the children of the triple household, they were not only on excellent terms with one another, and never thought of any distinction between their full and their half brothers and sisters; but they had the superior sociability which distinguishes the people who live in communities from those who live in small families.

The inference is that changes of partners are not in themselves injurious or undesirable. People are not demoralized by them when they are effected according to law. Therefore we need not hesitate to alter the law merely because the alteration would make such changes easier.

Home Manners are Bad Manners

On the other hand, we have all seen the bonds of marriage vilely abused by people who are never classed with shrews and wife-beaters: they are indeed sometimes held up as models of domesticity because they do not drink nor gamble nor neglect their children nor tolerate dirt and untidiness, and because they are not amiable enough to have what are called amiable weaknesses. These terrors conceive marriage as a dispensation from all the common civilities and delicacies which they have to observe among strangers, or, as they put it, "before company." And here the effects of indissoluble marriage-for-better-for-worse are very plainly and disagreeably seen. If such people took their domestic manners into general society, they would very soon find themselves without a friend or even an acquaintance in the world. There are women who, through total disuse, have lost the power of kindly human speech and can only scold and complain: there are men who grumble and nag from inveterate habit even when they are comfortable. But their unfortunate spouses and children cannot escape from them.

Spurious "Natural" Affection

What is more, they are protected from even such discomfort as the dislike of his prisoners may cause to a gaoler by the hypnotism of the convention that the natural relation between husband and wife and parent and child is one of intense affection, and that to feel any other sentiment towards a member of one's family is to be a monster. Under the influence of the emotion thus manufactured the most detestable people are spoilt with entirely undeserved deference, obedience, and even affection whilst they live, and mourned when they die by those whose lives they wantonly or maliciously made miserable. And this is what we call natural conduct. Nothing could well be less natural. That such a convention should have been established shews that the indissolubility of marriage creates such intolerable situations that only by beglamoring the human imagination with a hypnotic suggestion of wholly unnatural feelings can it be made to keep up appearances.

If the sentimental theory of family relationship encourages bad manners and personal slovenliness and uncleanness in the home, it also, in the case of sentimental people, encourages the practice of rousing and playing on the affections of children prematurely and far too frequently. The lady who says that as her religion is love, her children shall be brought up in an atmosphere of love, and institutes a system of sedulous endearments and exchanges of presents and conscious and studied acts of artificial kindness, may be defeated in a large family by the healthy derision and rebellion of children who have acquired hardihood and common sense in their conflicts with one another. But the small families, which are the rule just now, succumb more easily; and in the case of a single sensitive child the effect of being forced in a hothouse atmosphere of unnatural affection may be disastrous.

In short, whichever way you take it, the convention that marriage and family relationship produce special feelings which alter the nature of human intercourse is a mischievous one. The whole difficulty of bringing up a family well is the difficulty of making its members behave as considerately at home as on a visit in a strange house, and as frankly, kindly, and easily in a strange house as at home. In the middle classes, where the segregation of the artificially limited family in its little brick box is horribly complete, bad manners, ugly dresses, awkwardness, cowardice, peevishness, and all the

petty vices of unsociability flourish like mushrooms in a
cellar. In the upper class, where families are not limited
for money reasons; where at least two houses and sometimes
three or four are the rule (not to mention the
clubs); where there is travelling and hotel life; and
where the men are brought up, not in the family, but in
public schools, universities, and the naval and military
services, besides being constantly in social training in
other people's houses, the result is to produce what may
be called, in comparison with the middle class, something
that might almost pass as a different and much more
sociable species. And in the very poorest class, where
people have no homes, only sleeping places, and consequently
live practically in the streets, sociability again
appears, leaving the middle class despised and disliked
for its helpless and offensive unsociability as much by
those below it as those above it, and yet ignorant enough
to be proud of it, and to hold itself up as a model for
the reform of the (as it considers) elegantly vicious rich
and profligate poor alike.

Carrying the War into the Enemy's Country

Without pretending to exhaust the subject, I have
said enough to make it clear that the moment we lose the
desire to defend our present matrimonial and family arrangements,
there will be no difficulty in making out an
overwhelming case against them. No doubt until then
we shall continue to hold up the British home as the
Holy of Holies in the temple of honorable motherhood,
innocent childhood, manly virtue, and sweet and wholesome
national life. But with a clever turn of the hand
this holy of holies can be exposed as an Augean stable,
so filthy that it would seem more hopeful to burn it down
than to attempt to sweep it out. And this latter view

will perhaps prevail if the idolaters of marriage persist in refusing all proposals for reform and treating those who advocate it as infamous delinquents. Neither view is of any use except as a poisoned arrow in a fierce fight between two parties determined to discredit each other with a view to obtaining powers of legal coercion over one another.

Shelley and Queen Victoria

The best way to avert such a struggle is to open the eyes of the thoughtlessly conventional people to the weakness of their position in a mere contest of recrimination. Hitherto they have assumed that they have the advantage of coming into the field without a stain on their characters to combat libertines who have no character at all. They conceive it to be their duty to throw mud; and they feel that even if the enemy can find any mud to throw, none of it will stick. They are mistaken. There will be plenty of that sort of ammunition in the other camp; and most of it will stick very hard indeed. The moral is, do not throw any. If we can imagine Shelley and Queen Victoria arguing out their differences in another world, we may be sure that the Queen has long ago found that she cannot settle the question by classing Shelley with George IV. as a bad man; and Shelley is not likely to have called her vile names on the general ground that as the economic dependence of women makes marriage a money bargain in which the man is the purchaser and the woman the purchased, there is no essential difference between a married woman and the woman of the streets. Unfortunately, all the people whose methods of controversy are represented by our popular newspapers are not Queen Victorias and Shelleys. A great mass of them, when their prejudices are challenged, have no other impulse than to call the challenger names, and, when the crowd seems to be on their side, to maltreat him personally or hand him over to the law, if he is vulnerable to it. Therefore I cannot say that I have any certainty that the marriage question will be dealt with decently and tolerantly. But dealt with it will be, decently or indecently; for the present state of things in England is too strained and mischievous to last. Europe and America have left us a century behind in this matter.

A Probable Effect of Giving Women the Vote

The political emancipation of women is likely to lead to a comparatively stringent enforcement by law of sexual morality (that is why so many of us dread it); and this will soon compel us to consider what our sexual morality shall be. At present a ridiculous distinction is made between vice and crime, in order that men may be vicious with impunity. Adultery, for instance, though it is sometimes fiercely punished by giving an injured husband crushing damages in a divorce suit (injured wives are not considered in this way), is not now directly prosecuted; and this impunity extends to illicit relations between unmarried persons who have reached what is called the age of consent. There are other matters, such as notification of contagious disease and solicitation, in which the hand of the law has been brought down on one sex only. Outrages which were capital offences within the memory of persons still living when committed on women outside marriage, can still be inflicted by men on their wives without legal remedy. At all such points the code will be screwed up by the operation of Votes for Women, if there be any virtue in the franchise at all. The result will be that men will find the more ascetic side of our sexual morality taken seriously by the law. It is easy to foresee the consequences. No man will take much trouble to alter laws which he can evade, or which are either not enforced or enforced on women only. But when these laws take him by the collar and thrust him into prison, he suddenly becomes keenly critical of them, and of the arguments by which they are supported. Now we have seen that our marriage laws will not stand criticism, and that they have held out so far only because they are so worked as to fit roughly our state of society, in which women are neither politically nor personally free, in which indeed women are called womanly only when they regard themselves as existing solely for the use of men. When Liberalism enfranchises them politically, and Socialism emancipates them economically, they will no longer allow the law to take immorality so easily. Both men and women will be forced to behave morally in sex matters; and when they find that this is inevitable they will raise the question of what behavior really should be established as moral. If they decide in favor of our present professed morality, they will have to make a revolutionary change in their habits by becoming in fact what they only pretend to be at present. If, on the other hand, they find that this would be an unbearable tyranny, without even the excuse of justice or sound eugenics, they will reconsider their morality and remodel the law.

The Personal Sentimental Basis of Monogamy

Monogamy has a sentimental basis which is quite distinct from the political one of equal numbers of the sexes. Equal numbers in the sexes are quite compatible with a change of partners every day or every hour. Physically there is nothing to distinguish human society from the farm-yard except that children are more troublesome and costly than chickens and calves, and that men and women are not so completely enslaved as farm stock. Accordingly, the people whose conception of marriage is a farm-yard or slave-quarter conception are always more or less in a panic lest the slightest relaxation of the marriage laws should utterly demoralize society; whilst those to whom marriage is a matter of more highly evolved sentiments and needs (sometimes said to be distinctively human, though birds and animals in a state of freedom evince them quite as touchingly as we) are much more liberal, knowing as they do that monogamy will take care of itself provided the parties are free enough, and that promiscuity is a product of slavery and not of liberty.

The solid foundation of their confidence is the fact that the relationship set up by a comfortable marriage is so intimate and so persuasive of the whole life of the parties to it, that nobody has room in his or her life for more than one such relationship at a time. What is called a household of three is never really of three except in the sense that every household becomes a household of three when a child is born, and may in the same way become a household of four or fourteen if the union be fertile enough. Now no doubt the marriage tie means so little to some people that the addition to the household of half a dozen more wives or husbands would be as possible as the addition of half a dozen governesses or tutors or visitors or servants. A Sultan may have fifty wives as easily as he may have fifty dishes on his table, because in the English sense he has no wives at all; nor have his wives any husband: in short, he is not what we call a married man. And there are sultans and sultanas and seraglios existing in England under English forms. But when you come to the real modern marriage of sentiment, a relation is created which has never to my knowledge been shared by three persons except when all three have been extraordinarily fond of one another. Take for example the famous case of Nelson and Sir William and Lady Hamilton. The secret of this household of three was not only that both the husband and Nelson were devoted to Lady Hamilton, but that they were also apparently devoted to one another. When Hamilton died both Nelson and Emma seem to have been equally heartbroken. When there is a successful household of one man and two women the same unusual condition is fulfilled: the two women not only cannot live happily without the man but cannot live happily without each other. In every other case known to me, either from observation or record, the experiment is a hopeless failure: one of the two rivals for the really intimate affection of the third inevitably drives out the other. The driven-out party may accept the situation and remain in the house as a friend to save appearances, or for the sake of the children, or for economic reasons; but such an arrangement can subsist only when the forfeited relation is no longer really valued; and this indifference, like the triple bond of affection which carried Sir William Hamilton through, is so rare as to be practicably negligible in the establishment of a conventional morality of marriage. Therefore sensible and experienced people always assume that when a declaration of love is made to an already married person, the declaration binds the parties in honor never to see one another again unless they contemplate divorce and remarriage. And this is a sound convention, even for unconventional people. Let me illustrate by reference to a fictitious case: the one imagined in my own play Candida will do as well as another. Here a young man who has been received as a friend into the house of a clergyman falls in love with the clergyman's wife, and, being young and inexperienced, declares his feelings, and claims that he, and not the clergyman, is the more suitable mate for the lady. The clergyman, who has a temper, is first tempted to hurl the youth into the street by bodily violence: an impulse natural, perhaps, but vulgar and improper, and not open, on consideration, to decent men. Even coarse and inconsiderate men are restrained from it by the fact that the sympathy of the woman turns naturally to the victim of physical brutality and against the bully, the Thackerayan notion to the contrary being one of the illusions of literary masculinity. Besides, the husband is not necessarily the stronger man: an appeal to force has resulted in the ignominious defeat of the husband quite as often as in poetic justice as conceived in the conventional novelet. What an honorable and sensible man does when his household is invaded is what the Reverend James Mavor Morell does in my play. He recognizes that just as there is not room for two women in that sacredly intimate relation of sentimental domesticity which is what marriage means to him, so there is no room for two men in that relation with his wife; and he accordingly tells her firmly that she must choose which man will occupy the place that is large enough for one only. He is so far shrewdly unconventional as to recognize that if she chooses the other man, he must give way, legal tie or no legal tie; but he knows that either one or the other must go. And a sensible wife would act in the same way. If a romantic young lady came into her house and proposed to adore her husband on a tolerated footing, she would say "My husband has not room in his life for two wives: either you go out of the house or I go out of it." The situation is not at all unlikely: I had almost said not at all unusual. Young ladies and gentlemen in the greensickly condition which is called calf-love, associating with married couples at dangerous periods of mature life, quite often find themselves in it; and the extreme reluctance of proud and sensitive people to avoid any assertion of matrimonial rights, or to condescend to jealousy, sometimes makes the threatened husband or wife hesitate to take prompt steps and do the apparently conventional thing. But whether they hesitate or act the result is always the same. In a real marriage of sentiment the wife or husband cannot be supplanted by halves; and such a marriage will break very soon under the strain of polygyny or polyandry. What we want at present is a sufficiently clear teaching of this fact to ensure that prompt and decisive action shall always be taken in such cases without any false shame of seeming conventional (a shame to which people capable of such real marriage are specially susceptible), and a rational divorce law to enable the marriage to be dissolved and the parties honorably resorted and recoupled without disgrace and scandal if that should prove the proper solution.

It must be repeated here that no law, however stringent, can prevent polygamy among groups of people who choose to live loosely and be monogamous only in appearance. But such cases are not now under consideration. Also, affectionate husbands like Samuel Pepys, and affectionate wives of the corresponding temperament, may, it appears, engage in transient casual adventures out of doors without breaking up their home life. But within doors that home life may be regarded as naturally monogamous. It does not need to be protected against polygamy: it protects itself.

Divorce

All this has an important bearing on the question of divorce. Divorce reformers are so much preoccupied with the injustice of forbidding a woman to divorce her husband for unfaithfulness to his marriage vow, whilst allowing him that power over her, that they are apt to overlook the pressing need for admitting other and far more important grounds for divorce. If we take a document like Pepys' Diary, we learn that a woman may have an incorrigibly unfaithful husband, and yet be much better off than if she had an ill-tempered, peevish, maliciously sarcastic one, or was chained for life to a criminal, a drunkard, a lunatic, an idle vagrant, or a person whose religious faith was contrary to her own. Imagine being married to a liar, a borrower, a mischief maker, a teaser or tormentor of children and animals, or even simply to a bore! Conceive yourself tied for life to one of the perfectly "faithful" husbands who are sentenced to a month's imprisonment occasionally for idly leaving their wives in childbirth without food, fire, or attendance! What woman would not rather marry ten Pepyses? what man a dozen Nell Gwynnes? Adultery, far from being the first and only ground for divorce, might more reasonably be made the last, or wholly excluded. The present law is perfectly logical only if you once admit (as no decent person ever does) its fundamental assumption that there can be no companionship between men and women because the woman has a "sphere" of her own, that of housekeeping, in which the man must not meddle, whilst he has all the rest of human activity for his sphere: the only point at which the two spheres touch being that of replenishing the population. On this assumption the man naturally asks for a guarantee that the children shall be his because he has to find the money to support them. The power of divorcing a woman for adultery is this guarantee, a guarantee that she does not need to protect her against a similar imposture on his part, because he cannot bear children. No doubt he can spend the money that ought to be spent on her children on another woman and her children; but this is desertion, which is a separate matter. The fact for us to seize is that in the eye of the law, adultery without consequences is merely a sentimental grievance, whereas the planting on one man of another man's offspring is a substantial one. And so, no doubt, it is; but the day has gone by for basing laws on the assumption that a woman is less to a man than his dog, and thereby encouraging and accepting the standards of the husbands who buy meat for their bull-pups and leave their wives and children hungry. That basis is the penalty we pay for having borrowed our religion from the East, instead of building up a religion of our own out of our western inspiration and western sentiment. The result is that we all believe that our religion is on its last legs, whereas the truth is that it is not yet born, though the age walks visibly pregnant with it. Meanwhile, as women are dragged down by their oriental servitude to our men, and as, further, women drag down those who degrade them quite as effectually as men do, there are moments when it is difficult to see anything in our sex institutions except a *police des mœurs* keeping the field for a competition as to which sex shall corrupt the other most.

Importance of Sentimental Grievances

Any tolerable western divorce law must put the sentimental grievances first, and should carefully avoid singling out any ground of divorce in such a way as to create a convention that persons having that ground are bound in honor to avail themselves of it. It is generally admitted that people should not be encouraged to petition for a divorce in a fit of petulance. What is not so clearly seen is that neither should they be encouraged to petition in a fit of jealousy, which is certainly the most detestable and mischievous of all the passions that enjoy public credit. Still less should people who are not jealous be urged to behave as if they were jealous, and to enter upon duels and divorce suits in which they have no desire to be successful. There should be no publication of the grounds on which a divorce is sought or granted; and as this would abolish the only means the public now has of ascertaining that every possible effort has been made to keep the couple united against their wills, such privacy will only be tolerated when we at last admit that the sole and sufficient reason why people should be granted a divorce is that they want one. Then there will be no more reports of divorce cases, no more letters read in court with an indelicacy that makes every sensitive person shudder and recoil as from a profanation, no more washing of household linen, dirty or clean, in public. We must learn in these matters to mind our own business and not impose our individual notions of propriety on one another, even if it carries us to the length of openly admitting what we are now compelled to assume silently, that every human being has a right to sexual experience, and that the law is concerned only with parentage, which is now a separate matter.

Divorce Without Asking Why

The one question that should never be put to a petitioner for divorce is " Why ? " When a man appeals to a magistrate for protection from someone who threatens to kill him, on the simple ground that he desires to live, the magistrate might quite reasonably ask him why he desires to live, and why the person who wishes to kill him should not be gratified. Also whether he can prove that his life is a pleasure to himself or a benefit to anyone else, and whether it is good for him to be encouraged to exaggerate the importance of his short span in this vale of tears rather than to keep himself constantly ready to meet his God.

The only reason for not raising these very weighty points is that we find society unworkable except on the

assumption that every man has a natural right to live.
Nothing short of his own refusal to respect that right in
others can reconcile the community to killing him. From
this fundamental right many others are derived. The
American Constitution, one of the few modern political
documents drawn up by men who were forced by the
sternest circumstances to think out what they really had
to face instead of chopping logic in a university class-
room, specifies "liberty and the pursuit of happiness"
as natural rights. The terms are too vague to be of much
practical use; for the supreme right to life, extended as
it now must be to the life of the race, and to the quality
of life as well as to the mere fact of breathing, is making
short work of many ancient liberties, and exposing the
pursuit of happiness as perhaps the most miserable of
human occupations. Nevertheless, the American Constitution roughly expresses the conditions to which modern democracy commits us. To impose marriage on two
unmarried people who do not desire to marry one another would be admittedly an act of enslavement. But
it is no worse than to impose a continuation of marriage
on people who have ceased to desire to be married. It
will be said that the parties may not agree on that; that
one may desire to maintain the marriage the other wishes
to dissolve. But the same hardship arises whenever a
man in love proposes marriage to a woman and is refused. The refusal is so painful to him that he often
threatens to kill himself and sometimes even does it.
Yet we expect him to face his ill luck, and never dream
of forcing the woman to accept him. His case is the
same as that of the husband whose wife tells him she no
longer cares for him, and desires the marriage to be
dissolved. You will say, perhaps, if you are superstitious, that it is not the same—that marriage makes a
difference. You are wrong: there is no magic in marriage. If there were, married couples would never de-

sire to separate. But they do. And when they do, it is simple slavery to compel them to remain together.

Economic Slavery Again the Root Difficulty

The husband, then, is to be allowed to discard his wife when he is tired of her, and the wife the husband when another man strikes her fancy? One must reply unhesitatingly in the affirmative; for if we are to deny every proposition that can be stated in offensive terms by its opponents, we shall never be able to affirm anything at all. But the question reminds us that until the economic independence of women is achieved, we shall have to remain impaled on the other horn of the dilemma and maintain marriage as a slavery. And here let me ask the Government of the day (1910) a question with regard to the Labor Exchanges it has very wisely established throughout the country. What do these Exchanges do when a woman enters and states that her occupation is that of a wife and mother; that she is out of a job; and that she wants an employer? If the Exchanges refuse to entertain her application, they are clearly excluding nearly the whole female sex from the benefit of the Act. If not, they must become matrimonial agencies, unless, indeed, they are prepared to become something worse by putting the woman down as a housekeeper and introducing her to an employer without making marriage a condition of the hiring.

Labor Exchanges and the White Slavery

Suppose, again, a woman presents herself at the Labor Exchange, and states her trade as that of a White Slave, meaning the unmentionable trade pursued by many thousands of women in all civilized cities. Will the

Preface

Labor Exchange find employers for her? If not, what will it do with her? If it throws her back destitute and unhelped on the streets to starve, it might as well not exist as far as she is concerned; and the problem of unemployment remains unsolved at its most painful point. Yet if it finds honest employment for her and for all the unemployed wives and mothers, it must find new places in the world for women; and in so doing it must achieve for them economic independence of men. And when this is done, can we feel sure that any woman will consent to be a wife and mother (not to mention the less respectable alternative) unless her position is made as eligible as that of the women for whom the Labor Exchanges are finding independent work? Will not many women now engaged in domestic work under circumstances which make it repugnant to them, abandon it and seek employment under other circumstances? As unhappiness in marriage is almost the only discomfort sufficiently irksome to induce a woman to break up her home, and economic dependence the only compulsion sufficiently stringent to force her to endure such unhappiness, the solution of the problem of finding independent employment for women may cause a great number of childless unhappy marriages to break up spontaneously, whether the marriage laws are altered or not. And here we must extend the term childless marriages to cover households in which the children have grown up and gone their own way, leaving the parents alone together: a point at which many worthy couples discover for the first time that they have long since lost interest in one another, and have been united only by a common interest in their children. We may expect, then, that marriages which are maintained by economic pressure alone will dissolve when that pressure is removed; and as all the parties to them will certainly not accept a celibate life, the law must sanction the dissolution in order to prevent a recurrence of the scandal which has moved the Government to appoint the Commission now sitting to investigate the marriage question: the scandal, that is, of a great number of persons, condemned to celibacy by magisterial separation orders, and, of course, refusing to submit to the condemnation, forming illicit connections to an extent which threatens to familiarize the working classes with an open disuse of marriage. In short, once set women free from their economic slavery, and you will find that unless divorce is made as easy as the dissolution of a business partnership, the practice of dispensing with marriage will presently become so common that conventional couples will be ashamed to get married.

Divorce Favorable to Marriage

Divorce, in fact, is not the destruction of marriage, but the first condition of its maintenance. A thousand indissoluble marriages mean a thousand marriages and no more. A thousand divorces may mean two thousand marriages; for the couples may marry again. Divorce only re-assorts the couples: a very desirable thing when they are ill-assorted. Also, it makes people much more willing to marry, especially prudent people and proud people with a high sense of self-respect. Further, the fact that a divorce is possible often prevents its being petitioned for, not only because it puts married couples on their good behavior towards one another, but because, as no room feels like a prison if the door is left open, the removal of the sense of bondage would at once make marriage much happier than it is now. Also, if the door were always open, there would be no need to rush through it as there is now when it opens for one moment in a lifetime, and may never open again.

From this point of view England has the worst civil marriage law in the world, with the exception of silly

South Carolina. In every other reasonably civilized country the grounds on which divorce can be granted admit of so wide an interpretation that all unhappy marriages can be dissolved without resorting to the shameful shifts imposed by our law. Yet the figures just given to the Royal Commission shew that in the State of Washington, where there are eleven different grounds of divorce, and where, in fact, divorce can be had for the asking at a negligible cost, the divorce rate is only 184 per 100,000 of the population, which, if we assume that the 100,000 people represent 20,000 families, means less than one per cent of domestic failures. In Japan the rate is 215, which is said to be the highest on record. This is not very alarming: what is quite hideous is that the rate in England is only 2, a figure which, if we assume that human nature is much the same in Walworth as in Washington, must represent a frightful quantity of useless unhappiness and clandestine polygamy. I am not forgetting my own demonstration that the rate is kept down in Washington by the economic slavery of women; but I must point out that this is at its worst in the middle classes only, because a woman of the working class can turn to and support herself, however poorly; and a woman of the upper classes usually has some property. And in all classes we may guess that the object of many divorces is not the resumption of a single life, but a change of partners. As this change can be effected easily under the existing law in the State of Washington it is not certain that the economic emancipation of women would alter the rate there to any startling extent. What is certain is that it could not conceivably raise it to a figure at which even the most panicky alarmist could persuade sensible people that the whole social fabric was tumbling to pieces. When journalists and bishops and American Presidents and other simple people describe this Washington result as alarming, they are speaking as a peasant speaks of a motor car or an aeroplane when he sees one for the first time. All he means is that he is not used to it and therefore fears that it may injure him. Every advance in civilization frightens these honest folk. This is a pity; but if we were to spare their feelings we should never improve the world at all. To let them frighten us, and then pretend that their stupid timidity is virtue and purity and so forth, is simply moral cowardice.

Male Economic Slavery and The Rights of Bachelors

It must not be forgotten that the refusal to accept the indignities, risks, hardships, softships, and divided duties of marriage is not confined to our voluntary old maids. There are men of the mould of Beethoven and Samuel Butler, whom one can hardly conceive as married men. There are the great ecclesiastics, who will not own two loyalties: one to the Church and one to the hearth. There are men like Goethe, who marry late and reluctantly solely because they feel that they cannot in honest friendship refuse the status of marriage to any woman of whose attachment to them they have taken any compromizing advantage, either in fact or in appearance. No sensible man can, under existing circumstances, advise a woman to keep house with a man without insisting on his marrying her, unless she is independent of conventional society (a state of things which can occur only very exceptionally); and a man of honor cannot advise a woman to do for his sake what he would not advise her to do for anyone else's. The result is that our Beethovens and Butlers—of whom, in their ordinary human aspect, there are a good many—become barren old bachelors, and rather savage ones at that.

Preface

Another difficulty which we always think of in connection with women, but which is by no means without its application to men, is the economic one. The number of men who cannot afford to marry is large enough to produce very serious social results; and the higher the work the man is doing, the more likely he is to find himself in this class until he has reached or passed middle age. The higher departments of science, law, philosophy, poetry, and the fine arts are notoriously starved in youth and early manhood: the marriageable age there, economically speaking, is nearer fifty than twenty. Even in business the leading spirits seldom reach a position of security until they are far beyond the age at which celibacy is tolerable. Account must also be taken of the younger sons of the propertied classes, brought up in households in which the rate of expenditure, though ten times that possible on a younger son's portion, yet represents the only habit of life he has learnt.

Taking all these cases as representing a bachelor class, and bearing in mind that though a man who marries at forty is not called a bachelor, yet he has for twenty years of his adult life been one, and therefore produced all the social problems that arise out of the existence of unmarried men, we must not shrink from asking whether all these gentlemen are celibates, even though we know that the question must be answered very emphatically in the negative. Some of them marry women of property, thereby reproducing the economic dependence of women on men with the sexes reversed. But there are so few women of property available for this purpose in comparison with the number of bachelors who cannot afford to marry, that this resource does not solve the problem of the bachelor who cannot afford a wife. If there were no other resources available, bachelors would make love to the wives and daughters of their friends. This being morally inadmissible, a demand arises for a cheap temporary substitute for marriage. A class of women must be found to protect the wives and the daughters of the married by keeping company with the bachelors for hire for as long or as short a time as the bachelor can afford, on the understanding that no claim is to be made on him after the hiring is ended. And such an institution, as we know, exists among us. It is commonly spoken of and thought of as an offence against our marriage morality; but all the experts who write scientific treatises on marriage seem to be agreed that it is, on the contrary, a necessary part of that morality, and must stand and fall with it.

I do not myself think that this view will bear examination. In my play, Mrs Warren's Profession, I have shewn that the institution in question is an economic phenomenon, produced by our underpayment and illtreatment of women who try to earn an honest living. I am aware that for some reason scientific writers are perversely impatient of this view, and, to discredit it, quote police lists of the reasons given by the victims for adopting their trade, and insist on the fact that poverty is not often alleged. But this means only that the actual word is seldom used. If a prisonful of thieves were asked what induced them to take to thieving, and some replied Poverty, and others Hunger, and others Desire for Excitement, no one would deny that the three answers were really one answer—that poverty means hunger, an intolerable lack of variety and pleasure, and, in short, all sorts of privations. When a girl, similarly interrogated, says she wanted fine clothes, or more fun, or the like, she is really saying that she lacked what no woman with plenty of money need lack. The fact that, according to the testimony of men who profess experience in such matters, you may search Europe in vain for a woman in this trade who has the table manners of a lady, shews that prostitution is not a vocation but a slavery to which women are driven by the miseries of honest poverty. When every young woman has an honorable and comfortable livelihood open to her on reasonable terms, the streets will make no more recruits. When every young man can afford to marry, and marriage reform makes it easy to dissolve unions contracted by young and inexperienced people in the event of their turning out badly, or of one of the pair achieving a position neither comfortable nor suitable for the other, both prostitution and bachelordom will die a natural death. Until then, all talk of "purification" is idle. It is for that reason, and also because they have been so fully dealt with by Havelock Ellis and numerous foreign writers on the psychology and physiology of sex, that I lay little stress on prostitution here.

The Pathology of Marriage

I shall also say as little as possible of the pathology of marriage and its kerbstone breakwater. Only, as there seems to be no bottom to the abyss of public ignorance on the subject, I am compelled to warn my readers that marriage has a pathology and even a criminology. But they are both so frightful that they have been dealt with not only in such treatises as those of Havelock, Ellis, Fournier, Duclaux, and many German writers, but in such comparatively popular works as The Heavenly Twins by Sarah Grand, and several of the plays of Brieux: notably Les Avariés, Les Trois Filles de M. Dupont, and Maternité. I purposely pass them by quickly, not only because attention has already been called to them by these devoted writers, but because my mission is not to deal with obvious horrors, but to open the eyes of normal respectable men to evils which are escaping their consideration.

As to the evils of disease and contagion, our consciences are sound enough: what is wrong with us is ignorance of the facts. No doubt this is a very formidable ignorance in a country where the first cry of the soul is "Dont tell me: I dont want to know," and where frantic denials and furious suppressions indicate everywhere the cowardice and want of faith which conceives life as something too terrible to be faced. In this particular case " I dont want to know " takes a righteous air, and becomes "I dont want to know anything about the diseases which are the just punishment of wretches who should not be mentioned in my presence or in any book that is intended for family reading." Wicked and foolish as the spirit of this attitude is, the practice of it is so easy and lazy and uppish that it is very common. But its cry is drowned by a louder and more sincere one. We who do not want to know also do not want to go blind, to go mad, to be disfigured, to be barren, to become pestiferous, or to see such things happening to our children. We learn, at last, that the majority of the victims are not the people of whom we so glibly say "Serve them right," but quite innocent children and innocent parents, smitten by a contagion which, no matter in what vice it may or may not have originated, contaminates the innocent and the guilty alike once it is launched exactly as any other contagious disease does; that indeed it often hits the innocent and misses the guilty because the guilty know the danger and take elaborate precautions against it, whilst the innocent, who have been either carefully kept from any knowledge of their danger, or erroneously led to believe that contagion is possible through misconduct only, run into danger blindfold. Once knock this fact into people's minds, and their self-righteous indifference and intolerance soon change into lively concern for themselves and their families.

The Criminology of Marriage

The pathology of marriage involves the possibility of the most horrible crime imaginable: that of the person who, when suffering from contagious disease, forces the contagion on another person by an act of violence. Such an act occurring between unmarried people would, within the memory of persons now living, have exposed the aggressor to the penalty of death; and it is still punished unmercifully by an extreme term of penal servitude when it occurs, as it sometimes does, through the hideous countryside superstition that it effects a cure when the victim is a virgin. Marriage makes this outrage absolutely legal. You may with impunity do to the person to whom you are married what you may not do to the most despised outcast of the streets. And this is only the extreme instance of the outlawry which our marriage laws effect. In our anxiety to provide for ourselves a little private Alsatia in which we can indulge ourselves as we please without reproach or interference from law, religion, or even conscience (and this is what marriage has come to mean to many of us), we have forgotten that we cannot escape restraints without foregoing rights; that all the laws that are needed to compel strangers to respect us are equally if not more necessary to compel our husbands and wives to respect us; and that society without law, whether between two or two million persons, means tyranny and slavery.

If the incorrigible sentimentalists here raise their little pipe of " Not if they love one another," I tell them, with such patience as is possible, that if they had ever had five minutes experience of love they would know that love is itself a tyranny requiring special safeguards; that people will perpetrate " for the sake of " those they love, exactions and submissions that they would never dream of proposing to or suffering from those they dislike or regard with indifference; that healthy marriages are partnerships of companionable and affectionate friendship; that cases of chronic life-long love, whether sentimental or sensual, ought to be sent to the doctor if not to the executioner; and that honorable men and women, when their circumstances permit it, are so far from desiring to be placed helplessly at one another's mercy that they employ every device the law now admits of, from the most stringent marriage settlements to the employment of separate legal advisers, to neutralize the Alsatian evils of the marriage law.

Does it Matter?

A less obviously silly evasion, and one which has a greater air of common sense, is "After all, seeing that most couples get on very well together, does it matter so much?" The same reply might be made by a lazy magistrate when asked for a warrant to arrest a burglar, or by a sleepy fireman wakened by a midnight call for his fire-escape. "After all, very few people have their houses broken into; and fewer still have them burnt. Does it matter?" But tell the magistrate or fireman that it is *his* house that has been broken into, or *his* house that has been burnt, and you will be startled by the change in his attitude. Because a mass of people have shaken down into comfort enough to satisfy them, or at least to cause them no more discomfort than they are prepared to put up with for the sake of a quiet life, less lucky and more sensitive and conscientious people should not be condemned to expose themselves to intolerable wrongs. Besides, people ought not to be content with the marriage law as it is merely because it is not often unbearably uncomfortable. Slaves are very often much more comfortable both in body and mind than fully responsible free men. That does not excuse anybody for embracing slavery. It is no doubt a great pity, from many points of view, that we were not conquered by Napoleon, or even by Bismarck and Moltke. None the less we should have been rightly despised if we had not been prepared to fight them for the right to misgovern ourselves.

But, as I have said, I am content, in this matter of the evils of our marriage law, to take care of the pence and let the pounds take care of themselves. The crimes and diseases of marriage will force themselves on public attention by their own virulence. I mention them here only because they reveal certain habits of thought and feeling with regard to marriage of which we must rid ourselves if we are to act sensibly when we take the necessary reforms in hand.

Christian Marriage

First among these is the habit of allowing ourselves to be bound not only by the truths of the Christian religion but by the excesses and extravagances which the Christian movement acquired in its earlier days as a violent reaction against what it still calls paganism. By far the most dangerous of these, because it is a blasphemy against life, and, to put it in Christian terms, an accusation of indecency against God, is the notion that sex, with all its operations, is in itself absolutely an obscene thing, and that an immaculate conception is a miracle. So unwholesome an absurdity could only have gained ground under two conditions: one, a reaction against a society in which sensual luxury had been carried to revolting extremes, and, two, a belief that the world was coming to an end, and that therefore sex was no longer a necessity. Christianity, because it began under these conditions, made sexlessness and Communism the two main practical articles of its propaganda; and it has never quite lost its original bias in these directions. In spite of the putting off of the Second Coming from the lifetime of the apostles to the millennium, and of the great disappointment of the year 1000 A.D., in which multitudes of Christians seriously prepared for the end of the world, the prophet who announces that the end is at hand is still popular. Many of the people who ridicule his demonstrations that the fantastic monsters of the book of Revelation are among us in the persons of our own political contemporaries, and who proceed sanely in all their affairs on the assumption that the world is going to last, really do believe that there will be a Judgment Day, and that it *might* even be in their own time. A thunderstorm, an eclipse, or any very unusual weather will make them apprehensive and uncomfortable.

This explains why, for a long time, the Christian Church refused to have anything to do with marriage. The result was, not the abolition of sex, but its excommunication. And, of course, the consequences of persuading people that matrimony was an unholy state were so grossly carnal, that the Church had to execute a complete right-about-face, and try to make people understand that it was a holy state: so holy indeed that it could not be validly inaugurated without the blessing of the Church. And by this teaching it did something to atone for its earlier blasphemy. But the mischief of chopping and changing your doctrine to meet this or that practical emergency instead of keeping it adjusted to the whole scheme of life, is that you end by having half-a-dozen contradictory doctrines to suit half-a-dozen different emergencies. The Church solemnized and sanctified marriage without ever giving up its original Pauline doctrine on the subject. And it soon fell into another confusion. At the point at which it took up marriage and endeavored to make it holy, marriage was, as it still is, largely a survival of the custom of selling women to men.

Now in all trades a marked difference is made in price between a new article and a second-hand one. The moment we meet with this difference in value betwen human beings, we may know that we are in the slave-market, where the conception of our relations to the persons sold is neither religious nor natural nor human nor superhuman, but simply commercial. The Church, when it finally gave its blessing to marriage, did not, in its innocence, fathom these commercial traditions. Consequently it tried to sanctify them too, with grotesque results. The slave-dealer having always asked more money for virginity, the Church, instead of detecting the money-changer and driving him out of the temple, took him for a sentimental and chivalrous lover, and, helped by its only half-discarded doctrine of celibacy, gave virginity a heavenly value to ennoble its commercial pretensions. In short, Mammon, always mighty, put the Church in his pocket, where he keeps it to this day, in spite of the occasional saints and martyrs who contrive from time to time to get their heads and souls free to testify against him.

Divorce a Sacramental Duty

But Mammon overreached himself when he tried to impose his doctrine of inalienable property on the Church under the guise of indissoluble marriage. For the Church tried to shelter this inhuman doctrine and flat contradiction of the gospel by claiming, and rightly claiming, that marriage is a sacrament. So it is; but that is exactly what makes divorce a duty when the marriage has lost the inward and spiritual grace of which the marriage ceremony is the outward and visible sign. In vain do bishops stoop to pick up the discarded arguments of the atheists of fifty years ago by pleading that the words of Jesus were in an obscure Aramaic dialect, and were probably misunderstood, as Jesus, they think, could not have said anything a bishop would disapprove of. Unless they are prepared to add that the statement that those who take the sacrament with their lips but not with their hearts eat and drink their own damnation is also a mistranslation from the Aramaic, they are most solemnly bound to shield marriage from profanation, not merely by permitting divorce, but by making it compulsory in certain cases as the Chinese do.

When the great protest of the XVI century came, and the Church was reformed in several countries, the Reformation was so largely a rebellion against sacerdotalism that marriage was very nearly excommunicated again: our modern civil marriage, round which so many fierce controversies and political conflicts have raged, would have been thoroughly approved of by Calvin, and hailed with relief by Luther. But the instinctive doctrine that there is something holy and mystic in sex, a doctrine which many of us now easily dissociate from any priestly ceremony, but which in those days seemed to all who felt it to need a ritual affirmation, could not be thrown on the scrap-heap with the sale of Indulgences and the like; and so the Reformation left marriage where it was: a curious mixture of commercial sex slavery, early Christian sex abhorrence, and later Christian sex sanctification.

Othello and Desdemona

How strong was the feeling that a husband or a wife is an article of property, greatly depreciated in value at second-hand, and not to be used or touched by any person but the proprietor, may be learnt from Shakespear. His most infatuated and passionate lovers are Antony and Othello; yet both of them betray the commercial and proprietary instinct the moment they lose their tempers.

Preface

"I found you," says Antony, reproaching Cleopatra, "as a morsel cold upon dead Cæsar's trencher." Othello's worst agony is the thought of "keeping a corner in the thing he loves for others' uses." But this is not what a man feels about the thing he loves, but about the thing he owns. I never understood the full significance of Othello's outburst until I one day heard a lady, in the course of a private discussion as to the feasibility of "group marriage," say with cold disgust that she would as soon think of lending her toothbrush to another woman as her husband. The sense of outraged manhood with which I felt myself and all other husbands thus reduced to the rank of a toilet appliance gave me a very unpleasant taste of what Desdemona might have felt had she overheard Othello's outburst. I was so dumfounded that I had not the presence of mind to ask the lady whether she insisted on having a doctor, a nurse, a dentist, and even a priest and solicitor all to herself as well. But I had too often heard men speak of women as if they were mere personal conveniences to feel surprised that exactly the same view is held, only more fastidiously, by women.

All these views must be got rid of before we can have any healthy public opinion (on which depends our having a healthy population) on the subject of sex, and consequently of marriage. Whilst the subject is considered shameful and sinful we shall have no systematic instruction in sexual hygiene, because such lectures as are given in Germany, France, and even prudish America (where the great Miltonic tradition in this matter still lives) will be considered a corruption of that youthful innocence which now subsists on nasty stories and whispered traditions handed down from generation to generation of school-children: stories and traditions which conceal nothing of sex but its dignity, its honor, its sacredness, its rank as the first necessity of society and the deepest concern of the nation. We shall continue to maintain the White Slave Trade and protect its exploiters by, on the one hand, tolerating the white slave as the necessary breakwater of marriage; and, on the other, trampling on her and degrading her until she has nothing to hope from our Courts; and so, with policemen at every corner, and law triumphant all over Europe, she will still be smuggled and cattle-driven from one end of the civilized world to the other, cheated, beaten, bullied, and hunted into the streets to disgusting overwork, without daring to utter the cry for help that brings, not rescue, but exposure and infamy, yet revenging herself terribly in the end by scattering blindness and sterility, pain and disfigurement, insanity and death among us with the certainty that we are much too pious and genteel to allow such things to be mentioned with a view to saving either her or ourselves from them. And all the time we shall keep enthusiastically investing her trade with every allurement that the art of the novelist, the playwright, the dancer, the milliner, the painter, the limelight man, and the sentimental poet can devize, after which we shall continue to be very much shocked and surprised when the cry of the youth, of the young wife, of the mother, of the infected nurse, and of all the other victims, direct and indirect, arises with its invariable refrain: " Why did nobody warn me? "

What is to become of the Children?

I must not reply flippantly, Make them all Wards in Chancery; yet that would be enough to put any sensible person on the track of the reply. One would think, to hear the way in which people sometimes ask the question, that not only does marriage prevent the difficulty from ever arising, but that nothing except divorce can ever raise it. It is true that if you divorce the parents, the children have to be disposed of. But if you hang the parents, or imprison the parents, or take the children out of the custody of the parents because they hold Shelley's opinions, or if the parents die, the same difficulty arises. And as these things have happened again and again, and as we have had plenty of experience of divorce decrees and separation orders, the attempt to use children as an obstacle to divorce is hardly worth arguing with. We shall deal with the children just as we should deal with them if their homes were broken up by any other cause. There is a sense in which children are a real obstacle to divorce: they give parents a common interest which keeps together many a couple who, if childless, would separate. The marriage law is superfluous in such cases. This is shewn by the fact that the proportion of childless divorces is much larger than the proportion of divorces from all causes. But it must not be forgotten that the interest of the children forms one of the most powerful arguments for divorce. An unhappy household is a bad nursery. There is something to be said for the polygynous or polyandrous household as a school for children: children really do suffer from having too few parents: this is why uncles and aunts and tutors and governesses are often so good for children. But it is just the polygamous household which our marriage law allows to be broken up, and which, as we have seen, is not possible as a typical institution in a democratic country where the numbers of the sexes are about equal. Therefore polygyny and polyandry as a means of educating children fall to the ground, and with them, I think, must go the opinion which has been expressed by Gladstone and others, that an extension of divorce, whilst admitting many new grounds for it, might exclude the ground of adultery. There are, however, clearly many things that make some of our domestic interiors little private hells for children (especially when the children are quite content in them) which would justify any intelligent State in breaking up the home and giving the custody of the children either to the parent whose conscience had revolted against the corruption of the children, or to neither.

Which brings me to the point that divorce should no longer be confined to cases in which one of the parties petitions for it. If, for instance, you have a thoroughly rascally couple making a living by infamous means and bringing up their children to their trade, the king's proctor, instead of pursuing his present purely mischievous function of preventing couples from being divorced by proving that they both desire it, might very well intervene and divorce these children from their parents. At present, if the Queen herself were to rescue some unfortunate child from degradation and misery and place her in a respectable home, and some unmentionable pair of blackguards claimed the child and proved that they were its father and mother, the child would be given to them in the name of the sanctity of the home and the holiness of parentage, after perpetrating which crime, the law would calmly send an education officer to take the child out of the parents' hands several hours a day in the still more sacred name of compulsory education. (Of course what would really happen would be that the couple would blackmail the Queen for their consent to the salvation of the child, unless, indeed, a hint from a police inspector convinced them that bad characters cannot always rely on pedantically constitutional treatment when they come into conflict with persons in high station).

The truth is, not only must the bond between man and wife be made subject to a reasonable consideration of the welfare of the parties concerned and of the community, but the whole family bond as well. The theory that the wife is the property of the husband or the husband of the wife is not a whit less abhorrent and mischievous than the theory that the child is the property of the parent. Parental bondage will go the way of conjugal bondage: indeed the order of reform should rather be put the other way about; for the helplessness of children has already compelled the State to intervene between parent and child more than between husband and wife. If you pay less than £40 a year rent, you will sometimes feel tempted to say to the vaccination officer, the school attendance officer, and the sanitary inspector: " Is this child mine or yours?" The answer is that as the child is a vital part of the nation, the nation cannot afford to leave it at the irresponsible disposal of any individual or couple of individuals as a mere small parcel of private property. The only solid ground that the parent can take is that as the State, in spite of its imposing name, can, when all is said, do nothing with the child except place it in the charge of some human being or another, the parent is no worse a custodian than a stranger. And though this proposition may seem highly questionable at first sight to those who imagine that only parents spoil children, yet those who realize that children are as often spoilt by severity and coldness as by indulgence, and that the notion that natural parents are any worse than adopted parents is probably as complete an illusion as the notion that they are any better, see no serious likelihood that State action will detach children from their parents more than it does at present: nay, it is even likely that the present system of taking the children out of the parents' hands and having the parental duty performed by officials, will, as poverty and ignorance become the exception instead of the rule, give way to the system of simply requiring certain results, beginning with the baby's weight and ending perhaps with some sort of practical arts degree, but leaving parents and children to achieve the results as they best may. Such freedom is, of course, impossible in our present poverty-

stricken circumstances. As long as the masses of our
people are too poor to be good parents or good anything
else except beasts of burden, it is no use requiring much
more from them but hewing of wood and drawing of
water: whatever is to be done must be done *for* them,
mostly, alas! by people whose superiority is merely technical.
Until we abolish poverty it is impossible to push
rational measures of any kind very far: the wolf at the
door will compel us to live in a state of siege and to do
everything by a bureaucratic martial law that would be
quite unnecessary and indeed intolerable in a prosperous
community. But however we settle the question, we
must make the parent justify his custody of the child
exactly as we should make a stranger justify it. If a
family is not achieving the purposes of a family it should
be dissolved just as a marriage should when it, too, is
not achieving the purposes of marriage. The notion
that there is or ever can be anything magical and inviolable
in the legal relations of domesticity, and the curious
confusion of ideas which makes some of our bishops imagine
that in the phrase " Whom God hath joined," the
word God means the district registrar or the Reverend
John Smith or William Jones, must be got rid of. Means
of breaking up undesirable families are as necessary to
the preservation of the family as means of dissolving undesirable
marriages are to the preservation of marriage.
If our domestic laws are kept so inhuman that they at
last provoke a furious general insurrection against them
as they already provoke many private ones, we shall in
a very literal sense empty the baby out with the bath by
abolishing an institution which needs nothing more than
a little obvious and easy rationalizing to make it not only
harmless but comfortable, honorable, and useful.

The Cost of Divorce

But please do not imagine that the evils of indissoluble marriage can be cured by divorce laws administered on our present plan. The very cheapest undefended divorce, even when conducted by a solicitor for its own sake and that of humanity, costs at least £30 out-of-pocket expenses. To a client on business terms it costs about three times as much. Until divorce is as cheap as marriage, marriage will remain indissoluble for all except the handful of people to whom £100 is a procurable sum. For the enormous majority of us there is no difference in this respect between a hundred and a quadrillion. Divorce is the one thing you may not sue for *in forma pauperis*.

Let me, then, recommend as follows:

1. Make divorce as easy, as cheap, and as private as marriage.

2. Grant divorce at the request of either party, whether the other consents or not; and admit no other ground than the request, which should be made without stating any reasons.

3. Confine the power of dissolving marriage for misconduct to the State acting on the petition of the king's proctor or other suitable functionary, who may, however, be moved by either party to intervene in ordinary request cases, not to prevent the divorce taking place, but to enforce alimony if it be refused and the case is one which needs it.

4. Make it impossible for marriage to be used as a punishment as it is at present. Send the husband and wife to penal servitude if you disapprove of their conduct and want to punish them; but do not send them back to perpetual wedlock.

5. If, on the other hand, you think a couple perfectly innocent and well conducted, do not condemn them also

to perpetual wedlock against their wills, thereby making the treatment of what you consider innocence on both sides the same as the treatment of what you consider guilt on both sides.

6. Place the work of a wife and mother on the same footing as other work: that is, on the footing of labor worthy of its hire; and provide for unemployment in it exactly as for unemployment in shipbuilding or any other recognized bread-winning trade.

7. And take and deal with all the consequences of these acts of justice instead of letting yourself be frightened out of reason and good sense by fear of consequences. We must finally adapt our institutions to human nature. In the long run our present plan of trying to force human nature into a mould of existing abuses, superstitions, and corrupt interests, produces the explosive forces that wreck civilization.

8. Never forget that if you leave your law to judges and your religion to bishops, you will presently find yourself without either law or religion. If you doubt this, ask any decent judge or bishop. Do *not* ask somebody who does not know what a judge is, or what a bishop is, or what the law is, or what religion is. In other words, do not ask your newspaper. Journalists are too poorly paid in this country to know anything that is fit for publication.

Conclusions

To sum up, we have to depend on the solution of the problem of unemployment, probably on the principles laid down in the Minority Report of the Royal Commission on the Poor Law, to make the sexual relations between men and women decent and honorable by making women economically independent of men, and (in the younger son section of the upper classes) men economically independent of women. We also have to bring ourselves into line with the rest of Protestant civilization by providing means for dissolving all unhappy, improper, and inconvenient marriages. And, as it is our cautious custom to lag behind the rest of the world to see how their experiments in reform turn out before venturing ourselves, and then take advantage of their experience to get ahead of them, we should recognize that the ancient system of specifying grounds for divorce, such as adultery, cruelty, drunkenness, felony, insanity, vagrancy, neglect to provide for wife and children, desertion, public defamation, violent temper, religious heterodoxy, contagious disease, outrages, indignities, personal abuse, " mental anguish," conduct rendering life burdensome and so forth (all these are examples from some code actually in force at present), is a mistake, because the only effect of compelling people to plead and prove misconduct is that cases are manufactured and clean linen purposely smirched and washed in public, to the great distress and disgrace of innocent children and relatives, whilst the grounds have at the same time to be made so general that any sort of human conduct may be brought within them by a little special pleading and a little mental reservation on the part of witnesses examined on oath. When it comes to " conduct rendering life burdensome," it is clear that no marriage is any longer indissoluble; and the sensible thing to do then is to grant divorce whenever it is desired, without asking why.

GETTING MARRIED

On a fine morning in the spring of 1908 *the Norman kitchen in the Palace of the Bishop of Chelsea looks very spacious and clean and handsome and healthy.*

The Bishop is lucky enough to have a XII century palace. The palace itself has been lucky enough to escape being carved up into XV century Gothic, or shaved into XVIII century ashlar, or " restored " by a XIX century builder and a Victorian architect with a deep sense of the umbrella-like gentlemanliness of XIV century vaulting. The present occupant, A. Chelsea, unofficially Alfred Bridgenorth, appreciates Norman work. He has, by adroit complaints of the discomfort of the place, induced the Ecclesiastical Commissioners to give him some money to spend on it; and with this he has got rid of the wall papers, the paint, the partitions, the exquisitely planed and moulded casings with which the Victorian cabinetmakers enclosed and hid the huge black beams of hewn oak, and of all other expedients of his predecessors to make themselves feel at home and respectable in a Norman fortress. It is a house built to last for ever. The walls and beams are big enough to carry the tower of Babel, as if the builders, anticipating our modern ideas and instinctively defying them, had resolved to shew how much material they could lavish on a house built for the glory of God, instead of keeping a

competitive eye on the advantage of sending in the lowest
tender, and scientifically calculating how little material
would be enough to prevent the whole affair from tumbling down by its own weight.

    The kitchen is the Bishop's favorite room. This is not
at all because he is a man of humble mind; but because
the kitchen is one of the finest rooms in the house. The
Bishop has neither the income nor the appetite to have
his cooking done there. The windows, high up in the
wall, look north and south. The north window is the
largest; and if we look into the kitchen through it we see
facing us the south wall with small Norman windows
and an open door near the corner to the left. Through
this door we have a glimpse of the garden, and of a garden chair in the sunshine. In the right-hand corner is an
entrance to a vaulted circular chamber with a winding
stair leading up through a tower to the upper floors of
the palace. In the wall to our right is the immense fireplace, with its huge spit like a baby crane, and a collection of old iron and brass instruments which pass as the
original furniture of the fire, though as a matter of fact
they have been picked up from time to time by the
Bishop at secondhand shops. In the near end of the lefthand wall a small Norman door gives access to the Bishop's study, formerly a scullery. Further along, a great
oak chest stands against the wall. Across the middle of
the kitchen is a big timber table surrounded by eleven
stout rush-bottomed chairs: four on the far side, three
on the near side, and two at each end. There is a big
chair with railed back and sides on the hearth. On the
floor is a drugget of thick fibre matting. The only other
piece of furniture is a clock with a wooden dial about as
large as the bottom of a washtub, the weights, chains,
and pendulum being of corresponding magnitude; but
the Bishop has long since abandoned the attempt to keep
it going. It hangs above the oak chest.

The kitchen is occupied at present by the Bishop's lady, Mrs Bridgenorth, who is talking to Mr William Collins, the green-grocer. He is in evening dress, though it is early forenoon. Mrs Bridgenorth is a quiet happy-looking woman of fifty or thereabouts, placid, gentle, and humorous, with delicate features and fine grey hair with many white threads. She is dressed as for some festivity; but she is taking things easily as she sits in the big chair by the hearth, reading The Times.

Collins is an elderly man with a rather youthful waist. His muttonchop whiskers have a coquettish touch of Dundreary at their lower ends. He is an affable man, with those perfect manners which can be acquired only in keeping a shop for the sale of necessaries of life to ladies whose social position is so unquestionable that they are not anxious about it. He is a reassuring man, with a vigilant grey eye, and the power of saying anything he likes to you without offence, because his tone always implies that he does it with your kind permission. Withal by no means servile: rather gallant and compassionate, but never without a conscientious recognition, on public grounds, of social distinctions. He is at the oak chest counting a pile of napkins.

Mrs Bridgenorth reads placidly: Collins counts: a blackbird sings in the garden. Mrs Bridgenorth puts The Times down in her lap and considers Collins for a moment.

MRS BRIDGENORTH. Do you never feel nervous on these occasions, Collins?

COLLINS. Lord bless you, no, maam. It would be a joke, after marrying five of your daughters, if I was to get nervous over marrying the last of them.

MRS BRIDGENORTH. I have always said you were a wonderful man, Collins.

COLLINS [*almost blushing*] Oh, maam!

Mrs Bridgenorth. Yes. I never could arrange anything—a wedding or even a dinner—without some hitch or other.

Collins. Why should you give yourself the trouble, maam? Send for the greengrocer, maam: thats the secret of easy housekeeping. Bless you, it's his business. It pays him and you, let alone the pleasure in a house like this [*Mrs Bridgenorth bows in acknowledgment of the compliment*]. They joke about the greengrocer, just as they joke about the mother-in-law. But they cant get on without both.

Mrs Bridgenorth. What a bond between us, Collins!

Collins. Bless you, maam, theres all sorts of bonds between all sorts of people. You are a very affable lady, maam, for a Bishop's lady. I have known Bishop's ladies that would fairly provoke you to up and cheek them; but nobody would ever forget himself and his place with you, maam.

Mrs Bridgenorth. Collins: you are a flatterer. You will superintend the breakfast yourself as usual, of course, wont you?

Collins. Yes, yes, bless you, maam, of course. I always do. Them fashionable caterers send down such people as I never did set eyes on. Dukes you would take them for. You see the relatives shaking hands with them and asking them about the family—actually ladies saying "Where have we met before?" and all sorts of confusion. Thats my secret in business, maam. You can always spot me as the greengrocer. It's a fortune to me in these days, when you cant hardly tell who anyone is or isnt. [*He goes out through the tower, and immediately returns for a moment to announce*] The General, maam.

Mrs Bridgenorth rises to receive her brother-in-law, who enters resplendent in full-dress uniform, with many medals and orders. General Bridgenorth is a well set up man of fifty, with large brave nostrils, an iron mouth, faithful dog's eyes, and much natural simplicity and dignity of character. He is ignorant, stupid, and prejudiced, having been carefully trained to be so; and it is not always possible to be patient with him when his unquestionably good intentions become actively mischievous; but one blames society, not himself, for this. He would be no worse a man than Collins, had he enjoyed Collins's social opportunities. He comes to the hearth, where Mrs Bridgenorth is standing with her back to the fireplace.*

MRS BRIDGENORTH. Good morning, Boxer. [*They shake hands*]. Another niece to give away. This is the last of them.

THE GENERAL [*very gloomy*] Yes, Alice. Nothing for the old warrior uncle to do but give away brides to luckier men than himself. Has—[*he chokes*] has your sister come yet?

MRS BRIDGENORTH. Why do you always call Lesbia my sister? Dont you know that it annoys her more than any of the rest of your tricks?

THE GENERAL. Tricks! Ha! Well, I'll try to break myself of it; but I think she might bear with me in a little thing like that. She knows that her name sticks in my throat. Better call her your sister than try to call her L— [*he almost breaks down*] L— well, call her by her name and make a fool of myself by crying. [*He sits down at the near end of the table*].

MRS BRIDGENORTH [*going to him and rallying him*] Oh come, Boxer! Really, really! We are no longer boys and girls. You cant keep up a broken heart all your life. It must be nearly twenty years since she refused you. And you know that it's not because she dislikes you, but only that she's not a marrying woman.

THE GENERAL. It's no use. I love her still. And

I cant help telling her so whenever we meet, though I know it makes her avoid me. [*He all but weeps*].

MRS BRIDGENORTH. What does she say when you tell her?

THE GENERAL. Only that she wonders when I am going to grow out of it. I know now that I shall never grow out of it.

MRS BRIDGENORTH. Perhaps you would if you married her. I believe youre better as you are, Boxer.

THE GENERAL. I'm a miserable man. I'm really sorry to be a ridiculous old bore, Alice; but when I come to this house for a wedding—to these scenes—to—to—recollections of the past—always to give the bride to somebody else, and never to have my bride given to me—[*he rises abruptly*] May I go into the garden and smoke it off?

MRS BRIDGENORTH. Do, Boxer.

Collins returns with the wedding cake.

MRS BRIDGENORTH. Oh, heres the cake. I believe it's the same one we had for Florence's wedding.

THE GENERAL. I cant bear it [*he hurries out through the garden door*].

COLLINS [*putting the cake on the table*] Well, look at that, maam! Aint it odd that after all the weddings he's given away at, the General cant stand the sight of a wedding cake yet. It always seems to give him the same shock.

MRS BRIDGENORTH. Well, it's his last shock. You have married the whole family now, Collins. [*She takes up The Times again and resumes her seat*].

COLLINS. Except your sister, maam. A fine character of a lady, maam, is Miss Grantham. I have an ambition to arrange her wedding breakfast.

MRS BRIDGENORTH. She wont marry, Collins.

COLLINS. Bless you, maam, they all say that. You and me said it, I'll lay. I did, anyhow.

MRS BRIDGENORTH. No: marriage came natural to me. I should have thought it did to you too.

COLLINS [*pensive*] No, maam: it didnt come natural. My wife had to break me into it. It came natural to her: she's what you might call a regular old hen. Always wants to have her family within sight of her. Wouldnt go to bed unless she knew they was all safe at home and the door locked, and the lights out. Always wants her luggage in the carriage with her. Always goes and makes the engine driver promise her to be careful. She's a born wife and mother, maam. Thats why my children all ran away from home.

MRS BRIDGENORTH. Did you ever feel inclined to run away, Collins?

COLLINS. Oh yes, maam, yes: very often. But when it came to the point I couldnt bear to hurt her feelings. Shes a sensitive, affectionate, anxious soul; and she was never brought up to know what freedom is to some people. You see, family life is all the life she knows: she's like a bird born in a cage, that would die if you let it loose in the woods. When I thought how little it was to a man of my easy temper to put up with her, and how deep it would hurt her to think it was because I didnt care for her, I always put off running away till next time; and so in the end I never ran away at all. I daresay it was good for me to be took such care of; but it cut me off from all my old friends something dreadful, maam: especially the women, maam. She never gave them a chance: she didnt indeed. She never understood that married people should take holidays from one another if they are to keep at all fresh. Not that I ever got tired of her, maam; but my! how I used to get tired of home life sometimes. I used to catch myself envying my brother George: I positively did, maam.

MRS BRIDGENORTH. George was a bachelor then, I suppose?

COLLINS. Bless you, no, maam. He married a very fine figure of a woman; but she was that changeable and what you might call susceptible, you would not believe. She didnt seem to have any control over herself when she fell in love. She would mope for a couple of days, crying about nothing; and then she would up and say—no matter who was there to hear her—" I must go to him, George "; and away she would go from her home and her husband without with-your-leave or by-your-leave.

MRS BRIDGENORTH. But do you mean that she did this more than once? That she came back?

COLLINS. Bless you, maam, she done it five times to my own knowledge; and then George gave up telling us about it, he got so used to it.

MRS BRIDGENORTH. But did he always take her back?

COLLINS. Well, what could he do, maam? Three times out of four the men would bring her back the same evening and no harm done. Other times theyd run away from her. What could any man with a heart do but comfort her when she came back crying at the way they dodged her when she threw herself at their heads, pretending they was too noble to accept the sacrifice she was making. George told her again and again that if she'd only stay at home and hold off a bit theyd be at her feet all day long. She got sensible at last and took his advice. George always liked change of company.

MRS BRIDGENORTH. What an odious woman, Collins! Dont you think so?

COLLINS [*judicially*] Well, many ladies with a domestic turn thought so and said so, maam. But I will say for Mrs George that the variety of experience made her wonderful interesting. Thats where the flighty ones score off the steady ones, maam. Look at my old woman! She's never known any man but me; and she cant properly know me, because she dont know other men to compare me with. Of course she knows her parents in—well, in the way one does know one's parents: not knowing half their lives as you might say, or ever thinking that they was ever young; and she knew her children as children, and never thought of them as independent human beings till they ran away and nigh broke her heart for a week or two. But Mrs George she came to know a lot about men of all sorts and ages; for the older she got the younger she liked em; and it certainly made her interesting, and gave her a lot of sense. I have often taken her advice on things when my own poor old woman wouldnt have been a bit of use to me.

MRS BRIDGENORTH. I hope you dont tell your wife that you go elsewhere for advice.

COLLINS. Lord bless you, maam, I'm that fond of my old Matilda that I never tell her anything at all for fear of hurting her feelings. You see, she's such an out-and-out wife and mother that she's hardly a responsible human being out of her house, except when she's marketing.

MRS BRIDGENORTH. Does she approve of Mrs George?

COLLINS. Oh, Mrs George gets round her. Mrs George can get round anybody if she wants to. And then Mrs George is very particular about religion. And shes a clairvoyant.

MRS BRIDGENORTH [*surprised*] A clairvoyant!

COLLINS [*calm*] Oh yes, maam, yes. All you have to do is to mesmerize her a bit; and off she goes into a trance, and says the most wonderful things! not things about herself, but as if it was the whole human race giving you a bit of its mind. Oh, wonderful, maam, I assure you. You couldnt think of a game that Mrs George isnt up to.

Lesbia Grantham comes in through the tower. She is a tall, handsome, slender lady in her prime: that is, between 36 and 55. She has what is called a well-bred air, dressing very carefully to produce that effect without the least regard for the latest fashions, sure of herself, very terrifying to the young and shy, fastidious to the ends of her long finger-tips, and tolerant and amused rather than sympathetic.

LESBIA. Good morning, dear big sister.

MRS BRIDGENORTH. Good morning, dear little sister. [*They kiss*].

LESBIA. Good morning, Collins. How well you are looking! And how young! [*She turns the middle chair away from the table and sits down*].

COLLINS. Thats only my professional habit at a wedding, Miss. You should see me at a political dinner. I look nigh seventy. [*Looking at his watch*] Time's getting along, maam. May I send up word from you to Miss Edith to hurry a bit with her dressing?

MRS BRIDGENORTH. Do, Collins.

Collins goes out through the tower, taking the cake with him.

LESBIA. Dear old Collins! Has he told you any stories this morning?

MRS BRIDGENORTH. Yes. You were just late for a particularly thrilling invention of his.

LESBIA. About Mrs George?

MRS BRIDGENORTH. Yes. He says she's a clairvoyant.

LESBIA. I wonder whether he really invented Mrs George, or stole her out of some book.

MRS BRIDGENORTH. I wonder!

LESBIA. Wheres the Barmecide?

MRS BRIDGENORTH. In the study, working away at his new book. He thinks no more now of having a daughter married than of having an egg for breakfast.

The General, soothed by smoking, comes in from the garden.

THE GENERAL [*with resolute bonhomie*] Ah, Lesbia!

How do you do? [*They shake hands; and he takes the chair on her right*].

Mrs Bridgenorth goes out through the tower.

LESBIA. How are you, Boxer? You look almost as gorgeous as the wedding cake.

THE GENERAL. I make a point of appearing in uniform whenever I take part in any ceremony, as a lesson to the subalterns. It is not the custom in England; but it ought to be.

LESBIA. You look very fine, Boxer. What a frightful lot of bravery all these medals must represent!

THE GENERAL. No, Lesbia. They represent despair and cowardice. I won all the early ones by trying to get killed. You know why.

LESBIA. But you had a charmed life?

THE GENERAL. Yes, a charmed life. Bayonets bent on my buckles. Bullets passed through me and left no trace: thats the worst of modern bullets: Ive never been hit by a dum-dum. When I was only a company officer I had at least the right to expose myself to death in the field. Now I'm a General even that resource is cut off. [*Persuasively drawing his chair nearer to her*] Listen to me, Lesbia. For the tenth and last time—

LESBIA [*interrupting*] On Florence's wedding morning, two years ago, you said "For the ninth and last time."

THE GENERAL. We are two years older, Lesbia. I'm fifty: you are—

LESBIA. Yes, I know. It's no use, Boxer. When will you be old enough to take no for an answer?

THE GENERAL. Never, Lesbia, never. You have never given me a real reason for refusing me yet. I once thought it was somebody else. There were lots of fellows after you; but now theyve all given it up and married. [*Bending still nearer to her*] Lesbia: tell me your secret. Why—

LESBIA [*sniffing disgustedly*] Oh! Youve been smoking. [*She rises and goes to the chair on the hearth*] Keep away, you wretch.

THE GENERAL. But for that pipe, I could not have faced you without breaking down. It has soothed me and nerved me.

LESBIA [*sitting down with The Times in her hand*] Well, it has nerved me to tell you why I'm going to be an old maid.

THE GENERAL [*impulsively approaching her*] Dont say that, Lesbia. It's not natural: it's not right: it's—

LESBIA [*fanning him off*] No: no closer, Boxer, please. [*He retreats, discouraged*]. It may not be natural; but it happens all the time. Youll find plenty of women like me, if you care to look for them: women with lots of character and good looks and money and offers, who wont and dont get married. Cant you guess why?

THE GENERAL. I can understand when there is another.

LESBIA. Yes; but there isnt another. Besides, do you suppose I think, at my time of life, that the difference between one decent sort of man and another is worth bothering about?

THE GENERAL. The heart has its preferences, Lesbia. One image, and one only, gets indelibly—

LESBIA. Yes. Excuse my interrupting you so often; but your sentiments are so correct that I always know what you are going to say before you finish. You see, Boxer, everybody is not like you. You are a sentimental noodle: you dont see women as they really are. You dont see me as I really am. Now I do see men as they really are. I see you as you really are.

THE GENERAL [*murmuring*] No: dont say that, Lesbia.

LESBIA. I'm a regular old maid. I'm very particular

about my belongings. I like to have my own house, and to have it to myself. I have a very keen sense of beauty and fitness and cleanliness and order. I am proud of my independence and jealous for it. I have a sufficiently well-stocked mind to be very good company for myself if I have plenty of books and music. The one thing I never could stand is a great lout of a man smoking all over my house and going to sleep in his chair after dinner, and untidying everything. Ugh!

THE GENERAL. But love —

LESBIA. Oh, love! Have you no imagination? Do you think I have never been in love with wonderful men? heroes! archangels! princes! sages! even fascinating rascals! and had the strangest adventures with them? Do you know what it is to look at a mere real man after that? a man with his boots in every corner, and the smell of his tobacco in every curtain?

THE GENERAL [*somewhat dazed*] Well but—excuse my mentioning it—dont you want children?

LESBIA. I ought to have children. I should be a good mother to children. I believe it would pay the country very well to pay me very well to have children. But the country tells me that I cant have a child in my house without a man in it too; so I tell the country that it will have to do without my children. If I am to be a mother, I really cannot have a man bothering me to be a wife at the same time.

THE GENERAL. My dear Lesbia: you know I dont wish to be impertinent; but these are not the correct views for an English lady to express.

LESBIA. That is why I dont express them, except to gentlemen who wont take any other answer. The difficulty, you see, is that I really am an English lady, and am particularly proud of being one.

THE GENERAL. I'm sure of that, Lesbia: quite sure of it. I never meant—

LESBIA [*rising impatiently*] Oh, my dear Boxer, do please try to think of something else than whether you have offended me, and whether you are doing the correct thing as an English gentleman. You are faultless, and very dull. [*She shakes her shoulders intolerantly and walks across to the other side of the kitchen*].

THE GENERAL [*moodily*] Ha! thats whats the matter with me. Not clever. A poor silly soldier man.

LESBIA. The whole matter is very simple. As I say, I am an English lady, by which I mean that I have been trained to do without what I cant have on honorable terms, no matter what it is.

THE GENERAL. I really dont understand you, Lesbia.

LESBIA [*turning on him*] Then why on earth do you want to marry a woman you dont understand?

THE GENERAL. I dont know. I suppose I love you.

LESBIA. Well, Boxer, you can love me as much as you like, provided you look happy about it and dont bore me. But you cant marry me; and thats all about it.

THE GENERAL. It's so frightfully difficult to argue the matter fairly with you without wounding your delicacy by overstepping the bounds of good taste. But surely there are calls of nature—

LESBIA. Dont be ridiculous, Boxer.

THE GENERAL. Well, how am I to express it? Hang it all, Lesbia, dont you want a husband?

LESBIA. No. I want children; and I want to devote myself entirely to my children, and not to their father. The law will not allow me to do that; so I have made up my mind to have neither husband nor children.

THE GENERAL. But, great Heavens, the natural appetites—

LESBIA. As I said before, an English lady is not the slave of her appetites. That is what an English gentleman seems incapable of understanding. [*She sits down at the end of the table, near the study door*].

THE GENERAL [*huffily*] Oh well, if you refuse, you refuse. I shall not ask you again. I'm sorry I returned to the subject. [*He retires to the hearth and plants himself there, wounded and lofty*].

LESBIA. Dont be cross, Boxer.

THE GENERAL. I'm not cross, only wounded, Lesbia. And when you talk like that, I dont feel convinced: I only feel utterly at a loss.

LESBIA. Well, you know our family rule. When at a loss consult the greengrocer. [*Opportunely Collins comes in through the tower*]. Here he is.

COLLINS. Sorry to be so much in and out, Miss. I thought Mrs Bridgenorth was here. The table is ready now for the breakfast, if she would like to see it.

LESBIA. If you are satisfied, Collins, I am sure she will be.

THE GENERAL. By the way, Collins: I thought theyd made you an alderman.

COLLINS. So they have, General.

THE GENERAL. Then wheres your gown?

COLLINS. I dont wear it in private life, General.

THE GENERAL. Why? Are you ashamed of it?

COLLINS. No, General. To tell you the truth, I take a pride in it. I cant help it.

THE GENERAL. Attention, Collins. Come here. [*Collins comes to him*]. Do you see my uniform—all my medals?

COLLINS. Yes, General. They strike the eye, as it were.

THE GENERAL. They are meant to. Very well. Now you know, dont you, that your services to the community as a greengrocer are as important and as dignified as mine as a soldier?

COLLINS. I'm sure it's very honorable of you to say so, General.

THE GENERAL [*emphatically*] You know also, dont

you, that any man who can see anything ridiculous, or unmanly, or unbecoming in your work or in your civic robes is not a gentleman, but a jumping, bounding, snorting cad?

COLLINS. Well, strictly between ourselves, that is my opinion, General.

THE GENERAL. Then why not dignify my niece's wedding by wearing your robes?

COLLINS. A bargain's a bargain, General. Mrs Bridgenorth sent for the greengrocer, not for the alderman. It's just as unpleasant to get more than you bargain for as to get less.

THE GENERAL. I'm sure she will agree with me. I attach importance to this as an affirmation of solidarity in the service of the community. The Bishop's apron, my uniform, your robes: the Church, the Army, and the Municipality.

COLLINS [*retiring*] Very well, General. [*He turns dubiously to Lesbia on his way to the tower*]. I wonder what my wife will say, Miss?

THE GENERAL. What! Is your wife ashamed of your robes?

COLLINS. No, sir, not ashamed of them. But she grudged the money for them; and she will be afraid of my sleeves getting into the gravy.

Mrs Bridgenorth, her placidity quite upset, comes in with a letter; hurries past Collins; and comes between Lesbia and the General.

MRS BRIDGENORTH. Lesbia: Boxer: heres a pretty mess!

Collins goes out discreetly.

THE GENERAL. Whats the matter?

MRS BRIDGENORTH. Reginald's in London, and wants to come to the wedding.

THE GENERAL [*stupended*] Well, dash my buttons!

LESBIA. Oh, all right, let him come.

THE GENERAL. Let him come! Why, the decree has not been made absolute yet. Is he to walk in here to Edith's wedding, reeking from the Divorce Court?

MRS BRIDGENORTH [*vexedly sitting down in the middle chair*] It's too bad. No: I cant forgive him, Lesbia, really. A man of Reginald's age, with a young wife —the best of girls, and as pretty as she can be—to go off with a common woman from the streets! Ugh!

LESBIA. You must make allowances. What can you expect? Reginald was always weak. He was brought up to be weak. The family property was all mortgaged when he inherited it. He had to struggle along in constant money difficulties, hustled by his solicitors, morally bullied by the Barmecide, and physically bullied by Boxer, while they two were fighting their own way and getting well trained. You know very well he couldnt afford to marry until the mortgages were cleared and he was over fifty. And then of course he made a fool of himself marrying a child like Leo.

THE GENERAL. But to hit her! Absolutely to hit her! He knocked her down—knocked her flat down on a flowerbed in the presence of his gardener. He! the head of the family! the man that stands before the Barmecide and myself as Bridgenorth of Bridgenorth! to beat his wife and go off with a low woman and be divorced for it in the face of all England! in the face of my uniform and Alfred's apron! I can never forget what I felt: it was only the King's personal request—virtually a command—that stopped me from resigning my commission. I'd cut Reginald dead if I met him in the street.

MRS BRIDGENORTH. Besides, Leo's coming. Theyd meet. It's impossible, Lesbia.

LESBIA. Oh, I forgot that. That settles it. He mustnt come.

THE GENERAL. Of course he mustnt. You tell him

that if he enters this house, I'll leave it; and so will every decent man and woman in it.

COLLINS [*returning for a moment to announce*] Mr Reginald, maam. [*He withdraws when Reginald enters*].

THE GENERAL [*beside himself*] Well, dash my buttons!!

Reginald is just the man Lesbia has described. He is hardened and tough physically, and hasty and boyish in his manner and speech, belonging as he does to the large class of English gentlemen of property (solicitor-managed) who have never developed intellectually since their schooldays. He is a muddled, rebellious, hasty, untidy, forgetful, always late sort of man, who very evidently needs the care of a capable woman, and has never been lucky or attractive enough to get it. All the same, a likeable man, from whom nobody apprehends any malice nor expects any achievement. In everything but years he is younger than his brother the General.

REGINALD [*coming forward between the General and Mrs Bridgenorth*] Alice: it's no use. I cant stay away from Edith's wedding. Good morning, Lesbia. How are you, Boxer? [*He offers the General his hand*].

THE GENERAL [*with crushing stiffness*] I was just telling Alice, sir, that if you entered this house, I should leave it.

REGINALD. Well, dont let me detain you, old chap. When you start calling people, Sir, youre not particularly good company.

LESBIA. Dont you begin to quarrel. That wont improve the situation.

MRS BRIDGENORTH. I think you might have waited until you got my answer, Rejjy.

REGINALD. It's so jolly easy to say No in a letter. Wont you let me stay?

MRS BRIDGENORTH. How can I? Leo's coming.

REGINALD. Well, she wont mind.
THE GENERAL. Wont mind ! ! ! ! !
LESBIA. Dont talk nonsense, Rejjy; and be off with you.
THE GENERAL [*with biting sarcasm*] At school you had a theory that women liked being knocked down, I remember.
REGINALD. Youre a nice, chivalrous, brotherly sort of swine, you are.
THE GENERAL. Mr Bridgenorth: are you going to leave this house or am I?
REGINALD. You are, I hope. [*He emphasizes his intention to stay by sitting down*].
THE GENERAL. Alice: will you allow me to be driven from Edith's wedding by this—
LESBIA [*warningly*] Boxer!
THE GENERAL. —by this Respondent? Is Edith to be given away by him?
MRS BRIDGENORTH. Certainly not. Reginald: you were not asked to come; and I have asked you to go. You know how fond I am of Leo; and you know what she would feel if she came in and found you here.
COLLINS [*again apearing in the tower*] Mrs Reginald, maam.

LESBIA	No, no. Ask her to—	[*All three
MRS BRIDGENORTH	Oh how unfortunate!	clamoring
THE GENERAL	Well, dash my buttons!	together*].

It is too late: Leo is already in the kitchen. Collins goes out, mutely abandoning a situation which he deplores but has been unable to save.

Leo is very pretty, very youthful, very restless, and consequently very charming to people who are touched by youth and beauty, as well as to those who regard young women as more or less appetizing lollipops, and dont regard old women at all. Coldly studied, Leo's restless-

ness is much less lovable than the kittenishness which comes from a rich and fresh vitality. She is a born fusser about herself and everybody else for whom she feels responsible; and her vanity causes her to exaggerate her responsibilities officiously. All her fussing is about little things; but she often calls them by big names, such as Art, the Divine Spark, the world, motherhood, good breeding, the Universe, the Creator, or anything else that happens to strike her imagination as sounding intellectually important. She has more than common imagination and no more than common conception and penetration; so that she is always on the high horse about words and always in the perambulator about things. Considering herself clever, thoughtful, and superior to ordinary weaknesses and prejudices, she recklessly attaches herself to clever men on that understanding, with the result that they are first delighted, then exasperated, and finally bored. When marrying Reginald she told her friends that there was a great deal in him which needed bringing out. If she were a middle-aged man she would be the terror of his club. Being a pretty young woman, she is forgiven everything, proving that "Tout comprendre, c'est tout pardonner" is an error, the fact being that the secret of forgiving everything is to understand nothing.

She runs in fussily, full of her own importance, and swoops on Lesbia, who is much less disposed to spoil her than Mrs Bridgenorth is. But Leo affects a special intimacy with Lesbia, as of two thinkers among the Philistines.

LEO [to Lesbia, kissing her] Good morning. [Coming to Mrs Bridgenorth] How do, Alice? [Passing on towards the hearth] Why so gloomy, General? [Reginald rises between her and the General] Oh, Rejjy! What will the King's Proctor say?

REGINALD. Damn the King's Proctor!

LEO. Naughty. Well, I suppose I must kiss you; but dont any of you tell. [*She kisses him. They can hardly believe their eyes*]. Have you kept all your promises?

REGINALD. Oh, dont begin bothering about those—

LEO [*insisting*] Have? You? Kept? Your? Promises? Have you rubbed your head with the lotion every night?

REGINALD. Yes, yes. Nearly every night.

LEO. Nearly! I know what that means. Have you worn your liver pad?

THE GENERAL [*solmenly*] Leo: forgiveness is one of the most beautiful traits in a woman's nature; but there are things that should not be forgiven to a man. When a man knocks a woman down [*Leo gives a little shriek of laughter and collapses on a chair next Mrs Bridgenorth, on her left*]—

REGINALD [*sardonically*] The man that would raise his hand to a woman, save in the way of a kindness, is unworthy the name of Bridgenorth. [*He sits down at the end of the table nearest the hearth*].

THE GENERAL [*much huffed*] Oh, well, if Leo does not mind, of course I have no more to say. But I think you might, out of consideration for the family, beat your wife in private and not in the presence of the gardener.

REGINALD [*out of patience*] Whats the good of beating your wife unless theres a witness to prove it afterwards? You dont suppose a man beats his wife for the fun of it, do you? How could she have got her divorce if I hadnt beaten her? Nice state of things, that!

THE GENERAL [*gasping*] Do you mean to tell me that you did it in cold blood? simply to get rid of your wife?

REGINALD. No, I didn't: I did it to get her rid of me. What would you do if you were fool enough to marry a woman thirty years younger than yourself, and then found that she didnt care for you, and was in love with a young fellow with a face like a mushroom.

LEO. He has not. [*Bursting into tears*] And you are most unkind to say I didnt care for you. Nobody could have been fonder of you.

REGINALD. A nice way of shewing your fondness! I had to go out and dig that flower bed all over with my own hands to soften it. I had to pick all the stones out of it. And then she complained that I hadnt done it properly, because she got a worm down her neck. I had to go to Brighton with a poor creature who took a fancy to me on the way down, and got conscientious scruples about committing perjury after dinner. I had to put her down in the hotel book as Mrs Reginald Bridgenorth: Leo's name! Do you know what that feels like to a decent man? Do you know what a decent man feels about his wife's name? How would you like to go into a hotel before all the waiters and people with—with that on your arm? Not that it was the poor girl's fault, of course; only she started crying because I couldnt stand her touching me; and now she keeps writing to me. And then I'm held up in the public court for cruelty and adultery, and turned away from Edith's wedding by Alice, and lectured by you! a bachelor, and a precious green one at that. What do you know about it?

THE GENERAL. Am I to understand that the whole case was one of collusion?

REGINALD. Of course it was. Half the cases are collusions: what are people to do? [*The General, passing his hand dazedly over his bewildered brow, sinks into the railed chair*]. And what do you take me for, that you should have the cheek to pretend to believe all that rot about my knocking Leo about and leaving her for— for a—a— Ugh! you should have seen her.

THE GENERAL. This is perfectly astonishing to me. Why did you do it? Why did Leo allow it?

REGINALD. Youd better ask her.

LEO [*still in tears*] I'm sure I never thought it would be so horrid for Rejjy. I offered honorably to do it myself, and let him divorce me; but he wouldnt. And he said himself that it was the only way to do it—that it was the law that he should do it that way. I never saw that hateful creature until that day in Court. If he had only shewn her to me before, I should never have allowed it.

MRS BRIDGENORTH. You did all this for Leo's sake, Rejjy?

REGINALD [*with an unbearable sense of injury*] I shouldnt mind a bit if it were for Leo's sake. But to have to do it to make room for that mushroom-faced serpent—!

THE GENERAL [*jumping up*] What right had he to be made room for? Are you in your senses? What right?

REGINALD. The right of being a young man, suitable to a young woman. I had no right at my age to marry Leo: she knew no more about life than a child.

LEO. I knew a great deal more about it than a great baby like you. I'm sure I dont know how youll get on with no one to take care of you: I often lie awake at night thinking about it. And now youve made me thoroughly miserable.

REGINALD. Serve you right! [*She weeps*]. There: dont get into a tantrum, Leo.

LESBIA. May one ask who is the mushroom-faced serpent?

LEO. He isnt.

REGINALD. Sinjon Hotchkiss, of course.

MRS BRIDGENORTH. Sinjon Hotchkiss! Why, he's coming to the wedding!

REGINALD. What! In that case I'm off [*he makes for the tower*].

LEO — [*seizing him*] No you shant. You promised to be nice to him.

THE GENERAL [*all four rushing after him and capturing him on the threshold*] No, dont go, old chap. Not from Edith's wedding.

MRS BRIDGENORTH — Oh, do stay, Rejjy. I shall really be hurt if you desert us.

LESBIA — Better stay, Reginald. You must meet him sooner or later.

REGINALD. A moment ago, when I wanted to stay, you were all shoving me out of the house. Now that I want to go, you wont let me.

MRS BRIDGENORTH. I shall send a note to Mr Hotchkiss not to come.

LEO [*weeping again*] Oh, Alice! [*She comes back to her chair, heartbroken*].

REGINALD [*out of patience*] Oh well, let her have her way. Let her have her mushroom. Let him come. Let them all come.

He crosses the kitchen to the oak chest and sits sulkily on it. Mrs Bridgenorth shrugs her shoulders and sits at the table in Reginald's neighborhood listening in placid helplessness. Lesbia, out of patience with Leo's tears, goes into the garden and sits there near the door, snuffing up the open air in her relief from the domestic stuffiness of Reginald's affairs.

LEO. It's so cruel of you to go on pretending that I dont care for you, Rejjy.

REGINALD [*bitterly*] She explained to me that it was only that she had exhausted my conversation.

THE GENERAL [*coming paternally to Leo*] My dear girl: all the conversation in the world has been exhausted long ago. Heaven knows I have exhausted the conversation of the British Army these thirty years; but I dont leave it on that account.

LEO. It's not that Ive exhausted it; but he will keep on repeating it when I want to read or go to sleep. And Sinjon amuses me. He's so clever.

THE GENERAL [*stung*] Ha! The old complaint. You all want geniuses to marry. This demand for clever men is ridiculous. Somebody must marry the plain, honest, stupid fellows. Have you thought of that?

LEO. But there are such lots of stupid women to marry. Why do they want to marry us? Besides, Rejjy knows that I'm quite fond of him. I like him because he wants me; and I like Sinjon because I want him. I feel that I have a duty to Rejjy.

THE GENERAL. Precisely: you have.

LEO. And, of course, Sinjon has the same duty to me.

THE GENERAL. Tut, tut!

LEO. Oh, how silly the law is! Why cant I marry them both?

THE GENERAL [*shocked*] Leo!

LEO. Well, I love them both. I should like to marry a lot of men. I should like to have Rejjy for every day, and Sinjon for concerts and theatres and going out in the evenings, and some great austere saint for about once a year at the end of the season, and some perfectly blithering idiot of a boy to be quite wicked with. I so seldom feel wicked; and, when I do, it's such a pity to waste it merely because it's too silly to confess to a real grown-up man.

REGINALD. This is the kind of thing, you know—[*Helplessly*] Well, there it is!

THE GENERAL [*decisively*] Alice: this is a job for the Barmecide. He's a Bishop: it's his duty to talk to Leo. I can stand a good deal; but when it comes to flat polygamy and polyandry, we ought to do something.

Mrs Bridgenorth [*going to the study door*] Do come here a moment, Alfred. We're in a difficulty.

The Bishop [*within*] Ask Collins, I'm busy.

Mrs Bridgenorth. Collins wont do. It's something very serious. Do come just a moment, dear. [*When she hears him coming she takes a chair at the nearest end of the table*].

The Bishop comes out of his study. He is still a slim active man, spare of flesh, and younger by temperament than his brothers. He has a delicate skin, fine hands, a salient nose with chin to match, a short beard which accentuates his sharp chin by bristling forward, clever humorous eyes, not without a glint of mischief in them, ready bright speech, and the ways of a successful man who is always interested in himself and generally rather well pleased with himself. When Lesbia hears his voice she turns her chair towards him, and presently rises and stands in the doorway listening to the conversation.

The Bishop [*going to Leo*] Good morning, my dear. Hullo! Youve brought Reginald with you. Thats very nice of you. Have you reconciled them, Boxer?

The General. Reconciled them! Why, man, the whole divorce was a put-up job. She wants to marry some fellow named Hotchkiss.

Reginald. A fellow with a face like—

Leo. You shant, Rejjy. He has a very fine face.

Mrs Bridgenorth. And now she says she wants to marry both of them, and a lot of other people as well.

Leo. I didnt say I wanted to marry them: I only said I should like to marry them.

The Bishop. Quite a nice distinction, Leo.

Leo. Just occasionally, you know.

The Bishop [*sitting down cosily beside her*] Quite so. Sometimes a poet, sometimes a Bishop, sometimes a fairy prince, sometimes somebody quite indescribable, and sometimes nobody at all.

LEO. Yes: thats just it. How did you know?

THE BISHOP. Oh, I should say most imaginative and cultivated young women feel like that. I wouldnt give a rap for one who didnt. Shakespear pointed out long ago that a woman wanted a Sunday husband as well as a weekday one. But, as usual, he didnt follow up the idea.

THE GENERAL [*aghast*] Am I to understand—

THE BISHOP [*cutting him short*] Now, Boxer, am I the Bishop or are you?

THE GENERAL [*sulkily*] You.

THE BISHOP. Then dont ask me are you to understand. " Yours not to reason why: yours but to do and die "—

THE GENERAL. Oh, very well: go on. I'm not clever. Only a silly soldier man. Ha! Go on. [*He throws himself into the railed chair, as one prepared for the worst*].

MRS BRIDGENORTH. Alfred: dont tease Boxer.

THE BISHOP. If we are going to discuss ethical questions we must begin by giving the devil fair play. Boxer never does. England never does. We always assume that the devil is guilty; and we wont allow him to prove his innocence, because it would be against public morals if he succeeded. We used to do the same with prisoners accused of high treason. And the consequence is that we overreach ourselves; and the devil gets the better of us after all. Perhaps thats what most of us intend him to do.

THE GENERAL. Alfred: we asked you here to preach to Leo. You are preaching at me instead. I am not conscious of having said or done anything that calls for that unsolicited attention.

THE BISHOP. But poor little Leo has only told the simple truth; whilst you, Boxer, are striking moral attitudes.

THE GENERAL. I suppose thats an epigram. I dont understand epigrams. I'm only a silly soldier man. Ha! But I can put a plain question. Is Leo to be encouraged to be a polygamist?

THE BISHOP. Remember the British Empire, Boxer. Youre a British General, you know.

THE GENERAL. What has that to do with polygamy?

THE BISHOP. Well, the great majority of our fellow-subjects are polygamists. I cant as a British Bishop insult them by speaking disrespectfully of polygamy. It's a very interesting question. Many very interesting men have been polygamists: Solomon, Mahomet, and our friend the Duke of —of—hm! I never can remember his name.

THE GENERAL. It would become you better, Alfred, to send that silly girl back to her husband and her duty than to talk clever and mock at your religion. "What God hath joined together let no man put asunder." Remember that.

THE BISHOP. Dont be afraid, Boxer. What God hath joined together no man ever shall put asunder: God will take care of that. [*To Leo*] By the way, who was it that joined you and Reginald, my dear?

LEO. It was that awful little curate that afterwards drank, and travelled first class with a third-class ticket, and then tried to go on the stage. But they wouldnt have him. He called himself Egerton Fotheringay.

THE BISHOP. Well, whom Egerton Fotheringay hath joined, let Sir Gorell Barnes put asunder by all means.

THE GENERAL. I may be a silly soldier man; but I call this blasphemy.

THE BISHOP [*gravely*] Better for me to take the name of Mr Egerton Fotheringay in earnest than for you to take a higher name in vain.

LESBIA. Cant you three brothers ever meet without quarrelling?

THE BISHOP [*mildly*] This is not quarrelling, Lesbia: it's only English family life. Good morning.

LEO. You know, Bishop, it's very dear of you to take my part; but I'm not sure that I'm not a little shocked.

THE BISHOP. Then I think Ive been a little more successful than Boxer in getting you into a proper frame of mind.

THE GENERAL [*snorting*] Ha!

LEO. Not a bit; for now I'm going to shock you worse than ever. I think Solomon was an old beast.

THE BISHOP. Precisely what you ought to think of him, my dear. Dont apologize.

THE GENERAL [*more shocked*] Well, but hang it! Solomon was in the Bible. And, after all, Solomon was Solomon.

LEO. And I stick to it: I still want to have a lot of interesting men to know quite intimately—to say everything I think of to them, and have them say everything they think of to me.

THE BISHOP. So you shall, my dear, if you are lucky. But you know you neednt marry them all. Think of all the buttons you would have to sew on. Besides, nothing is more dreadful than a husband who keeps telling you everything he thinks, and always wants to know what you think.

LEO [*struck by this*] Well, thats very true of Rejjy: in fact, thats why I had to divorce him.

THE BISHOP [*condoling*] Yes: he repeats himself dreadfully, doesnt he?

REGINALD. Look here, Alfred. If I have my faults, let her find them out for herself without your help.

THE BISHOP. She has found them all out already, Reginald.

LEO [*a little huffily*] After all, there are worse men than Reginald. I daresay he's not so clever as you; but still he's not such a fool as you seem to think him!

THE BISHOP. Quite right, dear: stand up for your husband. I hope you will always stand up for all your husbands. [*He rises and goes to the hearth, where he stands complacently with his back to the fireplace, beaming at them all as at a roomful of children*].

LEO. Please dont talk as if I wanted to marry a whole regiment. For me there can never be more than two. I shall never love anybody but Rejjy and Sinjon.

REGINALD. A man with a face like a—

LEO. I wont have it, Rejjy. It's disgusting.

THE BISHOP. You see, my dear, youll exhaust Sinjon's conversation too in a week or so. A man is like a phonograph with half-a-dozen records. You soon get tired of them all; and yet you have to sit at table whilst he reels them off to every new visitor. In the end you have to be content with his common humanity; and when you come down to that, you find out about men what a great English poet of my acquaintance used to say about women: that they all taste alike. Marry whom you please: at the end of a month he'll be Reginald over again. It wasnt worth changing: indeed it wasnt.

LEO. Then it's a mistake to get married.

THE BISHOP. It is, my dear; but it's a much bigger mistake not to get married.

THE GENERAL [*rising*] Ha! You hear that, Lesbia? [*He joins her at the garden door*].

LESBIA. Thats only an epigram, Boxer.

THE GENERAL. Sound sense, Lesbia. When a man talks rot, thats epigram: when he talks sense, then I agree with him.

REGINALD [*coming off the oak chest and looking at his watch*] It's getting late. Wheres Edith? Hasnt she got into her veil and orange blossoms yet?

MRS BRIDGENORTH. Do go and hurry her, Lesbia.

LESBIA [*going out through the tower*] Come with me, Leo.

LEO [*following Lesbia out*] Yes, certainly.

The Bishop goes over to his wife and sits down, taking her hand and kissing it by way of beginning a conversation with her.

THE BISHOP. Alice: Ive had another letter from the mysterious lady who cant spell. I like that woman's letters. Theres an intensity of passion in them that fascinates me.

MRS BRIDGENORTH. Do you mean Incognita Appassionata?

THE BISHOP. Yes.

THE GENERAL [*turning abruptly: he has been looking out into the garden*] Do you mean to say that women write love-letters to you?

THE BISHOP. Of course.

THE GENERAL. They never do to me.

THE BISHOP. The army doesnt attract women: the Church does.

REGINALD. Do you consider it right to let them? They may be married women, you know.

THE BISHOP. They always are. This one is. [*To Mrs Bridgenorth*] Dont you think her letters are quite the best love-letters I get? [*To the two men*] Poor Alice has to read my love-letters aloud to me at breakfast, when theyre worth it.

MRS BRIDGENORTH. There really is something fascinating about Incognita. She never gives her address. Thats a good sign.

THE GENERAL. Mf! No assignations, you mean?

THE BISHOP. Oh yes: she began the correspondence by making a very curious but very natural assignation. She wants me to meet her in heaven. I hope I shall.

THE GENERAL. Well, I must say I hope not, Alfred. I hope not.

MRS BRIDGENORTH. She says she is happily married,

and that love is a necessary of life to her, but that she
must have, high above all her lovers—

THE BISHOP. She has several apparently—

MRS BRIDGENORTH. —some great man who will
never know her, never touch her, as she is on earth, but
whom she can meet in heaven when she has risen above
all the everyday vulgarities of earthly love.

THE BISHOP [*rising*] Excellent. Very good for her;
and no trouble to me. Everybody ought to have one of
these idealizations, like Dante's Beatrice. [*He clasps
his hands behind him, and strolls to the hearth and back,
singing*].

Lesbia appears in the tower, rather perturbed.

LESBIA. Alice: will you come upstairs? Edith is not
dressed.

MRS BRIDGENORTH [*rising*] Not dressed! Does she
know what hour it is?

LESBIA. She has locked herself into her room, reading.

The Bishop's song ceases: he stops dead in his stroll.

THE GENERAL. Reading!

THE BISHOP. What is she reading?

LESBIA. Some pamphlet that came by the eleven
o'clock post. She wont come out. She wont open the
door. And she says she doesnt know whether she's going
to be married or not till she's finished the pamphlet. Did
you ever hear such a thing? Do come and speak to her.

MRS BRIDGENORTH. Alfred: you had better go.

THE BISHOP. Try Collins.

LESBIA. Weve tried Collins already. He got all that
Ive told you out of her through the keyhole. Come,
Alice. [*She vanishes. Mrs Bridgenorth hurries after
her*].

THE BISHOP. This means a delay. I shall go back
to my work [*he makes for the study door*].

REGINALD. What are you working at now?

Getting Married

THE BISHOP [*stopping*] A chapter in my history of marriage. I'm just at the Roman business, you know.

THE GENERAL [*coming from the garden door to the chair Mrs Bridgenorth has just left, and sitting down*] Not more Ritualism, I hope, Alfred?

THE BISHOP. Oh no. I mean ancient Rome. [*He seats himself on the edge of the table*]. Ive just come to the period when the propertied classes refused to get married and went in for marriage settlements instead. A few of the oldest families stuck to the marriage tradition so as to keep up the supply of vestal virgins, who had to be legitimate; but nobody else dreamt of getting married. It's all very interesting, because we're coming to that here in England; except that as we dont require any vestal virgins, nobody will get married at all, except the poor, perhaps.

THE GENERAL. You take it devilishly coolly. Reginald: do you think the Barmecide's quite sane?

REGINALD. No worse than ever he was.

THE GENERAL [*to the Bishop*] Do you mean to say you believe such a thing will ever happen in England as that respectable people will give up being married?

THE BISHOP. In England especially they will. In other countries the introduction of reasonable divorce laws will save the situation; but in England we always let an institution strain itself until it breaks. Ive told our last four Prime Ministers that if they didnt make our marriage laws reasonable there would be a strike against marriage, and that it would begin among the propertied classes, where no Government would dare to interfere with it.

REGINALD. What did they say to that?

THE BISHOP. The usual thing. Quite agreed with me, but were sure that they were the only sensible men in the world, and that the least hint of marriage reform would lose them the next election. And then lost it all the same: on cordite, on drink, on Chinese labor in South Africa, on all sorts of trumpery.

REGINALD [*lurching across the kitchen towards the hearth with his hands in his pockets*] It's no use: they wont listen to our sort. [*Turning on them*] Of course they have to make you a Bishop and Boxer a General, because, after all, their blessed rabble of snobs and cads and half-starved shopkeepers cant do government work; and the bounders and week-enders are too lazy and vulgar. Theyd simply rot without us; but what do they ever do for us? what attention do they ever pay to what we say and what we want? I take it that we Bridgenorths are a pretty typical English family of the sort that has always set things straight and stuck up for the right to think and believe according to our conscience. But nowadays we are expected to dress and eat as the week-end bounders do, and to think and believe as the converted cannibals of Central Africa do, and to lie down and let every snob and every cad and every halfpenny journalist walk over us. Why, theres not a newspaper in England today that represents what I call solid Bridgenorth opinion and tradition. Half of them read as if they were published at the nearest mother's meeting, and the other half at the nearest motor garage. Do you call these chaps gentlemen? Do you call them Englishmen? I dont. [*He throws himself disgustedly into the nearest chair*].

THE GENERAL [*excited by Reginald's eloquence*] Do you see my uniform? What did Collins say? It strikes the eye. It was meant to. I put it on expressly to give the modern army bounder a smack in the eye. Somebody has to set a right example by beginning. Well, let it be a Bridgenorth. I believe in family blood and tradition, by George.

THE BISHOP [*musing*] I wonder who will begin the stand against marriage. It must come some day. I was married myself before I'd thought about it; and even if I had thought about it I was too much in love with Alice to let anything stand in the way. But, you know, Ive seen one of our daughters after another—Ethel, Jane, Fanny, and Christina and Florence—go out at that door in their veils and orange blossoms; and Ive always wondered whether theyd have gone quietly if theyd known what they were doing. Ive a horrible misgiving about that pamphlet. All progress means war with Society. Heaven forbid that Edith should be one of the combatants!

St John Hotchkiss comes into the tower ushered by Collins. He is a very smart young gentleman of twenty-nine or thereabouts, correct in dress to the last thread of his collar, but too much preoccupied with his ideas to be embarrassed by any concern as to his appearance. He talks about himself with energetic gaiety. He talks to other people with a sweet forbearance (implying a kindly consideration for their stupidity) which infuriates those whom he does not succeed in amusing. They either lose their tempers with him or try in vain to snub him.

COLLINS [*announcing*] Mr Hotchkiss. [*He withdraws*].

HOTCHKISS [*clapping Reginald gaily on the shoulder as he passes him*] Tootle loo, Rejjy.

REGINALD [*curtly, without rising or turning his head*] Morning.

HOTCHKISS. Good morning, Bishop.

THE BISHOP [*coming off the table*]. What on earth are you doing here, Sinjon? You belong to the bridegroom's party: youve no business here until after the ceremony.

HOTCHKISS. Yes, I know: thats just it. May I have a word with you in private? R e j j y or any of the family wont matter; but—[*he glances at the General, who has risen rather stiffly, as he strongly disapproves of the part played by Hotchkiss in Reginald's domestic affairs*].

THE BISHOP. All right, Sinjon. This is our brother, General Bridgenorth. [*He goes to the hearth and posts himself there, with his hands clasped behind him*].

HOTCHKISS. Oh, good! [*He turns to the General, and takes out a card-case*]. As you are in the service, allow me to introduce myself. Read my card, please. [*He presents his card to the astonished General*].

THE GENERAL [*reading*] "Mr St John Hotchkiss, the Celebrated Coward, late Lieutenant in the 165th Fusiliers."

REGINALD [*with a chuckle*] He was sent back from South Africa because he funked an order to attack, and spoiled his commanding officer's plan.

THE GENERAL [*very gravely*] I remember the case now. I had forgotten the name. I'll not refuse your acquaintance, Mr Hotchkiss; partly because youre my brother's guest, and partly because Ive seen too much active service not to know that every man's nerve plays him false at one time or another, and that some very honorable men should never go into action at all, because theyre not built that way. But if I were you I should not use that visiting card. No doubt it's an honorable trait in your character that you dont wish any man to give you his hand in ignorance of your disgrace; but you had better allow us to forget. We wish to forget. It isnt your disgrace alone: it's a disgrace to the army and to all of us. Pardon my plain speaking.

HOTCHKISS [*sunnily*] My dear General, I dont know what fear means in the military sense of the word. Ive fought seven duels with the sabre in Italy and Austria, and one with pistols in France, without turning a hair. There was no other way in which I could vindicate my motives in refusing to make that attack at Smutsfontein. I dont pretend to be a brave man. I'm afraid of wasps.

I'm afraid of cats. In spite of the voice of reason, I'm afraid of ghosts; and twice Ive fled across Europe from false alarms of cholera. But afraid to fight I am not. [*He turns gaily to Reginald and slaps him on the shoulder*]. Eh, Rejjy? [*Reginald grunts*].

THE GENERAL. Then why did you not do your duty at Smutsfontein?

HOTCHKISS. I did my duty—my higher duty. If I had made that attack, my commanding officer's plan would have been successful, and he would have been promoted. Now I happen to think that the British Army should be commanded by gentlemen, and by gentlemen alone. This man was not a gentleman. I sacrificed my military career—I faced disgrace and social ostracism—rather than give that man his chance.

THE GENERAL [*generously indignant*] Your commanding officer, sir, was my friend Major Billiter.

HOTCHKISS. Precisely. What a name!

THE GENERAL. And pray, sir, on what ground do you dare allege that Major Billiter is not a gentleman?

HOTCHKISS. By an infallible sign: one of those trifles that stamp a man. He eats rice pudding with a spoon.

THE GENERAL [*very angry*] Confound you, *I* eat rice pudding with a spoon. Now!

HOTCHKISS. Oh, so do I, frequently. But there are ways of doing these things. Billiter's way was unmistakable.

THE GENERAL. Well, I'll tell you something now. When I thought you were only a coward, I pitied you, and would have done what I could to help you back to your place in Society—

HOTCHKISS [*interrupting him*] Thank you: I havnt lost it. My motives have been fully appreciated. I was made an honorary member of two of the smartest clubs in London when the truth came out.

THE GENERAL. Well, sir, those clubs consist of snobs; and you are a jumping, bounding, prancing, snorting snob yourself.

THE BISHOP [*amused, but hospitably remonstrant*] My dear Boxer!

HOTCHKISS [*delighted*] How kind of you to say so, General! Youre quite right: I am a snob. Why not? The whole strength of England lies in the fact that the enormous majority of the English people are snobs. They insult poverty. They despise vulgarity. They love nobility. They admire exclusiveness. They will not obey a man risen from the ranks. They never trust one of their own class. I agree with them. I share their instincts. In my undergraduate days I was a Republican—a Socialist. I tried hard to feel toward a common man as I do towards a duke. I couldnt. Neither can you. Well, why should we be ashamed of this aspiration towards what is above us? Why dont I say that an honest man's the noblest work of God? Because I dont think so. If he's not a gentleman, I dont care whether he's honest or not: I shouldnt let his son marry my daughter. And thats the test, mind. Thats the test. You feel as I do. You are a snob in fact: I am a snob, not only in fact, but on principle. I shall go down in history, not as the first snob, but as the first avowed champion of English snobbery, and its first martyr in the army. The navy boasts two such martyrs in Captains Kirby and Wade, who were shot for refusing to fight under Admiral Benbow, a promoted cabin boy. I have always envied them their glory.

THE GENERAL. As a British General, sir, I have to inform you that if any officer under my command violated the sacred equality of our profession by putting a single jot of his duty or his risk on the shoulders of the humblest drummer boy, I'd shoot him with my own hand.

HOTCHKISS. That sentiment is not your equality,

General, but your superiority. Ask the Bishop. [*He seats himself on the edge of the table*].

THE BISHOP. I cant support you, Sinjon. My profession also compels me to turn my back on snobbery. You see, I have to do such a terribly democratic thing to every child that is brought to me. Without distinction of class I have to confer on it a rank so high and awful that all the grades in Debrett and Burke seem like the medals they give children in Infant Schools in comparison. I'm not allowed to make any class distinction. They are all soldiers and servants, not officers and masters.

HOTCHKISS. Ah, youre quoting the Baptism service. Thats not a bit real, you know. If I may say so, you would both feel so much more at peace with yourselves if you would acknowledge and confess your real convictions. You know you dont really think a Bishop the equal of a curate, or a lieutenant in a line regiment the equal of a general.

THE BISHOP. Of course I do. I was a curate myself.

THE GENERAL. And I was a lieutenant in a line regiment.

REGINALD. And I was nothing. But we're all our own and one another's equals, arnt we? So perhaps when youve quite done talking about yourselves, we shall get to whatever business Sinjon came about.

HOTCHKISS [*coming off the table hastily*] Oh! true, my dear fellow. I beg a thousand pardons. It's about the wedding?

THE GENERAL. What about the wedding?

HOTCHKISS. Well, we cant get our man up to the scratch. Cecil has locked himself in his room and wont see or speak to any one. I went up to his room and banged at the door. I told him I should look through the keyhole if he didnt answer. I looked through the keyhole. He was sitting on his bed, reading a book. [*Reginald rises in consternation. The General recoils*].

I told him not to be an ass, and so forth. He said he was not going to budge until he had finished the book. I asked him did he know what time it was, and whether he happened to recollect that he had a rather important appointment to marry Edith. He said the sooner I stopped interrupting him, the sooner he'd be ready. Then he stuffed his fingers in his ears; turned over on his elbows; and buried himself in his beastly book. I couldnt get another word out of him; so I thought I'd better come here and warn you.

REGINALD. This looks to me like a practical joke. Theyve arranged it between them.

THE BISHOP. No. Edith has no sense of humor. And Ive never seen a man in a jocular mood on his wedding morning.

Collins appears in the tower, ushering in the bridegroom, a young gentleman with good looks of the serious kind, somewhat careworn by an exacting conscience, and just now distracted by insoluble problems of conduct.

COLLINS [*announcing*] Mr Cecil Sykes. [*He retires*].

HOTCHKISS. Look here, Cecil: this is all wrong. Youve no business here until after the wedding. Hang it, man! youre the bridegroom.

SYKES [*coming to the Bishop, and addressing him with dogged desperation*] Ive come here to say this. When I proposed to Edith I was in utter ignorance of what I was letting myself in for legally. Having given my word, I will stand to it. You have me at your mercy: marry me if you insist. But take notice that I protest. [*He sits down distractedly in the railed chair*].

THE GENERAL.	[*Both highly incensed*]	What the devil do you mean by this? What the—
REGINALD.		Confound your impertinence, what do you—

Getting Married

HOTCHKISS. Easy, Rejjy. Easy, old man. Steady, steady, steady. [*Reginald subsides into his chair. Hotchkiss sits on his right, appeasing him*].

THE BISHOP. No, please, Rej. Control yourself, Boxer, I beg you.

THE GENERAL. I tell you I cant control myself. Ive been controlling myself for the last half-hour until I feel like bursting. [*He sits down furiously at the end of the table next the study*].

SYKES [*pointing to the simmering Reginald and the boiling General*] Thats just it, Bishop. Edith is her uncle's niece. She cant control herself any more than they can. And she's a Bishop's daughter. That means that she's engaged in social work of all sorts: organizing shop assistants and sweated work girls and all that. When her blood boils about it (and it boils at least once a week) she doesnt care what she says.

REGINALD. Well: you knew that when you proposed to her.

SYKES. Yes; but I didnt know that when we were married I should be legally responsible if she libelled anybody, though all her property is protected against me as if I were the lowest thief and cadger. This morning somebody sent me Belfort Bax's essays on Men's Wrongs; and they have been a perfect eye-opener to me. Bishop: I'm not thinking of myself: I would face anything for Edith. But my mother and sisters are wholly dependent on my property. I'd rather have to cut off an inch from my right arm than a hundred a year from my mother's income. I owe everything to her care of me.

Edith, in dressing-jacket and petticoat, comes in through the tower, swiftly and determinedly, pamphlet in hand, principles up in arms, more of a bishop than her father, yet as much a gentlewoman as her mother. She is the typical spoilt child of a clerical household: almost as terrible a product as the typical spoilt child of a Bohemian household: that is, all her childish affections of conscientious scruple and religious impulse have been applauded and deferred to until she has become an ethical snob of the first water. Her father's sense of humor and her mother's placid balance have done something to save her humanity; but her impetuous temper and energetic will, unrestrained by any touch of humor or scepticism, carry everything before them. Imperious and dogmatic, she takes command of the party at once.

EDITH [*standing behind Cecil's chair*] Cecil: I heard your voice. I must speak to you very particularly. Papa: go away. Go away everybody.

THE BISHOP [*crossing to the study door*] I think there can be no doubt that Edith wishes us to retire. Come. [*He stands in the doorway, waiting for them to follow*].

SYKES. Thats it, you see. It's just this outspokenness that makes my position hard, much as I admire her for it.

EDITH. Do you want me to flatter and be untruthful?

SYKES. No, not exactly that.

EDITH. Does anybody want me to flatter and be untruthful?

HOTCHKISS. Well, since you ask me, I do. Surely it's the very first qualification for tolerable social intercourse.

THE GENERAL [*markedly*] I hope you will always tell me the truth, my darling, at all events.

EDITH [*complacently coming to the fireplace*] You can depend on me for that, Uncle Boxer.

HOTCHKISS. Are you sure you have any adequate idea of what the truth about a military man really is?

REGINALD [*aggressively*] Whats the truth about you, I wonder?

HOTCHKISS. Oh, quite unfit for publication in its entirety. If Miss Bridgenorth begins telling it, I shall have to leave the room.

REGINALD. I'm not at all surprised to hear it. [*Rising*] But whats it got to do with our business here to-day? Is it you thats going to be married or is it Edith?

HOTCHKISS. I'm so sorry. I get so interested in myself that I thrust myself into the front of every discussion in the most insufferable way. [*Reginald, with an exclamation of disgust, crosses the kitchen towards the study door*]. But, my dear Rejjy, are you quite sure that Miss Bridgenorth is going to be married? Are you, Miss Bridgenorth?

Before Edith has time to answer her mother returns with Leo and Lesbia.

LEO. Yes, here she is, of course. I told you I heard her dash downstairs. [*She comes to the end of the table next the fireplace*].

MRS BRIDGENORTH [*transfixed in the middle of the kitchen*] And Cecil!!

LESBIA. And Sinjon!

THE BISHOP. Edith wishes to speak to Cecil. [*Mrs Bridgenorth comes to him. Lesbia goes into the garden, as before*]. Let us go into my study.

LEO. But she must come and dress. Look at the hour!

MRS BRIDGENORTH. Come, Leo dear. [*Leo follows her reluctantly. They are about to go into the study with the Bishop*].

HOTCHKISS. Do you know, Miss Bridgenorth, I should most awfully like to hear what you have to say to poor Cecil.

REGINALD [*scandalized*] Well!

EDITH. Who is poor Cecil, pray?

HOTCHKISS. One always calls a man that on his wedding morning: I dont know why. I'm his best man, you know. Dont you think it gives me a certain right to be present in Cecil's interest?

THE GENERAL [*gravely*] There is such a thing as delicacy, Mr Hotchkiss.

HOTCHKISS. There is such a thing as curiosity, General.

THE GENERAL [*furious*] Delicacy is thrown away here, Alfred. Edith: you had better take Sykes into the study.

The group at the study door breaks up. The General flings himself into the last chair on the long side of the table, near the garden door. Leo sits at the end, next him, and Mrs Bridgenorth next Leo. Reginald returns to the oak chest, to be near Leo; and the Bishop goes to his wife and stands by her.

HOTCHKISS [*to Edith*] Of course I'll go if you wish me to. But Cecil's objection to go through with it was so entirely on public grounds—

EDITH [*with quick suspicion*] His objection?

SYKES. Sinjon: you have no right to say that. I expressly said that I'm ready to go through with it.

EDITH. Cecil: do you mean to say that you have been raising difficulties about our marriage?

SYKES. I raise no difficulty. But I do beg you to be careful what you say about people. You must remember, my dear, that when we are married I shall be responsible for everything you say. Only last week you said on a public platform that Slattox and Chinnery were scoundrels. They could have got a thousand pounds damages apiece from me for that if we'd been married at the time.

EDITH [*austerely*] I never said anything of the sort. I never stoop to mere vituperation: what would my girls say of me if I did? I chose my words most carefully. I said they were tyrants, liars, and thieves; and so they are. Slattox is even worse.

HOTCHKISS. I'm afraid that would be at least five thousand pounds.

SYKES. If it were only myself, I shouldnt care. But my mother and sisters! Ive no right to sacrifice them.

EDITH. You neednt be alarmed. I'm not going to be married.

ALL THE REST. Not!

SYKES [*in consternation*] Edith! Are you throwing me over?

EDITH. How can I? you have been beforehand with me.

SYKES. On my honor, no. All I said was that I didnt know the law when I asked you to be my wife.

EDITH. And you wouldnt have asked me if you had. Is that it?

SYKES. No. I should have asked you for my sake to be a little more careful—not to ruin me uselessly.

EDITH. You think the truth useless?

HOTCHKISS. Much worse than useless, I assure you. Frequently most mischievous.

EDITH. Sinjon: hold your tongue. You are a chatterbox and a fool!

MRS BRIDGENORTH } [*shocked*] { Edith!
THE BISHOP   }   { My love!

HOTCHKISS [*mildly*] I shall not take an action, Cecil.

EDITH [*to Hotchkiss*] Sorry; but you are old enough to know better. [*To the others*] And now since there is to be no wedding, we had better get back to our work. Mamma: will you tell Collins to cut up the wedding cake into thirty-three pieces for the club girls? My not being married is no reason why they should be disappointed. [*She turns to go*].

HOTCHKISS [*gallantly*] If youll allow me to take Cecil's place, Miss Bridgenorth—

LEO. Sinjon!

HOTCHKISS. Oh, I forgot. I beg your pardon. [*To Edith, apologetically*] A prior engagement.

EDITH. What! You and Leo! I thought so. Well, hadnt you two better get married at once? I dont approve of long engagements. The breakfast's ready: the cake's ready: everything's ready. I'll lend Leo my veil and things.

THE BISHOP. I'm afraid they must wait until the decree is made absolute, my dear. And the license is not transferable.

EDITH. Oh well, it cant be helped. Is there anything else before I go off to the Club?

SYKES. You dont seem much disappointed, Edith. I cant help saying that much.

EDITH. And you cant help looking enormously relieved, Cecil. We shant be any worse friends, shall we?

SYKES [*distractedly*] Of course not. Still—I'm perfectly ready—at least—if it were not for my mother—Oh, I dont know what to do. Ive been so fond of you; and when the worry of the wedding was over I should have been so fond of you again—

EDITH [*petting him*] Come, come! dont make a scene, dear. Youre quite right. I dont think a woman doing public work ought to get married unless her husband feels about it as she does. I dont blame you at all for throwing me over.

REGINALD [*bouncing off the chest, and passing behind the General to the other end of the table*] No: dash it! I'm not going to stand this. Why is the man always to be put in the wrong? Be honest, Edith. Why werent you dressed? Were you going to throw him over? If you were, take your fair share of the blame; and dont put it all on him.

HOTCHKISS [*sweetly*] Would it not be better—
REGINALD [*violently*] Now look here, Hotchkiss. Who asked you to cut in? Is your name Edith? Am I your uncle?

HOTCHKISS. I wish you were: I should like to have an uncle, Reginald.

REGINALD. Yah! Sykes: are you ready to marry Edith or are you not?

SYKES. Ive already said that I'm quite ready. A promise is a promise.

REGINALD. We dont want to know whether a promise is a promise or not. Cant you answer yes or no without spoiling it and setting Hotchkiss here grinning like a Cheshire cat? If she puts on her veil and goes to Church, will you marry her?

SYKES. Certainly. Yes.

REGINALD. Thats all right. Now, Edie, put on your veil and off with you to the church. The bridegroom's waiting. [*He sits down at the table*].

EDITH. Is it understood that Slattox and Chinnery are liars and thieves, and that I hope by next Wednesday to have in my hands conclusive evidence that Slattox is something much worse?

SYKES. I made no conditions as to that when I proposed to you; and now I cant go back. I hope Providence will spare my poor mother. I say again I'm ready to marry you.

EDITH. Then I think you shew great weakness of character; and instead of taking advantage of it I shall set you a better example. I want to know is this true. [*She produces a pamphlet and takes it to the Bishop; then sits down between Hotchkiss and her mother*].

THE BISHOP [*reading the title*] DO YOU KNOW WHAT YOU ARE GOING TO DO? BY A WOMAN WHO HAS DONE IT. May I ask, my dear, what she did?

EDITH. She got married. When she had three children—the eldest only four years old—her husband committed a murder, and then attempted to commit suicide, but only succeeded in disfiguring himself. Instead of hanging him, they sent him to penal servitude for life, for the sake, they said, of his wife and infant children. And she could not get a divorce from that horrible murderer. They would not even keep him imprisoned for life. For twenty years she had to live singly, bringing up her children by her own work, and knowing that just when they were grown up and beginning life, this dreadful creature would be let out to disgrace them all, and prevent the two girls getting decently married, and drive the son out of the country perhaps. Is that really the law? Am I to understand that if Cecil commits a murder, or forges, or steals, or becomes an atheist, I cant get divorced from him?

THE BISHOP. Yes, my dear. That is so. You must take him for better for worse.

EDITH. Then I most certainly refuse to enter into any such wicked contract. What sort of servants? what sort of friends? what sort of Prime Ministers should we have if we took them for better for worse for all their lives? We should simply encourage them in every sort of wickedness. Surely my husband's conduct is of more importance to me than Mr Balfour's or Mr Asquith's. If I had known the law I would never have consented. I dont believe any woman would if she realized what she was doing.

SYKES. But I'm not going to commit murder.

EDITH. How do you know? Ive sometimes wanted to murder Slattox. Have you never wanted to murder somebody, Uncle Rejjy?

REGINALD [*at Hotchkiss, with intense expression*] Yes.

LEO. Rejjy!

REGINALD. I said yes; and I mean yes. There was

one night, Hotchkiss, when I jolly near shot you and Leo and finished up with myself; and thats the truth.

LEO [*suddenly whimpering*] Oh Rejjy [*she runs to him and kisses him*].

REGINALD [*wrathfully*] Be off. [*She returns weeping to her seat*].

MRS BRIDGENORTH [*petting Leo, but speaking to the company at large*] But isnt all this great nonsense? What likelihood is there of any of us committing a crime?

HOTCHKISS. Oh yes, I assure you. I went into the matter once very carefully; and I found things I have actually done—things that everybody does, I imagine—would expose me, if I were found out and prosecuted, to ten years' penal servitude, two years hard labor, and the loss of all civil rights. Not counting that I'm a private trustee, and, like all private trustees, a fraudulent one. Otherwise, the widow for whom I am trustee would starve occasionally, and the children get no education. And I'm probably as honest a man as any here.

THE GENERAL [*outraged*[Do you imply that I have been guilty of conduct that would expose me to penal servitude?

HOTCHKISS. I should think it quite likely. But of course I dont know.

MRS BRIDGENORTH. But bless me! marriage is not a question of law, is it? Have you children no affection for one another? Surely thats enough?

HOTCHKISS. If it's enough, why get married?

MRS BRIDGENORTH. Stuff, Sinjon! Of course people must get married. [*Uneasily*] Alfred: why dont you say something? Surely youre not going to let this go on.

THE GENERAL. Ive been waiting for the last twenty minutes, Alfred, in amazement! in stupefaction! to hear you put a stop to all this. We look to you: it's your place, your office, your duty. Exert your authority at once.

THE BISHOP. You must give the devil fair play, Boxer. Until you have heard and weighed his case you have no right to condemn him. I'm sorry you have been kept waiting twenty minutes; but I myself have waited twenty years for this to happen. Ive often wrestled with the temptation to pray that it might not happen in my own household. Perhaps it was a presentiment that it might become a part of our old Bridgenorth burden that made me warn our Governments so earnestly that unless the law of marriage were first made human, it could never become divine.

MRS BRIDGENORTH. Oh, do be sensible about this. People must get married. What would you have said if Cecil's parents had not been married?

THE BISHOP. They were not, my dear.

HOTCHKISS.	Hallo!
REGINALD.	What d'ye mean?
THE GENERAL.	Eh?
LEO.	Not married!
MRS BRIDGENORTH.	What!

SYKES [*rising in amazement*] What on earth do you mean, Bishop? My parents were married.

HOTCHKISS. You cant remember, Cecil.

SYKES. Well, I never asked my mother to shew me her marriage lines, if thats what you mean. What man ever has? I never suspected—I never knew—Are you joking? Or have we all gone mad?

THE BISHOP. Dont be alarmed, Cecil. Let me explain. Your parents were not Anglicans. You were not, I think, Anglican yourself, until your second year at Oxford. They were Positivists. They went through the Positivist ceremony at Newton Hall in Fetter Lane after entering into the civil contract before the Registrar of the West Strand District. I ask you, as an Anglican Catholic, was that a marriage?

SYKES [*overwhelmed*] Great Heavens, no! a thousand times, no. I never thought of that. I'm a child of sin. [*He collapses into the railed chair*].

THE BISHOP. Oh, come, come! You are no more a child of sin than any Jew, or Mohammedan, or Nonconformist, or anyone else born outside the Church. But you see how it affects my view of the situation. To me there is only one marriage that is holy: the Church's sacrament of marriage. Outside that, I can recognize no distinction between one civil contract and another. There was a time when all marriages were made in Heaven. But because the Church was unwise and would not make its ordinances reasonable, its power over men and women was taken away from it; and marriages gave place to contracts at a registry office. And now that our Governments refuse to make these contracts reasonable, those whom we in our blindness drove out of the Church will be driven out of the registry office; and we shall have the history of Ancient Rome repeated. We shall be joined by our solicitors for seven, fourteen, or twenty-one years—or perhaps months. Deeds of partnership will replace the old vows.

THE GENERAL. Would you, a Bishop, approve of such partnerships?

THE BISHOP. Do you think that I, a Bishop, approve of the Deceased Wife's Sister Act? That did not prevent its becoming law.

THE GENERAL. But when the Government sounded you as to whether youd marry a man to his deceased wife's sister you very naturally and properly told them youd see them damned first.

THE BISHOP [*horrified*] No, no, really, Boxer! You must not—

THE GENERAL [*impatiently*] Oh, of course I dont

mean that you used those words. But that was the meaning and the spirit of it.

THE BISHOP. Not the spirit, Boxer, I protest. But never mind that. The point is that State marriage is already divorced from Church marriage. The relations between Leo and Rejjy and Sinjon are perfectly legal; but do you expect me, as a Bishop, to approve of them?

THE GENERAL. I dont defend Reginald. He should have kicked you out of the house, Mr. Hotchkiss.

REGINALD [*rising*] How could I kick him out of the house? He's stronger than me: he could have kicked me out if it came to that. He did kick me out: what else was it but kicking out, to take my wife's affections from me and establish himself in my place? [*He comes to the hearth*].

HOTCHKISS. I protest, Reginald, I said all that a man could to prevent the smash.

REGINALD. Oh, I know you did: I dont blame you: people dont do these things to one another: they happen and they cant be helped. What was I to do? I was old: she was young. I was dull: he was brilliant. I had a face like a walnut: he had a face like a mushroom. I was as glad to have him in the house as she was: he amused me. And we were a couple of fools: he gave us good advice—told us what to do when we didnt know. She found out that I wasnt any use to her and he was; so she nabbed him and gave me the chuck.

LEO. If you dont stop talking in that disgraceful way about our married life, I'll leave the room and never speak to you again.

REGINALD. Youre not going to speak to me again, anyhow, are you? Do you suppose I'm going to visit you when you marry him?

HOTCHKISS. I hope so. Surely youre not going to be vindictive, Rejjy. Besides, youll have all the advantages I formerly enjoyed. Youll be the visitor, the relief, the new face, the fresh news, the hopeless attachment: *I* shall only be the husband.

REGINALD [*savagely*] Will you tell me this, any of you? how is it that we always get talking about Hotchkiss when our business is about Edith? [*He fumes up the kitchen to the tower and back to his chair*].

MRS BRIDGENORTH. Will somebody tell me how the world is to go on if nobody is to get married?

SYKES. Will somebody tell me what an honorable man and a sincere Anglican is to propose to a woman whom he loves and who loves him and wont marry him?

LEO. Will somebody tell me how I'm to arrange to take care of Rejjy when I'm married to Sinjon. Rejjy must not be allowed to marry anyone else, especially that odious nasty creature that told all those wicked lies about him in Court.

HOTCHKISS. Let us draw up the first English partnership deed.

LEO. For shame, Sinjon!

THE BISHOP. Somebody must begin, my dear. Ive a very strong suspicion that when it is drawn up it will be so much worse than the existing law that you will all prefer getting married. We shall therefore be doing the greatest possible service to morality by just trying how the new system would work.

LESBIA [*suddenly reminding them of her forgotten presence as she stands thoughtfully in the garden doorway*] Ive been thinking.

THE BISHOP [*to Hotchkiss*] Nothing like making people think: is there, Sinjon?

LESBIA [*coming to the table, on the General's left*] A woman has no right to refuse motherhood. That is clear, after the statistics given in The Times by Mr Sidney Webb.

THE GENERAL. Mr Webb has nothing to do with it. It is the Voice of Nature.

LESBIA. But if she is an English lady it is her right and her duty to stand out for honorable conditions. If we can agree on the conditions, I am willing to enter into an alliance with Boxer.

The General staggers to his feet, momentarily stupent and speechless.

EDITH [*rising*] And I with Cecil.

LEO [*rising*] And I with Rejjy and St John.

THE GENERAL [*aghast*] An alliance! Do you mean a—a—a—

REGINALD. She only means bigamy, as I understand her.

THE GENERAL. Alfred: how long more are you going to stand there and countenance this lunacy? Is it a horrible dream or am I awake? In the name of common sense and sanity, let us go back to real life—

Collins comes in through the tower, in alderman's robes. The ladies who are standing sit down hastily, and look as unconcerned as possible.

COLLINS. Sorry to hurry you, my lord; but the Church has been full this hour past; and the organist has played all the wedding music in *Lohengrin* three times over.

THE GENERAL. The very man we want. Alfred: I'm not equal to this crisis. You are not equal to it. The Army has failed. The Church has failed. I shall put aside all idle social distinctions and appeal to the Municipality.

MRS BRIDGENORTH. Do, Boxer. He is sure to get us out of this difficulty.

Collins, a little puzzled, comes forward affably to Hotchkiss's left.

HOTCHKISS [*rising, impressed by the aldermanic gown*] Ive not had the pleasure. Will you introduce me?

COLLINS [*confidentially*] All right, sir. Only the greengrocer, sir, in charge of the wedding breakfast. Mr Alderman Collins, sir, when I'm in my gown.

HOTCHKISS [*staggered*] Very pleased indeed [*he sits down again*].

THE BISHOP. Personally I value the counsel of my old friend, Mr Alderman Collins, very highly. If Edith and Cecil will allow him—

EDITH. Collins has known me from my childhood: I'm sure he will agree with me.

COLLINS. Yes, miss: you may depend on me for that. Might I ask what the difficulty is?

EDITH. Simply this. Do you expect me to get married in the existing state of the law?

SYKES [*rising and coming to Collin's left elbow*] I put it to you as a sensible man: is it any worse for her than for me?

REGINALD [*leaving his place and thrusting himself between Collins and Sykes, who returns to his chair*] Thats not the point. Let this be understood, Mr Collins. It's not the man who is backing out: it's the woman. [*He posts himself on the hearth*].

LESBIA. We do not admit that, Collins. The women are perfectly ready to make a reasonable arrangement.

LEO. With both men.

THE GENERAL. The case is now before you, Mr Collins. And I put it to you as one man to another: did you ever hear such crazy nonsense?

MRS BRIDGENORTH. The world must go on, mustnt it, Collins?

COLLINS [*snatching at this, the first intelligible proposition he has heard*] Oh, the world will go on, maam: dont you be afraid of that. It aint so easy to stop it as the earnest kind of people think.

EDITH. I knew you would agree with me, Collins. Thank you.

HOTCHKISS. Have you the least idea of what they are talking about, Mr Alderman?

COLLINS. Oh, thats all right, sir. The particulars dont matter. I never read the report of a Committee: after all, what can they say that you dont know? You pick it up as they go on talking. [*He goes to the corner of the table and speaks across it to the company*]. Well, my Lord and Miss Edith and Madam and Gentlemen, it's like this. Marriage is tolerable enough in its way if youre easygoing and dont expect too much from it. But it doesnt bear thinking about. The great thing is to get the young people tied up before they know what theyre letting themselves in for. Theres Miss Lesbia now. She waited till she started thinking about it; and then it was all over. If you once start arguing, Miss Edith and Mr Sykes, youll never get married. Go and get married first: youll have plenty of arguing afterwards, miss, believe me.

HOTCHKISS. Your warning comes too late. Theyve started arguing already.

THE GENERAL. But you dont take in the full—well, I dont wish to exaggerate; but the only word I can find is the full horror of the situation. These ladies not only refuse our honorable offers, but as I understand it—and I'm sure I beg your pardon most heartily, Lesbia, if I'm wrong, as I hope I am—they actually call on us to enter into—I'm sorry to use the expression; but what can I say?—into ALLIANCES with them under contracts to be drawn up by our confounded solicitors.

COLLINS. Dear me, General: thats something new when the parties belong to the same class.

THE BISHOP. Not new, Collins. The Romans did it.

COLLINS. Yes: they would, them Romans. When youre in Rome do as the Romans do, is an old saying. But we're not in Rome at present, my lord.

THE BISHOP. We have got into many of their ways. What do you think of the contract system, Collins?

COLLINS. Well, my lord, when theres a question of a contract, I always say, shew it to me on paper. If it's to be talk, let it be talk; but if it's to be a contract, down with it in black and white; and then we shall know what we're about.

HOTCHKISS. Quite right, Mr Alderman. Let us draft it at once. May I go into the study for writing materials, Bishop?

THE BISHOP. Do, Sinjon.

Hotchkiss goes into the library.

COLLINS. If I might point out a difficulty, my lord—

THE BISHOP. Certainly. [*He goes to the fourth chair from the General's left, but before sitting down, courteously points to the chair at the end of the table next the hearth*]. Wont you sit down, Mr Alderman? [*Collins, very appreciative of the Bishop's distinguished consideration, sits down. The Bishop then takes his seat*].

COLLINS. We are at present six men to four ladies. Thats not fair.

REGINALD. Not fair to the men, you mean.

LEO. Oh! Rejjy has said something clever! Can I be mistaken in him?

Hotchkiss comes back with a blotter and some paper. He takes the vacant place in the middle of the table between Lesbia and the Bishop.

COLLINS. I tell you the truth, my lord and ladies and gentlemen: I dont trust my judgment on this subject. Theres a certain lady that I always consult on delicate points like this. She has a very exceptional experience, and a wonderful temperament and instinct in affairs of the heart.

HOTCHKISS. Excuse me, Mr Alderman: I'm a snob; and I warn you that theres no use consulting anyone who will not advise us frankly on class lines. Marriage is good enough for the lower classes: they have facilities for desertion that are denied to us. What is the social position of this lady?

COLLINS. The highest in the borough, sir. She is the Mayoress. But you need not stand in awe of her, sir. She is my sister-in-law. [*To the Bishop*] Ive often spoken of her to your lady, my lord. [*To Mrs Bridgenorth*] Mrs George, maam.

MRS BRIDGENORTH [*startled*] Do you mean to say, Collins, that Mrs George is a real person?

COLLINS [*equally startled*] Didnt you believe in her, maam?

MRS BRIDGENORTH. Never for a moment.

THE BISHOP. We always thought that Mrs George was too good to be true. I still dont believe in her, Collins. You must produce her if you are to convince me.

COLLINS [*overwhelmed*] Well, I'm so taken aback by this that—Well I never ! ! ! Why! shes at the church at this moment, waiting to see the wedding.

THE BISHOP. Then produce her. [*Collins shakes his head*]. Come, Collins! confess. Theres no such person.

COLLINS. There is, my lord: there is, I assure you. You ask George. It's true *I* cant produce her; but you can, my lord.

THE BISHOP. I!

COLLINS. Yes, my lord, you. For some reason that I never could make out, she has forbidden me to talk about you, or to let her meet you. Ive asked her to come here of a wedding morning to help with the flowers or the like; and she has always refused. But if you order her to come as her Bishop, she'll come. She has some very strange fancies, has Mrs George. Send your ring to her, my lord—the official ring—send it by some very stylish gentleman—perhaps Mr Hotchkiss here would be good enough to take it—and she'll come.

Getting Married

THE BISHOP [*taking off his ring and handing it to Hotchkiss*] Oblige me by undertaking the mission.

HOTCHKISS. But how am I to know the lady?

COLLINS. She has gone to the church in state, sir, and will be attended by a Beadle with a mace. He will point her out to you; and he will take the front seat of the carriage on the way back.

HOTCHKISS. No, by heavens! Forgive me, Bishop; but you are asking too much. I ran away from the Boers because I was a snob. I run away from the Beadle for the same reason. I absolutely decline the mission.

THE GENERAL [*rising impressively*] Be good enough to give me that ring, Mr Hotchkiss.

HOTCHKISS. With pleasure. [*He hands it to him*].

THE GENERAL. I shall have the great pleasure, Mr Alderman, in waiting on the Mayoress with the Bishop's orders; and I shall be proud to return with municipal honors. [*He stalks out gallantly, Collins rising for a moment to bow to him with marked dignity*].

REGINALD. Boxer is rather a fine old josser in his way.

HOTCHKISS. His uniform gives him an unfair advantage. He will take all the attention off the Beadle.

COLLINS. I think it would be as well, my lord, to go on with the contract while we're waiting. The truth is, we shall none of us have much of a look-in when Mrs George comes; so we had better finish the writing part of the business before she arrives.

HOTCHKISS. I think I have the preliminaries down all right. [*Reading*] 'Memorandum of Agreement made this day of blank blank between blank blank of blank blank in the County of blank, Esquire, hereinafter called the Gentleman, of the one part, and blank blank of blank in the County of blank, hereinafter called the

Lady, of the other part, whereby it is declared and agreed as follows.'

LEO [*rising*] You might remember your manners, Sinjon. The lady comes first. [*She goes behind him and stoops to look at the draft over his shoulder*].

HOTCHKISS. To be sure. I beg your pardon. [*He alters the draft*].

LEO. And you have got only one lady and one gentleman. There ought to be two gentlemen.

COLLINS. Oh, thats a mere matter of form, maam. Any number of ladies or gentlemen can be put in.

LEO. Not any number of ladies. Only one lady. Besides, that creature wasnt a lady.

REGINALD. You shut your head, Leo. This is a general sort of contract for everybody: it's not your contract.

LEO. Then what use is it to me?

HOTCHKISS. You will get some hints from it for your own contract.

EDITH. I hope there will be no hinting. Let us have the plain straightforward truth and nothing but the truth.

COLLINS. Yes, yes, miss: it will be all right. Theres nothing underhand, I assure you. It's a model agreement, as it were.

EDITH [*unconvinced*] I hope so.

HOTCHKISS. What is the first clause in an agreement, usually? You know, Mr Alderman.

COLLINS [*at a loss*] Well, sir, the Town Clerk always sees to that. Ive got out of the habit of thinking for myself in these little matters. Perhaps his lordship knows.

THE BISHOP. I'm sorry to say I dont. But Soames will know. Alice, where is Soames?

HOTCHKISS. He's in there [*pointing to the study*].

THE BISHOP [*to his wife*] Coax him to join us, my

love. [*Mrs Bridgenorth goes into the study*]. Soames is my chaplain, Mr Collins. The great difficulty about Bishops in the Church of England to-day is that the affairs of the diocese make it necessary that a Bishop should be before everything a man of business, capable of sticking to his desk for sixteen hours a day. But the result of having Bishops of this sort is that the spiritual interests of the Church, and its influence on the souls and imaginations of the people, very soon begins to go rapidly to the devil—

EDITH [*shocked*] Papa!

THE BISHOP. I am speaking technically, not in Boxer's manner. Indeed the Bishops themselves went so far in that direction that they gained a reputation for being spiritually the stupidest men in the country and commercially the sharpest. I found a way out of this difficulty. Soames was my solicitor. I found that Soames, though a very capable man of business, had a romantic secret history. His father was an eminent Nonconformist divine who habitually spoke of the Church of England as The Scarlet Woman. Soames became secretly converted to Anglicanism at the age of fifteen. He longed to take holy orders, but didnt dare to, because his father had a weak heart and habitually threatened to drop dead if anybody hurt his feelings. You may have noticed that people with weak hearts are the tyrants of English family life. So poor Soames had to become a solicitor. When his father died—by a curious stroke of poetic justice he died of scarlet fever, and was found to have had a perfectly sound heart—I ordained Soames and made him my chaplain. He is now quite happy. He is a celibate; fasts strictly on Fridays and throughout Lent; wears a cassock and biretta; and has more legal business to do than ever he had in his old office in Ely Place. And he sets me free for the spiritual and scholarly pursuits proper to a Bishop.

MRS BRIDGENORTH [*coming back from the study with a knitting basket*] Here he is. [*She resumes her seat, and knits*].

Soames comes in in cassock and biretta. He salutes the company by blessing them with two fingers.

HOTCHKISS. Take my place, Mr Soames. [*He gives up his chair to him, and retires to the oak chest, on which he seats himself*].

THE BISHOP. No longer Mr Soames, Sinjon. Father Anthony.

SOAMES [*taking his seat*] I was christened Oliver Cromwell Soames. My father had no right to do it. I have taken the name of Anthony. When you become parents, young gentlemen, be very careful not to label a helpless child with views which it may come to hold in abhorrence.

THE BISHOP. Has Alice explained to you the nature of the document we are drafting?

SOAMES. She has indeed.

LESBIA. That sounds as if you disapproved.

SOAMES. It is not for me to approve or disapprove. I do the work that comes to my hand from my ecclesiastical superior.

THE BISHOP. Dont be uncharitable, Anthony. You must give us your best advice.

SOAMES. My advice to you all is to do your duty by taking the Christian vows of celibacy and poverty. The Church was founded to put an end to marriage and to put an end to property.

MRS BRIDGENORTH. But how could the world go on, Anthony?

SOAMES. Do your duty and see. Doing your duty is your business: keeping the world going is in higher hands.

LESBIA. Anthony: youre impossible.

SOAMES [*taking up his pen*] You wont take my advice. I didnt expect you would. Well, I await your instructions.

REGINALD. We got stuck on the first clause. What should we begin with?

SOAMES. It is usual to begin with the term of the contract.

EDITH. What does that mean?

SOAMES. The term of years for which it is to hold good.

LEO. But this is a marriage contract.

SOAMES. Is the marriage to be for a year, a week, or a day?

REGINALD. Come, I say, Anthony! Youre worse than any of us. A day!

SOAMES. Off the path is off the path. An inch or a mile: what does it matter?

LEO. If the marriage is not to be for ever, I'll have nothing to do with it. I call it immoral to have a marriage for a term of years. If the people dont like it they can get divorced.

REGINALD. It ought to be for just as long as the two people like. Thats what I say.

COLLINS. They may not agree on the point, sir. It's often fast with one and loose with the other.

LESBIA. I should say for as long as the man behaves himself.

THE BISHOP. Suppose the woman doesnt behave herself?

MRS BRIDGENORTH. The woman may have lost all her chances of a good marriage with anybody else. She should not be cast adrift.

REGINALD. So may the man! What about his home?

LEO. The wife ought to keep an eye on him, and see that he is comfortable and takes care of himself properly. The other man wont want her all the time.

LESBIA. There may not be another man.

LEO. Then why on earth should she leave him?

LESBIA. Because she wants to.

LEO. Oh, if people are going to be let do what they want to, then I call it simple immorality. [*She goes indignantly to the oak chest, and perches herself on it close beside Hotchkiss*].

REGINALD [*watching them sourly*] You do it yourself, dont you?

LEO. Oh, thats quite different. Dont make foolish witticisms, Rejjy.

THE BISHOP. We dont seem to be getting on. What do you say, Mr Alderman?

COLLINS. Well, my lord, you see people do persist in talking as if marriages was all of one sort. But theres almost as many different sorts of marriages as theres different sorts of people. Theres the young things that marry for love, not knowing what theyre doing, and the old things that marry for money and comfort and companionship. Theres the people that marry for children. Theres the people that dont intend to have children and that arnt fit to have them. Theres the people that marry because theyre so much run after by the other sex that they have to put a stop to it somehow. Theres the people that want to try a new experience, and the people that want to have done with experiences. How are you to please them all? Why, youll want half a dozen different sorts of contract.

THE BISHOP. Well, if so, let us draw them all up. Let us face it.

REGINALD. Why should we be held together whether we like it or not? Thats the question thats at the bottom of it all.

MRS BRIDGENORTH. Because of the children, Rejjy.

COLLINS. But even then, maam, why should we be held together when thats all over—when the girls are married and the boys out in the world and in business for themselves? When thats done with, the real work of the marriage is done with. If the two like to stay together, let them stay together. But if not, let them part, as old people in the workhouses do. Theyve had enough of one another. Theyve found one another out. Why should they be tied together to sit there grudging and hating and spiting one another like so many do? Put it twenty years from the birth of the youngest child.

SOAMES. How if there be no children?
COLLINS. Let em take one another on liking.
MRS BRIDGENORTH. Collins!
LEO. You wicked old man!
THE BISHOP [*remonstrating*] My dear, my dear!
LESBIA. And what is a woman to live on, pray, when she is no longer liked, as you call it?
SOAMES [*with sardonic formality*] It is proposed that the term of the agreement be twenty years from the birth of the youngest child when there are children. Any amendment?
LEO. I protest. It must be for life. It would not be a marriage at all if it were not for life.
SOAMES. Mrs Reginald Bridgenorth proposes life. Any seconder?
LEO. Dont be soulless, Anthony.
LESBIA. I have a very important amendment. If there are any children, the man must be cleared completely out of the house for two years on each occasion. At such times he is superfluous, importunate, and ridiculous.
COLLINS. But where is he to go, miss?
LESBIA. He can go where he likes as long as he does not bother the mother.
REGINALD. And is she to be left lonely—
LESBIA. Lonely! With her child. The poor woman

would be only too glad to have a moment to herself. Dont be absurd, Rejjy.

REGINALD. That father is to be a wandering wretched outcast, living at his club, and seeing nobody but his friends' wives!

LESBIA [*ironically*] Poor fellow!

HOTCHKISS. The friends' wives are perhaps the solution of the problem. You see, their husbands will also be outcasts; and the poor ladies will occasionally pine for male society.

LESBIA. There is no reason why a mother should not have male society. What she clearly should not have is a husband.

SOAMES. Anything else, Miss Grantham?

LESBIA. Yes: I must have my own separate house, or my own separate part of a house. Boxer smokes: I cant endure tobacco. Boxer believes that an open window means death from cold and exposure to the night air: I must have fresh air always. We can be friends; but we cant live together; and that must be put in the agreement.

EDITH. Ive no objection to smoking; and as to opening the windows, Cecil will of course have to do what is best for his health.

THE BISHOP. Who is to be the judge of that, my dear? You or he?

EDITH. Neither of us. We must do what the doctor orders.

REGINALD. Doctor be—!

LEO [*admonitorily*] Rejjy!

REGINALD [*to Soames*] You take my tip, Anthony. Put a clause into that agreement that the doctor is to have no say in the job. It's bad enough for the two people to be married to one another without their both being married to the doctor as well.

LESBIA. That reminds me of something very important. Boxer believes in vaccinnation: I do not. There must be a clause that I am to decide on such questions as I think best.

LEO [*to the Bishop*] Baptism is nearly as important as vaccination: isnt it?

THE BISHOP. It used to be considered so, my dear.

LEO. Well, Sinjon scoffs at it: he says that godfathers are ridiculous. I must be allowed to decide.

REGINALD. Theyll be his children as well as yours, you know.

LEO. Dont be indelicate, Rejjy.

EDITH. You are forgetting the very important matter of money.

COLLINS. Ah! Money! Now we're coming to it!

EDITH. When I'm married I shall have practically no money except what I shall earn.

THE BISHOP. I'm sorry, Cecil. A Bishop's daughter is a poor man's daughter.

SYKES. But surely you dont imagine that I'm going to let Edith work when we're married. I'm not a rich man; but Ive enough to spare her that; and when my mother dies—

EDITH. What nonsense! Of course I shall work when I'm married. I shall keep your house.

SYKES. Oh, that!

REGINALD. You call that work?

EDITH. Dont you? Leo used to do it for nothing; so no doubt you thought it wasnt work at all. Does your present housekeeper do it for nothing?

REGINALD. But it will be part of your duty as a wife.

EDITH. Not under this contract. I'll not have it so. If I'm to keep the house, I shall expect Cecil to pay me at least as well as he would pay a hired housekeeper. I'll not go begging to him every time I want a new dress or a cab fare, as so many women have to do.

SYKES. You know very well I would grudge you nothing, Edie.

EDITH. Then dont grudge me my self-respect and independence. I insist on it in fairness to you, Cecil, because in this way there will be a fund belonging solely to me; and if Slattox takes an action against you for anything I say, you can pay the damages and stop the interest out of my salary.

SOAMES. You forget that under this contract he will not be liable, because you will not be his wife in law.

EDITH. Nonsense! Of course I shall be his wife.

COLLINS [*his curiosity roused*] Is Slattox taking an action against you, miss? Slattox is on the Council with me. Could I settle it?

EDITH. He has not taken an action; but Cecil says he will.

COLLINS. What for, miss, if I may ask?

EDITH. Slattox is a liar and a thief; and it is my duty to expose him.

COLLINS. You surprise me, miss. Of course Slattox is in a manner of speaking a liar. If I may say so without offence, we're all liars, if it was only to spare one another's feelings. But I shouldnt call Slattox a thief. He's not all that he should be, perhaps; but he pays his way.

EDITH. If that is only your nice way of saying that Slattox is entirely unfit to have two hundred girls in his power as absolute slaves, then I shall say that too about him at the very next public meeting I address. He steals their wages under pretence of fining them. He steals their food under pretence of buying it for them. He lies when he denies having done it. And he does other things, as you evidently know, Collins. Therefore I give you notice that I shall expose him before all England without the least regard to the consequences to myself.

SYKES. Or to me?

EDITH. I take equal risks. Suppose you felt it to be your duty to shoot Slattox, what would become of me and the children? I'm sure I dont want anybody to be shot: not even Slattox; but if the public never will take any notice of even the most crying evil until somebody is shot, what are people to do but shoot somebody?

SOAMES [*inexorably*] I'm waiting for my instructions as to the term of the agreement.

REGINALD [*impatiently, leaving the hearth and going behind Soames*] It's no good talking all over the shop like this. We shall be here all day. I propose that the agreement holds good until the parties are divorced.

SOAMES. They cant be divorced. They will not be married.

REGINALD. But if they cant be divorced, then this will be worse than marriage.

MRS BRIDGENORTH. Of course it will. Do stop this nonsense. Why, who are the children to belong to?

LESBIA. We have already settled that they are to belong to the mother.

REGINALD. No: I'm dashed if you have. I'll fight for the ownership of my own children tooth and nail; and so will a good many other fellows, I can tell you.

EDITH. It seems to me that they should be divided between the parents. If Cecil wishes any of the children to be his exclusively, he should pay a certain sum for the risk and trouble of bringing them into the world: say a thousand pounds apiece. The interest on this could go towards the support of the child as long as we live together. But the principal would be my property. In that way, if Cecil took the child away from me, I should at least be paid for what it had cost me.

MRS BRIDGENORTH [*putting down her knitting in amazement*] Edith! Who ever heard of such a thing!!

EDITH. Well, how else do you propose to settle it?

THE BISHOP. There is such a thing as a favorite

child. What about the youngest child—the Benjamin—the child of its parents' matured strength and charity, always better treated and better loved than the unfortunate eldest children of their youthful ignorance and wilfulness? Which parent is to own the youngest child, payment or no payment?

COLLINS. Theres a third party, my lord. Theres the child itself. My wife is so fond of her children that they cant call their lives their own. They all run away from home to escape from her. A child hasnt a grown-up person's appetite for affection. A little of it goes a long way with them; and they like a good imitation of it better than the real thing, as every nurse knows.

SOAMES. Are you sure that any of us, young or old, like the real thing as well as we like an artistic imitation of it? Is not the real thing accursed? Are not the best beloved always the good actors rather than the true sufferers? Is not love always falsified in novels and plays to make it endurable? I have noticed in myself a great delight in pictures of the Saints and of Our Lady; but when I fall under that most terrible curse of the priest's lot, the curse of Joseph pursued by the wife of Potiphar, I am invariably repelled and terrified.

HOTCHKISS. Are you now speaking as a saint, Father Anthony, or as a solicitor?

SOAMES. There is no difference. There is not one Christian rule for solicitors and another for saints. Their hearts are alike; and their way of salvation is along the same road.

THE BISHOP. But "few there be that find it." Can you find it for us, Anthony?

SOAMES. It lies broad before you. It is the way to destruction that is narrow and tortuous. Marriage is an abomination which the Church was founded to cast out and replace by the communion of saints. I learnt that from every marriage settlement I drew up as a solicitor no less than from inspired revelation. You have set yourselves here to put your sin before you in black and white; and you cant agree upon or endure one article of it.

SYKES. It's certainly rather odd that the whole thing seems to fall to pieces the moment you touch it.

THE BISHOP. You see, when you give the devil fair play he loses his case. He has not been able to produce even the first clause of a working agreement; so I'm afraid we cant wait for him any longer.

LESBIA. Then the community will have to do without my children.

EDITH. And Cecil will have to do without me.

LEO [*getting off the chest*] And I positively will not marry Sinjon if he is not clever enough to make some provision for my looking after Rejjy. [*She leaves Hotchkiss, and goes back to her chair ct the end of the table behind Mrs Bridgenorth*].

MRS BRIDGENORTH. And the world will come to an end with this generation, I suppose.

COLLINS. Cant nothing be done, my lord?

THE BISHOP. You can make divorce reasonable and decent: that is all.

LESBIA. Thank you for nothing. If you will only make marriage reasonable and decent, you can do as you like about divorce. I have not stated my deepest objection to marriage; and I dont intend to. There are certain rights I will not give any person over me.

REGINALD. Well, I think it jolly hard that a man should support his wife for years, and lose the chance of getting a really good wife, and then have her refuse to be a wife to him.

LESBIA. I'm not going to discuss it with you, Rejjy. If your sense of personal honor doesnt make you understand, nothing will.

SOAMES [*implacably*] I'm still awaiting my instructions.

They look at one another, each waiting for one of the others to suggest something. Silence.

REGINALD [*blankly*] I suppose, after all, marriage is better than—well, than the usual alternative.

SOAMES [*turning fiercely on him*] What right have you to say so? You know that the sins that are wasting and maddening this unhappy nation are those committed in wedlock.

COLLINS. Well, the single ones cant afford to indulge their affections the same as married people.

SOAMES. Away with it all, I say. You have your Master's commandments. Obey them.

HOTCHKISS [*rising and leaning on the back of the chair left vacant by the General*] I really must point out to you, Father Anthony, that the early Christian rules of life were not made to last, because the early Christians did not believe that the world itself was going to last. Now we know that we shall have to go through with it. We have found that there are millions of years behind us; and we know that that there are millions before us. Mrs Bridgenorth's question remains unanswered. How is the world to go on? You say that that is our business —that it is the business of Providence. But the modern Christian view is that we are here to do the business of Providence and nothing else. The question is, how. Am I not to use my reason to find out why? Isnt that what my reason is for? Well, all my reason tells me at present is that you are an impracticable lunatic.

SOAMES. Does that help?

HOTCHKISS. No.

SOAMES. Then pray for light.

HOTCHKISS. No: I am a snob, not a beggar. [*He sits down in the General's chair*].

COLLINS. We dont seem to be getting on, do we? Miss Edith: you and Mr Sykes had better go off to church and settle the right and wrong of it afterwards. Itll ease your minds, believe me: I speak from experience. You will burn your boats, as one might say.

SOAMES. We should never burn our boats. It is death in life.

COLLINS. Well, Father, I will say for you that you have views of your own and are not afraid to out with them. But some of us are of a more cheerful disposition. On the Borough Council now, you would be in a minority of one. You must take human nature as it is.

SOAMES. Upon what compulsion must I? I'll take divine nature as it is. I'll not hold a candle to the devil.

THE BISHOP. Thats a very unchristian way of treating the devil.

REGINALD. Well, we dont seem to be getting any further, do we?

THE BISHOP. Will you give it up and get married, Edith?

EDITH. No. What I propose seems to me quite reasonable.

THE BISHOP. And you, Lesbia?

LESBIA. Never.

MRS BRIDGENORTH. Never is a long word, Lesbia. Dont say it.

LESBIA [with a flash of temper] Dont pity me, Alice, please. As I said before, I am an English lady, quite prepared to do without anything I cant have on honorable conditions.

SOAMES [after a silence expressive of utter deadlock] I am still awaiting my instructions.

REGINALD. Well, we dont seem to be getting along, do we?

LEO [out of patience] You said that before, Rejjy. Do not repeat yourself.

REGINALD. Oh, bother! [*He goes to the garden door and looks out gloomily*].

SOAMES [*rising with the paper in his hands*] Psha! [*He tears it in pieces*]. So much for the contract!

THE VOICE OF THE BEADLE. By your leave there, gentlemen. Make way for the Mayoress. Way for the worshipful the Mayoress, my lords and gentlemen. [*He comes in through the tower, in cocked hat and gold-braided overcoat, bearing the borough mace, and posts himself at the entrance*]. By your leave, gentlemen, way for the worshipful the Mayoress.

COLLINS [*moving back towards the wall*] Mrs George, my lord.

Mrs George is every inch a Mayoress in point of stylish dressing; and she does it very well indeed. There is nothing quiet about Mrs George: she is not afraid of colors, and knows how to make the most of them. Not at all a lady in Lesbia's use of the term as a class label, she proclaims herself to the first glance as the triumphant, pampered, wilful, intensely alive woman who has always been rich among poor people. In a historical museum she would explain Edward the Fourth's taste for shopkeepers' wives. Her age, which is certainly 40, and might be 50, is carried off by her vitality, her resilient figure, and her confident carriage. So far, a remarkably well-preserved woman. But her beauty is wrecked, like an ageless landscape ravaged by long and fierce war. Her eyes are alive, arresting and haunting; and there is still a turn of delicate beauty and pride in her indomitable chin; but her cheeks are wasted and lined, her mouth writhen and piteous. The whole face is a battlefield of the passions, quite deplorable until she speaks, when an alert sense of fun rejuvenates her in a moment, and makes her company irresistible.

All rise except Soames, who sits down. Leo joins Reginald at the garden door. Mrs Bridgenorth hurries to the tower to receive her guest, and gets as far as Soames's chair when Mrs George appears. Hotchkiss, apparently recognizing her, recoils in consternation to the study door at the furthest corner of the room from her.

MRS GEORGE [*coming straight to the Bishop with the ring in her hand*] Here is your ring, my lord; and here am I. It's your doing, remember: not mine.

THE BISHOP. Good of you to come.

MRS BRIDGENORTH. How do you do, Mrs Collins?

MRS GEORGE [*going to her past the Bishop, and gazing intently at her*] Are you his wife?

MRS BRIDGENORTH. The Bishop's wife? Yes.

MRS GEORGE. What a destiny! And you look like any other woman!

MRS BRIDGENORTH [*introducing Lesbia*] My sister, Miss Grantham.

MRS GEORGE. So strangely mixed up with the story of the General's life?

THE BISHOP. You know the story of his life, then?

MRS GEORGE. Not all. We reached the house before he brought it up to the present day. But enough to know the part played in it by Miss Grantham.

MRS BRIDGENORTH [*introducing Leo*] Mrs Reginald Bridgenorth.

REGINALD. The late Mrs Reginald Bridgenorth.

LEO. Hold your tongue, Rejjy. At least have the decency to wait until the decree is made absolute.

MRS GEORGE [*to Leo*] Well, youve more time to get married again than he has, havnt you?

MRS BRIDGENORTH [*introducing Hotchkiss*] Mr St John Hotchkiss.

Hotchkiss, still far aloof by the study door, bows.

MRS GEORGE. What! That! [*She makes a half tour of the kitchen and ends right in front of him*]. Young man: do you remember coming into my shop and telling me that my husband's coals were out of place in your cellar, as Nature evidently intended them for the roof?

HOTCHKISS. I remember that deplorable impertinence with shame and confusion. You were kind enough to answer that Mr Collins was looking out for a clever young man to write advertisements, and that I could take the job if I liked.

MRS GEORGE. It's still open. [*She turns to Edith*].

MRS BRIDGENORTH. My daughter Edith. [*She comes towards the study door to make the introduction*].

MRS GEORGE. The bride! [*Looking at Edith's dressing-jacket*] Youre not going to get married like that, are you?

THE BISHOP [*coming round the table to Edith's left*] Thats just what we are discussing. Will you be so good as to join us and allow us the benefit of your wisdom and experience?

MRS GEORGE. Do you want the Beadle as well? He's a married man.

They all turn involuntarily and contemplate the Beadle, who sustains their gaze with dignity.

THE BISHOP. We think there are already too many men to be quite fair to the women.

MRS GEORGE. Right, my lord. [*She goes back to the tower and addresses the Beadle*] Take away that bauble, Joseph. Wait for me wherever you find yourself most comfortable in the neighborhood. [*The Beadle withdraws. She notices Collins for the first time*]. Hullo, Bill: youve got em all on too. Go and hunt up a drink for Joseph: theres a dear. [*Collins goes out. She looks at Soames's cassock and biretta*] What! Another uniform! Are you the sexton? [*He rises*].

THE BISHOP. My chaplain, Father Anthony.

MRS GEORGE. Oh Lord! [*To Soames, coaxingly*] You dont mind, do you?

SOAMES. I mind nothing but my duties.
THE BISHOP. You know everybody now, I think.
MRS GEORGE [*turning to the railed chair*] Who's this?
THE BISHOP. Oh, I beg your pardon, Cecil. Mr Sykes. The bridegroom.
MRS GEORGE [*to Sykes*] Adorned for the sacrifice, arnt you?
SYKES. It seems doubtful whether there is going to be any sacrifice.
MRS GEORGE. Well, I want to talk to the women first. Shall we go upstairs and look at the presents and dresses?
MRS BRIDGENORTH. If you wish, certainly.
REGINALD. But the men want to hear what you have to say too.
MRS GEORGE. I'll talk to them afterwards: one by one.
HOTCHKISS [*to himself*] Great heavens!
MRS BRIDGENORTH. This way, Mrs Collins. [*She leads the way out through the tower, followed by Mrs George, Lesbia, Leo, and Edith*].
THE BISHOP. Shall we try to get through the last batch of letters whilst they are away, Soames?
SOAMES. Yes, certainly. [*To Hotchkiss, who is in his way*] Excuse me.
The Bishop and Soames go into the study, disturbing Hotchkiss, who, plunged in a strange reverie, has forgotten where he is. Awakened by Soames, he stares distractedly; then, with sudden resolution, goes swiftly to the middle of the kitchen.
HOTCHKISS. Cecil. Rejjy. [*Startled by his urgency, they hurry to him*]. I'm frightfully sorry to desert on this day; but I must bolt. This time it really is pure cowardice. I cant help it.
REGINALD. What are you afraid of?
HOTCHKISS. I dont know. Listen to me. I was a

young fool living by myself in London. I ordered my
first ton of coals from that woman's husband. At that
time I did not know that it is not true economy to buy
the lowest priced article: I thought all coals were alike,
and tried the thirteen shilling kind because it seemed
cheap. It proved unexpectedly inferior to the family
Silkstone; and in the irritation into which the first scuttle
threw me, I called at the shop and made an idiot of
myself as she described.

SYKES. Well, suppose you did! Laugh at it, man.

HOTCHKISS. At that, yes. But there was something
worse. Judge of my horror when, calling on the coal
merchant to make a trifling complaint at finding my
grate acting as a battery of quick-firing guns, and being
confronted by his vulgar wife, I felt in her presence an
extraordinary sensation of unrest, of emotion, of unsatisfied need. I'll not disgust you with details of the madness and folly that followed that meeting. But it went
as far as this: that I actually found myself prowling
past the shop at night under a sort of desperate necessity to be near some place where she had been. A hideous temptation to kiss the doorstep because her foot had
pressed it made me realize how mad I was. I tore myself away from London by a supreme effort; but I was
on the point of returning like a needle to the lodestone
when the outbreak of the war saved me. On the field of
battle the infatuation wore off. The Billiter affair made
a new man of me: I felt that I had left the follies and
puerilities of the old days behind me for ever. But halfan-hour ago—when the Bishop sent off that ring—a sudden grip at the base of my heart filled me with a nameless terror—me, the fearless! I recognized its cause
when she walked into the room. Cecil: this woman is a
harpy, a siren, a mermaid, a vampire. There is only
one chance for me: flight, instant precipitate flight.
Make my excuses. Forget me. Farewell. [*He makes*

*for the door and is confronted by Mrs George entering].
Too late: I'm lost. [He turns back and throws himself
desperately into the chair nearest the study door; that
being the furthest away from her].*

MRS GEORGE [*coming to the hearth and addressing
Reginald*] Mr Bridgenorth: will you oblige me by leaving me with this young man. I want to talk to him like a mother, on your business.

REGINALD. Do, maam. He needs it badly. Come along, Sykes. [*He goes into the study*].

SYKES [*looks irresolutely at Hotchkiss*]—?

HOTCHKISS. Too late: you cant save me now, Cecil. Go.

Sykes goes into the study. Mrs George strolls across to Hotchkiss and contemplates him curiously.

HOTCHKISS. Useless to prolong this agony. [*Rising*] Fatal woman—if woman you are indeed and not a fiend in human form—

MRS GEORGE. Is this out of a book? Or is it your usual society small talk?

HOTCHKISS [*recklessly*] Jibes are useless: the force that is sweeping me away will not spare you. I must know the worst at once. What was your father?

MRS GEORGE. A licensed victualler who married his barmaid. You would call him a publican, most likely.

HOTCHKISS. Then you are a woman totally beneath me. Do you deny it? Do you set up any sort of pretence to be my equal in rank, in age, or in culture?

MRS GEORGE. Have you eaten anything that has disagreed with you?

HOTCHKISS [*witheringly*] Inferior!

MRS GEORGE. Thank you. Anything else?

HOTCHKISS. This. I love you. My intentions are not honorable. [*She shows no dismay*]. Scream. Ring the bell. Have me turned out of the house.

MRS GEORGE [*with sudden depth of feeling*] Oh, if

you could restore to this wasted exhausted heart one ray of the passion that once welled up at the glance—at the touch of a lover! It's you who would scream then, young man. Do you see this face, once fresh and rosy like your own, now scarred and riven by a hundred burnt-out fires?

HOTCHKISS [*wildly*] Slate fires. Thirteen shillings a ton. Fires that shoot out destructive meteors, blinding and burning, sending men into the streets to make fools of themselves.

MRS GEORGE. You seem to have got it pretty bad, Sinjon.

HOTCHKISS. Dont dare call me Sinjon.

MRS GEORGE. My name is Zenobia Alexandrina. You may call me Polly for short.

HOTCHKISS. Your name is Ashtoreth—Durga—there is no name yet invented malign enough for you.

MRS GEORGE [*sitting down comfortably*] Come! Do you really think youre better suited to that young saucebox than her husband? You enjoyed her company when you were only the friend of the family—when there was the husband there to shew off against and to take all the responsibility. Are you sure youll enjoy it as much when you are the husband? She isnt clever, you know. She's only silly-clever.

HOTCHKISS [*uneasily leaning against the table and holding on to it to control his nervous movements*] Need you tell me? fiend that you are!

MRS GEORGE. You amused the husband, didnt you?

HOTCHKISS. He has more real sense of humor than she. He's better bred. That was not my fault.

MRS GEORGE. My husband has a sense of humor too.

HOTCHKISS. The coal merchant?—I mean the slate merchant.

MRS GEORGE [*appreciatively*] He would just love to

hear you talk. He's been dull lately for want of a change of company and a bit of fresh fun.

HOTCHKISS [*flinging a chair opposite her and sitting down with an overdone attempt at studied insolence*] And pray what is your wretched husband's vulgar conviviality to me?

MRS GEORGE. You love me?

HOTCHKISS. I loathe you.

MRS GEORGE. It's the same thing.

HOTCHKISS. Then I'm lost.

MRS GEORGE. You may come and see me if you promise to amuse George.

HOTCHKISS. I'll insult him, sneer at him, wipe my boots on him.

MRS GEORGE. No you wont, dear boy. Youll be a perfect gentleman.

HOTCHKISS [*beaten: appealing to her mercy*] Zenobia—

MRS GEORGE. Polly, please.

HOTCHKISS. Mrs Collins—

MRS GEORGE. Sir?

HOTCHKISS. Something stronger than my reason and common sense is holding my hands and tearing me along. I make no attempt to deny that it can drag me where you please and make me do what you like. But at least let me know your soul as you seem to know mine. Do you love this absurd coal merchant?

MRS GEORGE. Call him George.

HOTCHKISS. Do you love your Jorjy Porjy?

MRS GEORGE. Oh, I dont know that I love him. He's my husband, you know. But if I got anxious about George's health, and I thought it would nourish him, I would fry you with onions for his breakfast and think nothing of it. George and I are good friends. George belongs to me. Other men may come and go; but George goes on for ever.

HOTCHKISS. Yes: a husband soon becomes nothing but a habit. Listen: I suppose this detestable fascination you have for me is love.

MRS GEORGE. Any sort of feeling for a woman is called love nowadays.

HOTCHKISS. Do you love me?

MRS GEORGE [*promptly*] My love is not quite so cheap an article as that, my lad. I wouldnt cross the street to have another look at you—not yet. I'm not starving for love like the robins in winter, as the good ladies youre accustomed to are. Youll have to be very clever, and very good, and very real, if you are to interest me. If George takes a fancy to you, and you amuse him enough, I'll just tolerate you coming in and out occasionally for—well, say a month. If you can make a friend of me in that time so much the better for you. If you can touch my poor dying heart even for an instant, I'll bless you, and never forget you. You may try —if George takes to you.

HOTCHKISS. I'm to come on liking for the month?

MRS GEORGE. On condition that you drop Mrs Reginald.

HOTCHKISS. But she wont drop me. Do you suppose I ever wanted to marry her? I was a homeless bachelor; and I felt quite happy at their house as their friend. Leo was an amusing little devil; but I liked Reginald much more than I liked her. She didnt understand. One day she came to me and told me that the inevitable had happened. I had tact enough not to ask her what the inevitable was; and I gathered presently that she had told Reginald that their marriage was a mistake and that she loved me and could no longer see me breaking my heart for her in suffering silence. What could I say? What could I do? What can I say now? What can I do now?

MRS GEORGE. Tell her that the habit of falling in

love with other men's wives is growing on you; and that I'm your latest.

HOTCHKISS. What! Throw her over when she has thrown Reginald over for me!

MRS GEORGE [*rising*] You wont then? Very well. Sorry we shant meet again: I should have liked to see more of you for George's sake. Good-bye [*she moves away from him towards the hearth*].

HOTCHKISS [*appealing*] Zenobia—

MRS. GEORGE. I thought I had made a difficult conquest. Now I see you are only one of those poor petticoat-hunting creatures that any woman can pick up. Not for me, thank you. [*Inexorable, she turns towards the tower to go*].

HOTCHKISS [*following*] Dont be an ass, Polly.

MRS GEORGE [*stopping*] Thats better.

HOTCHKISS. Cant you see that I maynt throw Leo over just because I should be only too glad to. It would be dishonorable.

MRS GEORGE. Will you be happy if you marry her?

HOTCHKISS. No, great heaven, NO!

MRS GEORGE. Will she be happy when she finds you out?

HOTCHKISS. She's incapable of happiness. But she's not incapable of the pleasure of holding a man against his will.

MRS GEORGE. Right, young man. You will tell her, please, that you love me: before everybody, mind, the very next time you see her.

HOTCHKISS. But—

MRS GEORGE. Those are my orders, Sinjon. I cant have you marry another woman until George is tired of you.

HOTCHKISS. Oh, if I only didnt selfishly want to obey you!

The General comes in from the garden. Mrs George

goes half way to the garden door to speak to him. Hotchkiss posts himself on the hearth.

MRS GEORGE. Where have you been all this time?

THE GENERAL. I'm afraid my nerves were a little upset by our conversation. I just went into the garden and had a smoke. I'm all right now [*he strolls down to the study door and presently takes a chair at that end of the big table*].

MRS GEORGE. A smoke! Why, you said she couldnt bear it.

THE GENERAL. Good heavens! I forgot! It's such a natural thing to do, somehow.

Lesbia comes in through the tower.

MRS GEORGE. He's been smoking again.

LESBIA. So my nose tells me. [*She goes to the end of the table nearest the hearth, and sits down*].

THE GENERAL. Lesbia: I'm very sorry. But if I gave it up, I should become so melancholy and irritable that you would be the first to implore me to take to it again.

MRS GEORGE. Thats true. Women drive their husbands into all sorts of wickedness to keep them in good humor. Sinjon: be off with you: this doesnt concern you.

LESBIA. Please dont disturb yourself, Sinjon. Boxer's broken heart has been worn on his sleeve too long for any pretence of privacy.

THE GENERAL. You are cruel, Lesbia: devilishly cruel. [*He sits down, wounded*].

LESBIA. You are vulgar, Boxer.

HOTCHKISS. In what way? I ask, as an expert in vulgarity.

LESBIA. In two ways. First, he talks as if the only thing of any importance in life was which particular woman he shall marry. Second, he has no self-control.

THE GENERAL. Women are not all the same to me, Lesbia.

MRS GEORGE. Why should they be, pray? Women are all different: it's the men who are all the same. Besides, what does Miss Grantham know about either men or women? She's got too much self-control.

LESBIA [*widening her eyes and lifting her chin haughtily*] And pray how does that prevent me from knowing as much about men and women as people who have no self-control?

MRS GEORGE. Because it frightens people into behaving themselves before you; and then how can you tell what they really are? Look at me! I was a spoilt child. My brothers and sisters were well brought up, like all children of respectable publicans. So should I have been if I hadnt been the youngest: ten years younger than my youngest brother. My parents were tired of doing their duty by their children by that time; and they spoilt me for all they were worth. I never knew what it was to want money or anything that money could buy. When I wanted my own way, I had nothing to do but scream for it till I got it. When I was annoyed *I* didnt control myself: I scratched and called names. Did you ever, after you were grown up, pull a grown-up woman's hair? Did you ever bite a grown-up man? Did you ever call both of them every name you could lay your tongue to?

LESBIA [*shivering with disgust*] No.

MRS GEORGE. Well, I did. I know what a woman is like when her hair's pulled. I know what a man is like when he's bit. I know what theyre both like when you tell them what you really feel about them. And thats how I know more of the world than you.

LESBIA. The Chinese know what a man is like when he is cut into a thousand pieces, or boiled in oil. That sort of knowledge is of no use to me. I'm afraid we shall never get on with one another, Mrs George. I live like a fencer, always on guard. I like to be confronted with people who are always on guard. I hate sloppy people, slovenly people, people who cant sit up straight, sentimental people.

MRS GEORGE. Oh, sentimental your grandmother! You dont learn to hold your own in the world by standing on guard, but by attacking, and getting well hammered yourself.

LESBIA. I'm not a prize-fighter, Mrs. Collins. If I cant get a thing without the indignity of fighting for it, I do without it.

MRS GEORGE. Do you? Does it strike you that if we were all as clever as you at doing without, there wouldnt be much to live for, would there?

THE GENERAL. I'm afraid, Lesbia, the things you do without are the things you dont want.

LESBIA [*surprised at his wit*] Thats not bad for the silly soldier man. Yes, Boxer: the truth is, I dont want you enough to make the very unreasonable sacrifices required by marriage. And yet that is exactly why I ought to be married. Just because I have the qualities my country wants most I shall go barren to my grave; whilst the women who have neither the strength to resist marriage nor the intelligence to understand its infinite dishonor will make the England of the future. [*She rises and walks towards the study*].

THE GENERAL [*as she is about to pass him*] Well, I shall not ask you again, Lesbia.

LESBIA. Thank you, Boxer. [*She passes on to the study door*].

MRS GEORGE. Youre quite done with him, are you?

LESBIA. As far as marriage is concerned, yes. The field is clear for you, Mrs George. [*She goes into the study*].

The General buries his face in his hands. Mrs George comes round the table to him.

MRS GEORGE [*sympathetically*] She's a nice woman, that. And a sort of beauty about her too, different from anyone else.

THE GENERAL [*overwhelmed*] Oh Mrs Collins, thank you, thank you a thousand times. [*He rises effusively*]. You have thawed the long-frozen springs [*he kisses her hand*]. Forgive me; and thank you: bless you—[*he again takes refuge in the garden, choked with emotion*].

MRS GEORGE [*looking after him triumphantly*] Just caught the dear old warrior on the bounce, eh?

HOTCHKISS. Unfaithful to me already!

MRS GEORGE. I'm not your property, young man: dont you think it. [*She goes over to him and faces him*]. You understand that? [*He suddenly snatches her into his arms and kisses her*]. Oh! You dare do that again, you young blackguard; and I'll jab one of these chairs in your face [*she seizes one and holds it in readiness*]. Now you shall not see me for another month.

HOTCHKISS [*deliberately*] I shall pay my first visit to your husband this afternoon.

MRS GEORGE. Youll see what he'll say to you when I tell him what youve just done.

HOTCHKISS. What can he say? What dare he say?

MRS GEORGE. Suppose he kicks you out of the house?

HOTCHKISS. How can he? Ive fought seven duels with sabres. Ive muscles of iron. Nothing hurts me: not even broken bones. Fighting is absolutely uninteresting to me because it doesnt frighten me or amuse me; and I always win. Your husband is in all these respects an average man, probably. He will be horribly afraid of me; and if under the stimulus of your presence, and for your sake, and because it is the right thing to do among vulgar people, he were to attack me, I should simply defeat him and humiliate him [*he gradually gets his hands on the chair and takes it from her, as his words go home phrase by phrase*]. Sooner than expose him to that, you would suffer a thousand stolen kisses, wouldnt you?

MRS GEORGE [*in utter consternation*] You young viper!

HOTCHKISS. Ha ha! You are in my power. That is one of the oversights of your code of honor for husbands: the man who can bully them can insult their wives with impunity. Tell him if you dare. If I choose to take ten kisses, how will you prevent me?

MRS GEORGE. You come within reach of me and I'll not leave a hair on your head.

HOTCHKISS [*catching her wrists dexterously*] Ive got your hands.

MRS GEORGE. Youve not got my teeth. Let go; or I'll bite. I will, I tell you. Let go.

HOTCHKISS. Bite away: I shall taste quite as nice as George.

MRS GEORGE. You beast. Let me go. Do you call yourself a gentleman, to use your brute strength against a woman?

HOTCHKISS. You are stronger than me in every way but this. Do you think I will give up my one advantage? Promise youll receive me when I call this afternoon.

MRS GEORGE. After what youve just done? Not if it was to save my life.

HOTCHKISS. I'll amuse George.

MRS GEORGE. He wont be in.

HOTCHKISS [*taken aback*] Do you mean that we should be alone?

MRS GEORGE [*snatching away her hands triumphantly as his grasp relaxes*] Aha! Thats cooled you, has it?

HOTCHKISS [*anxiously*] When will George be at home?

MRS GEORGE. It wont matter to you whether he's at

home or not. The door will be slammed in your face whenever you call.

HOTCHKISS. No servant in London is strong enough to close a door that I mean to keep open. You cant escape me. If you persist, I'll go into the coal trade; make George's acquaintance on the coal exchange; and coax him to take me home with him to make your acquaintance.

MRS GEORGE. We have no use for you, young man: neither George nor I [*she sails away from him and sits down at the end of the table near the study door*].

HOTCHKISS [*following her and taking the next chair round the corner of the table*] Yes you have. George cant fight for you: I can.

MRS GEORGE [*turning to face him*] You bully. You low bully.

HOTCHKISS. You have courage and fascination: I have courage and a pair of fists. We're both bullies, Polly.

MRS GEORGE. You have a mischievous tongue. Thats enough to keep you out of my house.

HOTCHKISS. It must be rather a house of cards. A word from me to George—just the right word, said in the right way—and down comes your house.

MRS GEORGE. Thats why I'll die sooner than let you into it.

HOTCHKISS. Then as surely as you live, I enter the coal trade to-morrow. George's taste for amusing company will deliver him into my hands. Before a month passes your home will be at my mercy.

MRS GEORGE [*rising, at bay*] Do you think I'll let myself be driven into a trap like this?

HOTCHKISS. You are in it already. Marriage is a trap. You are married. Any man who has the power to spoil your marriage has the power to spoil your life. I have that power over you.

MRS GEORGE [*desperate*] You mean it?
HOTCHKISS. I do.
MRS GEORGE [*resolutely*] Well, spoil my marriage and be—
HOTCHKISS [*springing up*] Polly!
MRS GEORGE. Sooner than be your slave I'd face any unhappiness.
HOTCHKISS. What! Even for George?
MRS GEORGE. There must be honor between me and George, happiness or no happiness. Do your worst.
HOTCHKISS [*admiring her*] Are you really game, Polly? Dare you defy me?
MRS GEORGE. If you ask me another question I shant be able to keep my hands off you [*she dashes distractedly past him to the other end of the table, her fingers crisping*].
HOTCHKISS. That settles it. Polly: I adore you: we were born for one another. As I happen to be a gentleman, I'll never do anything to annoy or injure you except that I reserve the right to give you a black eye if you bite me; but youll never get rid of me now to the end of your life.
MRS GEORGE. I shall get rid of you if the beadle has to brain you with the mace for it [*she makes for the tower*].
HOTCHKISS [*running between the table and the oak chest and across to the tower to cut her off*] You shant.
MRS GEORGE [*panting*] Shant I though?
HOTCHKISS. No you shant. I have one card left to play that youve forgotten. Why were you so unlike yourself when you spoke to the Bishop?
MRS GEORGE [*agitated beyond measure*] Stop. Not that. You shall respect that if you respect nothing else. I forbid you. [*He kneels at her feet*]. What are you doing? Get up: dont be a fool.

HOTCHKISS. Polly: I ask you on my knees to let me make George's acquaintance in his home this afternoon; and I shall remain on my knees till the Bishop comes in and sees us. What will he think of you then?

MRS GEORGE [*beside herself*] Wheres the poker?

She rushes to the fireplace; seizes the poker; and makes for Hotchkiss, who flies to the study door. The Bishop enters just then and finds himself between them, narrowly escaping a blow from the poker.

THE BISHOP. Dont hit him, Mrs Collins. He is my guest.

Mrs George throws down the poker; collapses into the nearest chair; and bursts into tears. The Bishop goes to her and pats her consolingly on the shoulder. She shudders all through at his touch.

THE BISHOP. Come! you are in the house of your friends. Can we help you?

MRS GEORGE [*to Hotchkiss, pointing to the study*] Go in there, you. Youre not wanted here.

HOTCHKISS. You understand, Bishop, that Mrs Collins is not to blame for this scene. I'm afraid Ive been rather irritating.

THE BISHOP. I can quite believe it, Sinjon.

Hotchkiss goes into the study.

THE BISHOP [*turning to Mrs George with great kindness of manner*] I'm sorry you have been worried [*he sits down on her left*]. Never mind him. A little pluck, a little gaiety of heart, a little prayer; and youll be laughing at him.

MRS GEORGE. Never fear. I have all that. It was as much my fault as his; and I should have put him in his place with a clip of that poker on the side of his head if you hadnt come in.

THE BISHOP. You might have put him in his coffin that way, Mrs Collins. And I should have been very sorry; because we are all fond of Sinjon.

MRS GEORGE. Yes: it's your duty to rebuke me. But do you think I dont know?

THE BISHOP. I dont rebuke you. Who am I that I should rebuke you? Besides, I know there are discussions in which the poker is the only possible argument.

MRS GEORGE. My lord: be earnest with me. I'm a very funny woman, I daresay; but I come from the same workshop as you. I heard you say that yourself years ago.

THE BISHOP. Quite so; but then I'm a very funny Bishop. Since we are both funny people, let us not forget that humor is a divine attribute.

MRS GEORGE. I know nothing about divine attributes or whatever you call them; but I can feel when I am being belittled. It was from you that I learnt first to respect myself. It was through you that I came to be able to walk safely through many wild and wilful paths. Dont go back on your own teaching.

THE BISHOP. I'm not a teacher: only a fellow-traveller of whom you asked the way. I pointed ahead —ahead of myself as well as of you.

MRS GEORGE [*rising and standing over him almost threateningly*] As I'm a living woman this day, if I find you out to be a fraud, I'll kill myself.

THE BISHOP. What! Kill yourself for finding out something! For becoming a wiser and therefore a better woman! What a bad reason!

MRS GEORGE. I have sometimes thought of killing you, and then killing myself.

THE BISHOP. Why on earth should you kill yourself —not to mention me?

MRS GEORGE. So that we might keep our assignation in Heaven.

THE BISHOP [*rising and facing her, breathless*] Mrs. Collins! You are Incognita Appassionata!

MRS GEORGE. You read my letters, then? [*With a*

sigh of grateful relief, she sits down quietly, and says] Thank you.

THE BISHOP [*remorsefully*] And I have broken the spell by making you come here [*sitting down again*]. Can you ever forgive me?

MRS GEORGE. You couldnt know that it was only the coal merchant's wife, could you?

THE BISHOP. Why do you say only the coal merchant's wife?

MRS GEORGE. Many people would laugh at it.

THE BISHOP. Poor people! It's so hard to know the right place to laugh, isnt it?

MRS GEORGE. I didnt mean to make you think the letters were from a fine lady. I wrote on cheap paper; and I never could spell.

THE BISHOP. Neither could I. So that told me nothing.

MRS GEORGE. One thing I should like you to know.

THE BISHOP. Yes?

MRS GEORGE. We didnt cheat your friend. They were as good as we could do at thirteen shillings a ton.

THE BISHOP. Thats important. Thank you for telling me.

MRS GEORGE. I have something else to say; but will you please ask somebody to come and stay here while we talk? [*He rises and turns to the study door*]. Not a woman, if you dont mind. [*He nods understandingly and passes on*]. Not a man either.

THE BISHOP [*stopping*] Not a man and not a woman! We have no children left, Mrs Collins. They are all grown up and married.

MRS GEORGE. That other clergyman would do.

THE BISHOP. What! The sexton?

MRS GEORGE. Yes. He didnt mind my calling him that, did he? It was only my ignorance.

THE BISHOP. Not at all. [*He opens the study door*

and calls] Soames! Anthony! [*To Mrs George*] Call him Father: he likes it. [*Soames appears at the study door*]. Mrs Collins wishes you to join us, Anthony.

Soames looks puzzled.

MRS GEORGE. You dont mind, Dad, do you? [*As this greeting visibly gives him a shock that hardly bears out the Bishop's advice, she says anxiously*] That was what you told me to call him, wasnt it?

SOAMES. I am called Father Anthony, Mrs Collins. But it does not matter what you call me. [*He comes in, and walks past her to the hearth*].

THE BISHOP. Mrs Collins has something to say to me that she wants you to hear.

SOAMES. I am listening.

THE BISHOP [*going back to his seat next her*] Now.

MRS GEORGE. My lord: you should never have married.

SOAMES. This woman is inspired. Listen to her, my lord.

THE BISHOP [*taken aback by the directness of the attack*] I married because I was so much in love with Alice that all the difficulties and doubts and dangers of marriage seemed to me the merest moonshine.

MRS GEORGE. Yes: it's mean to let poor things in for so much while theyre in that state. Would you marry now that you know better if you were a widower?

THE BISHOP. I'm old now. It wouldnt matter.

MRS GEORGE. But would you if it did matter?

THE BISHOP. I think I should marry again lest anyone should imagine I had found marriage unhappy with Alice.

SOAMES [*sternly*] Are you fonder of your wife than of your salvation?

THE BISHOP. Oh, very much. When you meet a man who is very particular about his salvation, look out for a woman who is very particular about her character; and marry them to one another: theyll make a perfect pair. I advise you to fall in love, Anthony.

SOAMES [*with horror*] I!!

THE BISHOP. Yes, you! think of what it would do for you. For her sake you would come to care unselfishly and diligently for money instead of being selfishly and lazily indifferent to it. For her sake you would come to care in the same way for preferment. For her sake you would come to care for your health, your appearance, the good opinion of your fellow creatures, and all the really important things that make men work and strive instead of mooning and nursing their salvation.

SOAMES. In one word, for the sake of one deadly sin I should come to care for all the others.

THE BISHOP. Saint Anthony! Tempt him, Mrs Collins: tempt him.

MRS GEORGE [*rising and looking strangely before her*] Take care, my lord: you still have the power to make me obey your commands. And do you, Mr Sexton, beware of an empty heart.

THE BISHOP. Yes. Nature abhors a vacuum, Anthony. I would not dare go about with an empty heart: why, the first girl I met would fly into it by mere atmospheric pressure. Alice keeps them out now. Mrs Collins knows.

MRS GEORGE [*a faint convulsion passing like a wave over her*] I know more than either of you. One of you has not yet exhausted his first love: the other has not yet reached it. But I—I—[*she reels and is again convulsed*].

THE BISHOP [*saving her from falling*] Whats the matter? Are you ill, Mrs Collins? [*He gets her back into her chair*]. Soames: theres a glass of water in the study—quick. [*Soames hurries to the study door*].

MRS GEORGE. No. [*Soames stops*]. Dont call. Dont bring anyone. Cant you hear anything?

THE BISHOP. Nothing unusual. [*He sits by her, watching her with intense surprise and interest*].

MRS GEORGE. No music?

SOAMES. No. [*He steals to the end of the table and sits on her right, equally interested*].

MRS GEORGE. Do you see nothing—not a great light?

THE BISHOP. We are still walking in darkness.

MRS GEORGE. Put your hand on my forehead: the hand with the ring. [*He does so. Her eyes close*].

SOAMES [*inspired to prophesy*] There was a certain woman, the wife of a coal merchant, which had been a great sinner—

The Bishop, startled, takes his hand away. Mrs George's eyes open vividly as she interrupts Soames.

MRS GEORGE. You prophesy falsely, Anthony: never in all my life have I done anything that was not ordained for me. [*More quietly*] Ive been myself. Ive not been afraid of myself. And at last I have escaped from myself, and am become a voice for them that are afraid to speak, and a cry for the hearts that break in silence.

SOAMES [*whispering*] Is she inspired?

THE BISHOP. Marvellous. Hush.

MRS GEORGE. I have earned the right to speak. I have dared: I have gone through: I have not fallen withered in the fire: I have come at last out beyond, to the back of Godspeed?

THE BISHOP. And what do you see there, at the back of Godspeed?

SOAMES [*hungrily*] Give us your message.

MRS GEORGE [*with intensely sad reproach*] When you loved me I gave you the whole sun and stars to play with. I gave you eternity in a single moment, strength of the mountains in one clasp of your arms, and the volume of all the seas in one impulse of your souls. A moment only; but was it not enough? Were you not paid then for all the rest of your struggle on earth? Must I mend your clothes and sweep your floors as well? Was it not enough? I paid the price without bargaining: I bore the children without flinching: was that a reason for heaping fresh burdens on me? I carried the child in my arms: must I carry the father too? When I opened the gates of paradise, were you blind? was it nothing to you? When all the stars sang in your ears and all the winds swept you into the heart of heaven, were you deaf? were you dull? was I no more to you than a bone to a dog? Was it not enough? We spent eternity together; and you ask me for a little lifetime more. We possessed all the universe together; and you ask me to give you my scanty wages as well. I have given you the greatest of all things; and you ask me to give you little things. I gave you your own soul: you ask me for my body as a plaything. Was it not enough? Was it not enough?

SOAMES. Do you understand this, my lord?

THE BISHOP. I have that advantage over you, Anthony, thanks to Alice. [*He takes Mrs George's hand*]. Your hand is very cold. Can you come down to earth? Do you remember who I am, and who you are?

MRS GEORGE. It was enough for me. I did not ask to meet you—to touch you—[*the Bishop quickly releases her hand*]. When you spoke to my soul years ago from your pulpit, you opened the doors of my salvation to me; and now they stand open for ever. It was enough: I have asked you for nothing since: I ask you for nothing now. I have lived: it is enough. I have had my wages; and I am ready for my work. I thank you and bless you and leave you. You are happier in that than I am; for when I do for men what you did for me, I have no thanks, and no blessing: I am their prey; and there is no rest from their loving and no mercy from their loathing.

THE BISHOP. You must take us as we are, Mrs Collins.

SOAMES. No. Take us as we are capable of becoming.

MRS GEORGE. Take me as I am: I ask no more. [*She turns her head to the study door and cries*] Yes: come in, come in.

Hotchkiss comes softly in from the study.

HOTCHKISS. Will you be so kind as to tell me whether I am dreaming? In there I have heard Mrs Collins saying the strangest things, and not a syllable from you two.

SOAMES. My lord; is this possession by the devil?

THE BISHOP. Or the ecstasy of a saint?

HOTCHKISS. Or the convulsion of the pythoness on the tripod?

THE BISHOP. May not the three be one?

MRS GEORGE [*troubled*] You are paining and tiring me with idle questions. You are dragging me back to myself. You are tormenting me with your evil dreams of saints and devils and—what was it?—[*striving to fathom it*] the pythoness—the pythoness—[*giving it up*] I dont understand. I am a woman: a human creature like yourselves. Will you not take me as I am?

SOAMES. Yes; but shall we take you and burn you?

THE BISHOP. Or take you and canonize you?

HOTCHKISS [*gaily*] Or take you as a matter of course? [*Swiftly to the Bishop*] We must get her out of this: it's dangerous. [*Aloud to her*] May I suggest that you shall be Anthony's devil and the Bishop's saint and my adored Polly? [*Slipping behind her, he picks up her hand from her lap and kisses it over her shoulder*].

MRS GEORGE [*waking*] What was that? Who kissed

my hand? [*To the Bishop, eagerly*] Was it you? [*He shakes his head. She is mortified*]. I beg your pardon.

THE BISHOP. Not at all. I'm not repudiating that honor. Allow me [*he kisses her hand*].

MRS GEORGE. Thank you for that. It was not the sexton, was it?

SOAMES. I!

HOTCHKISS. It was I, Polly, your ever faithful.

MRS GEORGE [*turning and seeing him*] Let me catch you doing it again: thats all. How do you come there? I sent you away. [*With great energy, becoming quite herself again*] What the goodness gracious has been happening?

HOTCHKISS. As far as I can make out, you have been having a very charming and eloquent sort of fit.

MRS GEORGE [*delighted*] What! My second sight! [*To the Bishop*] Oh, how I have prayed that it might come to me if ever I met you! And now it has come. How stunning! You may believe every word I said: I cant remember it now; but it was something that was just bursting to be said; and so it laid hold of me and said itself. Thats how it is, you see.

Edith and Cecil Sykes come in through the tower. She has her hat on. Leo follows. They have evidently been out together. Sykes, with an unnatural air, half foolish, half rakish, as if he had lost all his self-respect and were determined not to let it prey on his spirits, throws himself into a chair at the end of the table near the hearth and thrusts his hands into his pockets, like Hogarth's Rake, without waiting for Edith to sit down. She sits in the railed chair. Leo takes the chair nearest the tower on the long side of the table, brooding, with closed lips.

THE BISHOP. Have you been out, my dear?

EDITH. Yes.

THE BISHOP. With Cecil?
EDITH. Yes.
THE BISHOP. Have you come to an understanding?
No reply. Blank silence.
SYKES. You had better tell them, Edie.
EDITH. Tell them yourself.
The General comes in from the garden.
THE GENERAL [*coming forward to the table*] Can anybody oblige me with some tobacco? Ive finished mine; and my nerves are still far from settled.
THE BISHOP. Wait a moment, Boxer. Cecil has something important to tell us.
SYKES. Weve done it. Thats all.
HOTCHKISS. Done what, Cecil?
SYKES. Well, what do you suppose?
EDITH. Got married, of course.
THE GENERAL. Married! Who gave you away?
SYKES [*jerking his head towards the tower*] This gentleman did. [*Seeing that they do not understand, he looks round and sees that there is no one there*]. Oh! I thought he came in with us. Hes gone downstairs, I suppose. The Beadle.
THE GENERAL. The Beadle! What the devil did he do that for?
SYKES. Oh, I dont know: I didnt make any bargain with him. [*To Mrs George*] How much ought I to give him, Mrs Collins?
MRS GEORGE. Five shillings. [*To the Bishop*] I want to rest for a moment: there! in your study. I saw it here [*she touches her forehead*].
THE BISHOP [*opening the study door for her*] By all means. Turn my brother out if he disturbs you. Soames: bring the letters out here.
SYKES. He wont be offended at my offering it, will he?
MRS GEORGE. Not he! He touches children with the

mace to cure them of ringworm for fourpence apiece. [*She goes into the study. Soames follows her*].

THE GENERAL. Well, Edith, I'm a little disappointed, I must say. However, I'm glad it was done by somebody in a public uniform.

Mrs Bridgenorth and Lesbia come in through the tower. Mrs Bridgenorth makes for the Bishop. He goes to her, and they meet near the oak chest. Lesbia comes between Sykes and Edith.

THE BISHOP. Alice, my love, theyre married.

MRS BRIDGENORTH [*placidly*] Oh, well, thats all right. Better tell Collins.

Soames comes back from the study with his writing materials. He seats himself at the nearest end of the table and goes on with his work. Hotchkiss sits down in the next chair round the table corner, with his back to him.

LESBIA. You have both given in, have you?

EDITH. Not at all. We have provided for everything.

SOAMES. How?

EDITH. Before going to the church, we went to the office of that insurance company—whats its name, Cecil?

SYKES. The British Family Insurance Corporation. It insures you against poor relations and all sorts of family contingencies.

EDITH. It has consented to insure Cecil against libel actions brought against him on my account. It will give us specially low terms because I am a Bishop's daughter.

SYKES. And I have given Edie my solemn word that if I ever commit a crime I'll knock her down before a witness and go off to Brighton with another lady.

LESBIA. Thats what you call providing for everything! [*She goes to the middle of the table on the garden side and sits down*].

LEO. Do make him see there are no worms before he knocks you down, Edith. Wheres Rejjy?

REGINALD [*coming in from the study*] Here. Whats the matter?

LEO [*springing up and flouncing round to him*] Whats the matter! You may well ask. While Edie and Cecil were at the insurance office I took a taxy and went off to your lodgings; and a nice mess I found everything in. Your clothes are in a disgraceful state. Your liver-pad has been made into a kettle-holder. Youre no more fit to be left to yourself than a one-year old baby.

REGINALD. Oh, I cant be bothered looking after things like that. I'm all right.

LEO. Youre not: youre a disgrace. You never consider that youre a disgrace to me: you think only of yourself. You must come home with me and be taken proper care of: my conscience will not allow me to let you live like a pig. [*She arranges his necktie*]. You must stay with me until I marry St John; and then we can adopt you or something.

REGINALD [*breaking loose from her and stumping off past Hotchkiss towards the hearth*] No, I'm dashed if I'll be adopted by St John. You can adopt him if you like.

HOTCHKISS [*rising*] I suggest that that would really be the better plan, Leo. Ive a confession to make to you. I'm not the man you took me for. Your objection to Rejjy was that he had low tastes.

REGINALD [*turning*] Was it? by George!

LEO. I said slovenly habits. I never thought he had really low tastes until I saw that woman in court. How he could have chosen such a creature and let her write to him after— .

REGINALD. Is this fair? I never—

HOTCHKISS. Of course you didnt, Rejjy. Dont be silly, Leo. It's I who really have low tastes.

LEO. You!

HOTCHKISS. Ive fallen in love with a coal merchant's wife. I adore her. I would rather have one of her boot-laces than a lock of your hair. [*He folds his arms and stands like a rock*].

REGINALD. You damned scoundrel, how dare you throw my wife over like that before my face? [*He seems on the point of assaulting Hotchkiss when Leo gets between them and draws Reginald away towards the study door*].

LEO. Dont take any notice of him, Rejjy. Go at once and get that odious decree demolished or annulled or whatever it is. Tell Sir Gorell Barnes that I have changed my mind. [*To Hotchkiss*] I might have known that you were too clever to be really a gentleman. [*She takes Reginald away to the oak chest and seats him there. He chuckles. Hotchkiss resumes his seat, brooding*].

THE BISHOP. All the problems appear to be solving themselves.

LESBIA. Except mine.

THE GENERAL. But, my dear Lesbia, you see what has happened here to-day. [*Coming a little nearer and bending his face towards hers*] Now I put it to you, does it not shew you the folly of not marrying?

LESBIA. No: I cant say it does. And [*rising*] you have been smoking again.

THE GENERAL. You drive me to it, Lesbia. I cant help it.

LESBIA [*standing behind her chair with her hands on the back of it and looking radiant*] Well, I wont scold you to-day. I feel in particularly good humor just now.

THE GENERAL. May I ask why, Lesbia?

LESBIA [*drawing a large breath*] To think that after all the dangers of the morning I am still unmarried! still independent! still my own mistress! still a glorious strong-minded old maid of old England!

Soames silently springs up and makes a long stretch from his end of the table to shake her hand across it.

THE GENERAL. Do you find any real happiness in being your own mistress? Would it not be more generous—would you not be happier as some one else's mistress—

LESBIA. Boxer!

THE GENERAL [*rising, horrified*] No, no, you must know, my dear Lesbia, that I was not using the word in its improper sense. I am sometimes unfortunate in my choice of expressions; but you know what I mean. I feel sure you would be happier as my wife.

LESBIA. I daresay I should, in a frowsy sort of way. But I prefer my dignity and my independence. I'm afraid I think this rage for happiness rather vulgar.

THE GENERAL. Oh, very well, Lesbia. I shall not ask you again. [*He sits down huffily*].

LESBIA. You will, Boxer; but it will be no use. [*She also sits down again and puts her hand almost affectionately on his*]. Some day I hope to make a friend of you; and then we shall get on very nicely.

THE GENERAL [*starting up again*] Ha! I think you are hard, Lesbia. I shall make a fool of myself if I remain here. Alice: I shall go into the garden for a while.

COLLINS [*appearing in the tower*] I think everything is in order now, maam.

THE GENERAL [*going to him*] Oh, by the way, could you oblige me—[*the rest of the sentence is lost in a whisper*].

COLLINS. Certainly, General. [*He takes out a tobacco pouch and hands it to the General, who takes it and goes into the garden*].

LESBIA. I dont believe theres a man in England who really and truly loves his wife as much as he loves his pipe.

THE BISHOP. By the way, what has happened to the wedding party?

SYKES. I dont know. There wasnt a soul in the church when we were married except the pew opener and the curate who did the job.

EDITH. They had all gone home.

MRS BRIDGENORTH. But the bridesmaids?

COLLINS. Me and the beadle have been all over the place in a couple of taxies, maam; and weve collected them all. They were a good deal disappointed on account of their dresses, and thought it rather irregular; but theyve agreed to come to the breakfast. The truth is, theyre wild with curiosity to know how it all happened. The organist held on until the organ was nigh worn out, and himself worse than the organ. He asked me particularly to tell you, my lord, that he held back Mendelssohn till the very last; but when that was gone he thought he might as well go too. So he played God Save The King and cleared out the church. He's coming to the breakfast to explain.

LEO. Please remember, Collins, that there is no truth whatever in the rumor that I am separated from my husband, or that there is, or ever has been, anything between me and Mr Hotchkiss.

COLLINS. Bless you, maam! one could always see that. [*To Mrs Bridgenorth*] Will you receive here or in the hall, maam?

MRS BRIDGENORTH. In the hall. Alfred: you and Boxer must go there and be ready to keep the first arrivals talking till we come. We have to dress Edith. Come, Lesbia: come, Leo: we must all help. Now, Edith. [*Lesbia, Leo, and Edith go out through the tower*]. Collins: we shall want you when Miss Edith's dressed to look over her veil and things and see that theyre all right.

COLLINS. Yes, maam. Anything you would like mentioned about Miss Lesbia, maam?

MRS BRIDGENORTH. No. She wont have the General. I think you may take that as final.

COLLINS. What a pity, maam! A fine lady wasted, maam. [*They shake their heads sadly; and Mrs Bridgenorth goes out through the tower*].

THE BISHOP. I'm going to the hall, Collins, to receive. Rejjy: go and tell Boxer; and come both of you to help with the small talk. Come, Cecil. [*He goes out through the tower, followed by Sykes*].

REGINALD [*to Hotchkiss*] Youve always talked a precious lot about behaving like a gentleman. Well, if you think youve behaved like a gentleman to Leo, youre mistaken. And I shall have to take her part, remember that.

HOTCHKISS. I understand. Your doors are closed to me.

REGINALD [*quickly*] Oh no. Dont be hasty. I think I should like you to drop in after a while, you know. She gets so cross and upset when theres nobody to liven up the house a bit.

HOTCHKISS. I'll do my best.

REGINALD [*relieved*] Righto. You dont mind, old chap, do you?

HOTCHKISS. It's Fate. Ive touched coal; and my hands are black; but theyre clean. So long, Rejjy. [*They shake hands: and Reginald goes into the garden to collect Boxer*].

COLLINS. Excuse me, sir; but do you stay to breakfast? Your name is on one of the covers; and I should like to change it if youre not remaining.

HOTCHKISS. How do I know? Is my destiny any

longer in my own hands? Go: ask SHE WHO MUST BE OBEYED.

COLLINS [awestruck] Has Mrs George taken a fancy to you, sir?

HOTCHKISS. Would she had! Worse, man, worse: Ive taken a fancy to Mrs George.

COLLINS. Dont despair, sir: if George likes your conversation youll find their house a very pleasant one: livelier than Mr Reginald's was, I daresay.

HOTCHKISS [calling] Polly.

COLLINS [promptly] Oh, if it's come to Polly already, sir, I should say you were all right.

Mrs George appears at the door of the study.

HOTCHKISS. Your brother-in-law wishes to know whether I'm to stay for the wedding breakfast. Tell him.

MRS GEORGE. He stays, Bill, if he chooses to behave himself.

HOTCHKISS [to Collins] May I, as a friend of the family, have the privilege of calling you Bill?

COLLINS. With pleasure, sir, I'm sure, sir.

HOTCHKISS. My own pet name in the bosom of my family is Sonny.

MRS GEORGE. Why didnt you tell me that before? Sonny is just the name I wanted for you. [*She pats his cheek familiarly: he rises abruptly and goes to the hearth, where he throws himself moodily into the ruled chair*] Bill: I'm not going into the hall until there are enough people there to make a proper little court for me. Send the Beadle for me when you think it looks good enough.

COLLINS. Right, maam. [*He goes out through the tower*].

Mrs George left alone with Hotchkiss and Soames, suddenly puts her hands on Soames's shoulders and bends over him.

MRS GEORGE. The Bishop said I was to tempt you, Anthony.
SOAMES [*without looking round*] Woman: go away.
MRS GEORGE. Anthony:
 "When other lips and other hearts
  Their tale of love shall tell
HOTCHKISS [*sardonically*]
  In language whose excess imparts
  The power they feel so well.
MRS GEORGE.
  Though hollow hearts may wear a mask
  Twould break your own to see,
  In such a moment I but ask
  That youll remember me."
And you will, Anthony. I shall put my spell on you.
SOAMES. Do you think that a man who has sung the Magnificat and adored the Queen of Heaven has any ears for such trash as that or any eyes for such trash as you—saving your poor little soul's presence. Go home to your duties, woman.
MRS GEORGE [*highly approving his fortitude*] Anthony: I adopt you as my father. Thats the talk! Give me a man whose whole life doesnt hang on some scrubby woman in the next street; and I'll never let him go [*she slaps him heartily on the back*].
SOAMES. Thats enough. You have another man to talk to. I'm busy.
MRS GEORGE [*leaving Soames and going a step or two nearer Hotchkiss*] Why arnt you like him, Sonny? Why do you hang on to a scrubby woman in the next street?
HOTCHKISS [*thoughtfully*] I must apologize to Billiter.
MRS GEORGE. Who is Billiter?
HOTCHKISS. A man who eats rice pudding with a spoon. Ive been eating rice pudding with a spoon ever

since I saw you first. [*He rises*]. We all eat our rice pudding with a spoon, dont we, Soames?

SOAMES. We are members of one another. There is no need to refer to me. In the first place, I'm busy: in the second, youll find it all in the Church Catechism, which contains most of the new discoveries with which the age is bursting. Of course you should apologize to Billiter. He is your equal. He will go to the same heaven if he behaves himself and to the same hell if he doesnt.

MRS GEORGE [*sitting down*] And so will my husband the coal merchant.

HOTCHKISS. If I were your husband's superior here I should be his superior in heaven or hell: equality lies deeper than that. The coal merchant and I are in love with the same woman. That settles the question for me for ever. [*He prowls across the kitchen to the garden door, deep in thought*].

SOAMES. Psha!

MRS GEORGE. You dont believe in women, do you, Anthony? He might as well say that he and George both like fried fish.

HOTCHKISS. I do not like fried fish. Dont be low, Polly.

SOAMES. Woman: do not presume to accuse me of unbelief. And do you, Hotchkiss, not despise this woman's soul because she speaks of fried fish. Some of the victims of the Miraculous Draught of Fishes were fried. And I eat fried fish every Friday and like it. You are as ingrained a snob as ever.

HOTCHKISS [*impatiently*] My dear Anthony: I find you merely ridiculous as a preacher, because you keep referring me to places and documents and alleged occurrences in which, as a matter of fact, I dont believe. I dont believe in anything but my own will and my own pride and honor. Your fishes and your catechisms and

all the rest of it make a charming poem which you call
your faith. It fits you to perfection; but it doesnt fit
me. I happen, like Napoleon, to prefer Mohammedanism.
[*Mrs George, associating Mohammedanism with polygamy, looks at him with quick suspicion*]. I believe the
whole British Empire will adopt a reformed Mohammedanism before the end of the century. The character
of Mahomet is congenial to me. I admire him, and share
his views of life to a considerable extent. That beats you,
you see, Soames. Religion is a great force—the only real
motive force in the world; but what you fellows dont understand is that you must get at a man through his own
religion and not through yours. Instead of facing that
fact, you persist in trying to convert all men to your
own little sect, so that you can use it against them afterwards. You are all missionaries and proselytizers trying
to uproot the native religion from your neighbor's flower-
beds and plant your own in its place. You would rather
let a child perish in ignorance than have it taught by a
rival sectary. You can talk to me of the quintessential
equality of coal merchants and British officers; and yet
you cant see the quintessential equality of all the religions. Who are you, anyhow, that you should know
better than Mahomet or Confucius or any of the other
Johnnies who have been on this job since the world
existed?

Mrs George [*admiring his eloquence*] George will
like you, Sonny. You should hear him talking about the
Church.

Soames. Very well, then: go to your doom, both of
you. There is only one religion for me: that which my
soul knows to be true; but even irreligion has one tenet;
and that is the sacredness of marriage. You two are
on the verge of deadly sin. Do you deny that?

Hotchkiss. You forget, Anthony: the marriage itself is the deadly sin according to you.

SOAMES. The question is not now what I believe, but what you believe. Take the vows with me; and give up that woman if you have the strength and the light. But if you are still in the grip of this world, at least respect its institutions. Do you believe in marriage or do you not?

HOTCHKISS. My soul is utterly free from any such superstition. I solemnly declare that between this woman, as you impolitely call her, and me, I see no barrier that my conscience bids me respect. I loathe the whole marriage morality of the middle classes with all my instincts. If I were an eighteenth century marquis I could feel no more free with regard to a Parisian citizen's wife than I do with regard to Polly. I despise all this domestic purity business as the lowest depth of narrow, selfish, sensual, wife-grabbing vulgarity.

MRS GEORGE [*rising promptly*] Oh, indeed. Then youre not coming home with me, young man. I'm sorry; for its refreshing to have met once in my life a man who wasnt frightened by my wedding ring; but I'm looking out for a friend and not for a French marquis; so youre not coming home with me.

HOTCHKISS [*inexorably*] Yes, I am.

MRS GEORGE. No.

HOTCHKISS. Yes. Think again. You know your set pretty well, I suppose, your petty tradesmen's set. You know all its scandals and hypocrisies, its jealousies and squabbles, its hundred of divorce cases that never come into court, as well as its tens that do.

MRS GEORGE. We're not angels. I know a few scandals; but most of us are too dull to be anything but good.

HOTCHKISS. Then you must have noticed that just as all murderers, judging by their edifying remarks on the scaffold, seem to be devout Christians, so all libertines, both male and female, are invariably people overflowing with domestic sentimentality and professions of respect for the conventions they violate in secret.

MRS GEORGE. Well, you dont expect them to give themselves away, do you?

HOTCHKISS. They are people of sentiment, not of honor. Now, I'm not a man of sentiment, but a man of honor. I know well what will happen to me when once I cross the threshold of your husband's house and break bread with him. This marriage bond which I despise will bind me as it never seems to bind the people who believe in it, and whose chief amusement it is to go to the theatres where it is laughed at. Soames: youre a Communist, arnt you?

SOAMES. I am a Christian. That obliges me to be a Communist.

HOTCHKISS. And you believe that many of our landed estates were stolen from the Church by Henry the eighth?

SOAMES. I do not merely believe that: I know it as a lawyer.

HOTCHKISS. Would you steal a turnip from one of the landlords of those stolen lands?

SOAMES [*fencing with the question*] They have no right to their lands.

HOTCHKISS. Thats not what I ask you. Would you steal a turnip from one of the fields they have no right to?

SOAMES. I do not like turnips.

HOTCHKISS. As you are a lawyer, answer me.

SOAMES. I admit that I should probably not do so. I should perhaps be wrong not to steal the turnip: I cant defend my reluctance to do so; but I think I should not do so. I know I should not do so.

HOTCHKISS. Neither shall I be able to steal George's wife. I have stretched out my hand for that forbidden fruit before; and I know that my hand will always come back empty. To disbelieve in marriage is easy: to love a married woman is easy; but to betray a comrade, to be disloyal to a host, to break the covenant of bread and salt, is impossible. You may take me home with you, Polly: you have nothing to fear.

MRS GEORGE. And nothing to hope?

HOTCHKISS. Since you put it in that more than kind way, Polly, absolutely nothing.

MRS GEORGE. Hm! Like most men, you think you know everything a woman wants, dont you? But the thing one wants most has nothing to do with marriage at all. Perhaps Anthony here has a glimmering of it. Eh, Anthony?

SOAMES. Christian fellowship?

MRS GEORGE. You call it that, do you?

SOAMES. What do you call it?

COLLINS [*appearing in the tower with the Beadle*]. Now, Polly, the hall's full; and theyre waiting for you.

THE BEADLE. Make way there, gentlemen, please. Way for the worshipful the Mayoress. If you please, my lords and gentlemen. By your leave, ladies and gentlemen: way for the Mayoress.

Mrs George takes Hotchkiss's arm, and goes out, preceded by the Beadle.

Soames resumes his writing tranquilly.

THE SHEWING-UP OF BLANCO POSNET

XVIII

1909

P,REFACE

The Censorship

THIS little play is really a religious tract in dramatic form. If our silly censorship would permit its performance, it might possibly help to set right-side-up the perverted conscience and re-invigorate the starved self-respect of our considerable class of loose-lived playgoers whose point of honor is to deride all official and conventional sermons. As it is, it only gives me an opportunity of telling the story of the Select Committee of both Houses of Parliament which sat last year to enquire into the working of the censorship, against which it was alleged by myself and others that as its imbecility and mischievousness could not be fully illustrated within the limits of decorum imposed on the press, it could only be dealt with by a parliamentary body subject to no such limits.

A Readable Bluebook

Few books of the year 1909 can have been cheaper and more entertaining than the report of this Committee. Its full title is REPORT FROM THE JOINT SELECT COMMITTEE OF THE HOUSE OF LORDS AND THE HOUSE OF COMMONS ON THE STAGE PLAYS (CENSORSHIP) TOGETHER WITH THE PROCEEDINGS OF THE COMMITTEE, MINUTES OF EVIDENCE, AND APPENDICES. What the phrase " the Stage Plays " means in this title I do not know; nor does anyone else. The number of the Bluebook is 214.

324 The Shewing-Up of Blanco Posnet

How interesting it is may be judged from the fact that it contains verbatim reports of long and animated interviews between the Committee and such witnesses as W. William Archer, Mr. Granville Barker, Mr. J. M. Barrie, Mr. Forbes Robertson, Mr. Cecil Raleigh, Mr. John Galsworthy, Mr. Laurence Housman, Sir Herbert Beerbohm Tree, Mr. W. L. Courtney, Sir William Gilbert, Mr. A. B. Walkley, Miss Lena Ashwell, Professor Gilbert Murray, Mr. George Alexander, Mr. George Edwardes, Mr. Comyns Carr, the Speaker of the House of Commons, the Bishop of Southwark, Mr. Hall Caine, Mr. Israel Zangwill, Sir Squire Bancroft, Sir Arthur Pinero, and Mr. Gilbert Chesterton, not to mention myself and a number of gentlemen less well known to the general public, but important in the world of the theatre. The publication of a book by so many famous contributors would be beyond the means of any commercial publishing firm. His Majesty's Stationery Office sells it to all comers by weight at the very reasonable price of three-and-threepence a copy.

How Not to Do It

It was pointed out by Charles Dickens in Little Dorrit, which remains the most accurate and penetrating study of the genteel littleness of our class governments in the English language, that whenever an abuse becomes oppressive enough to persuade our party parliamentarians that something must be done, they immediately set to work to face the situation and discover How Not To Do It. Since Dickens's day the exposures effected by the Socialists have so shattered the self-satisfaction of modern commercial civilization that it is no longer difficult to convince our governments that something must be done, even to the extent of attempts at a reconstruction of civilization on a thoroughly uncommercial basis. Consequently, the first part of the process described by Dickens: that in which the reformers were snubbed by front bench demonstrations that the administrative departments were consuming miles of red tape in the correctest forms of activity, and that everything was for the best in the best of all possible worlds, is out of fashion; and we are in that other phase, familiarized by the history of the French Revolution, in which the primary assumption is that the country is in danger, and that the first duty of all parties, politicians, and governments is to save it. But as the effect of this is to give governments a great many more things to do, it also gives a powerful stimulus to the art of How Not To Do Them: that is to say, the art of contriving methods of reform which will leave matters exactly as they are.

The report of the Joint Select Committee is a capital illustration of this tendency. The case against the censorship was overwhelming; and the defence was more damaging to it than no defence at all could have been. Even had this not been so, the mere caprice of opinion had turned against the institution; and a reform was expected, evidence or no evidence. Therefore the Committee was unanimous as to the necessity of reforming the censorship; only, unfortunately, the majority attached to this unanimity the usual condition that nothing should be done to disturb the existing state of things. How this was effected may be gathered from the recommendations finally agreed on, which are as follows.

1. The drama is to be set entirely free by the abolition of the existing obligation to procure a licence from the Censor before performing a play; but every theatre lease is in future to be construed as if it contained a clause giving the landlord power to break it and evict the lessee if he produces a play without first obtaining the usual licence from the Lord Chamberlain.

2. Some of the plays licensed by the Lord Chamber-

lain are so vicious that their present practical immunity
from prosecution must be put an end to; but no manager
who procures the Lord Chamberlain's licence for a play
can be punished in any way for producing it, though a
special tribunal may order him to discontinue the performance;
and even this order must not be recorded to
his disadvantage on the licence of his theatre, nor may it
be given as a judicial reason for cancelling that licence.

3. Authors and managers producing plays without
first obtaining the usual licence from the Lord Chamberlain
shall be perfectly free to do so, and shall be at no
disadvantage compared to those who follow the existing
practice, except that they may be punished, have the
licences of their theatres endorsed and cancelled, and
have the performance stopped pending the proceedings
without compensation in the event of the proceedings
ending in their acquittal.

4. Authors are to be rescued from their present subjection
to an irresponsible secret tribunal which can condemn
their plays without giving reasons, by the substitution
for that tribunal of a Committee of the Privy
Council, which is to be the final authority on the fitness
of a play for representation; and this Committee is to
sit *in camera* if and when it pleases.

5. The power to impose a veto on the production of
plays is to be abolished because it may hinder the growth
of a great national drama; but the Office of Examiner
of Plays shall be continued; and the Lord Chamberlain
shall retain his present powers to license plays, but shall
be made responsible to Parliament to the extent of making
it possible to ask questions there concerning his
proceedings, especially now that members have discovered
a method of doing this indirectly.

And so on, and so forth. The thing is to be done;
and it is not to be done. Everything is to be changed
and nothing is to be changed. The problem is to be

faced and the solution to be shirked. And the word of Dickens is to be justified.

The Story of the Joint Select Committee

Let me now tell the story of the Committee in greater detail, partly as a contribution to history; partly because, like most true stories, it is more amusing than the official story.

All commissions of public enquiry are more or less intimidated both by the interests on which they have to sit in judgment and, when their members are party politicians, by the votes at the back of those interests; but this unfortunate Committee sat under a quite exceptional cross fire. First, there was the king. The Censor is a member of his household retinue; and as a king's retinue has to be jealously guarded to avoid curtailment of the royal state no matter what may be the function of the particular retainer threatened, nothing but an express royal intimation to the contrary, which is a constitutional impossibility, could have relieved the Committee from the fear of displeasing the king by any proposal to abolish the censorship of the Lord Chamberlain. Now all the lords on the Committee and some of the commoners could have been wiped out of society (in their sense of the word) by the slightest intimation that the king would prefer not to meet them; and this was a heavy risk to run on the chance of "a great and serious national drama" ensuing on the removal of the Lord Chamberlain's veto on Mrs Warren's Profession. Second, there was the Nonconformist conscience, holding the Liberal Government responsible for the Committee it had appointed, and holding also, to the extent of votes enough to turn the scale in some constituencies, that the theatre is the gate of hell, to be tolerated, as vice is tolerated, only because the power to suppress it could not be given to any public body without too serious an interference with certain Liberal traditions of liberty which are still useful to Noncomformists in other directions. Third, there was the commercial interest of the theatrical managers and their syndicates of backers in the City, to whom, as I shall shew later on, the censorship affords a cheap insurance of enormous value. Fourth, there was the powerful interest of the trade in intoxicating liquors, fiercely determined to resist any extension of the authority of teetotaller-led local governing bodies over theatres. Fifth, there were the playwrights, without political power, but with a very close natural monopoly of a talent not only for play-writing but for satirical polemics. And since every interest has its opposition, all these influences had created hostile bodies by the operation of the mere impulse to contradict them, always strong in English human nature.

Why the Managers Love the Censorship

The only one of these influences which seems to be generally misunderstood is that of the managers. It has been assumed repeatedly that managers and authors are affected in the same way by the censorship. When a prominent author protests against the censorship, his opinion is supposed to be balanced by that of some prominent manager who declares that the censorship is the mainstay of the theatre, and his relations with the Lord Chamberlain and the Examiner of Plays a cherished privilege and an inexhaustible joy. This error was not removed by the evidence given before the Joint Select Committee. The managers did not make their case clear there, partly because they did not understand it, and partly because their most eminent witnesses were

Preface

not personally affected by it, and would not condescend to plead it, feeling themselves, on the contrary, compelled by their self-respect to admit and even emphasize the fact that the Lord Chamberlain in the exercise of his duties as licenser had done those things which he ought not to have done, and left undone those things which he ought to have done. Mr Forbes Robertson and Sir Herbert Tree, for instance, had never felt the real disadvantage of which managers have to complain. This disadvantage was not put directly to the Committee; and though the managers are against me on the question of the censorship, I will now put their case for them as they should have put it themselves, and as it can be read between the lines of their evidence when once the reader has the clue.

The manager of a theatre is a man of business. He is not an expert in politics, religion, art, literature, philosophy, or law. He calls in a playwright just as he calls in a doctor, or consults a lawyer, or engages an architect, depending on the playwright's reputation and past achievements for a satisfactory result. A play by an unknown man may attract him sufficiently to induce him to give that unknown man a trial; but this does not occur often enough to be taken into account: his normal course is to resort to a well-known author and take (mostly with misgiving) what he gets from him. Now this does not cause any anxiety to Mr Forbes Robertson and Sir Herbert Tree, because they are only incidentally managers and men of business: primarily they are highly cultivated artists, quite capable of judging for themselves anything that the most abstruse playwright is likely to put before them. But the plain sailing tradesman who must be taken as the typical manager (for the west end of London is not the whole theatrical world) is by no means equally qualified to judge whether a play is safe from prosecution or not. He may not understand it, may not like it, may not know what the author is driving at, may have no knowledge of the ethical, political, and sectarian controversies which may form the intellectual fabric of the play, and may honestly see nothing but an ordinary "character part" in a stage figure which may be a libellous and unmistakeable caricature of some eminent living person of whom he has never heard. Yet if he produces the play he is legally responsible just as if he had written it himself. Without protection he may find himself in the dock answering a charge of blasphemous libel, seditious libel, obscene libel, or all three together, not to mention the possibility of a private action for defamatory libel. His sole refuge is the opinion of the Examiner of Plays, his sole protection the licence of the Lord Chamberlain. A refusal to license does not hurt him, because he can produce another play: it is the author who suffers. The granting of the licence practically places him above the law; for though it may be legally possible to prosecute a licensed play, nobody ever dreams of doing it. The really responsible person, the Lord Chamberlain, could not be put into the dock; and the manager could not decently be convicted when he could procure in his defence a certificate from the chief officer of the King's household that the play was a proper one.

A Two Guinea Insurance Policy

The censorship, then, provides the manager, at the negligible premium of two guineas per play, with an effective insurance against the author getting him into trouble, and a complete relief from all conscientious responsibility for the character of the entertainment at his theatre. Under such circumstances, managers would be more than human if they did not regard the censorship as their most valuable privilege. This is the simple explanation of the rally of the managers and their Associations to the defence of the censorship, of their reiterated resolutions of confidence in the Lord Chamberlain, of their presentations of plate, and, generally, of their enthusiastic contentment with the present system, all in such startling contrast to the denunciations of the censorship by the authors. It also explains why the managerial witnesses who had least to fear from the Censor were the most reluctant in his defence, whilst those whose practice it is to strain his indulgence to the utmost were almost rapturous in his praise. There would be absolute unanimity among the managers in favor of the censorship if they were all simply tradesmen. Even those actor-managers who made no secret before the Committee of their contempt for the present operation of the censorship, and their indignation at being handed over to a domestic official as casual servants of a specially disorderly kind, demanded, not the abolition of the institution, but such a reform as might make it consistent with their dignity and unobstructive to their higher artistic aims. Feeling no personal need for protection against the author, they perhaps forgot the plight of many a manager to whom the modern advanced drama is so much Greek; but they did feel very strongly the need of being protected against Vigilance Societies and Municipalities and common informers in a country where a large section of the community still believes that art of all kinds is inherently sinful.

Why the Government Interfered

It may now be asked how a Liberal government had been persuaded to meddle at all with a question in which so many conflicting interests were involved, and which had probably no electoral value whatever. Many simple souls believed that it was because certain severely virtuous plays by Ibsen, by M. Brieux, by Mr Granville Barker, and by me, were suppressed by the censorship, whilst plays of a scandalous character were licensed without demur. No doubt this influenced public opinion; but those who imagine that it could influence British governments little know how remote from public opinion and how full of their own little family and party affairs British governments, both Liberal and Unionist, still are. The censorship scandal had existed for years without any parliamentary action being taken in the matter, and might have existed for as many more had it not happened in 1906 that Mr Robert Vernon Harcourt entered parliament as a member of the Liberal Party, of which his father had been one of the leaders during the Gladstone era. Mr Harcourt was thus a young man marked out for office both by his parentage and his unquestionable social position as one of the governing class. Also, and this was much less usual, he was brilliantly clever, and was the author of a couple of plays of remarkable promise. Mr Harcourt informed his leaders that he was going to take up the subject of the censorship. The leaders, recognizing his hereditary right to a parliamentary canter of some sort as a prelude to his public career, and finding that all the clever people seemed to be agreed that the censorship was an anti-Liberal institution and an abominable nuisance to boot, indulged him by appointing a Select Committee of both Houses to investigate the subject. The then Chancellor of the Duchy of Lancaster, Mr Herbert Samuel (now Postmaster-General), who had made his way into the Cabinet twenty years ahead of the usual age, was made Chairman. Mr Robert Harcourt himself was of course a member. With him, representing the Commons, were Mr Alfred Mason, a man of letters who had won a seat in parliament as offhandedly as he has since discarded it, or as he once appeared on the stage to help me out of a difficulty in casting Arms and the Man when that piece was the newest thing in the advanced drama. There was Mr Hugh Law, an Irish member, son of an Irish Chancellor, presenting a keen and joyous front to English intellectual sloth. Above all, there was Colonel Lockwood to represent at one stroke the Opposition and the average popular man. This he did by standing up gallantly for the Censor, to whose support the Opposition was in no way committed, and by visibly defying the most cherished conventions of the average man with a bunch of carnations in his buttonhole as large as a dinner-plate, which would have made a Bunthorne blench, and which very nearly did make Mr Granville Barker (who has an antipathy to the scent of carnations) faint.

The Peers on the Joint Select Committee

The House of Lords then proceeded to its selection. As fashionable drama in Paris and London concerns itself almost exclusively with adultery, the first choice fell on Lord Gorell, who had for many years presided over the Divorce Court. Lord Plymouth, who had been Chairman to the Shakespear Memorial project (now merged in the Shakespear Memorial National Theatre) was obviously marked out for selection; and it was generally expected that the Lords Lytton and Esher, who had taken a prominent part in the same movement, would have been added. This expectation was not fulfilled. Instead, Lord Willoughby de Broke, who had distinguished himself as an amateur actor, was selected along with Lord Newton, whose special qualifications for the Committee, if he had any, were unknown to the public. Finally Lord Ribblesdale, the argute son of a Scotch mother, was thrown in to make up for any shortcoming in intellectual subtlety that might arise in the case of his younger colleagues; and this completed the two teams.

The Committee's Attitude towards the Theatre

In England, thanks chiefly to the censorship, the theatre is not respected. It is indulged and despised as a department of what is politely called gaiety. It is therefore not surprising that the majority of the Committee began by taking its work uppishly and carelessly. When it discovered that the contemporary drama, licensed by the Lord Chamberlain, included plays which could be described only behind closed doors, and in the discomfort which attends discussions of very nasty subjects between men of widely different ages, it calmly put its own convenience before its public duty by ruling that there should be no discussion of particular plays, much as if a committee on temperance were to rule that drunkenness was not a proper subject of conversation among gentlemen.

A Bad Beginning

This was a bad beginning. Everybody knew that in England the censorship would not be crushed by the weight of the constitutional argument against it, heavy as that was, unless it were also brought home to the Committee and to the public that it had sanctioned and protected the very worst practicable examples of·the kind of play it professed to extirpate. For it must be remembered that the other half of the practical side of the case, dealing with the merits of the plays it had suppressed, could never secure a unanimous assent. If the Censor had suppressed Hamlet, as he most certainly would have done had it been submitted to him as a new play, he would have been supported by a large body of people to whom incest is a tabooed subject which must not be mentioned on the stage or anywhere else outside a criminal court. Hamlet, Oedipus, and The Cenci, Mrs Warren's Profession, Brieux's Maternité, and Les Avariés, Maeterlinck's Monna Vanna and Mr. Granville Barker's Waste may or may not be great poems, or edifying sermons, or important documents, or charming romances: our tribal citizens know nothing about that and do not want to know anything: all that they do know is that incest, prostitution, abortion, contagious diseases, and nudity are improper, and that all conversations, or books, or plays in which they are discussed are improper conversations, improper books, improper plays, and should not be allowed. The Censor may prohibit all such plays with complete certainty that there will be a chorus of "Quite right too" sufficient to drown the protests of the few who know better. The Achilles heel of the censorship is therefore not the fine plays it has suppressed, but the abominable plays it has licensed: plays which the Committee itself had to turn the public out of the room and close the doors before it could discuss, and which I myself have found it impossible to expose in the press because no editor of a paper or magazine intended for general family reading could admit into his columns the baldest narration of the stories which the Censor has not only tolerated but expressly certified as fitting for presentation on the stage. When the Committee ruled out this part of the case it shook the confidence of the authors in its impartiality and its seriousness. Of course it was not able to enforce its ruling thoroughly. Plays which were merely lightminded and irresponsible in their viciousness were repeatedly mentioned by Mr Harcourt and others. But the really detestable plays, which would have damned the censorship beyond all apology or salvation, were never referred to; and the moment Mr Harcourt or anyone else made the Committee uncomfortable by a move in their direction, the ruling was appealed to at once, and the censorship saved.

A Comic Interlude

It was part of this nervous dislike of the unpleasant part of its business that led to the comic incident of the Committee's sudden discovery that I had insulted it, and its suspension of its investigation for the purpose of elaborately insulting me back again. Comic to the lookers-on, that is; for the majority of the Committee made no attempt to conceal the fact that they were wildly angry with me; and I, though my public experience and skill in acting enabled me to maintain an appearance of imperturbable good-humor, was equally furious. The friction began as follows.

The precedents for the conduct of the Committee were to be found in the proceedings of the Committee of 1892. That Committee, no doubt recognizing the absurdity of calling on distinguished artists to give their views before it, and then refusing to allow them to state their views except in nervous replies to such questions as it might suit members to put to them, allowed Sir Henry Irving and Sir John Hare to prepare and read written statements, and formally invited them to read them to the Committee before being questioned. I accordingly prepared such a statement. For the greater convenience of the Committee, I offered to have this statement printed at my own expense, and to supply the members with copies. The offer was accepted; and the copies supplied. I also offered to provide the Committee with copies of those plays of mine which had been refused a licence by the Lord Chamberlain. That offer also was accepted; and the books duly supplied.

An Anti-Shavian Panic

As far as I can guess, the next thing that happened was that some timid or unawakened member of the Committee read my statement and was frightened or scandalized out of his wits by it. At all events it is certain that the majority of the Committee allowed themselves to be persuaded to refuse to allow any statement to be read; but to avoid the appearance of pointing this expressly at me, the form adopted was a resolution to adhere strictly to precedent, the Committee being then unaware that the precedents were on my side. Accordingly, when I appeared before the Committee, and proposed to read my statement " according to precedent," the Committee was visibly taken aback. The Chairman was bound by the letter of the decision arrived at to allow me to read my statement, since that course was according to precedent; but as this was exactly what the decision was meant to prevent, the majority of the Committee would have regarded this hoisting of them with their own petard as a breach of faith on the part of the Chairman, who, I infer, was not in agreement with the suppressive majority. There was nothing for it, after a somewhat awkward pause, but to clear me and the public out of the room and reconsider the situation *in camera*. When the doors were opened again I was informed simply that the Committee would not hear my statement. But as the Committee could not very decently refuse my evidence altogether, the Chairman, with a printed copy of my statement in his hand as " proof," was able to come to the rescue to some extent by putting to me a series of questions to which no doubt I might have replied by taking another copy out of my pocket, and quoting my statement paragraph by paragraph, as some of the later witnesses did. But as in offering the Committee my statement for burial in their bluebook I had made a considerable sacrifice, being able to secure greater publicity for it by independent publication on my own account; and as, further, the circumstances of the refusal made it offensive enough to take all heart out of the scrupulous consideration with which I had so far treated the Committee, I was not disposed to give its majority a second chance, or to lose the opportunity offered me by the questions to fire an additional broadside into the censorship. I pocketed my statement, and answered the questions *viva voce*. At the conclusion of this, my examination-in-chief, the Committee adjourned, asking me to present myself again for (virtually) cross-examination. But this cross-examination never came off, as the sequel will shew.

A Rare and Curious First Edition

The refusal of the Committee to admit my statement had not unnaturally created the impression that it must be a scandalous document; and a lively demand for copies at once set in. And among the very first applicants were members of the majority which had carried the decision to exclude the document. They had given so little attention to the business that they did not know, or had forgotten, that they had already been supplied with copies at their own request. At all events, they came to me publicly and cleaned me out of the handful of copies I had provided for distribution to the press. And after the sitting it was intimated to me that yet more copies were desired for the use of the Committee: a demand, under the circumstances, of breath-bereaving coolness. At the same time, a brisk demand arose outside the Committee, not only among people who were anxious to read what I had to say on the subject, but among victims of the craze for collecting first editions, copies of privately circulated pamphlets, and other real or imaginary rarities, and who will cheerfully pay five guineas for any piece of discarded old rubbish of mine when they will not pay four-and-sixpence for this book because everyone else can get it for four-and-sixpence too.

The Times to the Rescue

The day after the refusal of the Committee to face my statement, I transferred the scene of action to the columns of The Times, which did yeoman's service to the public on this, as on many other occasions, by treating the question as a public one without the least regard to the supposed susceptibilities of the Court on the one side, or the avowed prejudices of the Free Churches or the interests of the managers or theatrical speculators on the other. The Times published the summarized conclusions of my statement, and gave me an opportunity of saying as much as it was then advisable to say of what had occurred. For it must be remembered that, however impatient and contemptuous I might feel of the intellectual cowardice shewn by the majority of the Committee face to face with myself, it was none the less necessary to keep up its prestige in every possible way, not only for the sake of the dignity and importance of the matter with which it had to deal, and in the hope that the treatment of subsequent witnesses and the final report might make amends for a feeble beginning, but also out of respect and consideration for the minority. For it is fair to say that the majority was never more than a bare majority, and that the worst thing the Committee did—the exclusion of references to particular plays—was perpetrated in the absence of the Chairman.

I, therefore, had to treat the Committee in The Times very much better than its majority deserved, an injustice for which I now apologize. I did not, however, resist the temptation to hint, quite good-humoredly, that my politeness to the Committee had cost me quite enough already, and that I was not prepared to supply the members of the Committee, or anyone else, with extra copies merely as collectors' curiosities.

The Council of Ten

Then the fat was in the fire. The majority, chaffed for its eagerness to obtain copies of scarce pamphlets retailable at five guineas, went dancing mad. When I presented myself, as requested, for cross-examination, I found the doors of the Committee room shut, and the corridors of the House of Lords filled by a wondering crowd, to whom it had somehow leaked out that something terrible was happening inside. It could not be another licensed play too scandalous to be discussed in public, because the Committee had decided to discuss no more of these examples of the Censor's notions of purifying the stage; and what else the Committee might have to discuss that might not be heard by all the world was not easily guessable.

Without suggesting that the confidence of the Committee was in any way violated by any of its members further than was absolutely necessary to clear them from suspicion of complicity in the scene which followed, I think I may venture to conjecture what was happening. It was felt by the majority, first, that it must be cleared at all costs of the imputation of having procured more than one copy each of my statement, and that one not from any interest in an undesirable document by an irreverent author, but in the reluctant discharge of its solemn public duty; second, that a terrible example must be made of me by the most crushing public snub in the power of the Committee to administer. To throw my wretched little pamphlet at my head and to kick me out of the room was the passionate impulse which prevailed

Preface

in spite of all the remonstrances of the Commoners, seasoned to the give-and-take of public life, and of the single peer who kept his head. The others, for the moment, had no heads to keep. And the fashion in which they proposed to wreak their vengeance was as follows.

The Sentence

I was to be admitted, as a lamb to the slaughter, and allowed to take my place as if for further examination. The Chairman was then to inform me coldly that the Committee did not desire to have anything more to say to me. The members were thereupon solemnly to hand me back the copies of my statement as so much waste paper, and I was to be suffered to slink away with what countenance I could maintain in such disgrace.

But this plan required the active co-operation of every member of the Committee; and whilst the majority regarded it as an august and impressive vindication of the majesty of parliament, the minority regarded it with equal conviction as a puerile tomfoolery, and declined altogether to act their allotted parts in it. Besides, they did not all want to part with the books. For instance, Mr Hugh Law, being an Irishman, with an Irishman's sense of how to behave like a gallant gentleman on occasion, was determined to be able to assure me that nothing should induce him to give up my statement or prevent him from obtaining and cherishing as many copies as possible. (I quote this as an example to the House of Lords of the right thing to say in such emergencies). So the program had to be modified. The minority could not prevent the enraged majority from refusing to examine me further; nor could the Chairman refuse to communicate that decision to me. Neither could the minority object to the secretary handing me back such copies as he could collect from the majority. And at that the matter was left. The doors were opened; the audience trooped in; I was called to my place in the dock (so to speak); and all was ready for the sacrifice.

The Execution

Alas! the majority reckoned without Colonel Lockwood. That hardy and undaunted veteran refused to shirk his share in the scene merely because the minority was recalcitrant and the majority perhaps subject to stage fright. When Mr Samuel had informed me that the Committee had no further questions to ask me with an urbanity which gave the public no clue as to the temper of the majority; when I had jumped up with the proper air of relief and gratitude; when the secretary had handed me his little packet of books with an affability which effectually concealed his dramatic function as executioner; when the audience was simply disappointed at being baulked of the entertainment of hearing Mr Robert Harcourt cross-examine me; in short, when the situation was all but saved by the tact of the Chairman and secretary, Colonel Lockwood rose, with all his carnations blazing, and gave away the whole case by handing me, with impressive simplicity and courtesy, his *two* copies of the precious statement. And I believe that if he had succeeded in securing ten, he would have handed them all back to me with the most sincere conviction that every one of the ten must prove a crushing addition to the weight of my discomfiture. I still cherish that second copy, a little blue-bound pamphlet, methodically autographed " Lockwood B " among my most valued literary trophies.

An innocent lady told me afterwards that she never knew that I could smile so beautifully, and that she thought it shewed very good taste on my part. I was not conscious of smiling; but I should have embraced the Colonel had I dared. As it was, I turned expectantly to his colleagues, mutely inviting them to follow his example. But there was only one Colonel Lockwood on that Committee. No eye met mine except minority eyes, dancing with mischief. There was nothing more to be said. I went home to my morning's work, and returned in the afternoon to receive the apologies of the minority for the conduct of the majority, and to see Mr Granville Barker, overwhelmed by the conscience-stricken politeness of the now almost abject Committee, and by a powerful smell of carnations, heading the long list of playwrights who came there to testify against the censorship, and whose treatment, I am happy to say, was everything they could have desired.

After all, ridiculous as the scene was, Colonel Lockwood's simplicity and courage were much more serviceable to his colleagues than their own inept *coup de théâtre* would have been if he had not spoiled it. It was plain to every one that he had acted in entire good faith, without a thought as to these apparently insignificant little books being of any importance or having caused me or anybody else any trouble, and that he was wounded in his most sensitive spot by the construction my Times letter had put on his action. And in Colonel Lockwood's case one saw the case of his party on the Committee. They had simply been thoughtless in the matter.

I hope nobody will suppose that this in any way exonerates them. When people accept public service for one of the most vital duties that can arise in our society, they have no right to be thoughtless. In spite of the fun of the scene on the surface, my public sense was, and still is, very deeply offended by it. It made an end for me of the claim of the majority to be taken seriously. When the Government comes to deal with the question, as it presumably will before long, I invite it to be guided by the Chairman, the minority, and by the witnesses ac-

344 The Shewing-Up of Blanco Posnet

cording to their weight, and to pay no attention whatever to those recommendations which were obviously inserted solely to conciliate the majority and get the report through and the Committee done with.

My evidence will be found in the Bluebook, pp. 46-53. And here is the terrible statement which the Committee went through so much to suppress.

THE REJECTED STATEMENT

PART I

The Witness's Qualifications

I AM by profession a playwright. I have been in practice since 1892. I am a member of the Managing Committee of the Society of Authors and of the Dramatic Sub-Committee of that body. I have written nineteen plays, some of which have been translated and performed in all European countries except Turkey, Greece, and Portugal. They have been performed extensively in America. Three of them have been refused licences by the Lord Chamberlain. In one case a licence has since been granted. The other two are still unlicensed. I have suffered both in pocket and reputation by the action of the Lord Chamberlain. In other countries I have not come into conflict with the censorship except in Austria, where the production of a comedy of mine was postponed for a year because it alluded to the part taken by Austria in the Servo-Bulgarian war. This comedy was not one of the plays suppressed in England by the Lord Chamberlain. One of the plays so suppressed was prosecuted in America by the police in consequence of an immense crowd of disorderly persons having been attracted to the first performance by the Lord Chamberlain's condemnation of it; but on appeal to a higher court it was decided that the representation was lawful and the intention innocent, since when it has been repeatedly performed.

I am not an ordinary playwright in general practice.

I am a specialist in immoral and heretical plays. My reputation has been gained by my persistent struggle to force the public to reconsider its morals. In particular, I regard much current morality as to economic and sexual relations as disastrously wrong; and I regard certain doctrines of the Christian religion as understood in England to-day with abhorrence. I write plays with the deliberate object of converting the nation to my opinions in these matters. I have no other effectual incentive to write plays, as I am not dependent on the theatre for my livelihood. If I were prevented from producing immoral and heretical plays, I should cease to write for the theatre, and propagate my views from the platform and through books. I mention these facts to shew that I have a special interest in the achievement by my profession of those rights of liberty of speech and conscience which are matters of course in other professions. I object to censorship not merely because the existing form of it grievously injures and hinders me individually, but on public grounds.

The Definition of Immorality

In dealing with the question of the censorship, everything depends on the correct use of the word immorality, and a careful discrimination between the powers of a magistrate or judge to administer a code, and those of a censor to please himself.

Whatever is contrary to established manners and customs is immoral. An immoral act or doctrine is not necessarily a sinful one: on the contrary, every advance in thought and conduct is by definition immoral until it has converted the majority. For this reason it is of the most enormous importance that immorality should be protected jealously against the attacks of those who have no standard except the standard of custom, and who regard any attack on custom—that is, on morals—as an attack on society, on religion, and on virtue.

A censor is never intentionally a protector of immorality. He always aims at the protection of morality. Now morality is extremely valuable to society. It imposes conventional conduct on the great mass of persons who are incapable of original ethical judgment, and who would be quite lost if they were not in leading-strings devised by lawgivers, philosophers, prophets and poets for their guidance. But morality is not dependent on censorship for protection. It is already powerfully fortified by the magistracy and the whole body of law. Blasphemy, indecency, libel, treason, sedition, obscenity, profanity, and all the other evils which a censorship is supposed to avert, are punishable by the civil magistrate with all the severity of vehement prejudice. Morality has not only every engine that lawgivers can devise in full operation for its protection, but also that enormous weight of public opinion enforced by social ostracism which is stronger than all the statutes. A censor pretending to protect morality is like a child pushing the cushions of a railway carriage to give itself the sensation of making the train travel at sixty miles an hour. It is immorality, not morality, that needs protection: it is morality, not immorality, that needs restraint; for morality, with all the dead weight of human inertia and superstition to hang on the back of the pioneer, and all the malice of vulgarity and prejudice to threaten him, is responsible for many persecutions and many martyrdoms.

Persecutions and martyrdoms, however, are trifles compared to the mischief done by censorships in delaying the general march of enlightenment. This can be brought home to us by imagining what would have been the effect of applying to all literature the censorship we still apply to the stage. The works of Linnæus and the evolutionists of 1790–1830, of Darwin, Wallace, Huxley, Helmholtz, Tyndall, Spencer, Carlyle, Ruskin, and Samuel Butler, would not have been published, as they were all immoral and heretical in the very highest degree, and gave pain to many worthy and pious people. They are at present condemned by the Greek and Roman Catholic censorships as unfit for general reading. A censorship of conduct would have been equally disastrous. The disloyalty of Hampden and of Washington; the revolting immorality of Luther in not only marrying when he was a priest, but actually marrying a nun; the heterodoxy of Galileo; the shocking blasphemies and sacrileges of Mohammed against the idols whom he dethroned to make way for his conception of one god; the still more startling blasphemy of Jesus when he declared God to be the son of man and himself to be the son of God, are all examples of shocking immoralities (every immorality shocks somebody), the suppression and extinction of which would have been more disastrous than the utmost mischief that can be conceived as ensuing from the toleration of vice.

These facts, glaring as they are, are disguised by the promotion of immoralities into moralities which is constantly going on. Christianity and Mohammedanism, once thought of and dealt with exactly as Anarchism is thought of and dealt with today, have become established religions; and fresh immoralities are presecuted in their name. The truth is that the vast majority of persons professing these religions have never been anything but simple moralists. The respectable Englishman who is a Christian because he was born in Clapham would be a Mohammedan for the cognate reason if he had been born in Constantinople. He has never willingly tolerated immorality. He did not adopt any innovation until it had become moral; and then he adopted it, not on its merits, but solely because it had become moral. In doing so he never realized that it had ever been immoral: consequently its early struggles taught him no lesson; and he has opposed the next step in human progress as indignantly as if neither manners, customs, nor thought had ever changed since the beginning of the world. Toleration must be imposed on him as a mystic and painful duty by his spiritual and political leaders, or he will condemn the world to stagnation, which is the penalty of an inflexible morality.

What Toleration Means

This must be done all the more arbitrarily because it is not possible to make the ordinary moral man understand what toleration and liberty really mean. He will accept them verbally with alacrity, even with enthusiasm, because the word toleration has been moralized by eminent Whigs; but what he means by toleration is toleration of doctrines that he considers enlightened, and, by liberty, liberty to do what he considers right: that is, he does not mean toleration or liberty at all; for there is no need to tolerate what appears enlightened or to claim liberty to do what most people consider right. Toleration and liberty have no sense or use except as toleration of opinions that are considered damnable, and liberty to do what seems wrong. Setting Englishmen free to marry their deceased wife's sisters is not tolerated by the people who approve of it, but by the people who regard it as incestuous. Catholic Emancipation and the admission of Jews to parliament needed no toleration from Catholics and Jews: the toleration they needed was that of the people who regarded the one measure as a facilitation of idolatry, and the other as a condonation of the crucifixion. Clearly such toleration is not clamored for by the multitude or by the press which reflects its prejudices. It is essentially one of those abnegations of passion and prejudice which the common man submits to because uncommon men whom he respects as wiser than himself assure him that it must be so, or the higher affairs of human destiny will suffer.

Such admission is the more difficult because the arguments against tolerating immorality are the same as the arguments against tolerating murder and theft; and this is why the Censor seems to the inconsiderate as obviously desirable a functionary as the police magistrate. But there is this simple and tremendous difference between the cases: that whereas no evil can conceivably result from the total suppression of murder and theft, and all communities prosper in direct proportion to such suppression, the total suppression of immorality, especially in matters of religion and sex, would stop enlightenment, and produce what used to be called a Chinese civilization until the Chinese lately took to immoral courses by permitting railway contractors to desecrate the graves of their ancestors, and their soldiers to wear clothes which indecently revealed the fact that they had legs and waists and even posteriors. At about the same moment a few bold Englishwomen ventured on the immorality of riding astride their horses, a practice that has since established itself so successfully that before another generation has passed away there may not be a new side-saddle in England or a woman who could use it if there was.

The Case for Toleration

Accordingly, there has risen among wise and far-sighted men a perception of the need for setting certain departments of human activity entirely free from legal interference. This has nothing to do with any sympathy these liberators may themselves have with immoral views. A man with the strongest conviction of the Divine ordering of the universe and of the superiority of monarchy to all forms of government may nevertheless quite consistently and conscientiously be ready to lay down his life for the right of every man to advocate Atheism or Republicanism if he believes in them. An attack on morals may turn out to be the salvation of the race. A hundred years ago nobody foresaw that Tom Paine's centenary would be the subject of a laudatory special article in The Times; and only a few understood that the persecution of his works and the transportation of men for the felony of reading them was a mischievous mistake. Even less, perhaps, could they have guessed that Proudhon, who became notorious by his essay entitled "What is Property? It is Theft" would have received, on the like occasion and in the same paper, a respectful consideration which nobody would now dream of according to Lord Liverpool or Lord Brougham. Nevertheless there was a mass of evidence to shew that such a development was not only possible but fairly probable, and that the risks of suppressing liberty of propaganda were far greater than the risk of Paine's or Proudhon's writings wrecking civilization. Now there was no such evidence in favor of tolerating the cutting of throats and the robbing of tills. No case whatever can be made out for the statement that a nation cannot do without common thieves and homicidal ruffians. But an overwhelming case can be made out for the statement that no nation can prosper or even continue to exist without heretics and advocates of shockingly immoral doctrines. The Inquisition and the Star Chamber, which were nothing but censorships, made ruthless war on impiety and immorality. The result was once familiar to Englishmen, though of late years it seems to have been forgotten. It cost England a revolution to get rid of the Star Chamber. Spain did not get rid of the Inquisition, and paid for that omission by becoming a barely third-rate power politically, and intellectually no power at all, in the Europe she had once dominated as the mightiest of the Christian empires.

The Limits to Toleration

But the large toleration these considerations dictate has limits. For example, though we tolerate, and rightly tolerate, the propaganda of Anarchism as a political theory which embraces all that is valuable in the doctrine of Laisser-Faire and the method of Free Trade as well as all that is shocking in the views of Bakounine, we clearly cannot, or at all events will not, tolerate assassination of rulers on the ground that it is "propaganda by deed" or sociological experiment. A play inciting to such an assassination cannot claim the privileges of heresy or immorality, because no case can be made out in support of assassination as an indispensable instrument of progress. Now it happens that we have in the Julius Cæsar of Shakespear a play which the Tsar of Russia or the Governor-General of India would hardly care to see performed in their capitals just now. It is an artistic treasure; but it glorifies a murder which Goethe described as the silliest crime ever committed. It may quite possibly have helped the regicides of 1649 to see themselves, as it certainly helped generations of Whig statesmen to see them, in a heroic light; and it unquestionably vindicates and ennobles a conspirator who assassinated the head of the Roman State not because he abused his position but solely because he occupied it, thus affirming the extreme republican principle that all kings, good or bad, should be killed because kingship and freedom cannot live together. Under certain circumstances this vindication and ennoblement might act as an incitement to an actual assassination as well as to Plutarchian republicanism; for it is one thing to advo-

cate republicanism or royalism: it is quite another to
make a hero of Brutus or Ravaillac, or a heroine of
Charlotte Corday. Assassination is the extreme form of
censorship; and it seems hard to justify an incitement to
it on anti-censorial principles. The very people who
would have scouted the notion of prohibiting the performances of Julius Cæsar at His Majesty's Theatre in
London last year, might now entertain very seriously a
proposal to exclude Indians from them, and to suppress
the play completely in Calcutta and Dublin; for if the
assassin of Cæsar was a hero, why not the assassins of
Lord Fredcrick Cavendish, Presidents Lincoln and
McKinley, and Sir Curzon Wyllie? Here is a strong
case for some constitutional means of preventing the performance of a play. True, it is an equally strong case
for preventing the circulation of the Bible, which was
always in the hands of our regicides; but as the Roman
Catholic Church does not hesitate to accept that consequence of the censorial principle, it does not invalidate
the argument.

Take another actual case. A modern comedy, Arms
and The Man, though not a comedy of politics, is nevertheless so far historical that it reveals the unacknowledged fact that as the Servo-Bulgarian War of 1885
was much more than a struggle between the Servians
and Bulgarians, the troops engaged were officered by
two European Powers of the first magnitude. In consequence, the performance of the play was for some time
forbidden in Vienna, and more recently it gave offence
in Rome at a moment when popular feeling was excited
as to the relations of Austria with the Balkan States.
Now if a comedy so remote from political passion as
Arms and The Man can, merely because it refers to political facts, become so inconvenient and inopportune
that Foreign Offices take the trouble to have its production postponed, what may not be the effect of what is

called a patriotic drama produced at a moment when the balance is quivering between peace and war? Is there not something to be said for a political censorship, if not for a moral one? May not those continental governments who leave the stage practically free in every other respect, but muzzle it politically, be justified by the practical exigencies of the situation?

The Difference between Law and Censorship

The answer is that a pamphlet, a newspaper article, or a resolution moved at a political meeting can do all the mischief that a play can, and often more; yet we do not set up a permanent censorship of the press or of political meetings. Any journalist may publish an article, any demagogue may deliver a speech without giving notice to the government or obtaining its licence. The risk of such freedom is great; but as it is the price of our political liberty, we think it worth paying. We may abrogate it in emergencies by a Coercion Act, a suspension of the Habeas Corpus Act, or a proclamation of martial law, just as we stop the traffic in a street during a fire, or shoot thieves at sight if they loot after an earthquake. But when the emergency is past, liberty is restored everywhere except in the theatre. The Act of 1843 is a permanent Coercion Act for the theatre, a permanent suspension of the Habeas Corpus Act as far as plays are concerned, a permanent proclamation of martial law with a single official substituted for a court martial. It is, in fact, assumed that actors, playwrights, and theatre managers are dangerous and dissolute characters whose existence creates a chronic state of emergency, and who must be treated as earthquake looters are treated. It is not necessary now to discredit this assumption. It was broken down by the late Sir Henry Irving when he finally shamed the Government into extending to his profession the official recognition enjoyed by the other branches of fine art. To-day we have on the roll of knighthood actors, authors, and managers. The rogue and vagabond theory of the depravity of the theatre is as dead officially as it is in general society; and with it has perished the sole excuse for the Act of 1843 and for the denial to the theatre of the liberties secured, at far greater social risk, to the press and the platform.

There is no question here of giving the theatre any larger liberties than the press and the platform, or of claiming larger powers for Shakespear to eulogize Brutus than Lord Rosebery has to eulogize Cromwell. The abolition of the censorship does not involve the abolition of the magistrate and of the whole civil and criminal code. On the contrary it would make the theatre more effectually subject to them than it is at present; for once a play now runs the gauntlet of the censorship, it is practically placed above the law. It is almost humiliating to have to demonstrate the essential difference between a censor and a magistrate or a sanitary inspector; but it is impossible to ignore the carelessness with which even distinguished critics of the theatre assume that all the arguments proper to the support of a magistracy and body of jurisprudence apply equally to a censorship.

A magistrate has laws to administer: a censor has nothing but his own opinion. A judge leaves the question of guilt to the jury: the Censor is jury and judge as well as lawgiver. A magistrate may be strongly prejudiced against an atheist or an anti-vaccinator, just as a sanitary inspector may have formed a careful opinion that drains are less healthy than cesspools; but the magistrate must allow the atheist to affirm instead of to swear, and must grant the anti-vaccinator an exemption certificate, when their demands are lawfully made; and in cities the inspector must compel the builder to make drains and must prosecute him if he makes cesspools. The law may be only the intolerance of the community; but it is a defined and limited intolerance. The limitation is sometimes carried so far that a judge cannot inflict the penalty for housebreaking on a burglar who can prove that he found the door open and therefore made only an unlawful entry. On the other hand, it is sometimes so vague, as for example in the case of the American law against obscenity, that it makes the magistrate virtually a censor. But in the main a citizen can ascertain what he may do and what he may not do; and, though no one knows better than a magistrate that a single ill-conducted family may demoralize a whole street, no magistrate can imprison or otherwise restrain its members on the ground that their immorality may corrupt their neighbors. He can prevent any citizen from carrying certain specified weapons, but not from handling pokers, table-knives, bricks or bottles of corrosive fluid, on the ground that he might use them to commit murder or inflict malicious injury. He has no general power to prevent citizens from selling unhealthy or poisonous substances, or judging for themselves what substances are unhealthy and what wholesome, what poisonous and what innocuous: what he *can* do is to prevent anybody who has not a specific qualification from selling certain specified poisons of which a schedule is kept. Nobody is forbidden to sell minerals without a licence; but everybody is forbidden to sell silver without a licence. When the law has forgotten some atrocious sin—for instance, contracting marriage whilst suffering from contagious disease—the magistrate cannot arrest or punish the wrongdoer, however he may abhor his wickedness. In short, no man is lawfully at the mercy of the magistrate's personal caprice, prejudice, ignorance, superstition, temper, stupidity, resentment, timidity, ambition, or private conviction. But a playwright's livelihood, his reputation, and his inspiration and mission are at the personal mercy of the Censor. The two do not stand, as the criminal and the judge stand, in the presence of a law that binds them both equally, and was made by neither of them, but by the deliberative collective wisdom of the community. The only law that affects them is the Act of 1843, which empowers one of them to do absolutely and finally what he likes with the other's work. And when it is remembered that the slave in this case is the man whose profession is that of Eschylus and Euripides, of Shakespear and Goethe, of Tolstoy and Ibsen, and the master the holder of a party appointment which by the nature of its duties practically excludes the possibility of its acceptance by a serious statesman or great lawyer, it will be seen that the playwrights are justified in reproaching the framers of that Act for having failed not only to appreciate the immense importance of the theatre as a most powerful instrument for teaching the nation how and what to think and feel, but even to conceive that those who make their living by the theatre are normal human beings with the common rights of English citizens. In this extremity of inconsiderateness it is not surprising that they also did not trouble themselves to study the difference between a censor and a magistrate. And it will be found that almost all the people who disinterestedly defend the censorship today are defending him on the assumption that there is no constitutional difference between him and any other functionary whose duty it is to restrain crime and disorder.

One further difference remains to be noted. As a magistrate grows old his mind may change or decay; but the law remains the same. The censorship of the theatre fluctuates with every change in the views and character of the man who exercises it. And what this implies can only be appreciated by those who can imagine what the effect on the mind must be of the duty of reading through every play that is produced in the kingdom year in, year out.

Why the Lord Chamberlain?

What may be called the high political case against censorship as a principle is now complete. The pleadings are those which have already freed books and pulpits and political platforms in England from censorship, if not from occasional legal persecution. The stage alone remains under a censorship of a grotesquely unsuitable kind. No play can be performed if the Lord Chamberlain happens to disapprove of it. And the Lord Chamberlain's functions have no sort of relationship to dramatic literature. A great judge of literature, a farseeing statesman, a born champion of liberty of conscience and intellectual integrity—say a Milton, a Chesterfield, a Bentham—would be a very bad Lord Chamberlain: so bad, in fact, that his exclusion from such a post may be regarded as decreed by natural law. On the other hand, a good Lord Chamberlain would be a stickler for morals in the narrowest sense, a busy-body, a man to whom a matter of two inches in the length of a gentleman's sword or the absence of a feather from a lady's head-dress would be a graver matter than the Habeas Corpus Act. The Lord Chamberlain, as Censor of the theatre, is a direct descendant of the King's Master of the Revels, appointed in 1544 by Henry VIII. to keep order among the players and musicians of that day when they performed at Court. This first appearance of the theatrical censor in politics as the whipper-in of the player, with its conception of the player as a rich man's servant hired to amuse him, and, outside his professional duties, as a gay, disorderly, anarchic spoilt child, half privileged, half outlawed, probably as much vagabond as actor, is the real foundation of the subjection of the whole profession, actors, managers, authors and all, to the despotic authority of an officer whose business it is to preserve decorum among menials. It must be remembered that it was not until a hundred years later, in the reaction against the Puritans, that a woman could appear on the English stage without being pelted off as the Italian actresses were. The theatrical profession was regarded as a shameless one; and it is only of late years that actresses have at last succeeded in living down the assumption that actress and prostitute are synonymous terms, and made good their position in respectable society. This makes the survival of the old ostracism in the Act of 1843 intolerably galling; and though it explains the apparently unaccountable absurdity of choosing as Censor of dramatic literature an official whose functions and qualifications have nothing whatever to do with literature, it also explains why the present arrangement is not only criticized as an institution, but resented as an insult.

The Diplomatic Objection to the Lord Chamberlain

There is another reason, quite unconnected with the susceptibilities of authors, which makes it undesirable that a member of the King's Household should be responsible for the character and tendency of plays. The drama, dealing with all departments of human life, is necessarily political. Recent events have shown—what indeed needed no demonstration—that it is impossible to prevent inferences being made, both at home and abroad, from the action of the Lord Chamberlain. The most talked-about play of the present year (1909), An Englishman's Home, has for its main interest an invasion of England by a fictitious power which is under-

360 The Shewing-Up of Blanco Posnet

stood, as it is meant to be understood, to represent Germany. The lesson taught by the play is the danger of invasion and the need for every English citizen to be a soldier. The Lord Chamberlain licensed this play, but refused to license a parody of it. Shortly afterwards he refused to license another play in which the fear of a German invasion was ridiculed. The German press drew the inevitable inference that the Lord Chamberlain was an anti-German alarmist, and that his opinions were a reflection of those prevailing in St. James's Palace. Immediately after this, the Lord Chamberlain licensed the play. Whether the inference, as far as the Lord Chamberlain was concerned, was justified, is of no consequence. What is important is that it was sure to be made, justly or unjustly, and extended from the Lord Chamberlain to the Throne.

The Objection of Court Etiquet

There is another objection to the Lord Chamberlain's censorship which affects the author's choice of subject. Formerly very little heed was given in England to the susceptibilities of foreign courts. For instance, the notion that the Mikado of Japan should be as sacred to the English playwright as he is to the Japanese Lord Chamberlain would have seemed grotesque a generation ago. Now that the maintenance of *entente cordiale* between nations is one of the most prominent and most useful functions of the crown, the freedom of authors to deal with political subjects, even historically, is seriously threatened by the way in which the censorship makes the King responsible for the contents of every play. One author—the writer of these lines, in fact—has long desired to dramatize the life of Mahomet. But the possibility of a protest from the Turkish Ambassador—or the fear of it—causing the Lord Chamberlain to refuse to license such a play has prevented the play from being written. Now, if the censorship were abolished, nobody but the author could be held responsible for the play. The Turkish Ambassador does not now protest against the publication of Carlyle's essay on the prophet, or of the English translations of the Koran in the prefaces to which Mahomet is criticized as an impostor, or of the older books in which he is reviled as Mahound and classed with the devil himself. But if these publications had to be licensed by the Lord Chamberlain it would be impossible for the King to allow the licence to be issued, as he would thereby be made responsible for the opinions expressed. This restriction of the historical drama is an unmixed evil. Great religious leaders are more interesting and more important subjects for the dramatist than great conquerors. It is a misfortune that public opinion would not tolerate a dramatization of Mahomet in Constantinople. But to prohibit it here, where public opinion would tolerate it, is an absurdity which, if applied in all directions, would make it impossible for the Queen to receive a Turkish ambassador without veiling herself, or the Dean and Chapter of St. Paul's to display a cross on the summit of their Cathedral in a city occupied largely and influentially by Jews. Court etiquet is no doubt an excellent thing for court ceremonies; but to attempt to impose it on the drama is about as sensible as an attempt to make everybody in London wear court dress.

Why not an Enlightened Censorship?

In the above cases the general question of censorship is separable from the question of the present form of it. Every one who condemns the principle of censorship must also condemn the Lord Chamberlain's control of the drama; but those who approve of the principle do not necessarily approve of the Lord Chamberlain being the Censor *ex officio*. They may, however, be entirely opposed to popular liberties, and may conclude from what has been said, not that the stage should be made as free as the church, press, or platform, but that these institutions should be censored as strictly as the stage. It will seem obvious to them that nothing is needed to remove all objections to a censorship except the placing of its powers in better hands.

Now though the transfer of the censorship to, say, the Lord Chancellor, or the Primate, or a Cabinet Minister, would be much less humiliating to the persons immediately concerned, the inherent vices of the institution would not be appreciably less disastrous. They would even be aggravated, for reasons which do not appear on the surface, and therefore need to be followed with some attention.

It is often said that the public is the real censor. That this is to some extent true is proved by the fact that plays which are licensed and produced in London have to be expurgated for the provinces. This does not mean that the provinces are more strait-laced, but simply that in many provincial towns there is only one theatre for all classes and all tastes, whereas in London there are separate theatres for separate sections of playgoers; so that, for example, Sir Herbert Beerbohm Tree can conduct His Majesty's Theatre without the slightest regard to the tastes of the frequenters of the Gaiety Theatre; and Mr. George Edwardes can conduct the Gaiety Theatre without catering in any way for lovers of Shakespear. Thus the farcical comedy which has scandalized the critics in London by the libertinage of its jests is played to the respectable dress circle of Northampton with these same jests slurred over so as to be imperceptible by even the most prurient spectator. The public, in short, takes care that nobody shall outrage it.

The Rejected Statement

But the public also takes care that nobody shall starve it, or regulate its dramatic diet as a schoolmistress regulates the reading of her pupils. Even when it wishes to be debauched, no censor can—or at least no censor does —stand out against it. If a play is irresistibly amusing, it gets licensed no matter what its moral aspect may be. A brilliant instance is the Divorçons of the late Victorien Sardou, which may not have been the naughtiest play of the 19th century, but was certainly the very naughtiest that any English manager in his senses would have ventured to produce. Nevertheless, being a very amusing play, it passed the licenser with the exception of a reference to impotence as a ground for divorce which no English actress would have ventured on in any case. Within the last few months a very amusing comedy with a strongly polygamous moral was found irresistible by the Lord Chamberlain. Plenty of fun and a happy ending will get anything licensed, because the public will have it so, and the Examiner of Plays, as the holder of the office testified before the Commission of 1892 (Report, page 330), feels with the public, and knows that his office could not survive a widespread unpopularity. In short, the support of the mob—that is, of the unreasoning, unorganized, uninstructed mass of popular sentiment—is indispensable to the censorship as it exists today in England. This is the explanation of the toleration by the Lord Chamberlain of coarse and vicious plays. It is not long since a judge before whom a licensed play came in the course of a lawsuit expressed his scandalized astonishment at the licensing of such a work. Eminent churchmen have made similar protests. In some plays the simulation of criminal assaults on the stage has been carried to a point at which a step further would have involved the interference of the police. Provided the treatment of the theme is gaily or hypocritically popular, and the ending happy, the indulgence of

the Lord Chamberlain can be counted on. On the other
hand, anything unpleasing and unpopular is rigorously
censored. Adultery and prostitution are tolerated and
even encouraged to such an extent that plays which do
not deal with them are commonly said not to be plays
at all. But if any of the unpleasing consequences of
adultery and prostitution—for instance, an *unsuccessful*
illegal operation (successful ones are tolerated) or vene-
real disease—are mentioned, the play is prohibited.
This principle of shielding the playgoer from unpleasant reflections is carried so far that when a play was submitted for license in which the relations of a prostitute
with all the male characters in the piece was described
as "immoral," the Examiner of Plays objected to that
passage, though he made no objection to the relations
themselves. The Lord Chamberlain dare not, in short,
attempt to exclude from the stage the tragedies of murder and lust, or the farces of mendacity, adultery, and
dissoluteness gaiety in which vulgar people delight. But
when these same vulgar people are threatened with an
unpopular play in which dissoluteness is shown to be no
laughing matter, it is prohibited at once amid the vulgar
applause, the net result being that vice is made delightful and virtue banned by the very institution which is
supported on the understanding that it produces exactly
the opposite result.

The Weakness of the Lord Chamberlain's Department

Now comes the question, Why is our censorship,
armed as it is with apparently autocratic powers, so
scandalously timid in the face of the mob? Why is it
not as autocratic in dealing with playwrights below the
average as with those above it? The answer is that its
position is really a very weak one. It has no direct co-

ercive forces, no funds to institute prosecutions and recover the legal penalties of defying it, no powers of arrest or imprisonment, in short, none of the guarantees of autocracy. What it can do is to refuse to renew the licence of a theatre at which its orders are disobeyed. When it happens that a theatre is about to be demolished, as was the case recently with the Imperial Theatre after it had passed into the hands of the Wesleyan Methodists, unlicensed plays can be performed, technically in private, but really in full publicity, without risk. The prohibited plays of Brieux and Ibsen have been performed in London in this way with complete impunity. But the impunity is not confined to condemned theatres. Not long ago a West End manager allowed a prohibited play to be performed at his theatre, taking his chance of losing his licence in consequence. The event proved that the manager was justified in regarding the risk as negligible; for the Lord Chamberlain's remedy—the closing of a popular and well-conducted theatre—was far too extreme to be practicable. Unless the play had so outraged public opinion as to make the manager odious and provoke a clamor for his exemplary punishment, the Lord Chamberlain could only have had his revenge at the risk of having his powers abolished as unsupportably tyrannical.

The Lord Chamberlain then has his powers so adjusted that he is tyrannical just where it is important that he should be tolerant, and tolerant just where he could screw up the standard a little by being tyrannical. His plea that there are unmentionable depths to which managers and authors would descend if he did not prevent them is disproved by the plain fact that his indulgence goes as far as the police, and sometimes further than the public, will let it. If our judges had so little power there would be no law in England. If our churches had so much, there would be no theatre, no literature, no science, no art, possibly no England. The institution is at once absurdly despotic and abjectly weak.

An Enlightened Censorship still worse than the Lord Chamberlain's

Clearly a censorship of judges, bishops, or statesmen would not be in this abject condition. It would no doubt make short work of the coarse and vicious pieces which now enjoy the protection of the Lord Chamberlain, or at least of those of them in which the vulgarity and vice are discoverable by merely reading the prompt copy. But it would certainly disappoint the main hope of its advocates: the hope that it would protect and foster the higher drama. It would do nothing of the sort. On the contrary, it would inevitably suppress it more completely than the Lord Chamberlain does, because it would understand it better. The one play of Ibsen's which is prohibited on the English stage, Ghosts, is far less subversive than A Doll's House. But the Lord Chamberlain does not meddle with such far-reaching matters as the tendency of a play. He refuses to license Ghosts exactly as he would refuse to license Hamlet if it were submitted to him as a new play. He would license even Hamlet if certain alterations were made in it. He would disallow the incestuous relationship between the King and Queen. He would probably insist on the substitution of some fictitious country for Denmark in deference to the near relations of our reigning house with that realm. He would certainly make it an absolute condition that the closet scene, in which a son, in an agony of shame and revulsion, reproaches his mother for her relations with his uncle, should be struck out as unbearably horrifying and improper. But compliance with these conditions would satisfy him. He would raise no speculative objections to the tendency of the play.

This indifference to the larger issues of a theatrical performance could not be safely predicated of an enlightened censorship. Such a censorship might be more liberal in its toleration of matters which are only objected to on the ground that they are not usually discussed in general social conversation or in the presence of children; but it would presumably have a far deeper insight to and concern for the real ethical tendency of the play. For instance, had it been in existence during the last quarter of a century, it would have perceived that those plays of Ibsen's which have been licensed without question are fundamentally immoral to an altogether extraordinary degree. Every one of them is a deliberate act of war on society as at present constituted. Religion, marriage, ordinary respectability, are subjected to a destructive exposure and criticism which seems to mere moralists—that is, to persons of no more than average depth of mind—to be diabolical. It is no exaggeration to say that Ibsen gained his overwhelming reputation by undertaking a task of no less magnitude than changing the mind of Europe with the view of changing its morals. Now you cannot license work of that sort without making yourself responsible for it. The Lord Chamberlain accepted the responsibility because he did not understand it or concern himself about it. But what really enlightened and conscientious official dare take such a responsibility? The strength of character and range of vision which made Ibsen capable of it are not to be expected from any official, however eminent. It is true that an enlightened censor might, whilst shrinking even with horror from Ibsen's views, perceive that any nation which suppressed Ibsen would presently find itself falling behind the nations which tolerated him just as Spain fell behind England; but the proper action to take on such a conviction is the abdication of censorship, not the practise of it. As long as a censor is a censor, he cannot endorse by his licence opinions which seem to him dangerously heretical.

We may, therefore, conclude that the more enlightened a censorship is, the worse it would serve us. The Lord Chamberlain, an obviously unenlightened Censor, prohibits Ghosts and licenses all the rest of Ibsen's plays. An enlightened censorship would possibly license Ghosts; but it would certainly suppress many of the other plays. It would suppress subversiveness as well as what is called bad taste. The Lord Chamberlain prohibits one play by Sophocles because, like Hamlet, it mentions the subject of incest; but an enlightened censorship might suppress all the plays of Euripides because Euripides, like Ibsen, was a revolutionary Freethinker. Under the Lord Chamberlain, we can smuggle a good deal of immoral drama and almost as much coarsely vulgar and furtively lascivious drama as we like. Under a college of cardinals, or bishops, or judges, or any other conceivable form of experts in morals, philosophy, religion, or politics, we should get little except stagnant mediocrity.

The Practical Impossibilities of Censorship

There is, besides, a crushing material difficulty in the way of an enlightened censorship. It is not too much to say that the work involved would drive a man of any intellectual rank mad. Consider, for example, the Christmas pantomimes. Imagine a judge of the High Court, or an archbishop, or a Cabinet Minister, or an eminent man of letters, earning his living by reading through the mass of trivial doggerel represented by all the pantomimes which are put into rehearsal simultaneously at the end of every year. The proposal to put

The Rejected Statement 369

such mind-destroying drudgery upon an official of the class implied by the demand for an enlightened censorship falls through the moment we realize what it implies in practice.

Another material difficulty is that no play can be judged by merely reading the dialogue. To be fully effective a censor should witness the performance. The *mise-en-scène* of a play is as much a part of it as the words spoken on the stage. No censor could possibly object to such a speech as "Might I speak to you for a moment, miss"; yet that apparently innocent phrase has often been made offensively improper on the stage by popular low comedians, with the effect of changing the whole character and meaning of the play as understood by the official Examiner. In one of the plays of the present season, the dialogue was that of a crude melodrama dealing in the most conventionally correct manner with the fortunes of a good-hearted and virtuous girl. Its morality was that of the Sunday school. But the principal actress, between two speeches which contained no reference to her action, changed her underclothing on the stage? It is true that in this case the actress was so much better than her part that she succeeded in turning what was meant as an impropriety into an inoffensive stroke of realism; yet it is none the less clear that stage business of this character, on which there can be no check except the actual presence of a censor in the theatre, might convert any dialogue, however innocent, into just the sort of entertainment against which the Censor is supposed to protect the public.

It was this practical impossibility that prevented the London County Council from attempting to apply a censorship of the Lord Chamberlain's pattern to the London music halls. A proposal to examine all entertainments before permitting their performance was actually made; and it was abandoned, not in the least as contrary to the liberty of the stage, but because the executive problem of how to do it at once reduced the proposal to absurdity. Even if the Council devoted all its time to witnessing rehearsals of variety performances, and putting each item to the vote, possibly after a prolonged discussion followed by a division, the work would still fall into arrear. No committee could be induced to undertake such a task. The attachment of an inspector of morals to each music hall would have meant an appreciable addition to the ratepayers' burden. In the face of such difficulties the proposal melted away. Had it been pushed through, and the inspectors appointed, each of them would have become a censor, and the whole body of inspectors would have become a *police des mœurs*. Those who know the history of such police forces on the continent will understand how impossible it would be to procure inspectors whose characters would stand the strain of their opportunities of corruption, both pecuniary and personal, at such salaries as a local authority could be persuaded to offer.

It has been suggested that the present censorship should be supplemented by a board of experts, who should deal, not with the whole mass of plays sent up for license, but only those which the Examiner of Plays refuses to pass. As the number of plays which the Examiner refuses to pass is never great enough to occupy a Board in permanent session with regular salaries, and as casual employment is not compatible with public responsibility, this proposal would work out in practice as an addition to the duties of some existing functionary. A Secretary of State would be objectionable as likely to be biased politically. An ecclesiastical referee might be biassed against the theatre altogether. A judge in chambers would be the proper authority. This plan would combine the inevitable intolerance of an enlightened censorship with the popular laxity of the Lord Chamberlain.

The Rejected Statement

The judge would suppress the pioneers, whilst the Examiner of Plays issued two guinea certificates for the vulgar and vicious plays. For this reason the plan would no doubt be popular; but it would be very much as a relaxation of the administration of the Public Health Acts accompanied by the cheapening of gin would be popular.

The Arbitration Proposal

On the occasion of a recent deputation of playwrights to the Prime Minister it was suggested that if a censorship be inevitable, provision should be made for an appeal from the Lord Chamberlain in cases of refusal of licence. The authors of this suggestion propose that the Lord Chamberlain shall choose one umpire and the author another. The two umpires shall then elect a referee, whose decision shall be final.

This proposal is not likely to be entertained by constitutional lawyers. It is a naïve offer to accept the method of arbitration in what is essentially a matter, not between one private individual or body and another, but between a public offender and the State. It will presumably be ruled out as a proposal to refer a case of manslaughter to arbitration would be ruled out. But even if it were constitutionally sound, it bears all the marks of that practical inexperience which leads men to believe that arbitration either costs nothing or is at least cheaper than law. Who is to pay for the time of the three arbitrators, presumably men of high professional standing? The author may not be able: the manager may not be willing: neither of them should be called upon to pay for a public service otherwise than by their contributions to the revenue. Clearly the State should pay. But even so, the difficulties are only beginning. A licence is seldom refused except on grounds which are controversial.

372 The Shewing-Up of Blanco Posnet

The two arbitrators selected by the opposed parties to the controversy are to agree to leave the decision to a third party unanimously chosen by themselves. That is very far from being a simple solution. An attempt to shorten and simplify the passing of the Finance Bill by referring it to an arbitrator chosen unanimously by Mr. Asquith and Mr. Balfour might not improbably cost more and last longer than a civil war. And why should the chosen referee—if he ever succeeded in getting chosen—be assumed to be a safer authority than the Examiner of Plays? He would certainly be a less responsible one: in fact, being (however eminent) a casual person called in to settle a single case, he would be virtually irresponsible. Worse still, he would take all responsibility away from the Lord Chamberlain, who is at least an official of the King's Household and a nominee of the Government. The Lord Chamberlain, with all his shortcomings, thinks twice before he refuses a licence, knowing that his refusal is final and may promptly be made public. But if he could transfer his responsibility to an arbitrator, he would naturally do so whenever he felt the slightest misgiving, or whenever, for diplomatic reasons, the licence would come more gracefully from an authority unconnected with the court. These considerations, added to the general objection to the principle of censorship, seem sufficient to put the arbitration expedient quite out of the question.

END OF THE FIRST PART OF THE REJECTED STATEMENT.

THE REJECTED STATEMENT

PART II

THE LICENSING OF THEATRES

The Distinction between Licensing and Censorship

IT must not be concluded that the uncompromising abolition of all censorship involves the abandonment of all control and regulation of theatres. Factories are regulated in the public interest; but there is no censorship of factories. For example, many persons are sincerely convinced that cotton clothing is unhealthy; that alcoholic drinks are demoralizing; and that playing-cards are the devil's picture-books. But though the factories in which cotton, whiskey, and cards are manufactured are stringently regulated under the factory code and the Public Health and Building Acts, the inspectors appointed to carry out these Acts never go to a manufacturer and inform him that unless he manufactures woollens instead of cottons, ginger-beer instead of whiskey, Bibles instead of playing-cards, he will be forbidden to place his products on the market. In the case of premises licensed for the sale of spirits the authorities go a step further. A public-house differs from a factory in the essential particular that whereas disorder in a factory is promptly and voluntarily suppressed, because every moment of its duration involves a measurable pecuniary loss to the proprietor, disorder in a public-house may be a source of profit to the proprietor by its attraction for disorderly customers. Consequently a publican is compelled to obtain a licence to pursue his trade; and this licence lasts only a year, and need not be renewed if his house has been conducted in a disorderly manner in the meantime.

Prostitution and Drink in Theatres

The theatre presents the same problem as the public-house in respect to disorder. To begin with, a theatre is actually a place licensed for the sale of spirits. The bars at a London theatre can be let without difficulty for £30 a week and upwards. And though it is clear that nobody will pay from a shilling to half a guinea for access to a theatre bar when he can obtain access to an ordinary public-house for nothing, there is no law to prevent the theatre proprietor from issuing free passes broadcast and recouping himself by the profit on the sale of drink. Besides, there may be some other attraction than the sale of drink. When this attraction is that of the play no objection need be made. But it happens that the auditorium of a theatre, with its brilliant lighting and luxurious decorations, makes a very effective shelter and background for the display of fine dresses and pretty faces. Consequently theatres have been used for centuries in England as markets by prostitutes. From the Restoration to the days of Macready all theatres were made use of in this way as a matter of course; and to this, far more than to any prejudice against dramatic art, we owe the Puritan formula that the theatre door is the gate of hell. Macready had a hard struggle to drive the prostitutes from his theatre; and since his time the London theatres controlled by the Lord Chamberlain have become respectable and even socially pretentious. But some of the variety theatres still derive a revenue by selling admissions to women who do not look at the performance, and men who go to purchase or admire the women. And in the provinces this state of things is by no means confined to the variety theatres.

The real attraction is sometimes not the performance at
all. The theatre is not really a theatre: it is a drink
shop and a prostitution market; and the last shred of its
disguise is stripped by the virtually indiscriminate issue
of free tickets to the men. Access to the stage is so
easily obtained; and the plays preferred by the man-
agement are those in which the stage is filled with young
women who are not in any serious technical sense of the
word actresses at all. Considering that all this is now
possible at any theatre, and actually occurs at some theatres, the fact that our best theatres are as respectable
as they are is much to their credit; but it is still an
intolerable evil that respectable managers should have to
fight against the free tickets and disorderly housekeeping of unscrupulous competitors. The dramatic author
is equally injured. He finds that unless he writes plays
which make suitable sideshows for drinking-bars and
brothels, he may be excluded from towns where there
is not room for two theatres, and where the one existing theatre is exploiting drunkenness and prostitution
instead of carrying on a legitimate dramatic business.
Indeed everybody connected with the theatrical profession suffers in reputation from the detestable tradition of
such places, against which the censorship has proved
quite useless.

Here we have a strong case for applying either the
licensing system or whatever better means may be devized for securing the orderly conduct of houses of
public entertainment, dramatic or other. Liberty must,
no doubt, be respected in so far that no manager should
have the right to refuse admission to decently dressed,
sober, and well-conducted persons, whether they are
prostitutes, soldiers in uniform, gentlemen not in evening
dress, Indians, or what not; but when disorder is
stopped, disorderly persons will either cease to come or
else reform their manners. It is, however, quite argu-

able that the indiscriminate issue of free admissions, though an apparently innocent and good-natured, and certainly a highly popular proceeding, should expose the proprietor of the theatre to the risk of a refusal to renew his licence.

Why the Managers dread Local Control

All this points to the transfer of the control of theatres from the Lord Chamberlain to the municipality. And this step is opposed by the long-run managers, partly because they take it for granted that municipal control must involve municipal censorship of plays, so that plays might be licensed in one town and prohibited in the next, and partly because, as they have no desire to produce plays which are in advance of public opinion, and as the Lord Chamberlain in every other respect gives more scandal by his laxity than trouble by his severity, they find in the present system a cheap and easy means of procuring a certificate which relieves them of all social responsibility, and provides them with so strong a weapon of defence in case of a prosecution that it acts in practice as a bar to any such proceedings. Above all, they know that the Examiner of Plays is free from the pressure of that large body of English public opinion already alluded to, which regards the theatre as the Prohibitionist Teetotaller regards the public-house: that is, as an abomination to be stamped out unconditionally. The managers rightly dread this pressure more than anything else; and they believe that it is so strong in local governments as to be a characteristic bias of municipal authority. In this they are no doubt mistaken. There is not a municipal authority of any importance in the country in which a proposal to stamp out the theatre, or even to treat it illiberally, would have a chance of adoption. Municipal control of the variety theatres (formerly called music halls) has been very far from liberal, except in the one particular in which the Lord Chamberlain is equally illiberal. That particular is the assumption that a draped figure is decent and an undraped one indecent. It is useless to point to actual experience, which proves abundantly that naked or apparently naked figures, whether exhibited as living pictures, animated statuary, or in a dance, are at their best not only innocent, but refining in their effect, whereas those actresses and skirt dancers who have brought the peculiar aphrodisiac effect which is objected to to the highest pitch of efficiency wear twice as many petticoats as an ordinary lady does, and seldom exhibit more than their ankles. Unfortunately, municipal councillors persist in confusing decency with drapery; and both in London and the provinces certain positively edifying performances have been forbidden or withdrawn under pressure, and replaced by coarse and vicious ones. There is not the slightest reason to suppose that the Lord Chamberlain would have been any more tolerant; but this does not alter the fact that the municipal licensing authorities have actually used their powers to set up a censorship which is open to all the objections to censorship in general, and which, in addition, sets up the objection from which central control is free: namely, the impossibility of planning theatrical tours without the serious commercial risk of having the performance forbidden in some of the towns booked. How can this be prevented?

Desirable Limitations of Local Control

The problem is not a difficult one. The municipality can be limited just as the monarchy is limited. The Act transferring theatres to local control can be a charter of the liberties of the stage as well as an Act to reform administration. The power to refuse to grant or renew a licence to a theatre need not be an arbitrary one. The municipality may be required to state the ground of refusal; and certain grounds can be expressly declared as unlawful; so that it shall be possible for the manager to resort to the courts for a mandamus to compel the authority to grant a licence. It can be declared unlawful for a licensing authority to demand from the manager any disclosure of the nature of any entertainment he proposes to give, or to prevent its performance, or to refuse to renew his licence on the ground that the tendency of his entertainments is contrary to religion and morals, or that the theatre is an undesirable institution, or that there are already as many theatres as are needed, or that the theatre draws people away from the churches, chapels, mission halls, and the like in its neighborhood. The assumption should be that every citizen has a right to open and conduct a theatre, and therefore has a right to a licence unless he has forfeited that right by allowing his theatre to become a disorderly house, or failing to provide a building which complies with the regulations concerning sanitation and egress in case of fire, or being convicted of an offence against public decency. Also, the licensing powers of the authority should not be delegated to any official or committee; and the manager or lessee of the theatre should have a right to appear in person or by counsel to plead against any motion to refuse to grant or renew his licence. With these safeguards the licensing power could not be stretched to censorship. The manager would enjoy liberty of conscience as far as the local authority is concerned; but on the least attempt on his part to keep a disorderly house under cover of opening a theatre he would risk his licence.

But the managers will not and should not be satisfied with these limits to the municipal power. If they are

deprived of the protection of the Lord Chamberlain's
licence, and at the same time efficiently protected against
every attempt at censorship by the licensing authority.
the enemies of the theatre will resort to the ordinary
law, and try to get from the prejudices of a jury what
they are debarred from getting from the prejudices of
a County Council or City Corporation. Moral Reform
Societies, "Purity" Societies, Vigilance Societies, exist
in England and America for the purpose of enforcing
the existing laws against obscenity, blasphemy, Sabbath-
breaking, the debauchery of children, prostitution and so
forth. The paid officials of these societies, in their
anxiety to produce plenty of evidence of their activity
in the annual reports which go out to the subscribers, do
not always discriminate between an obscene postcard and
an artistic one, or to put it more exactly, between a
naked figure and an indecent one. They often combine
a narrow but terribly sincere sectarian bigotry with a
complete ignorance of art and history. Even when they
have some culture, their livelihood is at the mercy of
subscribers and committee men who have none. If these
officials had any power of distinguishing between art and
blackguardism, between morality and virtue, between immorality and vice, between conscientious heresy and mere
baseness of mind and foulness of mouth, they might be
trusted by theatrical managers not to abuse the powers of the common informer. As it is, it has been found
necessary, in order to enable good music to be performed
on Sunday, to take away these powers in that particular,
and vest them solely in the Attorney-General. This
disqualification of the common informer should be extended to the initiation of all proceedings of a censorial
character against theatres. Few people are aware of the
monstrous laws against blasphemy which still disgrace
our statute book. If any serious attempt were made to
carry them out, prison accommodation would have to be

provided for almost every educated person in the country, beginning with the Archbishop of Canterbury. Until some government with courage and character enough to repeal them comes into power, it is not too much to ask that such infamous powers of oppression should be kept in responsible hands and not left at the disposal of every bigot ignorant enough to be unaware of the social dangers of persecution. Besides, the common informer is not always a sincere bigot, who believes he is performing an action of signal merit in silencing and ruining a heretic. He is unfortunately just as often a blackmailer, who has studied his powers as a common informer in order that he may extort money for refraining from exercising them. If the manager is to be responsible he should be made responsible to a responsible functionary. To be responsible to every fanatical ignoramus who chooses to prosecute him for exhibiting a cast of the Hermes of Praxiteles in his vestibule, or giving a performance of Measure for Measure, is mere slavery. It is made bearable at present by the protection of the Lord Chamberlain's certificate. But when that is no longer available, the common informer must be disarmed if the manager is to enjoy security.

SUMMARY

THE general case against censorship as a principle, and the particular case against the existing English censorship and against its replacement by a more enlightened one, is now complete. The following is a recapitulation of the propositions and conclusions contended for.

1. The question of censorship or no censorship is a question of high political principle and not of petty policy.

2. The toleration of heresy and shocks to morality on the stage, and even their protection against the prejudices and superstitions which necessarily enter largely into morality and public opinion, are essential to the welfare of the nation.

3. The existing censorship of the Lord Chamberlain does not only intentionally suppress heresy and challenges to morality in their serious and avowed forms, but unintentionally gives the special protection of its official licence to the most extreme impropriety that the lowest section of London playgoers will tolerate in theatres especially devoted to their entertainment, licensing everything that is popular and forbidding any attempt to change public opinion or morals.

4. The Lord Chamberlain's censorship is open to the special objection that its application to political plays is taken to indicate the attitude of the Crown on questions of domestic and foreign policy, and that it imposes the limits of etiquet on the historical drama.

5. A censorship of a more enlightened and independ-

ent kind, exercised by the most eminent available authorities, would prove in practice more disastrous than the censorship of the Lord Chamberlain, because the more eminent its members were the less possible it would be for them to accept the responsibility for heresy or immorality by licensing them, and because the many heretical and immoral plays which now pass the Lord Chamberlain because he does not understand them, would be understood and suppressed by a more highly enlightened censorship.

6. A reconstructed and enlightened censorship would be armed with summary and effective powers which would stop the evasions by which heretical and immoral plays are now performed in spite of the Lord Chamberlain; and such powers would constitute a tyranny which would ruin the theatre spiritually by driving all independent thinkers from the drama into the uncensored forms of art.

7. The work of critically examining all stage plays in their written form, and of witnessing their performance in order to see that the sense is not altered by the stage business, would, even if it were divided among so many officials as to be physically possible, be mentally impossible to persons of taste and enlightenment.

8. Regulation of theatres is an entirely different matter from censorship, inasmuch as a theatre, being not only a stage, but a place licensed for the sale of spirits, and a public resort capable of being put to disorderly use, and needing special provision for the safety of audiences in cases of fire, etc., cannot be abandoned wholly to private control, and may therefore reasonably be made subject to an annual licence like those now required before allowing premises to be used publicly for music and dancing.

9. In order to prevent the powers of the licensing au-

The Rejected Statement 383

thority being abused so as to constitute a virtual censorship, any Act transferring the theatres to the control of a licensing authority should be made also a charter of the rights of dramatic authors and managers by the following provisions:

A. The public prosecutor (the Attorney-General) alone should have the right to set the law in operation against the manager of a theatre or the author of a play in respect of the character of the play or entertainment.

B. No disclosure of the particulars of a theatrical entertainment shall be required before performance.

C. Licences shall not be withheld on the ground that the existence of theatres is dangerous to religion and morals, or on the ground that any entertainment given or contemplated is heretical or immoral.

D. The licensing area shall be no less than that of a County Council or City Corporation, which shall not delegate its licensing powers to any minor local authority or to any official or committee; it shall decide all questions affecting the existence of a theatrical licence by vote of the entire body; managers, lessees, and proprietors of theatres shall have the right to plead, in person or by counsel, against a proposal to withhold a licence; and the licence shall not be withheld except for stated reasons, the validity of which shall be subject to the judgment of the high courts.

E. The annual licence, once granted, shall not be cancelled or suspended unless the manager has been convicted by public prosecution of an offence against the ordinary laws against disorderly housekeeping, indecency, blasphemy, etc., except in cases where some structural or sanitary defect in the building necessitates immediate action for the protection of the public against physical injury.

F. No licence shall be refused on the ground that

the proximity of the theatre to a church, mission hall, school, or other place of worship, edification, instruction, or entertainment (including another theatre) would draw the public away from such places into its own doors.

PREFACE RESUMED

Mr. George Alexander's Protest

ON the facts mentioned in the foregoing statement, and in my evidence before the Joint Select Committee, no controversy arose except on one point. Mr. George Alexander protested vigorously and indignantly against my admission that theatres, like public-houses, need special control on the ground that they can profit by disorder, and are sometimes conducted with that end in view. Now, Mr. Alexander is a famous actor-manager; and it is very difficult to persuade the public that the more famous an actor-manager is the less he is likely to know about any theatre except his own. When the Committee of 1892 reported, I was considered guilty of a perverse paradox when I said that the witness who knew least about the theatre was Henry Irving. Yet a moment's consideration would have shown that the paradox was a platitude. For about quarter of a century Irving was confined night after night to his own theatre and his own dressing-room, never seeing a play even there because he was himself part of the play; producing the works of long-departed authors; and, to the extent to which his talent was extraordinary, necessarily making his theatre unlike any other theatre. When he went to the provinces or to America, the theatres to which he went were swept and garnished for him, and their staffs replaced—as far as he came in contact with them—by his own lieutenants. In the end, there was hardly a first-nighter in his gallery who did not know more about the London theatres and the progress of dramatic art than he; and as to the provinces, if any chief constable had told him the real history and character of many provincial theatres, he would have denounced that chief constable as an ignorant libeller of a noble profession. But the constable would have been right for all that. Now if this was true of Sir Henry Irving, who did not become a London manager until he had roughed it for years in the provinces, how much more true must it be of, say, Mr. George Alexander, whose successful march through his profession has passed as far from the purlieus of our theatrical world as the king's naval career from the Isle of Dogs? The moment we come to that necessary part of the censorship question which deals with the control of theatres from the point of view of those who know how much money can be made out of them by managers who seek to make the auditorium attractive rather than the stage, you find the managers divided into two sections. The first section consists of honorable and successful managers like Mr. Alexander, who know nothing of such abuses, and deny, with perfect sincerity and indignant vehemence, that they exist except, perhaps, in certain notorious variety theatres. The other is the silent section which knows better, but is very well content to be publicly defended and privately amused by Mr. Alexander's innocence. To accept a West End manager as an expert in theatres because he is an actor is much as if we were to accept the organist of St. Paul's Cathedral as an expert on music halls because he is a musician. The real experts are all in the conspiracy to keep the police out of the theatre. And they are so successful that even the police do not know as much as they should.

The police should have been examined by the Committee, and the whole question of the extent to which theatres are disorderly houses in disguise sifted to the bottom. For it is on this point that we discover behind the phantoms of the corrupt dramatists who are restrained by the censorship from debauching the stage, the reality of the corrupt managers and theatre proprietors who actually do debauch it without let or hindrance from the censorship. The whole case for giving control over theatres to local authorities rests on this reality.

Eliza and Her Bath

The persistent notion that a theatre is an Alsatia where the king's writ does not run, and where any wickedness is possible in the absence of a special tribunal and a special police, was brought out by an innocent remark made by Sir William Gilbert, who, when giving evidence before the Committee, was asked by Colonel Lockwood whether a law sufficient to restrain impropriety in books would also restrain impropriety in plays. Sir William replied: " I should say there is a very wide distinction between what is read and what is seen. In a novel one may read that 'Eliza stripped off her dressing-gown and stepped into her bath' without any harm; but I think if that were presented on the stage it would be shocking." All the stupid and inconsiderate people seized eagerly on this illustration as if it were a successful attempt to prove that without a censorship we should be unable to prevent actresses from appearing naked on the stage. As a matter of fact, if an actress could be persuaded to do such a thing (and it would be about as easy to persuade a bishop's wife to appear in church in the same condition) the police would simply arrest her on a charge of indecent exposure. The extent to which this obvious safeguard was overlooked may be taken as a measure of the thoughtlessness and frivolity of the excuses made for the censorship. It should be added that the artistic representation of a bath, with every suggestion of nakedness that the law as to decency allows, is one of the most familiar subjects of scenic art. From the Rhine maidens in Wagner's Trilogy, and the bathers in the second act of Les Huguenots, to the ballets of water nymphs in our Christmas pantomimes and at our variety theatres, the sound hygienic propaganda of the bath, and the charm of the undraped human figure, are exploited without offence on the stage to an extent never dreamt of by any novelist.

A King's Proctor

Another hare was started by Professor Gilbert Murray and Mr. Laurence Housman, who, in pure kindness to the managers, asked whether it would not be possible to establish for their assistance a sort of King's Proctor to whom plays might be referred for an official legal opinion as to their compliance with the law before production. There are several objections to this proposal; and they may as well be stated in case the proposal should be revived. In the first place, no lawyer with the most elementary knowledge of the law of libel in its various applications to sedition, obscenity, and blasphemy, could answer for the consequences of producing any play whatsoever as to which the smallest question could arise in the mind of any sane person. I have been a critic and an author in active service for thirty years; and though nothing I have written has ever been prosecuted in England or made the subject of legal proceedings, yet I have never published in my life an article, a play, or a book, as to which, if I had taken legal advice, an expert could have assured me that I was proof against prosecution or against an action for damages by the persons criticized. No doubt a sensible solicitor might have advised me that the risk was no greater than all men have to take in dangerous trades; but such an opinion, though it may encourage a client, does not protect him. For example, if a publisher asks his solicitor whether he may venture on an edition of Sterne's Sentimental Journey, or a manager whether he may produce King Lear without risk of prosecution, the solicitor will advise him to go ahead. But if the solicitor or counsel consulted by him were asked for a guarantee that neither of these works was a libel, he would have to reply that he could give no such guarantee; that, on the contrary, it was his duty to warn his client that both of them are obscene libels; that King Lear, containing as it does perhaps the most appalling blasphemy that despair ever uttered, is a blasphemous libel, and that it is doubtful whether it could not be construed as a seditious libel as well. As to Ibsen's Brand (the play which made him popular with the most earnestly religious people) no sane solicitor would advise his client even to chance it except in a broadly cultivated and tolerant (or indifferent) modern city. The lighter plays would be no better off. What lawyer could accept any responsibility for the production of Sardou's Divorçons or Clyde Fitch's The Woman in the Case? Put the proposed King's Proctor in operation to-morrow; and what will be the result? The managers will find that instead of insuring them as the Lord Chamberlain does, he will warn them that every play they submit to him is vulnerable to the law, and that they must produce it not only on the ordinary risk of acting on their own responsibility, but at the very grave additional risk of doing so in the teeth of an official warning. Under such circumstances, what manager would resort a second time to the Proctor; and how would the Proctor live without fees, unless indeed the Government gave him a salary for doing nothing? The institution would not last a year, except as a job for somebody.

Counsel's Opinion

The proposal is still less plausible when it is considered that at present, without any new legislation at all, any manager who is doubtful about a play can obtain the advice of his solicitor, or Counsel's opinion, if he thinks it will be of any service to him. The verdict of the proposed King's Proctor would be nothing but Counsel's opinion without the liberty of choice of counsel, possibly cheapened, but sure to be adverse; for an official cannot give practical advice as a friend and a man of the world: he must stick to the letter of the law and take no chances. And as far as the law is concerned, journalism, literature, and the drama exist only by custom or sufferance.

Wanted: A New Magna Charta

This leads us to a very vital question. Is it not possible to amend the law so as to make it possible for a lawyer to advise his client that he may publish the works of Blake, Zola, and Swinburne, or produce the plays of Ibsen and Mr. Granville Barker, or print an ordinary criticism in his newspaper, without the possibility of finding himself in prison, or mulcted in damages and costs in consequence? No doubt it is; but only by a declaration of constitutional right to blaspheme, rebel, and deal with tabooed subjects. Such a declaration is not just now within the scope of practical politics, although we are compelled to act to a great extent as if it was actually part of the constitution. All that can be done is to take my advice and limit the necessary public control of the theatres in such a manner as to prevent its being abused as a censorship. We have ready to our hand the machinery of licensing as applied to public-houses. A licensed victualler can now be assured confidently by his lawyer that a magistrate cannot refuse to renew his licence on the ground that he (the magistrate) is a teetotaller and has seen too much of the evil of drink to sanction its sale. The magistrate must give a judicial reason for his refusal, meaning really a constitutional reason; and his teetotalism is not such a reason. In the same way you can protect a theatrical manager by ruling out certain reasons as unconstitutional, as suggested in my statement. Combine this with the abolition of the common informer's power to initiate proceedings, and you will have gone as far as seems possible at present. You will have local control of the theatres for police purposes and sanitary purposes without censorship; and I do not see what more is possible until we get a formal Magna Charta declaring all the categories of libel and the blasphemy laws contrary to public liberty, and repealing and defining accordingly.

Proposed: A New Star Chamber

Yet we cannot mention Magna Charta without recalling how useless such documents are to a nation which has no more political comprehension nor political virtue than King John. When Henry VII. calmly proceeded to tear up Magna Charta by establishing the Star Chamber (a criminal court consisting of a committee of the Privy Council without a jury) nobody objected until, about a century and a half later, the Star Chamber began cutting off the ears of eminent XVII. century Nonconformists and standing them in the pillory; and then the Nonconformists, and nobody else, abolished the Star Chamber. And if anyone doubts that we are quite ready to establish the Star Chamber again, let him read the Report of the Joint Select Committee, on which I now venture to offer a few criticisms.

The report of the Committee, which will be found in

the bluebook, should be read with attention and respect as far as page x., up to which point it is an able and well-written statement of the case. From page x. onward, when it goes on from diagnosing the disease to prescribing the treatment, it should be read with even greater attention but with no respect whatever, as the main object of the treatment is to conciliate the How Not To Do It majority. It contains, however, one very notable proposal, the same being nothing more or less than to revive the Star Chamber for the purpose of dealing with heretical or seditious plays and their authors, and indeed with all charges against theatrical entertainments except common police cases of indecency. The reason given is that for which the Star Chamber was created by Henry VII: that is, the inadequacy of the ordinary law. "We consider," says the report, "that the law which prevents or punishes indecency, blasphemy and libel in printed publications [it does not, by the way, except in the crudest police cases] would not be adequate for the control of the drama." Therefore a committee of the Privy Council is to be empowered to suppress plays and punish managers and authors at its pleasure, on the motion of the Attorney-General, without a jury. The members of the Committee will, of course, be men of high standing and character: otherwise they would not be on the Privy Council. That is to say, they will have all the qualifications of Archbishop Laud.

Now I have no guarantee that any member of the majority of the Joint Select Committee ever heard of the Star Chamber or of Archbishop Laud. One of them did not know that politics meant anything more than party electioneering. Nothing is more alarming than the ignorance of our public men of the commonplaces of our history, and their consequent readiness to repeat experiments which have in the past produced national catastrophes. At all events, whether they knew what they were doing or not, there can be no question as to what they did. They proposed virtually that the Act of the Long Parliament in 1641 shall be repealed, and the Star Chamber re-established, in order that playwrights and managers may be punished for unspecified offences unknown to the law. When I say unspecified, I should say specified as follows (see page xi. of the report) in the case of a play.

(*a*) To be indecent.
(*b*) To contain offensive personalities.
(*c*) To represent on the stage in an invidious manner a living person, or any person recently dead.
(*d*) To do violence to the sentiment of religious reverence.
(*e*) To be calculated to conduce to vice or crime.
(*f*) To be calculated to impair friendly relations with any foreign power.
(*g*) To be calculated to cause a breach of the peace.

Now it is clear that there is no play yet written, or possible to be written, in this world, that might not be condemned under one or other of these heads. How any sane man, not being a professed enemy of public liberty, could put his hand to so monstrous a catalogue passes my understanding. Had a comparatively definite and innocent clause been added forbidding the affirmation or denial of the doctrine of Transubstantiation, the country would have been up in arms at once. Lord Ribblesdale made an effort to reduce the seven categories to the old formula "not to be fitting for the preservation of good manners, decorum, or the public peace"; but this proposal was not carried; whilst on Lord Gorell's motion a final widening of the net was achieved by adding the phrase "to be calculated to"; so that even if a play does not produce any of the results feared, the author can still be punished on the ground that his play is " calculated " to produce them. I have no hesitation in saying that a committee capable of such an outrageous display of thoughtlessness and historical ignorance as this paragraph of its report implies deserves to be haled before the tribunal it has itself proposed, and dealt with under a general clause levelled at conduct " calculated to " overthrow the liberties of England.

Possibilities of the Proposal

Still, though I am certainly not willing to give Lord Gorell the chance of seeing me in the pillory with my ears cut off if I can help it, I daresay many authors would rather take their chance with a Star Chamber than with a jury, just as some soldiers would rather take their chance with a court-martial than at Quarter Sessions. For that matter, some of them would rather take their chance with the Lord Chamberlain than with either. And though this is no reason for depriving the whole body of authors of the benefit of Magna Charta, still, if the right of the proprietor of a play to refuse the good offices of the Privy Council and to perform the play until his accusers had indicted him at law, and obtained the verdict of a jury against him, were sufficiently guarded, the proposed committee might be set up and used for certain purposes. For instance, it might be made a condition of the intervention of the Attorney-General or the Director of Public Prosecutions that he should refer an accused play to the committee, and obtain their sanction before taking action, offering the proprietor of the play, if the Committee thought fit, an opportunity of voluntarily accepting trial by the Committee as an alternative to prosecution in the ordinary course of law. But the Committee should have no powers of punishment beyond the power (formidable enough) of suspending performances of the play. If it thought that additional punishment was called for, it could order a prosecution without allowing the proprietor or author of the play the alternative of a trial by itself. The author of the play should be made a party to all proceedings of the Committee, and have the right to defend himself in person or by counsel. This would provide a check on the Attorney-General (who might be as bigoted as any of the municipal aldermen who are so much dreaded by the actor-managers) without enabling the Committee to abuse its powers for party, class, or sectarian ends beyond that irreducible minimum of abuse which a popular jury would endorse, for which minimum there is no remedy.

But when everything is said for the Star Chamber that can be said, and every precaution taken to secure to those whom it pursues the alternative of trial by jury, the expedient still remains a very questionable one, to be endured for the sake of its protective rather than its repressive powers. It should abolish the present quaint toleration of rioting in theatres. For example, if it is to be an offence to perform a play which the proposed new Committee shall condemn, it should also be made an offence to disturb a performance which the Committee has not condemned. "Brawling" at a theatre should be dealt with as severely as brawling in church if the censorship is to be taken out of the hands of the public. At present Jenny Geddes may throw her stool at the head of a playwright who preaches unpalatable doctrine to her, or rather, since her stool is a fixture, she may hiss and hoot and make it impossible to proceed with the performance, even although nobody has compelled her to come to the theatre or suspended her liberty to stay away, and although she has no claim on an unendowed theatre for her spiritual necessities, as she has on her parish church. If mob censorship cannot be trusted to keep naughty playwrights in order, still less can it be trusted to keep the pioneers of thought in countenance; and I submit that anyone hissing a play permitted by the new censorship should be guilty of contempt of court.

Star Chamber Sentimentality

But what is most to be dreaded in a Star Chamber is not its sternness but its sentimentality. There is no worse censorship than one which considers only the feelings of the spectators, except perhaps one which considers the feelings of people who do not even witness the performance. Take the case of the Passion Play at Oberammergau. The offence given by a representation of the Crucifixion on the stage is not bounded by frontiers: further, it is an offence of which the voluntary spectators are guilty no less than the actors. If it is to be tolerated at all: if we are not to make war on the German Empire for permitting it, nor punish the English people who go to Bavaria to see it and thereby endow it with English money, we may as well tolerate it in London, where nobody need go to see it except those who are not offended by it. When Wagner's Parsifal becomes available for representation in London, many people will be sincerely horrified when the miracle of the Mass is simulated on the stage of Covent Garden, and the Holy Ghost descends in the form of a dove. But if the Committee of the Privy Council, or the Lord Chamberlain, or anyone else, were to attempt to keep Parsifal from us to spare the feelings of these people, it would not be long before even the most thoughtless champions of the censorship would see that the principle of doing nothing that could shock anybody had reduced itself to absurdity. No quarter whatever should be given to the bigotry of people so unfit for social life

Preface

as to insist not only that their own prejudices and superstitions should have the fullest toleration but that everybody else should be compelled to think and act as they do. Every service in St. Paul's Cathedral is an outrage to the opinions of the congregation of the Roman Catholic Cathedral of Westminster. Every Liberal meeting is a defiance and a challenge to the most cherished opinions of the Unionists. A law to compel the Roman Catholics to attend service at St. Paul's, or the Liberals to attend the meetings of the Primrose League would be resented as an insufferable tyranny. But a law to shut up both St. Paul's and the Westminster Cathedral, and to put down political meetings and associations because of the offence given by them to many worthy and excellent people, would be a far worse tyranny, because it would kill the religious and political life of the country outright, whereas to compel people to attend the services and meetings of their opponents would greatly enlarge their minds, and would actually be a good thing if it were enforced all round. I should not object to a law to compel everybody to read two newspapers, each violently opposed to the other in politics; but to forbid us to read newspapers at all would be to maim us mentally and cashier our country in the ranks of civilization. I deny that anybody has the right to demand more from me, over and above lawful conduct in a general sense, than liberty to stay away from the theatre in which my plays are represented. If he is unfortunate enough to have a religion so petty that it can be insulted (any man is as welcome to insult my religion, if he can, as he is to insult the universe) I claim the right to insult it to my heart's content, if I choose, provided I do not compel him to come and hear me. If I think this country ought to make war on any other country, then, so long as war remains lawful, I claim full liberty to write and perform a play inciting the country to that war without interference from the ambassadors of the menaced country. I may "give pain to many worthy people, and pleasure to none," as the Censor's pet phrase puts it: I may even make Europe a cockpit and Asia a shambles: no matter: if preachers and politicians, statesmen and soldiers, may do these things—if it is right that such things should be done, then I claim my share in the right to do them. If the proposed Committee is meant to prevent me from doing these things whilst men of other professions are permitted to do them, then I protest with all my might against the formation of such a Committee. If it is to protect me, on the contrary, against the attacks that bigots and corrupt pornographers may make on me by appealing to the ignorance and prejudices of common jurors, then I welcome it; but is that really the object of its proposers? And if it is, what guarantee have I that the new tribunal will not presently resolve into a mere committee to avoid unpleasantness and keep the stage "in good taste"? It is no more possible for me to do my work honestly as a playwright without giving pain than it is for a dentist. The nation's morals are like its teeth: the more decayed they are the more it hurts to touch them. Prevent dentists and dramatists from giving pain, and not only will our morals become as carious as our teeth, but toothache and the plagues that follow neglected morality will presently cause more agony than all the dentists and dramatists at their worst have caused since the world began.

Anything for a Quiet Life

Another doubt: would a Committee of the Privy Council really face the risks that must be taken by all communities as the price of our freedom to evolve? Would it not rather take the popular English view that freedom and virtue generally are sweet and desirable only when

Preface

they cost nothing? Nothing worth having is to be had without risk. A mother risks her child's life every time she lets it ramble through the countryside, or cross the street, or clamber over the rocks on the shore by itself. A father risks his son's morals when he gives him a latchkey. The members of the Joint Select Committee risked my producing a revolver and shooting them when they admitted me to the room without having me handcuffed. And these risks are no unreal ones. Every day some child is maimed or drowned and some young man infected with disease; and political assassinations have been appallingly frequent of late years. Railway travelling has its risks; motoring has its risks; aeroplaning has its risks; every advance we make costs us a risk of some sort. And though these are only risks to the individual, to the community they are certainties. It is not certain that I will be killed this year in a railway accident; but it is certain that somebody will. The invention of printing and the freedom of the press have brought upon us, not merely risks of their abuse, but the establishment as part of our social routine of some of the worst evils a community can suffer from. People who realize these evils shriek for the suppression of motor cars, the virtual imprisonment and enslavement of the young, the passing of Press Laws (especially in Egypt, India, and Ireland), exactly as they shriek for a censorship of the stage. The freedom of the stage will be abused just as certainly as the complaisance and innocence of the censorship is abused at present. It will also be used by writers like myself for raising very difficult and disturbing questions, social, political, and religious, at moments which may be extremely inconvenient to the government. Is it certain that a Committee of the Privy Council would stand up to all this as the price of liberty? I doubt it. If I am to be at the mercy of a nice amiable Committee of elderly gentlemen (I know all about elderly gentlemen, being one myself) whose motto is the highly popular one, " Anything for a quiet life," and who will make the inevitable abuses of freedom by our blackguards an excuse for interfering with any disquieting use of it by myself, then I shall be worse off than I am with the Lord Chamberlain, whose mind is not broad enough to obstruct the whole range of thought. If it were, he would be given a more difficult post.

Shall the Examiner of Plays Starve?

And here I may be reminded that if I prefer the Lord Chamberlain I can go to the Lord Chamberlain, who is to retain all his present functions for the benefit of those who prefer to be judged by him. But I am not so sure that the Lord Chamberlain will be able to exercise those functions for long if resort to him is to be optional. Let me be kinder to him than he has been to me, and uncover for him the pitfalls which the Joint Select Committee have dug (and concealed) in his path. Consider how the voluntary system must inevitably work. The Joint Select Committee expressly urges that the Lord Chamberlain's licence must not be a bar to a prosecution. Granted that in spite of this reservation the licence would prove in future as powerful a defence as it has been in the past, yet the voluntary clause nevertheless places the manager at the mercy of any author who makes it a condition of his contract that his play shall not be submitted for licence. I should probably take that course without opposition from the manager. For the manager, knowing that three of my plays have been refused a licence, and that it would be far safer to produce a play for which no licence had been asked than one for which it had been asked and refused, would agree that it was more prudent, in my case, to avail himself of the power of dispensing with the Lord Chamberlain's licence. But now mark the consequences. The manager, having thus discovered that his best policy was to dispense with the licence in the few doubtful cases, would presently ask himself why he should spend two guineas each on licences for the many plays as to which no question could conceivably arise. What risk does any manager run in producing such works as Sweet Lavender, Peter Pan, The Silver King, or any of the 99 per cent of plays that are equally neutral on controversial questions? Does anyone seriously believe that the managers would continue to pay the Lord Chamberlain two guineas a play out of mere love and loyalty, only to create an additional risk in the case of controversial plays, and to guard against risks that do not exist in the case of the great bulk of other productions? Only those would remain faithful to him who produce such plays as the Select Committee began by discussing *in camera*, and ended by refusing to discuss at all because they were too nasty. These people would still try to get a licence, and would still no doubt succeed as they do today. But could the King's Reader of Plays live on his fees from these plays alone; and if he could how long would his post survive the discredit of licensing only pornographic plays? It is clear to me that the Examiner would be starved out of existence, and the censorship perish of desuetude. Perhaps that is exactly what the Select Committee contemplated. If so, I have nothing more to say, except that I think sudden death would be more merciful.

Lord Gorell's Awakening

In the meantime, conceive the situation which would arise if a licensed play were prosecuted. To make it clearer, let us imagine any other offender—say a company promoter with a fraudulent prospectus—pleading in Court that he had induced the Lord Chamberlain to issue a certificate that the prospectus contained nothing objectionable, and that on the strength of that certificate he issued it; also, that by law the Court could do nothing to him except order him to wind up his company. Some such vision as this must have come to Lord Gorell when he at last grappled seriously with the problem. Mr. Harcourt seized the opportunity to make a last rally. He seconded Lord Gorell's proposal that the Committee should admit that its scheme of an optional censorship was an elaborate absurdity, and report that all censorship before production was out of the question. But it was too late: the *volte face* was too sudden and complete. It was Lord Gorell whose vote had turned the close division which took place on the question of receiving my statement. It was Lord Gorell without whose countenance and authority the farce of the books could never have been performed. Yet here was Lord Gorell, after assenting to all the provisions for the optional censorship paragraph by paragraph, suddenly informing his colleagues that they had been wrong all through and that I had been right all through, and inviting them to scrap half their work and adopt my conclusion. No wonder Lord Gorell got only one vote: that of Mr. Harcourt. But the incident is not the less significant. Lord Gorell carried more weight than any other member of the Committee on the legal and constitutional aspect of the question. Had he begun where he left off—had he at the outset put down his foot on the notion that an optional penal law could ever be anything but a gross contradiction in terms, that part of the Committee's proposals would never have come into existence.

Preface

Judges: Their Professional Limitations

I do not, however, appeal to Lord Gorell's judgment on all points. It is inevitable that a judge should be deeply impressed by his professional experience with a sense of the impotence of judges and laws and courts to deal satisfactorily with evils which are so Protean and elusive as to defy definition, and which yet seem to present quite simple problems to the common sense of men of the world. You have only to imagine the Privy Council as consisting of men of the world highly endowed with common sense, to persuade yourself that the supplementing of the law by the common sense of the Privy Council would settle the whole difficulty. But no man knows what he means by common sense, though every man can tell you that it is very uncommon, even in Privy Councils. And since every ploughman is a man of the world, it is evident that even the phrase itself does not mean what it says. As a matter of fact, it means in ordinary use simply a man who will not make himself disagreeable for the sake of a principle: just the sort of man who should never be allowed to meddle with political rights. Now to a judge a political right, that is, a dogma which is above our laws and conditions our laws, instead of being subject to them, is anarchic and abhorrent. That is why I trust Lord Gorell when he is defending the integrity of the law against the proposal to make it in any sense optional, whilst I very strongly mistrust him, as I mistrust all professional judges, when political rights are in danger.

Conclusion

I must conclude by recommending the Government to take my advice wherever it conflicts with that of the Joint Select Committee. It is, I think, obviously more

deeply considered and better informed, though I say it
that should not. At all events, I have given my reasons; and at that I must leave it. As the tradition which
makes Malvolio not only Master of the Revels but Master of the Mind of England, and which has come down
to us from Henry VIII., is manifestly doomed to the
dustbin, the sooner it goes there the better; for the democratic control which naturally succeeds it can easily be
limited so as to prevent it becoming either a censorship
or a tyranny. The Examiner of Plays should receive a
generous pension, and be set free to practise privately
as an expert adviser of theatrical managers. There is
no reason why they should be deprived of the counsel
they so highly value.

It only remains to say that public performances of
The Shewing-Up of Blanco Posnet are still prohibited
in Great Britain by the Lord Chamberlain. An attempt
was made to prevent even its performance in Ireland by
some indiscreet Castle officials in the absence of the
Lord Lieutenant. This attempt gave extraordinary publicity to the production of the play; and every possible
effort was made to persuade the Irish public that the
performance would be an outrage to their religion, and
to provoke a repetition of the rioting that attended the
first performances of Synge's Playboy of the Western
World before the most sensitive and, on provocation, the
most turbulent audience in the kingdom. The directors
of the Irish National Theatre, Lady Gregory and Mr.
William Butler Yeats, rose to the occasion with inspiriting courage. I am a conciliatory person, and was willing, as I always am, to make every concession in return
for having my own way. But Lady Gregory and Mr.
Yeats not only would not yield an inch, but insisted,
within the due limits of gallant warfare, on taking the
field with every circumstance of defiance, and winning
the battle with every trophy of victory. Their triumph

was as complete as they could have desired. The performance exhausted the possibilities of success, and provoked no murmur, though it inspired several approving sermons. Later on, Lady Gregory and Mr. Yeats brought the play to London and performed it under the Lord Chamberlain's nose, through the instrumentality of the Stage Society.

After this, the play was again submitted to the Lord Chamberlain. But, though beaten, he, too, understands the art of How Not To Do It. He licensed the play, but endorsed on his licence the condition that all the passages which implicated God in the history of Blanco Posnet must be omitted in representation. All the coarseness, the profligacy, the prostitution, the violence, the drinking-bar humor into which the light shines in the play are licensed, but the light itself is extinguished. I need hardly say that I have not availed myself of this licence, and do not intend to. There is enough licensed darkness in our theatres today without my adding to it.

AYOT ST. LAWRENCE,
14th July 1910.

POSTSCRIPT.—Since the above was written the Lord Chamberlain has made an attempt to evade his responsibility and perhaps to postpone his doom by appointing an advisory committee, unknown to the law, on which he will presumably throw any odium that may attach to refusals of licences in the future. This strange and lawless body will hardly reassure our moralists, who object much more to the plays he licenses than to those he suppresses, and are therefore unmoved by his plea that his refusals are few and far between. It consists of two eminent actors (one retired), an Oxford professor of literature, and two eminent barristers. As their assembly is neither created by statute nor sanctioned by custom, it is difficult to know what to call it until it advises the Lord Chamberlain to deprive some author of his means of livelihood, when it will, I presume, become a conspiracy, and be indictable accordingly; unless, indeed, it can persuade the Courts to recognize it as a new Estate of the Realm, created by the Lord Chamberlain. This constitutional position is so questionable that I strongly advise the members to resign promptly before the Lord Chamberlain gets them into trouble.

THE SHEWING-UP OF BLANCO POSNET

A number of women are sitting working together in a big room not unlike an old English tithe barn in its timbered construction, but with windows high up next the roof. It is furnished as a courthouse, with the floor raised next the walls, and on this raised flooring a seat for the Sheriff, a rough jury box on his right, and a bar to put prisoners to on his left. In the well in the middle is a table with benches round it. A few other benches are in disorder round the room. The autumn sun is shining warmly through the windows and the open door. The women, whose dress and speech are those of pioneers of civilization in a territory of the United States of America, are seated round the table and on the benches, shucking nuts. The conversation is at its height.

BABSY [*a bumptious young slattern, with some good looks*] I say that a man that would steal a horse would do anything.

LOTTIE [*a sentimental girl, neat and clean*] Well, I never should look at it in that way. I do think killing a man is worse any day than stealing a horse.

HANNAH [*elderly and wise*] I dont say it's right to kill a man. In a place like this, where every man has to have a revolver, and where theres so much to try people's tempers, the men get to be a deal too free with one another in the way of shooting. God knows it's hard enough to have to bring a boy into the world and nurse him up to be a man only to have him brought home to you on a shutter, perhaps for nothing, or only just to shew that the man that killed him wasnt afraid of him. But men are like children when they get a gun in their hands: theyre not content til theyve used it on somebody.

JESSIE [*a good-natured but sharp-tongued, hoity-toity young woman; Babsy's rival in good looks and her superior in tidiness*] They shoot for the love of it. Look at them at a lynching. Theyre not content to hang the man; but directly the poor creature is swung up they all shoot him full of holes, wasting their cartridges that cost solid money, and pretending they do it in horror of his wickedness, though half of them would have a rope round their own necks if all they did was known— let alone the mess it makes.

LOTTIE. I wish we could get more civilized. I dont like all this lynching and shooting. I dont believe any of us like it, if the truth were known.

BABSY. Our Sheriff is a real strong man. You want a strong man for a rough lot like our people here. He aint afraid to shoot and he aint afraid to hang. Lucky for us quiet ones, too.

JESSIE. Oh, dont talk to me. I know what men are. Of course he aint afraid to shoot and he aint afraid to hang. Wheres the risk in that with the law on his side and the whole crowd at his back longing for the lynching as if it was a spree? Would one of them own to it or let him own to it if they lynched the wrong man? Not them. What they call justice in this place is nothing but a breaking out of the devil thats in all of us. What I want to see is a Sheriff that aint afraid not to shoot and not to hang.

EMMA [*a sneak who sides with Babsy or Jessie, ac-*

cording to the fortune of war] Well, I must say it does sicken me to see Sheriff Kemp putting down his foot, as he calls it. Why dont he put it down on his wife? She wants it worse than half the men he lynches. He and his Vigilance Committee, indeed!

BABSY [*incensed*] Oh, well! if people are going to take the part of horse-thieves against the Sheriff—!

JESSIE. Who's taking the part of horse-thieves against the Sheriff?

BABSY. You are. Waite your own horse is stolen, and youll know better. I had an uncle that died of thirst in the sage brush because a negro stole his horse. But they caught him and burned him; and serve him right, too.

EMMA. I have known that a child was born crooked because its mother had to do a horse's work that was stolen.

BABSY. There! You hear that? I say stealing a horse is ten times worse than killing a man. And if the Vigilance Committee ever gets hold of you, youd better have killed twenty men than as much as stole a saddle or bridle, much less a horse.

Elder Daniels comes in.

ELDER DANIELS. Sorry to disturb you, ladies; but the Vigilance Committee has taken a prisoner; and they want the room to try him in.

JESSIE. But they cant try him til Sheriff Kemp comes back from the wharf.

ELDER DANIELS. Yes; but we have to keep the prisoner here til he comes.

BABSY. What do you want to put him here for? Cant you tie him up in the Sheriff's stable?

ELDER DANIELS. He has a soul to be saved, almost like the rest of us. I am bound to try to put some religion into him before he goes into his Maker's presence after the trial.

HANNAH. What has he done, Mr Daniels?

ELDER DANIELS. Stole a horse.

BABSY. And are we to be turned out of the town hall for a horse-thief? Aint a stable good enough for his religion?

ELDER DANIELS. It may be good enough for his, Babsy; but, by your leave, it is not good enough for mine. While I am Elder here, I shall umbly endeavour to keep up the dignity of Him I serve to the best of my small ability. So I must ask you to be good enough to clear out. Allow me. [*He takes the sack of husks and put it out of the way against the panels of the jury box*].

THE WOMEN [*murmuring*] Thats always the way. Just as we'd settled down to work. What harm are we doing? Well, it is tiresome. Let them finish the job themselves. Oh dear, oh dear! We cant have a minute to ourselves. Shoving us out like that!

HANNAH. Whose horse was it, Mr Daniels?

ELDER DANIELS [*returning to move the other sack*] I am sorry to say that it was the Sheriff's horse—the one he loaned to young Strapper. Strapper loaned it to me; and the thief stole it, thinking it was mine. If it had been mine, I'd have forgiven him cheerfully. I'm sure I hoped he would get away; for he had two hours start of the Vigilance Committee. But they caught him. [*He disposes of the other sack also*].

JESSIE. It cant have been much of a horse if they caught him with two hours start.

ELDER DANIELS [*coming back to the centre of the group*] The strange thing is that he wasnt on the horse when they took him. He was walking; and of course he denies that he ever had the horse. The Sheriff's brother wanted to tie him up and lash him till he confessed what he'd done with it; but I couldnt allow that: it's not the law.

The Shewing-Up of Blanco Posnet 411

BABSY. Law! What right has a horse-thief to any law? Law is thrown away on a brute like that.

ELDER DANIELS. Dont say that, Babsy. No man should be made to confess by cruelty until religion has been tried and failed. Please God I'll get the whereabouts of the horse from him if youll be so good as to clear out from this. [*Disturbance outside*]. They are bringing him in. Now ladies! please, please.

They rise reluctantly. Hannah, Jessie, and Lottie retreat to the Sheriff's bench, shepherded by Daniels; but the other women crowd forward behind Babsy and Emma to see the prisoner.

Blanco Posnet is brought in by Strapper Kemp, the Sheriff's brother, and a cross-eyed man called Squinty. Others follow. Blanco is evidently a blackguard. It would be necessary to clean him to make a close guess at his age; but he is under forty, and an upturned, red moustache, and the arrangement of his hair in a crest on his brow, proclaim the dandy in spite of his intense disreputableness. He carries his head high, and has a fairly resolute mouth, though the fire of incipient delirium tremens is in his eye.

His arms are bound with a rope with a long end, which Squinty holds. They release him when he enters; and he stretches himself and lounges across the courthouse in front of the women. Strapper and the men remain between him and the door.

BABSY [*spitting at him as he passes her*] Horse-thief! horse-thief!

OTHERS. You will hang for it; do you hear? And serve you right. Serve you right. That will teach you. I wouldnt wait to try you. Lynch him straight off, the varmint. Yes, yes. Tell the boys. Lynch him.

BLANCO [*mocking*] "Angels ever bright and fair—"

BABSY. You call me an angel, and I'll smack your dirty face for you.

BLANCO. " Take, oh take me to your care."
EMMA. There wont be any angels where youre going to.
OTHERS. Aha! Devils, more likely. And too good company for a horse-thief.
ALL. Horse-thief! Horse-thief! Horse-thief!
BLANCO. Do women make the law here, or men? Drive these heifers out.
THE WOMEN. Oh! [*They rush at him, vituperating, screaming passionately, tearing at him. Lottie puts her fingers in her ears and runs out. Hannah follows, shaking her head. Blanco is thrown down*]. Oh, did you hear what he called us? You foul-mouthed brute! You liar! How dare you put such a name to a decent woman? Let me get at him. You coward! Oh, he struck me: did you see that? Lynch him! Pete, will you stand by and hear me called names by a skunk like that? Burn him: burn him! Thats what I'd do with him. Aye, burn him!
THE MEN [*pulling the women away from Blanco, and getting them out partly by violence and partly by coaxing*] Here! come out of this. Let him alone. Clear the courthouse. Come on now. Out with you. Now, Sally: out you go. Let go my hair, or I'll twist your arm out. Ah, would you? Now, then: get along. You know you must go. Whats the use of scratching like that? Now, ladies, ladies, ladies. How would you like it if you were going to be hanged?

At last the women are pushed out, leaving Elder Daniels, the Sheriff's brother Strapper Kemp, and a few others with Blanco. Strapper is a lad just turning into a man: strong, selfish, sulky, and determined.

BLANCO [*sitting up and tidying himself*]—

   Oh woman, in our hours of ease,
   Uncertain, coy, and hard to please—

Is my face scratched? I can feel their damned claws all over me still. Am I bleeding? [*He sits on the nearest bench*].

ELDER DANIELS. Nothing to hurt. Theyve drawn a drop or two under your left eye.

STRAPPER. Lucky for you to have an eye left in your head.

BLANCO [*wiping the blood off*]—

> When pain and anguish wring the brow,
> A ministering angel thou.

Go out to them, Strapper Kemp; and tell them about your big brother's little horse that some wicked man stole. Go and cry in your mammy's lap.

STRAPPER [*furious*] You jounce me any more about that horse, Blanco Posnet; and I'll—I'll—

BLANCO. Youll scratch my face, wont you? Yah! Your brother's the Sheriff, aint he?

STRAPPER. Yes, he is. He hangs horse-thieves.

BLANCO [*with calm conviction*] He's a rotten Sheriff. Oh, a rotten Sheriff. If he did his first duty he'd hang himself. This is a rotten town. Your fathers came here on a false alarm of gold-digging; and when the gold didnt pan out, they lived by licking their young into habits of honest industry.

STRAPPER. If I hadnt promised Elder Daniels here to give him a chance to keep you out of Hell, I'd take the job of twisting your neck off the hands of the Vigilance Committee.

BLANCO [*with infinite scorn*] You and your rotten Elder, and your rotten Vigilance Committee!

STRAPPER. Theyre sound enough to hang a horse-thief, anyhow.

BLANCO. Any fool can hang the wisest man in the country. Nothing he likes better. But you cant hang me.

STRAPPER. Cant we?

BLANCO. No, you cant. I left the town this morning before sunrise, because it's a rotten town, and I couldnt bear to see it in the light. Your brother's horse did the same, as any sensible horse would. Instead of going to look for the horse, you went looking for me. That was a rotten thing to do, because the horse belonged to your brother—or to the man he stole it from—and I dont belong to him. Well, you found me; but you didn't find the horse. If I had took the horse, I'd have been on the horse. Would I have taken all that time to get to where I did if I'd a horse to carry me?

STRAPPER. I dont believe you started not for two hours after you say you did.

BLANCO. Who cares what you believe or dont believe? Is a man worth six of you to be hanged because youve lost your big brother's horse, and youll want to kill somebody to relieve your rotten feelings when he licks you for it? Not likely. Till you can find a witness that saw me with that horse you cant touch me; and you know it.

STRAPPER. Is that the law, Elder?

ELDER DANIELS. The Sheriff knows the law. I wouldnt say for sure; but I think it would be more seemly to have a witness. Go and round one up, Strapper; and leave me here alone to wrestle with his poor blinded soul.

STRAPPER. I'll get a witness all right enough. I know the road he took; and I'll ask at every house within sight of it for a mile out. Come boys.

Strapper goes out with the others, leaving Blanco and Elder Daniels together. Blanco rises and strolls over to the Elder, surveying him with extreme disparagement.

BLANCO. Well, brother? Well, Boozy Posnet, alias Elder Daniels? Well, thief? Well, drunkard?

The Shewing-Up of Blanco Posnet

ELDER DANIELS. It's no good, Blanco. Theyll never believe we're brothers.

BLANCO. Never fear. Do you suppose I want to claim you? Do you suppose I'm proud of you? Youre a rotten brother, Boozy Posnet. All you ever did when I owned you was to borrow money from me to get drunk with. Now you lend money and sell drink to other people. I was ashamed of you before; and I'm worse ashamed of you now. I wont have you for a brother. Heaven gave you to me; but I return the blessing without thanks. So be easy: I shant blab. [*He turns his back on him and sits down*].

ELDER DANIELS. I tell you they wouldnt believe you; so what does it matter to me whether you blab or not? Talk sense, Blanco: theres no time for your foolery now; for youll be a dead man an hour after the Sheriff comes back. What possessed you to steal that horse?

BLANCO. I didnt steal it. I distrained on it for what you owed me. I thought it was yours. I was a fool to think that you owned anything but other people's property. You laid your hands on everything father and mother had when they died. I never asked you for a fair share. I never asked you for all the money I'd lent you from time to time. I asked you for mother's old necklace with the hair locket in it. You wouldnt give me that: you wouldnt give me anything. So as you refused me my due I took it, just to give you a lesson.

ELDER DANIELS. Why didnt you take the necklace if you must steal something? They wouldnt have hanged you for that.

BLANCO. Perhaps I'd rather be hanged for stealing a horse than let off for a damned piece of sentimentality.

ELDER DANIELS. Oh, Blanco, Blanco: spiritual pride has been your ruin. If youd only done like me, youd be a free and respectable man this day instead of laying there with a rope round your neck.

BLANCO [*turning on him*] Done like you! What do you mean? Drink like you, eh? Well, Ive done some of that lately. I see things.

ELDER DANIELS. Too late, Blanco: too late. [*Convulsively*] Oh, why didnt you drink as I used to? Why didnt you drink as I was led to by the Lord for my good, until the time came for me to give it up? It was drink that saved my character when I was a young man; and it was the want of it that spoiled yours. Tell me this. Did I ever get drunk when I was working?

BLANCO. No; but then you never worked when you had money enough to get drunk.

ELDER DANIELS. That just shews the wisdom of Providence and the Lord's mercy. God fulfils himself in many ways: ways we little think of when we try to set up our own shortsighted laws against his Word. When does the Devil catch hold of a man? Not when he's working and not when he's drunk; but when he's idle and sober. Our own natures tell us to drink when we have nothing else to do. Look at you and me! When we'd both earned a pocketful of money, what did we do? Went on the spree, naturally. But I was humble minded. I did as the rest did. I gave my money in at the drinkshop; and I said, " Fire me out when I have drunk it all up." Did you ever see me sober while it lasted?

BLANCO. No; and you looked so disgusting that I wonder it didnt set me against drink for the rest of my life.

ELDER DANIELS. That was your spiritual pride, Blanco. You never reflected that when I was drunk I was in a state of innocence. Temptations and bad company and evil thoughts passed by me like the summer wind as you might say: I was too drunk to notice them. When the money was gone, and they fired me out, I was fired out like gold out of the furnace, with my character unspoiled and unspotted; and when I went back to work, the work kept me steady. Can you say as much, Blanco? Did your holidays leave your character unspoiled? Oh, no, no. It was theatres: it was gambling: it was evil company: it was reading in vain romances: it was women, Blanco, women: it was wrong thoughts and gnawing discontent. It ended in your becoming a rambler and a gambler: it is going to end this evening on the gallows tree. Oh, what a lesson against spiritual pride! Oh, what a— [*Blanco throws his hat at him*].

BLANCO. Stow it, Boozy. Sling it. Cut it. Cheese it. Shut up. "Shake not the dying sinner's sand."

ELDER DANIELS. Aye: there you go, with your scraps of lustful poetry. But you cant deny what I tell you. Why, do you think I would put my soul in peril by selling drink if I thought it did no good, as them silly temperance reformers make out, flying in the face of the natural tastes implanted in us all for a good purpose? Not if I was to starve for it to-morrow. But I know better. I tell you, Blanco, what keeps America to-day the purest of the nations is that when she's not working she's too drunk to hear the voice of the tempter.

BLANCO. Dont deceive yourself, Boozy. You sell drink because you make a bigger profit out of it than you can by selling tea. And you gave up drink yourself because when you got that fit at Edwardstown the doctor told you youd die the next time; and that frightened you off it.

ELDER DANIELS [*fervently*] Oh thank God selling drink pays me! And thank God he sent me that fit as a warning that my drinking time was past and gone, and that he needed me for another service!

BLANCO. Take care, Boozy. He hasnt finished with you yet. He always has a trick up His sleeve—

ELDER DANIELS. Oh, is that the way to speak of the ruler of the universe—the great and almighty God?

BLANCO. He's a sly one. He's a mean one. He lies low for you. He plays cat and mouse with you. He lets you run loose until you think youre shut of him; and then, when you least expect it, he's got you.

ELDER DANIELS. Speak more respectful, Blanco—more reverent.

BLANCO [*springing up and coming at him*] Reverent! Who taught you your reverent cant? Not your Bible. It says He cometh like a thief in the night—aye, like a thief—a horse-thief—

ELDER DANIELS [*shocked*] Oh!

BLANCO [*overhearing him*] And it's true. Thats how He caught me and put my neck into the halter. To spite me because I had no use for Him—because I lived my own life in my own way, and would have no truck with His "Dont do this," and "You mustnt do that," and "Youll go to Hell if you do the other." I gave Him the go-bye and did without Him all these years. But He caught me out at last. The laugh is with Him as far as hanging me goes. [*He thrusts his hands into his pockets and lounges moodily away from Daniels, to the table, where he sits facing the jury box*].

ELDER DANIELS. Dont dare to put your theft on Him, man. It was the Devil tempted you to steal the horse.

BLANCO. Not a bit of it. Neither God nor Devil tempted me to take the horse: I took it on my own. He had a cleverer trick than that ready for me. [*He takes his hands out of his pockets and clenches his fists*]. Gosh! When I think that I might have been safe and fifty miles away by now with that horse; and here I am waiting to be hung up and filled with lead! What came to me? What made me such a fool? Thats what I want to know. Thats the great secret.

The Shewing-Up of Blanco Posnet 419

ELDER DANIELS [*at the opposite side of the table*] Blanco: the great secret now is, what did you do with the horse?

BLANCO [*striking the table with his fist*] May my lips be blighted like my soul if ever I tell that to you or any mortal men! They may roast me alive or cut me to ribbons; but Strapper Kemp shall never have the laugh on me over that job. Let them hang me. Let them shoot. So long as they are shooting a man and not a sniveling skunk and softy, I can stand up to them and take all they can give me—game.

ELDER DANIELS. Dont be headstrong, Blanco. Whats the use? [*Slyly*] They might let up on you if you put Strapper in the way of getting his brother's horse back.

BLANCO. Not they. Hanging's too big a treat for them to give up a fair chance. Ive done it myself. Ive yelled with the dirtiest of them when a man no worse than myself was swung up. Ive emptied my revolver into him, and persuaded myself that he deserved it and that I was doing justice with strong stern men. Well, my turn's come now. Let the men I yelled at and shot at look up out of Hell and see the boys yelling and shooting at me as *I* swing up.

ELDER DANIELS. Well, even if you want to be hanged, is that any reason why Strapper shouldnt have his horse? I tell you I'm responsible to him for it. [*Bending over the table and coaxing him*]. Act like a brother, Blanco: tell me what you done with it.

BLANCO [*shortly, getting up and leaving the table*] Never you mind what I done with it. I was done out of it. Let that be enough for you.

ELDER DANIELS [*following him*] Then why dont you put us on to the man that done you out of it?

BLANCO. Because he'd be too clever for you, just as he was too clever for me.

ELDER DANIELS. Make your mind easy about that, Blanco. He wont be too clever for the boys and Sheriff Kemp if you put them on his trail.

BLANCO. Yes he will. It wasnt a man.

ELDER DANIELS. Then what was it?

BLANCO [*pointing upward*] Him.

ELDER DANIELS. Oh what a way to utter His holy name!

BLANCO. He done me out of it. He meant to pay off old scores by bringing me here. He means to win the deal and you cant stop Him. Well, He's made a fool of me; but He cant frighten me. I'm not going to beg off. I'll fight off if I get a chance. I'll lie off if they cant get a witness against me. But back down I never will, not if all the hosts of heaven come to snivel at me in white surplices and offer me my life in exchange for an umble and a contrite heart.

ELDER DANIELS. Youre not in your right mind, Blanco. I'll tell em youre mad. I believe theyll let you off on that. [*He makes for the door*].

BLANCO [*seizing him, with horror in his eyes*] Dont go: dont leave me alone: do you hear?

ELDER DANIELS. Has your conscience brought you to this, that youre afraid to be left alone in broad daylight, like a child in the dark?

BLANCO. I'm afraid of Him and His tricks. When I have you to raise the devil in me—when I have people to shew off before and keep me game, I'm all right; but Ive lost my nerve for being alone since this morning. It's when youre alone that He takes His advantage. He might turn my head again. He might send people to me—not real people perhaps. [*Shivering*] By God, I dont believe that woman and the child were real. I dont. I never noticed them till they were at my elbow.

ELDER DANIELS. What woman and what child? What

are you talking about? Have you been drinking too hard?

BLANCO. Never you mind. Youve got to stay with me: thats all; or else send someone else—someone rottener than yourself to keep the devil in me. Strapper Kemp will do. Or a few of those scratching devils of women.

Strapper Kemp comes back.

ELDER DANIELS [*to Strapper*] He's gone off his head.

STRAPPER. Foxing, more likely. [*Going past Daniels and talking to Blanco nose to nose*] It's no good: we hang madmen here; and a good job too!

BLANCO. I feel safe with you, Strapper. Youre one of the rottenest.

STRAPPER. You know youre done, and that you may as well be hanged for a sheep as a lamb. So talk away. Ive got my witness; and I'll trouble you not to make a move towards her when she comes in to identify you.

BLANCO [*retreating in terror*] A woman? She aint real: neither is the child.

ELDER DANIELS. He's raving about a woman and a child. I tell you he's gone off his chump.

STRAPPER [*calling to those without*] Shew the lady in there.

Feemy Evans comes in. She is a young woman of 23 or 24, with impudent manners, battered good looks, and dirty-fine dress.

ELDER DANIELS. Morning, Feemy.

FEEMY. Morning, Elder. [*She passes on and slips her arm familiarly through Strapper's*].

STRAPPER. Ever see him before, Feemy?

FEEMY. Thats the little lot that was on your horse this morning, Strapper. Not a doubt of it.

BLANCO [*implacably contemptuous*] Go home and wash yourself, you slut.

FEEMY [*reddening, and disengaging her arm from Strapper's*] I'm clean enough to hang you, anyway. [*Going over to him threateningly*]. Youre no true American man, to insult a woman like that.

BLANCO. A woman! Oh Lord! You saw me on a horse, did you?

FEEMY. Yes I did.

BLANCO. Got up early on purpose to do it, didnt you?

FEEMY. No I didnt: I stayed up late on a spree.

BLANCO. I was on a horse, was I?

FEEMY. Yes you were; and if you deny it youre a liar.

BLANCO [*to Strapper*] She saw a man on a horse when she was too drunk to tell which was the man and which was the horse—

FEEMY [*breaking in*] You lie. I wasnt drunk—at least not as drunk as that.

BLANCO [*ignoring the interruption*]—and you found a man without a horse. Is a man on a horse the same as a man on foot? Yah! Take your witness away. Who's going to believe her? Shove her into the dustbin. Youve got to find that horse before you get a rope round my neck. [*He turns away from her contemptuously, and sits at the table with his back to the jury box*].

FEEMY [*following him*] I'll hang you, you dirty horse-thief; or not a man in this camp will ever get a word or a look from me again. Youre just trash: thats what you are. White trash.

BLANCO. And what are you, darling? What are you? Youre a worse danger to a town like this than ten horse-thieves.

FEEMY. Mr Kemp: will you stand by and hear me insulted in that low way? [*To Blanco, spitefully*] I'll see you swung up and I'll see you cut down: I'll see you high and I'll see you low, as dangerous as I am. [*He*

The Shewing-Up of Blanco Posnet

laughs]. Oh you neednt try to brazen it out. Youll look white enough before the boys are done with you.

BLANCO. You do me good, Feemy. Stay by me to the end, wont you? Hold my hand to the last; and I'll die game. [*He puts out his hand: she strikes savagely at it; but he withdraws it in time and laughs at her discomfiture*].

FEEMY. You—

ELDER DANIELS. Never mind him, Feemy: he's not right in his head to-day. [*She receives the assurance with contemptuous credulity, and sits down on the step of the Sheriff's dais*].

Sheriff Kemp comes in: a stout man, with large flat ears, and a neck thicker than his head.

ELDER DANIELS. Morning, Sheriff.

THE SHERIFF. Morning, Elder. [*Passing on*]. Morning, Strapper. [*Passing on*]. Morning, Miss Evans. [*Stopping between Strapper and Blanco*]. Is this the prisoner?

BLANCO [*rising*] Thats so. Morning, Sheriff.

THE SHERIFF. Morning. You know, I suppose, that if youve stole a horse and the jury find against you, you wont have any time to settle your affairs. Consequently, if you feel guilty, youd better settle em now.

BLANCO. Affairs be damned! Ive got none.

THE SHERIFF. Well, are you in a proper state of mind? Has the Elder talked to you?

BLANCO. He has. And I say it's against the law. It's torture: thats what it is.

ELDER DANIELS. He's not accountable. He's out of his mind, Sheriff. He's not fit to go into the presence of his Maker.

THE SHERIFF. You are a merciful man, Elder; but you wont take the boys with you there. [*To Blanco*]. If it comes to hanging you, youd better for your own sake be hanged in a proper state of mind than in an improper one. But it wont make any difference to us: make no mistake about that.

BLANCO. Lord keep me wicked till I die! Now Ive said my little prayer. I'm ready. Not that I'm guilty, mind you; but this is a rotten town, dead certain to do the wrong thing.

THE SHERIFF. You wont be asked to live long in it, I guess. [*To Strapper*] Got the witness all right, Strapper?

STRAPPER. Yes, got everything.

BLANCO. Except the horse.

THE SHERIFF. Whats that? Aint you got the horse?

STRAPPER. No. He traded it before we overtook him, I guess. But Feemy saw him on it.

FEEMY. She did.

STRAPPER. Shall I call in the boys?

BLANCO. Just a moment, Sheriff. A good appearance is everything in a low-class place like this. [*He takes out a pocket comb and mirror, and retires towards the dais to arrange his hair*].

ELDER DANIELS. Oh, think of your immortal soul, man, not of your foolish face.

BLANCO. I cant change my soul, Elder: it changes me—sometimes. Feemy: I'm too pale. Let me rub my cheek against yours, darling.

FEEMY. You lie: my color's my own, such as it is. And a pretty color youll be when youre hung white and shot red.

BLANCO. Aint she spiteful, Sheriff?

THE SHERIFF. Time's wasted on you. [*To Strapper*] Go and see if the boys are ready. Some of them were short of cartridges, and went down to the store to buy them. They may as well have their fun; and itll be shorter for him.

STRAPPER. Young Jack has brought a boxful up. Theyre all ready.

The Shewing-Up of Blanco Posnet

THE SHERIFF [*going to the dais and addressing Blanco*] Your place is at the bar there. Take it. [*Blanco bows ironically and goes to the bar*]. Miss Evans: youd best sit at the table. [*She does so, at the corner nearest the bar. The Elder takes the opposite corner. The Sheriff takes his chair*]. All ready, Strapper.

STRAPPER [*at the door*] All in to begin.

The crowd comes in and fills the court. Babsy, Jessie, and Emma come to the Sheriff's right; Hannah and Lottie to his left.

THE SHERIFF. Silence there. The jury will take their places as usual. [*They do so*].

BLANCO. I challenge this jury, Sheriff.

THE FOREMAN. Do you, by Gosh?

THE SHERIFF. On what ground?

BLANCO. On the general ground that it's a rotten jury. [*Laughter*].

THE SHERIFF. Thats not a lawful ground of challenge.

THE FOREMAN. It's a lawful ground for me to shoot yonder skunk at sight, first time I meet him, if he survives this trial.

BLANCO. I challenge the Foreman because he's prejudiced.

THE FOREMAN. I say you lie. We mean to hang you, Blanco Posnet; but you will be hanged fair.

THE JURY. Hear, hear!

STRAPPER [*to the Sheriff*] George: this is rot. How can you get an unprejudiced jury if the prisoner starts by telling them theyre all rotten? If theres any prejudice against him he has himself to thank for it.

THE BOYS. Thats so. Of course he has. Insulting the court! Challenge be jiggered! Gag him.

NESTOR [*a juryman with a long white beard, drunk, the oldest man present*] Besides, Sheriff, I go so far as to say that the man that is not prejudiced against a horse-thief is not fit to sit on a jury in this town.

THE BOYS. Right. Bully for you, Nestor! Thats the straight truth. Of course he aint. Hear, hear!

THE SHERIFF. That is no doubt true, old man. Still, you must get as unprejudiced as you can. The critter has a right to his chance, such as he is. So now go right ahead. If the prisoner dont like this jury, he should have stole a horse in another town; for this is all the jury he'll get here.

THE FOREMAN. Thats so, Blanco Posnet.

THE SHERIFF [*to Blanco*] Dont you be uneasy. You will get justice here. It may be rough justice; but it is justice.

BLANCO. What is justice?

THE SHERIFF. Hanging horse-thieves is justice; so now you know. Now then: weve wasted enough time. Hustle with your witness there, will you?

BLANCO [*indignantly bringing down his fist on the bar*] Swear the jury. A rotten Sheriff you are not to know that the jury's got to be sworn.

THE FOREMAN [*galled*] Be swore for you! Not likely. What do you say, old son?

NESTOR [*deliberately and solemnly*] I say: GUILTY!

THE BOYS [*tumultuously rushing at Blanco*] Thats it. Guilty, guilty. Take him out and hang him. He's found guilty. Fetch a rope. Up with him. [*They are about to drag him from the bar*].

THE SHERIFF [*rising, pistol in hand*] Hands off that man. Hands off him, I say, Squinty, or I drop you, and would if you were my own son. [*Dead silence*]. I'm Sheriff here; and it's for me to say when he may lawfully be hanged. [*They release him*].

BLANCO. As the actor says in the play, "a Daniel come to judgment." Rotten actor he was, too.

THE SHERIFF. Elder Daniel is come to judgment all

right, my lad. Elder: the floor is yours. [*The Elder rises*]. Give your evidence. The truth and the whole truth and nothing but the truth, so help you God.

ELDER DANIELS. Sheriff: let me off this. I didnt ought to swear away this man's life. He and I are, in a manner of speaking, brothers.

THE SHERIFF. It does you credit, Elder: every man here will acknowledge it. But religion is one thing: law is another. In religion we're all brothers. In law we cut our brother off when he steals horses.

THE FOREMAN. Besides, you neednt hang him, you know. Theres plenty of willing hands to take that job off your conscience. So rip ahead, old son.

STRAPPER. Youre accountable to me for the horse until you clear yourself, Elder: remember that.

BLANCO. Out with it, you fool.

ELDER DANIELS. You might own up, Blanco, as far as my evidence goes. Everybody knows I borrowed one of the Sheriff's horses from Strapper because my own's gone lame. Everybody knows you arrived in the town yesterday and put up in my house. Everybody knows that in the morning the horse was gone and you were gone.

BLANCO [*in a forensic manner*] Sheriff: the Elder, though known to you and to all here as no brother of mine and the rottenest liar in this town, is speaking the truth for the first time in his life as far as what he says about me is concerned. As to the horse, I say nothing; except that it was the rottenest horse you ever tried to sell.

THE SHERIFF. How do you know it was a rotten horse if you didnt steal it?

BLANCO. I dont know of my own knowledge. I only argue that if the horse had been worth its keep, you wouldnt have lent it to Strapper, and Strapper wouldnt have lent it to this eloquent and venerable ram. [*Sup-

pressed laughter]. And now I ask him this. [*To the Elder*] Did we or did we not have a quarrel last evening about a certain article that was left by my mother, and that I considered I had a right to more than you? And did you say one word to me about the horse not belonging to you?

ELDER DANIELS. Why should I? We never said a word about the horse at all. How was I to know what it was in your mind to do?

BLANCO. Bear witness all that I had a right to take a horse from him without stealing to make up for what he denied me. I am no thief. But you havnt proved yet that I took the horse. Strapper Kemp: had I the horse when you took me, or had I not?

STRAPPER. No, nor you hadnt a railway train neither. But Feemy Evans saw you pass on the horse at four o'clock twenty-five miles from the spot where I took you at seven on the road to Pony Harbor. Did you walk twenty-five miles in three hours? That so, Feemy, eh?

FEEMY. Thats so. At four I saw him. [*To Blanco*] Thats done for you.

THE SHERIFF. You say you saw him on my horse?

FEEMY. I did.

BLANCO. And I ate it, I suppose, before Strapper fetched up with me. [*Suddenly and dramatically*] Sheriff: I accuse Feemy of immoral relations with Strapper.

FEEMY. Oh you liar!

BLANCO. I accuse the fair Euphemia of immoral relations with every man in this town, including yourself, Sheriff. I say this is a conspiracy to kill me between Feemy and Strapper because I wouldnt touch Feemy with a pair of tongs. I say you darent hang any white man on the word of a woman of bad character. I stand on the honor and virtue of my American manhood. I

say that she's not had the oath, and that you darent for
the honor of the town give her the oath because her lips
would blaspheme the holy Bible if they touched it. I
say thats the law; and if you are a proper United States
Sheriff and not a low-down lyncher, youll hold up the
law and not let it be dragged in the mud by your brother's kept woman.

Great excitement among the women. The men much puzzled.

JESSIE. Thats right. She didnt ought to be let kiss the Book.

EMMA. How could the like of her tell the truth?

BABSY. It would be an insult to every respectable woman here to believe her.

FEEMY. It's easy to be respectable with nobody ever offering you a chance to be anything else.

THE WOMEN [*clamoring all together*] Shut up, you hussy. Youre a disgrace. How dare you open your lips to answer your betters? Hold your tongue and learn your place, miss. You painted slut! Whip her out of the town!

THE SHERIFF. Silence. Do you hear? Silence. [*The clamor ceases*]. Did anyone else see the prisoner with the horse?

FEEMY [*passionately*] Aint I good enough?

BABSY. No. Youre dirt: thats what you are.

FEEMY. And you—

THE SHERIFF. Silence. This trial is a man's job; and if the women forget their sex they can go out or be put out. Strapper and Miss Evans: you cant have it two ways. You can run straight, or you can run gay, so to speak; but you cant run both ways together. There is also a strong feeling among the men of this town that a line should be drawn between those that are straight wives and mothers and those that are, in the words of the Book of Books, taking the primrose path. We dont wish to be hard on any woman; and most of us have a personal regard for Miss Evans for the sake of old times; but theres no getting out of the fact that she has private reasons for wishing to oblige Strapper, and that —if she will excuse my saying so—she is not what I might call morally particular as to what she does to oblige him. Therefore I ask the prisoner not to drive us to give Miss Evans the oath. I ask him to tell us fair and square, as a man who has but a few minutes between him and eternity, what he done with my horse.

THE BOYS. Hear, hear! Thats right. Thats fair. That does it. Now Blanco. Own up.

BLANCO. Sheriff: you touch me home. This is a rotten world; but there is still one thing in it that remains sacred even to the rottenest of us, and that is a horse.

THE BOYS. Good. Well said, Blanco. Thats straight.

BLANCO. You have a right to your horse, Sheriff; and if I could put you in the way of getting it back, I would. But if I had that horse I shouldnt be here. As I hope to be saved, Sheriff—or rather as I hope to be damned; for I have no taste for pious company and no talent for playing the harp—I know no more of that horse's whereabouts than you do yourself.

STRAPPER. Who did you trade him to?

BLANCO. I did not trade him. I got nothing for him or by him. I stand here with a rope round my neck for the want of him. When you took me, did I fight like a thief or run like a thief; and was there any sign of a horse on me or near me?

STRAPPER. You were looking at a rainbow like a damned silly fool instead of keeping your wits about you; and we stole up on you and had you tight before you could draw a bead on us.

THE SHERIFF. That dont sound like good sense. What would he look at a rainbow for?

BLANCO. I'll tell you, Sheriff. I was looking at it because there was something written on it.

SHERIFF. How do you mean written on it?

BLANCO. The words were, " Ive got the cinch on you this time, Blanco Posnet." Yes, Sheriff, I saw those words in green on the red streak of the rainbow; and as I saw them I felt Strapper's grab on my arm and Squinty's on my pistol.

THE FOREMAN. He's shammin mad: thats what he is. Aint it about time to give a verdict and have a bit of fun, Sheriff?

THE BOYS. Yes, lets have a verdict. We're wasting the whole afternoon. Cut it short.

THE SHERIFF [making up his mind] Swear Feemy Evans, Elder. She dont need to touch the Book. Let her say the words.

FEEMY. Worse people than me has kissed that Book. What wrong Ive done, most of you went shares in. Ive to live, havnt I? same as the rest of you. However, it makes no odds to me. I guess the truth is the truth and a lie is a lie, on the Book or off it.

BABSY. Do as youre told. Who are you, to be let talk about it?

THE SHERIFF. Silence there, I tell you. Sail ahead, Elder.

ELDER DANIELS. Feemy Evans: do you swear to tell the truth and the whole truth and nothing but the truth, so help you God?

FEEMY. I do, so help me—

SHERIFF. Thats enough. Now, on your oath, did you see the prisoner on my horse this morning on the road to Pony Harbor?

FEEMY. On my oath—[*Disturbance and crowding at the door*].

AT THE DOOR. Now then, now then! Where are you shovin to? Whats up? Order in court. Chuck him out. Silence. You cant come in here. Keep back.

Strapper rushes to the door and forces his way out.

SHERIFF [*savagely*] Whats this noise? Cant you keep quiet there? Is this a Sheriff's court or is it a saloon?

BLANCO. Dont interrupt a lady in the act of hanging a gentleman. Wheres your manners?

FEEMY. I'll hang you, Blanco Posnet. I will. I wouldnt for fifty dollars hadnt seen you this morning. I'll teach you to be civil to me next time, for all I'm not good enough to kiss the Book.

BLANCO. Lord keep me wicked till I die! I'm game for anything while youre spitting dirt at me, Feemy.

RENEWED TUMULT AT THE DOOR. Here, whats this? Fire them out. Not me. Who are you that I should get out of your way? Oh, stow it. Well, she cant come in. What woman? What horse? Whats the good of shoving like that? Who says? No! you dont say!

THE SHERIFF. Gentlemen of the Vigilance Committee: clear that doorway. Out with them in the name of the law.

STRAPPER [*without*] Hold hard, George. [*At the door*] Theyve got the horse. [*He comes in, followed by Waggoner Jo, an elderly carter, who crosses the court to the jury side. Strapper pushes his way to the Sheriff and speaks privately to him*].

THE BOYS. What! No! Got the horse! Sheriff's horse? Who took it, then? Where? Get out. Yes it is, sure. I tell you it is. It's the horse all right enough. Rot. Go and look. By Gum!

THE SHERIFF [*to Strapper*] You dont say!

STRAPPER. It's here, I tell you.

WAGGONER JO. It's here all right enough, Sheriff.

STRAPPER. And theyve got the thief too.

ELDER DANIELS. Then it aint Blanco.

The Shewing-Up of Blanco Posnet 433

STRAPPER. No: it's a woman. [*Blanco yells and covers his eyes with his hands*].

THE WHOLE CROWD. A woman!

THE SHERIFF. Well, fetch her in. [*Strapper goes out. The Sheriff continues, to Feemy*] And what do you mean, you lying jade, by putting up this story on us about Blanco?

FEEMY. I aint put up no story on you. This is a plant: you see if it isnt.

Strapper returns with a woman. Her expression of intense grief silences them as they crane over one another's heads to see her. Strapper takes her to the corner of the table. The Elder moves up to make room for her.

BLANCO [*terrified*]: that woman aint real. You take care. That woman will make you do what you never intended. Thats the rainbow woman. Thats the woman that brought me to this.

THE SHERIFF. Shut your mouth, will you. Youve got the horrors. [*To the woman*] Now you. Who are you? and what are you doing with a horse that doesnt belong to you?

THE WOMAN. I took it to save my child's life. I thought it would get me to a doctor in time. It was choking with croup.

BLANCO [*strangling, and trying to laugh*] A little choker: thats the word for him. His choking wasnt real: wait and see mine. [*He feels his neck with a sob*].

THE SHERIFF. Where's the child?

STRAPPER. On Pug Jackson's bench in his shed. He's makin a coffin for it.

BLANCO [*with a horrible convulsion of the throat—frantically*] Dead! The little Judas kid! The child I gave my life for! [*He breaks into hideous laughter*].

THE SHERIFF [*jarred beyond endurance by the sound*]

Hold you noise! will you? Shove his neckerchief into his mouth if he dont stop. [*To the woman*] Dont you mind him, maam: he's mad with drink and devilment. I suppose theres no fake about this, Strapper. Who found her?

WAGGONER JO. I did, Sheriff. Theres no fake about it. I came on her on the track round by Red Mountain. She was settin on the ground with the dead body on her lap, stupid-like. The horse was grazin on the other side of the road.

THE SHERIFF [*puzzled*] Well, this is blamed queer. [*To the woman*] What call had you to take the horse from Elder Daniels' stable to find a doctor? Theres a doctor in the very next house.

BLANCO [*mopping his dabbled red crest and trying to be ironically gay*] Story simply wont wash, my angel. You got it from the man that stole the horse. He gave it to you because he was a softy and went to bits when you played off the sick kid on him. Well, I guess that clears me. I'm not that sort. Catch me putting my neck in a noose for anybody's kid!

THE FOREMAN. Dont you go putting her up to what to say. She said she took it.

THE WOMAN. Yes: I took it from a man that met me. I thought God sent him to me. I rode here joyfully thinking so all the time to myself. Then I noticed that the child was like lead in my arms. God would never have been so cruel as to send me the horse to disappoint me like that.

BLANCO. Just what He would do.

STRAPPER. We aint got nothin to do with that. This is the man, aint he? [*pointing to Blanco*].

THE WOMAN [*pulling herself together after looking scaredly at Blanco, and then at the Sheriff and at the jury*] No.

THE FOREMAN. You lie.

THE SHERIFF. Youve got to tell us the truth. Thats the law, you know.

THE WOMAN. The man looked a bad man. He cursed me; and he cursed the child: God forgive him! But something came over him. I was desperate. I put the child in his arms; and it got its little fingers down his neck and called him Daddy and tried to kiss him; for it was not right in its head with the fever. He said it was a little Judas kid, and that it was betraying him with a kiss, and that he'd swing for it. And then he gave me the horse, and went away crying and laughing and singing dreadful dirty wicked words to hymn tunes like as if he had seven devils in him.

STRAPPER. She's lying. Give her the oath, George.

THE SHERIFF. Go easy there. Youre a smart boy, Strapper; but youre not Sheriff yet. This is my job. You just wait. I submit that we're in a difficulty here. If Blanco was the man, the lady cant, as a white woman, give him away. She oughtnt to be put in the position of having either to give him away or commit perjury. On the other hand, we dont want a horse-thief to get off through a lady's delicacy.

THE FOREMAN. No we dont; and we dont intend he shall. Not while I am foreman of this jury.

BLANCO [*with intense expression*] A rotten foreman! Oh, what a rotten foreman!

THE SHERIFF. Shut up, will you. Providence shows us a way out here. Two women saw Blanco with a horse. One has a delicacy about saying so. The other will excuse me saying that delicacy is not her strongest holt. She can give the necessary witness. Feemy Evans: youve taken the oath. You saw the man that took the horse.

FEEMY. I did. And he was a low-down rotten drunken lying hound that would go further to hurt a woman any day than to help her. And if he ever did a good action it was because he was too drunk to know what he was doing. So it's no harm to hang him. She said he cursed her and went away blaspheming and singing things that were not fit for the child to hear.

BLANCO [*troubled*] I didnt mean them for the child to hear, you venomous devil.

THE SHERIFF. All thats got nothing to do with us. The question you have to answer is, was that man Blanco Posnet?

THE WOMAN. No. I say no. I swear it. Sheriff: dont hang that man: oh dont. You may hang me instead if you like: Ive nothing to live for now. You darent take her word against mine. She never had a child: I can see it in her face.

FEEMY [*stung to the quick*] I can hang him in spite of you, anyhow. Much good your child is to you now, lying there on Pug Jackson's bench!

BLANCO [*rushing at her with a shriek*] I'll twist your heart out of you for that. [*They seize him before he can reach her*].

FEEMY [*mocking at him as he struggles to get at her*] Ha, ha, Blanco Posnet. You cant touch me; and I can hang you. Ha, ha! Oh, I'll do for you. I'll twist your heart and I'll twist your neck. [*He is dragged back to the bar and leans on it, gasping and exhausted.*] Give me the oath again, Elder. I'll settle him. And do you [*to the woman*] take your sickly face away from in front of me.

STRAPPER. Just turn your back on her there, will you?

THE WOMAN. God knows I dont want to see her commit murder. [*She folds her shawl over her head*].

THE SHERIFF. Now, Miss Evans: cut it short. Was the prisoner the man you saw this morning or was he not? Yes or no?

The Shewing-Up of Blanco Posnet

FEEMY [*a little hysterically*] I'll tell you fast enough. Dont think I'm a softy.

THE SHERIFF [*losing patience*] Here: weve had enough of this. You tell the truth, Feemy Evans; and let us have no more of your lip. Was the prisoner the man or was he not? On your oath?

FEEMY. On my oath and as I'm a living woman—[*flinching*] Oh God! he felt the little child's hands on his neck—I cant [*bursting into a flood of tears and scolding at the other woman*] It's you with your snivelling face that has put me off it. [*Desperately*] No: it wasnt him. I only said it out of spite because he insulted me. May I be struck dead if I ever saw him with the horse!

Everybody draws a long breath. Dead silence.

BLANCO [*whispering at her*] Softy! Cry-baby! Landed like me! Doing what you never intended! [*Taking up his hat and speaking in his ordinary tone*] I presume I may go now, Sheriff.

STRAPPER. Here, hold hard.

THE FOREMAN. Not if we know it, you dont.

THE BOYS [*barring the way to the door*] You stay where you are. Stop a bit, stop a bit. Dont you be in such a hurry. Dont let him go. Not much.

Blanco stands motionless, his eye fixed, thinking hard, and apparently deaf to what is going on.

THE SHERIFF [*rising solemnly*] Silence there. Wait a bit. I take it that if the Sheriff is satisfied and the owner of the horse is satisfied, theres no more to be said. I have had to remark on former occasions that what is wrong with this court is that theres too many Sheriffs in it. To-day there is going to be one, and only one; and that one is your humble servant. I call that to the notice of the Foreman of the jury, and also to the notice of young Strapper. I am also the owner of the horse. Does any man say that I am not? [*Silence*].

438 The Shewing-Up of Blanco Posnet

Very well, then. In my opinion, to commandeer a horse for the purpose of getting a dying child to a doctor is not stealing, provided, as in the present case, that the horse is returned safe and sound. I rule that there has been no theft.

NESTOR. That aint the law.

THE SHERIFF. I fine you a dollar for contempt of court, and will collect it myself off you as you leave the building. And as the boys have been disappointed of their natural sport, I shall give them a little fun by standing outside the door and taking up a collection for the bereaved mother of the late kid that shewed up Blanco Posnet.

THE BOYS. A collection. Oh, I say! Calls that sport? Is this a mothers' meeting? Well, I'll be jiggered! Where does the sport come in?

THE SHERIFF [*continuing*] The sport comes in, my friends, not so much in contributing as in seeing others fork out. Thus each contributes to the general enjoyment; and all contribute to his. Blanco Posnet: you go free under the protection of the Vigilance Committee for just long enough to get you out of this town, which is not a healthy place for you. As you are in a hurry, I'll sell you the horse at a reasonable figure. Now, boys, let nobody go out till I get to the door. The court is adjourned. [*He goes out*].

STRAPPER [*to Feemy, as he goes to the door*] I'm done with you. Do you hear? I'm done with you. [*He goes out sulkily*].

FEEMY [*calling after him*] As if I cared about a stingy brat like you! Go back to the freckled maypole you left for me: youve been fretting for her long enough.

THE FOREMAN [*To Blanco, on his way out*] A man like you makes me sick. Just sick. [*Blanco makes no sign. The Foreman spits disgustedly, and follows Strap-*

The Shewing-Up of Blanco Posnet

per out. *The Jurymen leave the box, except Nestor, who collapses in a drunken sleep*].

BLANCO [*Suddenly rushing from the bar to the table and jumping up on it*] Boys, I'm going to preach you a sermon on the moral of this day's proceedings.

THE BOYS [*crowding round him*] Yes: lets have a sermon. Go ahead, Blanco. Silence for Elder Blanco. Tune the organ. Let us pray.

NESTOR [*staggering out of his sleep*] Never hold up your head in this town again. I'm done with you.

BLANCO [*pointing inexorably to Nestor*] Drunk in church. Disturbing the preacher. Hand him out.

THE BOYS [*chivying Nestor out*] Now, Nestor, outside. Outside, Nestor. Out you go. Get your subscription ready for the Sheriff. Skiddoo, Nestor.

NESTOR. Afraid to be hanged! Afraid to be hanged! [*At the door*] Coward! [*He is thrown out*].

BLANCO. Dearly beloved brethren—

A BOY. Same to you, Blanco. [*Laughter*].

BLANCO. And many of them. Boys: this is a rotten world.

ANOTHER BOY. Lord have mercy on us, miserable sinners. [*More laughter*].

BLANCO [*Forcibly*] No: thats where youre wrong. Dont flatter yourselves that youre miserable sinners. Am I a miserable sinner? No: I'm a fraud and a failure. I started in to be a bad man like the rest of you. You all started in to be bad men or you wouldnt be in this jumped-up, jerked-off, hospital-turned-out camp that calls itself a town. I took the broad path because I thought I was a man and not a snivelling canting turning-the-other-cheek apprentice angel serving his time in a vale of tears. They talked Christianity to us on Sundays; but when they really meant business they told us never to take a blow without giving it back, and to get dollars. When they talked the

golden rule to me, I just looked at them as if they
werent there, and spat. But when they told me to try
to live my life so that I could always look my fellowman
straight in the eye and tell him to go to hell, that
fetched me.

THE BOYS. Quite right. Good. Bully for you,
Blanco, old son. Right good sense too. Aha-a-ah!

BLANCO. Yes; but whats come of it all? Am I a
real bad man? a man of game and grit? a man that does
what he likes and goes over or through other people
to his own gain? or am I a snivelling cry-baby that let
a horse his life depended on be took from him by a
woman, and then sat on the grass looking at the rainbow and let himself be took like a hare in a trap by
Strapper Kemp: a lad whose back I or any grown man
here could break against his knee? I'm a rottener fraud
and failure than the Elder here. And youre all as rotten as me, or youd have lynched me.

A BOY. Anything to oblige you, Blanco.

ANOTHER. We can do it yet if you feel really bad
about it.

BLANCO. No: the devil's gone out of you. We're all
frauds. Theres none of us real good and none of us
real bad.

ELDER DANIELS. There is One above, Blanco.

BLANCO. What do you know about Him? you that
always talk as if He never did anything without asking
your rotten leave first? Why did the child die? Tell
me that if you can. He cant have wanted to kill the
child. Why did He make me go soft on the child if
He was going hard on it Himself? Why should He go
hard on the innocent kid and go soft on a rotten thing
like me? Why did I go soft myself? Why did the Sheriff go soft? Why did Feemy go soft? Whats this game
that upsets our game? For seems to me theres two
games bein played. Our game is a rotten game that

The Shewing-Up of Blanco Posnet

makes me feel I'm dirt and that youre all as rotten dirt as me. T'other game may be a silly game; but it aint rotten. When the Sheriff played it he stopped being rotten. When Feemy played it the paint nearly dropped off her face. When I played it I cursed myself for a fool; but I lost the rotten feel all the same.

ELDER DANIELS. It was the Lord speaking to your soul, Blanco.

BLANCO. Oh yes: you know all about the Lord, dont you? Youre in the Lord's confidence. He wouldnt for the world do anything to shock you, would He, Boozy dear? Yah! What about the croup? It was early days when He made the croup, I guess. It was the best He could think of then; but when it turned out wrong on His hands He made you and me to fight the croup for him. You bet He didnt make us for nothing; and He wouldnt have made us at all if He could have done His work without us. By Gum, that must be what we're for! He'd never have made us to be rotten drunken blackguards like me, and good-for-nothing rips like Feemy. He made me because He had a job for me. He let me run loose til the job was ready; and then I had to come along and do it, hanging or no hanging. And I tell you it didnt feel rotten: it felt bully, just bully. Anyhow, I got the rotten feel off me for a minute of my life; and I'll go through fire to get it off me again. Look here! which of you will marry Feemy Evans?

THE BOYS [*uproariously*] Who speaks first? Who'll marry Feemy? Come along, Jack. Nows your chance, Peter. Pass along a husband for Feemy. Oh my! Feemy!

FEEMY [*shortly*] Keep your tongue off me, will you?

BLANCO. Feemy was a rose of the broad path, wasnt she? You all thought her the champion bad woman of this district. Well, she's a failure as a bad woman; and

I'm a failure as a bad man. So let Brother Daniels marry us to keep all the rottenness in the family. What do you say, Feemy?

FEEMY. Thank you; but when I marry I'll marry a man that could do a decent action without surprising himself out of his senses. Youre like a child with a new toy: you and your bit of human kindness!

THE WOMAN. How many would have done it with their life at stake?

FEEMY. Oh well, if youre so much taken with him, marry him yourself. Youd be what people call a good wife to him, wouldnt you?

THE WOMAN. I was a good wife to the child's father. I dont think any woman wants to be a good wife twice in her life. I want somebody to be a good husband to me now.

BLANCO. Any offer, gentlemen, on that understanding? [*The boys shake their heads*]. Oh, it's a rotten game, our game. Here's a real good woman; and she's had enough of it, finding that it only led to being put upon.

HANNAH. Well, if there was nothing wrong in the world there wouldnt be anything left for us to do, would there?

ELDER DANIELS. Be of good cheer, brothers. Fight on. Seek the path.

BLANCO. No. No more paths. No more broad and narrow. No more good and bad. Theres no good and bad; but by Jiminy, gents, theres a rotten game, and theres a great game. I played the rotten game; but the great game was played on me; and now I'm for the great game every time. Amen. Gentlemen: let us adjourn to the saloon. I stand the drinks. [*He jumps down from the table*].

THE BOYS. Right you are, Blanco. Drinks round. Come along, boys. Blanco's standing. Right along to the Elder's. Hurrah! [*They rush out, dragging the Elder with them*].

BLANCO [*to Feemy, offering his hand*] Shake, Feemy.

FEEMY. Get along, you blackguard.

BLANCO. It's come over me again, same as when the kid touched me. Shake, Feemy.

FEEMY. Oh well, here. [*They shake hands*].

www.ingramcontent.com/pod-product-compliance
Lightning Source LLC
Chambersburg PA
CBHW030236170426
43202CB00007B/28